Software Architecture with Spring

Design scalable and high-performance Java applications
with Spring

Wanderson Xesquevixos

Software Architecture with Spring

Copyright © 2025 Packt Publishing

All rights reserved. No part of this book may be reproduced, stored in a retrieval system, or transmitted in any form or by any means, without the prior written permission of the publisher, except in the case of brief quotations embedded in critical articles or reviews.

The author acknowledges the use of cutting-edge AI, such as ChatGPT, with the sole aim of enhancing the language and clarity within the book, thereby ensuring a smooth reading experience for readers. It's important to note that the content itself has been crafted by the author and edited by a professional publishing team.

Every effort has been made in the preparation of this book to ensure the accuracy of the information presented. However, the information contained in this book is sold without warranty, either express or implied. Neither the author nor Packt Publishing or its dealers and distributors, will be held liable for any damages caused or alleged to have been caused directly or indirectly by this book.

Packt Publishing has endeavored to provide trademark information about all of the companies and products mentioned in this book by the appropriate use of capitals. However, Packt Publishing cannot guarantee the accuracy of this information.

Portfolio Director: Ashwin Nair

Relationship Lead: Aaron Lazar

Project Manager: Ruvika Rao

Content Engineer: Kinnari Chohan

Technical Editor: Sweety Pagaria

Copy Editor: Safis Editing

Proofreader: Kinnari Chohan

Indexer: Tejal Soni

Production Designer: Shankar Kalbhor

Growth Lead: Anamika Singh

First published: June 2025

Production reference: 3071125

Published by Packt Publishing Ltd.

Grosvenor House

11 St Paul's Square

Birmingham

B3 1RB, UK.

ISBN 978-1-83588-060-9

www.packtpub.com

To my wife, Caroline Xesquevixos, for being my loving partner throughout our joint life journey; this book would not have been possible without you. To my mother, Maria Xesquevixos (in memory), and my father, Aroldo Siqueira, for their sacrifices and examples of determination and kindness; you are my examples. To my son, Alexander, and my daughter, Stephany, you are my reason for moving forward and setting an example.

- Wanderson Xesquevixos

Contributors

About the author

Wanderson Xesquevixos is a seasoned software engineer and architect with over twenty-five years of experience. He has dedicated his career to developing and designing complex systems for many global companies in the banking, telecom, tourism, retail, and e-commerce industries. He earned his computer science degree from UNIVAP in 2005. He holds an MBA in data science and analytics and is pursuing another MBA in software engineering from the prestigious Universidade de São Paulo (USP). He holds certifications as a Java Programmer, Web Component Developer, JEE Business Component Developer, and AWS Certified Solutions Architect. Originally from Jacareí, SP, Wanderson resides in São Francisco do Sul, SC, with his wife Caroline and son Alexander.

This book was made possible by the invaluable support of many. My deepest thanks to my family for their love and encouragement and my colleagues for their insights and collaboration; you don't know how much I've learned from you. To the readers, I hope this work inspires you. Special thanks to the Packt team for their professionalism in bringing this book to life. You are superb!

About the reviewer

Madhavi Yeduguri Sandinti, MBA, MS, is a seasoned systems lead developer, senior IT technical lead, and technical architect with over 20 years of expertise in Java application design, web development, and IT management. Skilled in Agile methodologies, she excels in gathering requirements, software analysis, UI development, and cross-functional team leadership. Madhavi is adept at migrations, implementations, testing, and deployment while optimizing performance for continuous improvement. Known for thriving in fast-paced, high-pressure environments, she combines technical acumen with strong organizational and interpersonal skills.

Maciej Walkowiak is an independent Java consultant specializing in the Spring Boot ecosystem and AWS. He helps companies design and build complex, business-critical systems with a focus on quality, maintainability, and clear architecture. He advocates for Domain-Driven Design, values clean and easy-to-understand code, and promotes pragmatic, reliable testing strategies. Maciej is the project lead of Spring Cloud AWS, a conference speaker, and an active open source contributor. He also shares practical knowledge with the developer community through his blog and YouTube channel aimed at helping developers build reliable, production-grade Java applications.

Enderson Siqueira has nearly two decades of experience in IT, with a strong background in the banking industry and payment solutions. He holds a postgraduate degree in Information Architecture from Faculdade Impacta in São Paulo. For the last eight years, Enderson has focused on developing microservices with Java, applying Agile methodologies, and working with cloud platforms such as AWS and Azure. His expertise includes SQL, NoSQL databases, and implementing observability in distributed systems, always aiming for robust, scalable, and reliable solutions.

Table of Contents

2

Decision-Making Processes in Software Architecture 33

3

Understanding the System Context 55

Part 2: Exploring Architectural Styles

4

Monolithic Architecture   81

5

Client-Server Architecture   109

6

Microservices Architecture   137

7

Microservices Patterns with Spring Cloud   167

8

Event-Driven Architecture 203

9

Pipe-and-Filter and Serverless Architecture — 231

Part 3: Advanced Topics in Modern Software Development

10

Security — 259

14

Orchestration with Kubernetes   369

15

Continuous Integration and Continuous Deployment   393

Preface

Software architecture is the cornerstone of software systems, shaping their scalability, performance, and maintainability. As software demands evolve, so does the need for flexible, efficient, and secure architectures. Spring Framework 6, with its comprehensive ecosystem and advanced features, serves as an excellent foundation for building scalable and resilient applications.

This book embarks on a journey through software architecture, starting with the fundamentals, introducing decision-making processes in software architecture, and exploring the importance of understanding the system context.

Using an online auction application as a case study, we evolve it through various architectural styles to reflect real-world software needs, addressing both functional and non-functional requirements. This approach ensures each concept is explained theoretically and brought to life through practical examples. You'll witness the application's transformation from a monolithic structure to distributed microservices and beyond, showcasing the progression of architectural decisions in modern software projects.

The book also delves into vital areas such as security, observability, testing, performance optimization, microservices orchestration, and CI/CD pipelines, providing a comprehensive toolkit for building enterprise-ready applications.

Who this book is for

This book is perfect for experienced Java software engineers aiming to become software architects or current architects looking to deepen their knowledge of software architecture styles using Spring 6.0.

What this book covers

Chapter 1, Diving into Software Architecture, explores the fundamentals of software architecture, distinguishing it from design. It introduces architectural principles, styles such as monolithic and microservices, and the CAP theorem, offering guidance on aligning technical requirements with business goals and choosing databases to support different architectural needs.

Chapter 2, Decision-Making Processes in Software Architecture, highlights the importance of architectural decisions. It covers key choices, trade-offs, and systematic methods such as ATAM. The chapter emphasizes aligning decisions with business goals, documenting them with ADRs, and using case studies to demonstrate the impact of thoughtful, collaborative decision-making.

Chapter 3, Understanding the System Context, explores the distinction between system context and architecture, emphasizing their integration into design. It covers stakeholder engagement, functional and non-functional requirements, and agile methodologies for dynamic management. It also introduces the C4 model for clear, hierarchical documentation, enhancing communication, and architectural visualization.

Chapter 4, Monolithic Architecture, explores monolithic architecture, detailing its definition, pros and cons, and patterns such as N-Layer and MVC. It explains stateful and stateless operations and demonstrates implementing a monolithic application with Spring Boot, Spring Web MVC, Thymeleaf, and Spring Security, using an online auction system as a case study. It also emphasizes automated testing.

Chapter 5, Client-Server Architecture, explores client-server architecture and its components. It covers RESTful API design and token-based authentication using JWT. A case study transitions the monolithic auction application to a client-server architecture, demonstrating API documentation using OpenAPI, security, and testing practices such as code coverage testing with JaCoCo.

Chapter 6, Microservices Architecture, highlights microservices' autonomy and specialization, along with their benefits and challenges. It focuses on transitioning the online auction application to microservices. It explores **domain-driven design (DDD)**, CAP theorem-driven database strategies, clean architecture, monitoring with Spring Boot Actuator, and containerizing microservices using Docker and Docker Compose.

Chapter 7, Microservices Patterns with Spring Cloud, explores patterns such as service discovery, load balancing, centralized configuration, gateways, and resilience with Spring Cloud tools.

Chapter 8, Event-Driven Architecture, examines event-driven systems and their asynchronous nature. It covers essential components, event types, and patterns. The chapter concludes with an implementation using Apache Kafka for message handling in an online auction application.

Chapter 9, Pipe-and-Filter and Serverless Architecture, examines modular workflows with pipe-and-filter patterns and implements them using Spring Batch. It also explores serverless architecture with FaaS solutions, using Spring Cloud Functions to run and deploy the application locally and in AWS Lambda.

Chapter 10, Security, emphasizes integrating security from the start, covering encryption, authentication, authorization, and safeguarding data at rest and in transit. It addresses threats such as DoS, input injection, CSRF, and XSS alongside defense mechanisms. It introduces frameworks such as Zero Trust Architecture, threat modeling, and OWASP and provides an in-depth discussion of OAuth2 and OpenID Connect with practical steps for implementing authentication and authorization.

Chapter 11, Observability, introduces logs, metrics, and traces for system reliability and explores and presents tools such as APM, ELK, OpenTelemetry, and Zipkin for distributed tracing, centralized logging, and metric collection in modern architectures.

Chapter 12, Testing, emphasizes quality assurance, showcasing how automated testing ensures faster, more reliable releases. It explores the testing pyramid, covering unit, integration, and UI tests, and tools such as Testcontainers for stable, dependency-free tests. The chapter also highlights performance testing and delves into TDD and BDD, demonstrating their role in improving code quality and aligning tests with business requirements.

Chapter 13, Performance and Optimizations, discusses enhancing application efficiency and scalability through JVM architecture and Garbage Collector tuning. It offers strategies for heap size configuration to reduce latency and improve throughput and caching techniques to boost performance and reduce server load. The chapter also introduces reactive programming with Spring WebFlux.

Chapter 14, Orchestration with Kubernetes, introduces Kubernetes for containerized application management. It covers cluster components, deployment manifests, and practical guidance for deploying services in a scalable, self-healing environment.

Chapter 15, Continuous Integration and Continuous Deployment, explores the concepts of CI/CD and guides the construction of Jenkins pipelines for automated integration, testing, and deployment. Practical steps include Docker containerization, GitHub integration, and application deployment to a Kubernetes environment using Minikube.

To get the most out of this book

To get the most out of this book, you should be familiar with Git and Maven, have basic knowledge of databases, Docker, and Docker Compose, be proficient in Java development with an object-oriented programming background, and have a solid understanding of the Spring Framework.

Software/hardware covered in the book	Operating system requirements
Java 21	Windows, macOS, or Linux
Maven 3.9.9	Windows, macOS, or Linux
Docker 27.4.0	Windows, macOS, or Linux
Docker Compose 2.32.2	Windows, macOS, or Linux
Git 2.39.5	Windows, macOS, or Linux

If you are using the digital version of this book, we advise you to type the code yourself or access the code from the book's GitHub repository (a link is available in the next section). Doing so will help you avoid any potential errors related to the copying and pasting of code.

Download the example code files

You can download the example code files for this book from GitHub at `https://github.com/PacktPublishing/Software-Architecture-with-Spring`. If there's an update to the code, it will be updated in the GitHub repository.

Conventions used

There are a number of text conventions used throughout this book.

`Code in text`: Indicates code words in text, database table names, folder names, filenames, file extensions, pathnames, dummy URLs, user input, and Twitter handles. Here is an example: "Mount the downloaded `WebStorm-10*.dmg` disk image file as another disk in your system."

A block of code is set as follows:

```
public interface Payment { void processPayment(double amount); }
```

When we wish to draw your attention to a particular part of a code block, the relevant lines or items are set in bold:

```
public Book implements ValidateIsbn, Publication{
    void displayInfo(){ ... }
    void validateIsbn(String isbn){ ... }
}
Voicemail(s0)
```

Any command-line input or output is written as follows:

```
keytool -genkeypair -alias myappkey -keyalg RSA -keysize 2048
-keystore mykeystore.jks -validity 365
```

Bold: Indicates a new term, an important word, or words that you see onscreen. For instance, words in menus or dialog boxes appear in **bold**. Here is an example: "Select **System info** from the **Administration** panel."

> **Tips or important notes**
> Appear like this.

Get in touch

Feedback from our readers is always welcome.

General feedback: If you have questions about any aspect of this book, email us at `customercare@packtpub.com` and mention the book title in the subject of your message.

Errata: Although we have taken every care to ensure the accuracy of our content, mistakes do happen. If you have found a mistake in this book, we would be grateful if you would report this to us. Please visit `www.packtpub.com/support/errata` and fill in the form.

Piracy: If you come across any illegal copies of our works in any form on the internet, we would be grateful if you would provide us with the location address or website name. Please contact us at `copyright@packt.com` with a link to the material.

If you are interested in becoming an author: If there is a topic that you have expertise in and you are interested in either writing or contributing to a book, please visit `authors.packtpub.com`.

Share your thoughts

Once you've read *Software Architecture with Spring*, we'd love to hear your thoughts! Scan the QR code below to go straight to the Amazon review page for this book and share your feedback.

`https://packt.link/r/1835880614`

Your review is important to us and the tech community and will help us make sure we're delivering excellent quality content.

Free Benefits with Your Book

This book comes with free benefits to support your learning. Activate them now for instant access (see the "*How to Unlock*" section for instructions).

Here's a quick overview of what you can instantly unlock with your purchase:

PDF and ePub Copies

Next-Gen Web-Based Reader

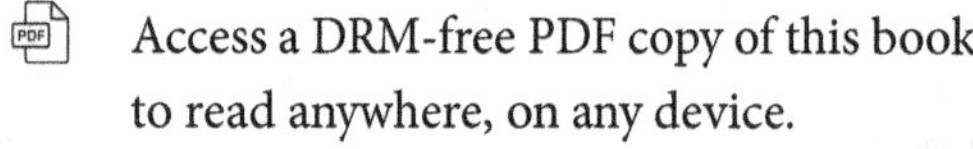
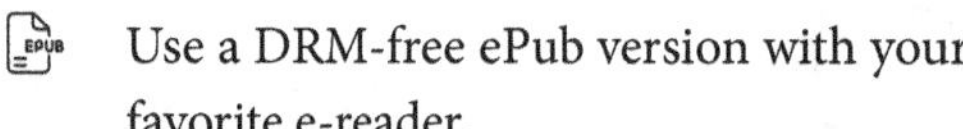

Access a DRM-free PDF copy of this book to read anywhere, on any device.

Use a DRM-free ePub version with your favorite e-reader.

Multi-device progress sync: Pick up where you left off, on any device.

Highlighting and notetaking: Capture ideas and turn reading into lasting knowledge.

Bookmarking: Save and revisit key sections whenever you need them.

Dark mode: Reduce eye strain by switching to dark or sepia themes

How to Unlock

Scan the QR code (or go to `packtpub.com/unlock`). Search for this book by name, confirm the edition, and then follow the steps on the page.

Note: Keep your invoice handly. Purchase made directly from packt don't require one.

Part 1: Foundations of Software Architecture

In this part, you will create a solid foundation in software architecture by exploring its core principles and the critical elements that guide successful system design. You will explore the fundamental concepts of software architecture, gain insights into effective decision-making processes, and understand how to evaluate the system context to align architecture with business and technical requirements. These chapters provide the groundwork for understanding, designing, and implementing robust and scalable software systems.

This part has the following chapters:

- *Chapter 1, Diving into Software Architecture*
- *Chapter 2, Decision-Making Processes in Software Architecture*
- *Chapter 3, Understanding the System Context*

1

Diving into Software Architecture

Software architecture is the cornerstone of successful software development, bridging the gap between complex technical requirements and strategic business objectives. It not only shapes the blueprint for system design and implementation but also ensures the delivery of high-quality, robust, and efficient software solutions. Beyond guiding strategic decisions, software architecture is pivotal in managing the software development life cycle, optimizing costs, and mitigating risks while enhancing communication with stakeholders.

This chapter delves into the essence of software architecture, shedding light on its critical role in the strategic planning of software projects and clarifying the nuanced distinctions between software design and architecture. We will explore key architectural principles, examine prevalent architectural styles, and unravel the implications of the CAP theorem and architectural styles to select the most suitable database for your projects.

This chapter will cover the following topics:

- Definition and the importance of software architecture
- A journey through software design and architecture
- Key principles of software architecture
- Overview of the most common architectural styles
- Selecting a database by architectural style

By the end of this chapter, you'll have grasped the fundamentals of software architecture and appreciate its profound impact, enabling you to make informed choices about database selection and architectural styles tailored to your projects. Prepare to embark on a journey through concepts of software architecture designed to equip you with the knowledge to craft robust software systems that resonate with the needs of stakeholders.

Technical requirements

All the code for this chapter can be found on GitHub at `https://github.com/PacktPublishing/ Software-Architecture-with-Spring/tree/main/ch1`. Ellipses in the code blocks indicate that parts of the code have been omitted, and the complete code is available on GitHub.

> **Free Benefits with Your Book**
>
> Your purchase includes a free PDF copy of this book along with other exclusive benefits. Check the *Free Benefits with Your Book* section in the Preface to unlock them instantly and maximize your learning experience.

Definition and the importance of software architecture

Much like the architectural blueprint for a building, software architecture is foundational in developing successful software systems. It can be briefly described as the fundamental structure of a software system that defines components, their interactions, and the overarching principles guiding its evolution. This blueprint ensures that software meets technical specifications and business objectives while remaining flexible, secure, and efficient over time.

> **Importance of software architecture**
>
> Software architecture is a crucial and indispensable aspect of software development. Without it, projects can quickly become disorganized and chaotic, leading to costly mistakes and missed deadlines. So, if you want your software development projects to succeed, note the critical role of software architecture. Are you curious about the crucial elements that make software architecture indispensable to software development?

Let's dive in and explore the essential aspects of software architecture that can make or break any software project!

- **Blueprint for development**: It offers a blueprint to guide the development process from conception to deployment, ensuring every phase aligns with the specified requirements for the whole software development cycle.

- **Strategic decision-making**: Architectural choices significantly influence the project's direction, such as selecting the right technologies, databases, and frameworks that determine scalability and maintenance efficiency.

- **Identifies risks early**: By foreseeing potential system issues, software architecture allows for preemptive solutions, safeguarding against future problems that could derail project success.

- **Ensures quality**: It addresses essential non-functional requirements, ensuring the system is performant, secure, and reliable.

- **Facilitates communication**: It provides a common language that enhances understanding and consensus among all stakeholders, from developers to business executives.

- **Supports scalability and reusability**: It encourages design practices such as modularity, abstractions, loose coupling, and design patterns that accommodate growth and change, enhancing system longevity.

- **Optimizes resources**: It streamlines development and maintenance, reducing costs and improving efficiency.

- **Enables smooth integration**: It eases the integration of diverse system components and external systems, ensuring cohesive operation.

Software architecture's strategic importance cannot be overstated – it is integral to developing systems that are functional, adaptable, maintainable, and aligned with business goals. As we progress, we'll delve into the nuanced differences between software architecture and design, further clarifying their distinct roles in shaping successful software solutions.

A journey through software design and architecture

Having established a solid grasp of software architecture and its significance, we'll now progress to the subsequent stage of the software development cycle: the intricacies of software design.

Setting apart the realms of software architecture and software design

Using a brief analogy of the construction of a home, we could say that software architecture is like the blueprint of a house – outlining its overall structure, defining the rooms and their relationships, and ensuring it meets broader objectives and regulations. Software design, however, delves into the specifics, akin to choosing interior finishes, planning the electrical and plumbing details, and selecting construction materials. While architecture sets the foundational vision, design handles the detailed execution that brings this vision to life.

Software architecture and software design are critical phases in software development, focusing on structuring and organizing software solutions. They work together to ensure that a software system meets its requirements while being maintainable, scalable, and reliable. However, they differ in some aspects, and understanding these differences is crucial for successful software development.

- **Scope and abstraction**: Software architecture is more about the high-level structure of software; on the other hand, software design delves into the "micro" aspects, detailing the implementation specifics of the system. It is concerned with the behavior and structure of software components such as modules, objects, classes, and their interactions. The design takes architectural decisions and translates them into detailed instructions for solving specific problems. For example, software architecture selects the appropriate architecture and database. In contrast, software design is responsible for data modeling, deciding whether services require a cache, which type of cryptography to use for data storage, and the type of authentication, such as OAuth2 or basic authentication.

- **Granularity**: Software architecture looks at the system as a whole or major components, focusing on how these elements interact. In contrast, software design breaks down those components into smaller, more detailed parts. It describes the internal details of the components, including algorithms, data structure choices, and detailed interfaces between system components.

- **Timeframe**: Software architecture decisions are made early in the software development life cycle, setting the direction for the design and implementation phases. In contrast, software design is a continuous activity that can evolve more frequently over the development cycle, refining the architectural vision into implementable solutions.

- **Decision scope**: Software architecture involves strategic decisions such as selecting the proper architecture, database, and communication type that have long-term effects on the system's structure, performance, security, and quality. Software design involves tactical decisions focused on solving specific problems within the decisions of software architecture, such as the framework, database, and communication type set by the architecture, often requiring detailed technical knowledge and expertise. For instance, if the software architecture decides that the microservices will use RESTful APIs for communication, the software design must determine whether it will be synchronous or asynchronous calls using reactive programming.

- **Stakeholders**: Software architecture is typically of interest to high-level stakeholders, including system architects, business managers, and product owners. It aligns the software's strategic direction with business goals. Software design is more relevant to the development team, including software designers and developers, who need to understand the specifics of how to implement the system's components.

- **Changes**: Changes to the software architecture are significantly more impactful and costly as they affect the overall system structure. Modifications to the software design are less impactful on the overall system, although they can still be significant within the scope of specific components.

- **Documentation**: Software architecture documentation focuses on high-level diagrams and descriptions, such as architectural blueprints, that outline the system's structure and its components. Software design documentation is more detailed, including diagrams such as components, classes, sequences, and other detailed design documents that guide developers in implementation.

While software architecture provides a high-level roadmap and guidelines for the system, software design focuses on the detailed creation of the system within those guidelines. Both are essential for developing robust, scalable, and maintainable software systems. Still, they operate at different levels of abstraction and detail, serve different purposes, and address the needs of different stakeholders. Understanding the distinctions between them is vital for everyone involved in software development, from architects and developers to project managers and business analysts.

Grasping the software architect role

The software architect has a critical role in complex software projects by designing system structures, making critical technological decisions, establishing coding standards, and collaborating with stakeholders. They lead technical teams, manage risks, ensure quality and compliance, and drive continuous improvement. This multifaceted role demands technical expertise, up-to-date knowledge of new trends and technologies, leadership, and practical communication skills to deliver complex software systems successfully.

The impact of software architecture in recent times

In today's fast-evolving digital age, software architecture remains vital, with dedicated architects and even a software architecture team in larger organizations and collaborative approaches in smaller teams or start-ups where software engineers assume the role of software architect. While dedicated software architecture roles remain essential, how software architecture is approached and implemented might vary widely depending on the context and organizational culture. The key is to ensure that architectural decisions are well informed, aligned with business objectives, and continuously refined through collaboration and feedback.

Having gained an understanding of the differences between software architecture and design, the pivotal role of the software architect, and the significance of software architecture in today's digital landscape, let's explore the fundamental principles of software architecture.

Principles of software architecture

In the ever-evolving landscape of software development, architects and developers are continually challenged to design systems that are not only functional and performant but also maintainable, scalable, and resilient to change. The key to achieving such a balance lies in adhering to foundational principles that have been distilled from decades of collective experience and wisdom in software engineering. These principles are the bedrock upon which reliable and efficient software systems are built.

Exploring coupling and cohesion

Coupling is often compared to **cohesion**. Typically, low coupling is associated with high cohesion, and the reverse is also true. Larry Constantine introduced the software quality metrics of coupling and cohesion in the late 1960s within the framework of structured design, emphasizing "good" programming practices aimed at minimizing costs related to maintenance and modifications.

Mastering coupling

Coupling denotes the level of interdependence among modules, packages, and components. When there is low coupling, it is generally a sign of a well-structured computer system with good design. This provides the system with better maintainability and scalability. However, when there is high coupling, the modules are highly dependent on each other. This means that if you make a change in one module, you will also have to make changes in the other module.

High coupling

Some typical code that is highly coupled is presented here:

```java
public class ShoppingCart {
  private CreditCardPayment cc = new CreditCardPayment();
  private DebitCardPayment debit = new DebitCardPayment();
  public void checkout(String typePayment, double amount){
    if (typePayment.equals("CC")) {
      cc.processCreditCardPayment(amount);
    } else {
      debit.processDebitCardPayment(amount);
```

The `ShoppingCart` class creates instances of the `CreditCardPayment` and `DebitCardPayment` classes by directly using the new keyword. This approach presents problems concerning future updates and maintenance. If we change the method signatures of those classes or add new payment methods, we will have to modify the `ShoppingCart` class due to the tight coupling between them. To add new payment options, we must always instantiate a new class and include a new payment condition, such as `if(typePayment.equals("new_payment"))`.

Low coupling

Now, let's work on the same example as previously to implement **low coupling**. Low coupling is often achieved by using interfaces or abstract classes, which serve as contracts between different parts of a program, and we pass them to the class that needs them through the constructor method.

First, we create `interface Payment`, which contains the abstract `processPayment` method, which receives a double parameter:

```java
public interface Payment {
  void processPayment(double amount);
}
```

Then, we change the `CreditCardPayment` and `DebitCardPayment` classes to implement `interface Payment`, such as the `implements Payment` code:

```java
public class CreditCardPayment implements Payment {
  public void processPayment(double amount) {…}
```

```
}
public class DebitCardPayment implements Payment {
  public void processPayment(double amount) {…}
```

In the `ShoppingCart` class, we declare a private and final variable of `Payment` at the class level and create a constructor method, `ShoppingCart(Payment payment)`, that will receive the proper instance. The class that uses the `ShoppingCart` class will provide this instance through the constructor. Finally, in the `checkout` method, we removed the `typePayment` parameter; we don't need it anymore since all kinds of payment implement the `processPayment` method:

```
public class ShoppingCart {
  private final Payment payment;
  public ShoppingCart(Payment payment) {
    this.payment = payment;
  }
  public void checkout(double amount) {
    payment.processPayment(amount);
  }
}
```

With this approach, we achieve low-coupled code because we don't need to change the `ShoppingCart` class when changes occur inside the `processPayment` methods in the `CreditCardPayment` and `DebitCardPayment` classes. If we need to add a new way of payment, we just need to create a new class and make it implement the `Payment` interface, then the client class just needs to pass it through the constructor method to the `ShoppingCart` class.

Class diagram of the low-coupling solution

In *Figure 1.1*, we present the class diagram of the low-coupling solution.

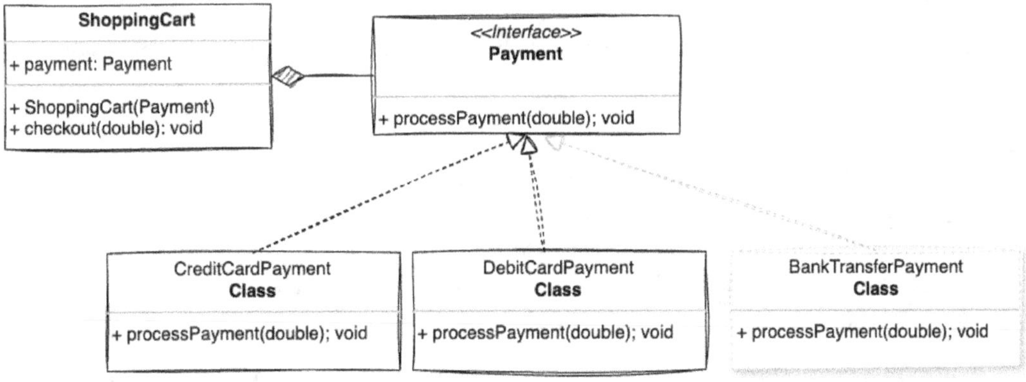

Figure 1.1: Class diagram of the low-coupling solution

The low coupling diagram highlights that to add a new form of payment, we just need to create a class that implements the `Payment` interface, in this case, the `BankTransferPayment` class, and we don't need to change any code in the `ShoppingCart` class.

Keeping the modules cohesive

Cohesion in software development refers to how closely related and focused the responsibilities of a single module, class, or function are. When a module's components are closely related, it's easier to maintain, understand, and reuse. High cohesion is a measure of how well the module's internal elements work together to achieve a single, well-defined purpose. The higher the cohesion, the better, as it typically leads to more robust and reliable software.

For instance, let's consider a hypothetical application that requires user information management. A class focusing on managing user information would be highly cohesive if it only had methods related to managing users, such as adding, updating, and deleting. Take a look at the `UserManager` class:

```
public class UserManager {
   public void addUser(User user) {…}
   public void updateUser(User user) {…}
```

The `UserManager` class shows high cohesion because all methods and properties are closely related to the single responsibility of managing user information.

On the other hand, a low cohesion would be the same class comporting the methods to `validateEmail` and `sendEmail`. They should be in another class, such as an `Email` class:

```
public void addUser(User user) {…}
public void updateUser(User user) {…}
public void validateEmail(String email) {…}To
public void sendEmail() {…}
```

Maintaining high cohesion in our modules will facilitate the maintenance and comprehension of our project.

Separation of concerns

The core concept of the **Separation of Concerns** (**SoC**) principle involves dividing the software application into distinct sections, where each section focuses on a specific concern with minimal overlap with other sections. It is applied at various levels of software development, such as the architectural and programming levels.

At an architectural level, it would separate the application into layers, for instance, using design patterns, such as **Model-View-Controller** (**MVC**). At the programming level, it will break down the components, services, functions, or modules into well-defined domains, ensuring that each part of the program focuses on a specific aspect of the application's functionality.

Figure 1.2 illustrates the SoC at the architectural and programming levels.

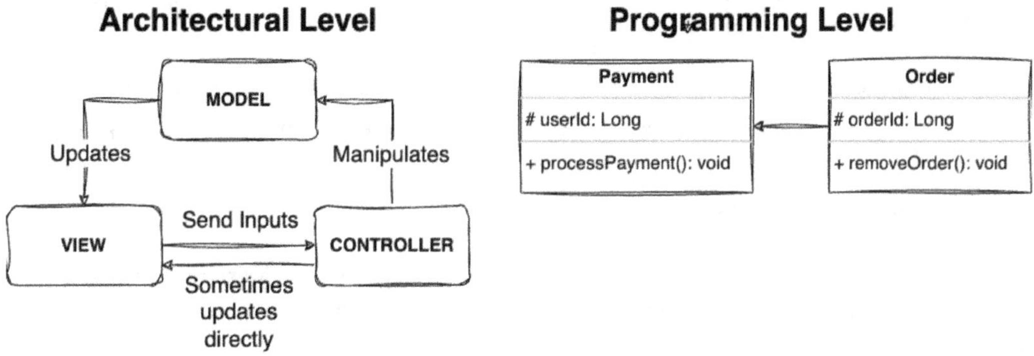

Figure 1.2: SoC of the architectural and programming levels

The MVC design pattern is employed at the architectural level, while at the programming level, the `Payment` and `Order` classes each handle their specific responsibilities.A breach of this design principle would occur if, for instance, the `Payment` class contained a method such as `removeOrder()`.

Implementing SOLID principles

The **SOLID** principles constitute a collection of five design guidelines aimed at enhancing the understandability, flexibility, and maintainability of software designs. Embedded within the framework of object-oriented design, these principles were unveiled by Robert C. Martin, often referred to as Uncle Bob, during the early 2000s. They have gained widespread acceptance within the software engineering community as essential strategies for structuring software systems. **SOLID** is an acronym that stands for **Single Responsibility Principle, Open and Closed Principle, Liskov Substitution Principle, Interface Segregation Principle, and Dependency Inversion Principle**.

Single Responsibility Principle

The **Single Responsibility Principle (SRP)** suggests that a class should have only one responsibility and should change for only one reason. Adhering to it makes your code more modular, allowing changes to be made to one part of the system without affecting others. It also ensures high cohesion, making it easier to maintain, understand, and test the class.

Implementing the Single Responsibility Principle

Let's implement a library to exemplify the SRP:

```
public class Book {
    private String title;
    private String author;
    public Book(String title, String author) {…}
```

```
}
public class BookPersistence {
  public void save(Book book){...}
```

The Book class is focused on representing a book's properties and behaviors. The `BookPersistence` class is responsible for saving books. This separates the concern of persistence from the Book class, adhering to the SRP.

Open and Closed Principle

The **Open and Closed Principle (OCP)** states that modules can be open for extension but closed for modification, which means they should be able to add new functionality to an object or method without changing its existing code.

Implementing the Open and Closed Principle

Building on the previous library example with books and persistence, let's demonstrate how to apply the OCP by saving a book in different data sources without modifying the existing `BookPersistence` class. We can do this by introducing an abstraction for saving books and then providing implementations for different formats, such as text files and databases.

First, we abstract the concept of book saving into an interface, the `BookSaveFormat` interface:

```
public interface BookSaveFormat {
  void save(Book book);
}
```

Then, we provide concrete implementations for each format in which we want to save the book, the `TextFileSaveFormat` and `DbSaveFormat` classes:

```
public class TextFileSaveFormat implements BookSaveFormat {
  public void save(Book book) {
    System.out.println("Saving book '" + book.getTitle() + "' to
        file.");
  }
}
public class DbSaveFormat implements BookSaveFormat {
  public void save(Book book) {
    System.out.println("Saving book '" + book.getTitle() + "' to DB");
  }
}
```

Lastly, the `BookPersistence` class is designed to accept an instance of `BookSaveFormat` through its constructor, adhering to the principle of being open for extension yet closed for modification. For example, to save the book in JSON format, we must develop a new class, such as the `JsonSaveFormat` class, which implements the `BookSaveFormat` interface and supplies it to `BookPersistence` via the constructor:

```java
public class BookPersistence {
  private BookSaveFormat saveFormat;

  public BookPersistence(BookSaveFormat saveFormat) {
    this.saveFormat = saveFormat;
  }
  public void saveBook(Book book) {
    this.saveFormat.save(book);
  }
}
```

With the OCP implemented in our example, we leave it open for extension, that is, adding new save formats, and closed to modification because to add new save formats, we don't need to change the `BookPersistence` class.

Liskov Substitution Principle

The **Liskov Substitution Principle** (**LSP**) states that objects of a superclass should be replaceable with objects of a subclass without affecting program correctness.

Implementing the Liskov Substitution Principle

Using the previous library example, let's create an Ebook class that extends the Book class:

```java
public class EBook extends Book {
  private String url;
  // Getters and Setters
}
```

Then, the `displayBookDetails` method inside the following `Application` class is designed to accept Book objects but can also handle EBook objects, demonstrating compliance with the LSP. The check with `instanceof` allows for EBook-specific behavior while maintaining compatibility with the Book class. This use of `instanceof` is to illustrate the LSP in practice, though in a well-designed system, such type checks should be avoided or handled through more polymorphic designs:

```java
public class Application {
  public static void displayBookDetails(Book book) {
  System.out.println(book.getTitle());
    if (book instanceof EBook) {
      System.out.println(((EBook)book).getDownloadUrl());
```

Interface Segregation Principle

The **Interface Segregation Principle (ISP)** in object-oriented design advocates that clients should not be compelled to rely on interfaces that include methods they do not utilize. It suggests splitting large, cumbersome interfaces into smaller, more specific ones to reduce side effects.

Implementing the Interface Segregation Principle

Given a `Publication` interface implemented by the `Book` and `Magazine` classes, where `Book` has an ISBN and `Magazine` an ISSN, it's impractical for `Book` to implement a `validateIssn()` method, and likewise for `Magazine` to implement `validateIsbn()`:

```
public interface Publication {
  void displayInfo();
  void validateIsbn(String isbn);
  void validateIssn(String issn);
}
```

A better solution is to separate these validation methods into distinct interfaces specific to each publication type, ensuring classes only implement methods pertinent to their attributes:

```
public interface ValidateIsbn {
  void validate(String isbn);
}
public interface ValidateIssn {
  void validate(String issn);
}
public interface Publication {
  void displayInfo();
}
```

Now, for instance, a `Book` class could only implement the `Publication` and `ValidateIsbn` interfaces:

```
public Book implements ValidateIsbn, Publication{
    void displayInfo(){ ... }
    void validateIsbn(String isbn){ ... }
}
```

Now, the `Book` class does not need to implement the `validateIssn` method; thus, it respects the ISP.

Dependency Inversion Principle

The **Dependency Inversion Principle (DIP)** in object-oriented design advises that high-level modules should avoid relying on low-level modules; instead, both should rely on abstractions. Additionally, abstractions should not depend on details but details should depend upon abstractions. This principle aims to reduce dependencies between the code modules, making the system easier to scale, refactor, and maintain. By adhering to the DIP, software developers can create more modular, flexible, and resilient systems.

Implementing the Dependency Inversion Principle

To illustrate the DIP in the context of our library example, we will create `BookPersistence` and `BookFormat` interfaces, which abstract the book-saving process, allowing both high-level (application logic) and low-level (specific save formats) modules to rely on this abstraction for flexibility and modularity:

```java
public interface BookPersistence{
  void save(Book book);
}
public interface BookSaveFormat {
  void save(Book book);
}
```

The `BookPersistenceImpl` class implements `BookPersistence` without being tied to a specific saving format, using the abstract `BookSaveFormat` to save books:

```java
public class BookPersistenceImpl implements BookPersistence
{

  private BookSaveFormat saveFormat;

  public BookPersistenceImpl(BookSaveFormat saveFormat){
    this.saveFormat = saveFormat;
}

  public void saveBook(Book book) {
    saveFormat.save(book);
  }
```

Now, we can create implementation classes that save the book as a file or a database or even send it over the network. The following code snippet presents the `TextFileSaveFormat` class, which extends `BookSaveFormat`:

```java
public class TextFileSaveFormat implements BookSaveFormat {
public void save(Book book) {

  System.out.println("Saving book '" + book.getTitle() + "' to
      file.");
  }
}
```

In a client class, we need to instantiate the desired format for saving the book and pass it through the constructor of `BookPersistenceImpl`. The following code snippet checks whether the user pressed *T* and then creates a `BookPersistenceImpl` object using `TextFileSaveFormat` to save the book to a text file or `DbSaveFormat` to save the book to a database. Finally, the `bookPersistence.saveBook(book)` instruction is called to execute the save operation based on the determined persistence type:

```java
Book book = new Book(title, author);
BookPersistence bookPersistence = null;
if (saveType.equals("T")) {
    bookPersistence = new BookPersistenceImpl(
        new TextFileSaveFormat());
} else {
    bookPersistence = new BookPersistenceImpl(
        new DbSaveFormat());
}
bookPersistence.saveBook(book);
```

This design ensures the application's saving mechanism can be smoothly altered or extended by adding new formats with minimal impact, promoting a maintainable and flexible architecture by decoupling high-level functions from low-level implementations.

To understand the concepts of SOLID principles more deeply, I suggest reading Robert C. Martin's book *Clean Architecture: A Craftsman's Guide to Software Structure and Design*. Now, let's also learn about other important principles, such as KISS, DRY, YAGNI, and the Law of Demeter.

Embodying KISS, DRY, YAGNI, and the Law of Demeter

Like the SOLID principles, there are other important principles that you need in your toolbox; let's delve into them.

Keep It Simple, Stupid (KISS)

The **Keep It Simple, Stupid (KISS)** principle highlights the importance of simplicity in system design and implementation across software development, engineering, and other design disciplines. It encourages reducing complexity in both design and execution, underpinning the notion that simpler systems are more reliable, comprehensible, and easier to maintain. The fundamental concept of KISS is to steer clear of unnecessary complications, aiming for the simplest possible solution.

Don't Repeat Yourself (DRY)

The **Don't Repeat Yourself (DRY)** principle is a concept in software development aimed at reducing repetition within code. Originating from the book *The Pragmatic Programmer* by Andy Hunt and

Dave Thomas, DRY emphasizes the importance of avoiding duplication by abstracting common functionalities into a single location. This approach ensures that every piece of knowledge or logic in the system has a single, unambiguous representation.

You Aren't Gonna Need It (YAGNI)

YAGNI stands for **you aren't gonna need it**. It's a software development principle that advises against adding functionalities until they are necessary. It emphasizes simplicity and efficiency, urging developers to focus on immediate requirements rather than future speculations. The principle reminds developers to prioritize immediate value and avoid adding unnecessary complexity until it is proven necessary. Following YAGNI can lead to more efficient development processes and a code base that's easier to maintain and evolve.

The Law of Demeter

The **Law of Demeter** (**LoD**), also known as the principle of least knowledge, serves as a design recommendation in software engineering, promoting reduced coupling among modules or classes. Originating from Northeastern University in the late 1980s, it suggests that a method of an object should only call the following methods:

- The object itself
- Objects passed as arguments
- Objects it creates
- Its direct components

This principle encourages objects to interact mainly with close associates to decrease dependencies and improve encapsulation. While it boosts modularity and reduces coupling, overly applying it can complicate designs due to excessive wrapper methods.

Now that we are familiar with software architecture principles, let's get an overview of the most common architectural styles.

Overview of the most common architectural styles

In software development, architectural styles are crucial in determining how systems are structured and how they will function. Each architectural style has its own set of principles and patterns that address specific problems and requirements. Selecting a software architectural style is a critical decision in the software development process, as it impacts the application's performance, maintainability, scalability, and overall success. We will discuss some common concerns that developers and architects may have when selecting an architectural style. We will then provide an overview of some of the most common architectural styles.

Common concerns when selecting a software architectural style

Here are some common concerns that developers and architects must have in mind when selecting a software architectural style:

- **Cost**: Consideration of the financial aspects, including initial development, deployment, maintenance, and scalability costs.

- **Maintainability**: The ease with which the system can be modified to add features, fix bugs, or improve performance without introducing defects.

- **Testability**: The degree to which the system can be effectively tested to ensure it works correctly and meets its requirements.

- **Scalability and performance**: The system's ability to handle growth in workload, such as increased data volume or number of users, without compromising performance. It also relates to the architecture's complexity and efficiency in scaling out or up.

- **Security**: The architecture must support the necessary security measures to protect data and ensure secure operations. This includes considerations for authentication, authorization, encryption, and secure data storage (at rest) and transmission (in traffic).

- **Flexibility and adaptability**: The ability of the architecture to adapt to future changes in technology, business requirements, or user needs. A rigid architecture may hinder the evolution of the application.

- **Reliability and availability**: The system's ability to operate without failure and to be available when needed. The architecture should support redundancy, failover mechanisms, and disaster recovery plans.

Now that we know the common concerns when selecting an architectural style, we will discuss one of them, scalability, and learn about the ways we can use to scale a system.

Scalability – vertical scaling versus horizontal scaling

Vertical and horizontal scaling are two strategies for increasing the capacity of a system to handle more workload or to improve its performance. Grasping the differences between these strategies is vital for informed choices regarding infrastructure and application scalability.

Vertical scaling (scaling up)

Vertical scaling increases server capacity/performance by upgrading hardware, such as CPU, RAM, and disk space. It's easier to implement but has limitations such as physical limits and high costs beyond a certain point. Relying on a single server or a few high-capacity servers can lead to a single point of failure and affect system availability.

Horizontal scaling (scaling out)

Horizontal scaling involves adding more servers or nodes to distribute workload. It's flexible, easy to adjust, enhances fault tolerance, and reduces the risk of a single point of failure. It's better suited for distributed systems and applications designed to run in parallel across multiple servers. However, it requires more sophisticated management, load balancing, and changes to the application to distribute the workload effectively. Initially, adding more standard servers may be more cost-effective than investing in high-capacity upgrades for a single server.

In *Figure 1.3*, vertical and horizontal scaling are presented.

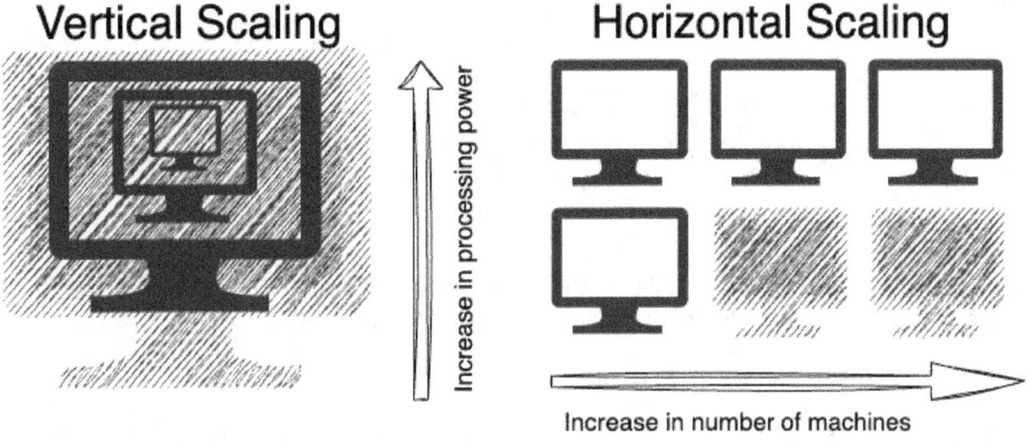

Figure 1.3: Vertical scaling versus horizontal scaling

We can observe in the figure that while vertical scaling is accomplished by adding more processing power, horizontal scaling is accomplished by adding more machines. Now, let's learn about the architectural style Monolithic.

Monolithic architecture

Monolithic architecture is a traditional model for designing and developing software applications. The application is built as a unified unit in this architectural style, where all its components and functionalities are tightly integrated and deployed.

In *Figure 1.4*, we can see a traditional monolithic application.

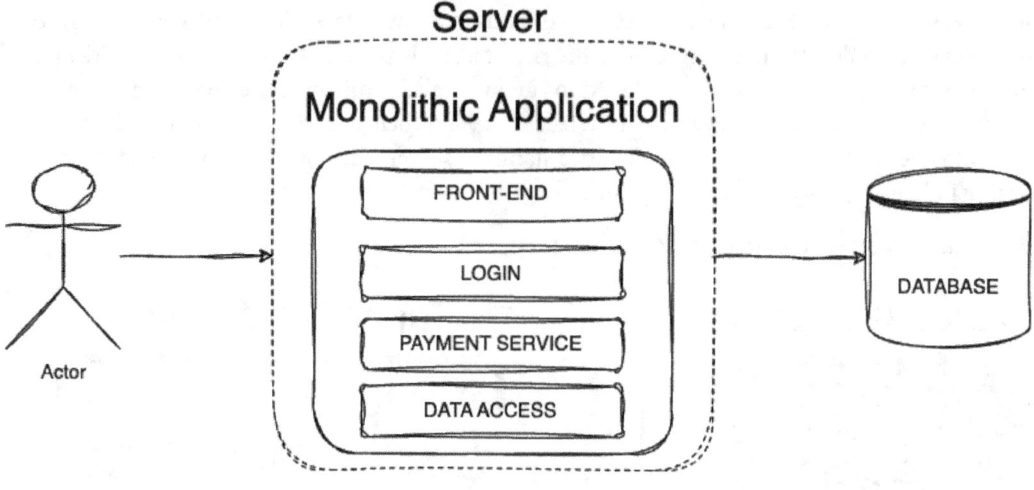

Figure 1.4: Monolithic application

The monolithic application is deployed into a single server, and all components and functionalities are in an artifact. In Java, a WAR file is generally deployed into an application server such as Tomcat.

Benefits of monolithic architecture

Monolithic architecture consolidates the code for various components, such as the database, application layer, and user interface, into a single code base, enhancing development efficiency, simplifying debugging and testing, and ensuring transactional integrity due to the unified environment. This setup can offer better performance due to the absence of network delays seen in microservices architectures and allows for straightforward scaling by replicating the application across servers.

Drawbacks of monolithic architecture

As applications expand in complexity, monolithic architectures can hinder scalability and slow down development, updates, and technology adoption due to being tightly coupled to their initial technology stack. The architecture's inherent coupling can also obstruct independent development efforts within teams, as changes in one component may inadvertently affect others, leading to coordination challenges and potential productivity losses.

Client-server architecture

Client-server architecture is a foundational framework in computing that separates systems into two distinct applications: *clients* and *servers*. This model facilitates interaction between user-facing applications, such as those on personal computers, smartphones, or web browsers (clients), and robust systems managing databases, file services, and applications (servers). The architecture enables multiple clients to interact simultaneously with a server across local or internet-based networks, centralizing access to resources.

In *Figure 1.5*, we illustrate a client-server application.

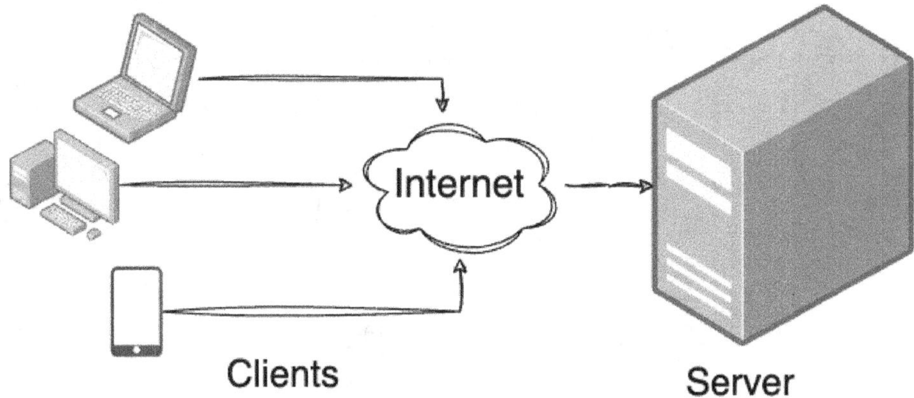

Figure 1.5: Client-server architecture

In the figure, we can observe a variety of client applications, such as web browsers, mobile applications, and terminals, accessing the server application through the internet.

Benefits of client-server architecture

Client server architecture centralizes data management, updates, and security on a server, facilitating consistency, ease of maintenance, and resource optimization. It offers scalability and improved accessibility, allowing users to access applications from any connected device.

Drawbacks of client-server architecture

Client-server architecture's reliance on network connectivity can impact performance and accessibility in offline scenarios. Scaling, particularly vertically, can be costly, and horizontal scaling introduces complexity with potential data consistency challenges. Centralized servers also pose attractive targets for cyber-attacks, necessitating ongoing, sophisticated security measures. Without proper design, servers can become performance bottlenecks or single points of failure, leading to potential data loss or downtime. Managing a client-server system, especially on a large scale, demands substantial administrative effort and expertise to maintain security, performance, and reliability.

Microservices architecture

Microservices architecture, in contrast to monolithic architecture, advocates for dividing the application into smaller, loosely coupled services that communicate over well-defined APIs or events.

Every microservice manages a distinct business capability and has the flexibility to be developed, deployed, and scaled autonomously from the other microservices.

Figure 1.6 provides a simplified view of the microservices architecture of an e-commerce business.

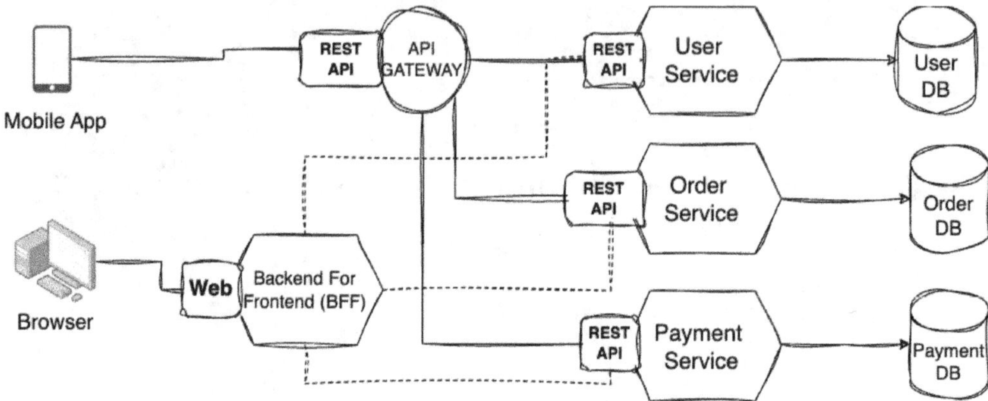

Figure 1.6: Microservices architecture

Microservices architecture decomposes the domain into services such as user, order, and payment. Each microservice has its database, and communication is through the REST API. The mobile app reaches the microservices through the API gateway, which is an entry point for all client requests. It directs requests to the appropriate microservices and may also handle cross-cutting concerns, such as authentication, SSL termination, and request logging. The web application accesses the services via the **Backend for Frontend (BFF)** component. BFF is a service that caters to a particular frontend application or user experience; that is, it acts like an API gateway for frontend requests. Now, let's check the benefits and drawbacks of microservices architecture.

Benefits of microservices architecture

Microservices architecture is a method that emphasizes flexible, scalable software development, offering significant benefits and certain challenges. The advantages include the ability to scale services independently, use the most suitable technology stacks, enhance system resilience, deploy updates faster, improve team agility, and isolate faults effectively.

Drawbacks of microservices architecture

It also introduces complexities in managing multiple services, data consistency issues, potential network latency, security vulnerabilities, testing difficulties, increased operational overhead, and deployment challenges.

Despite these challenges, the architecture's scalability, flexibility, and resilience make it attractive.

Event-driven architecture

Event-Driven Architecture (EDA) is an approach that relies on events for initiating and facilitating communication among loosely coupled services, a prevalent approach in contemporary applications developed using microservices. An event is defined as a significant change in state or an occurrence that necessitates awareness and response from other parts of the system.

Core components and their roles

In EDA, there are four core components and we will present them further:

- **Events**: The central element of EDA represents a noteworthy change in the system or an occurrence that triggers a response.

- **Producers**: Entities that generate or emit events, which could be user actions, sensor outputs, or any source capable of initiating an event.

- **Consumers**: Components that listen for and act upon events, executing actions in response to the events they subscribe to.

- **Event broker (or event channel)**: This is middleware that enables event-driven communication between different components or services within a system. It acts as an intermediary that handles the transmission of events from event producers (publishers) to event consumers (subscribers). Event brokers decouple the production of an event from its consumption, meaning that the producer does not need to know about the consumer's identity, location, or even the number of consumers.

Figure 1.7 presents the Event-driven architecture.

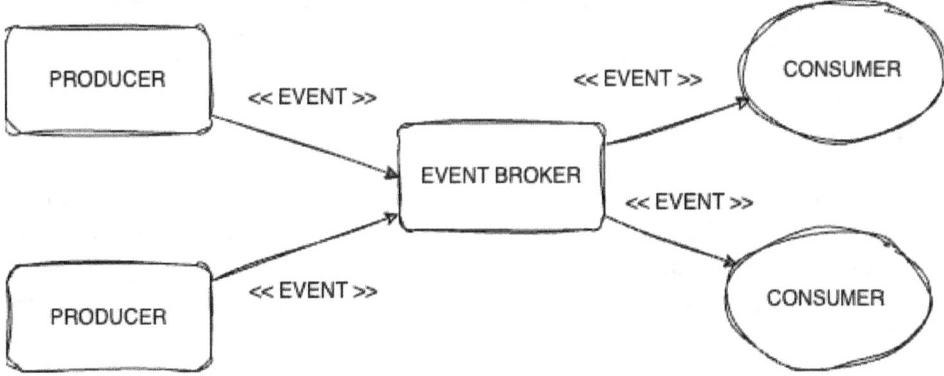

Figure 1.7: Event-driven architecture

We can see the four core components in action: producers, consumers, events, and the event broker. Producers and consumers don't know each other's existence, and they communicate through the event broker via events.

Event-driven architecture patterns

EDA encompasses several patterns. The most known are the publisher/subscriber and event streaming models, each catering to different system requirements:

- **Publisher/subscriber pattern**: Enhances scalability and flexibility by allowing publishers to emit events without knowing the consumers who subscribe to events of interest.

- **Event streaming architecture**: Focuses on the real-time processing of continuous data flows, which is suitable for applications needing immediate data analysis and action.

It focuses on the real-time processing of continuous data flows, which is suitable for applications needing immediate data analysis and action.

Benefits of event-driven architecture

EDA offers advantages such as scalability through independent component scaling, flexibility, and loose coupling for modifications and maintenance; real-time responsiveness via asynchronous processing; and resilience, allowing components to fail without systemic failures, that is, a failure at one component won't affect others components of the system.

Drawbacks of event-driven architecture

EDA faces challenges such as increased complexity in event flow management, difficulties in testing and debugging due to its asynchronous and distributed nature, challenges in maintaining data consistency across services, and a dependency on brokers for system performance and reliability.

Serverless architecture

Serverless architecture allows the development and operation of applications and services without the necessity of overseeing infrastructure. Within this architecture, the cloud provider is responsible for automatically allocating, scaling, and maintaining the infrastructure needed to execute the code. The developers focus solely on writing the application code without worrying about the underlying servers, runtime environments, or maintenance.

Types of serverless architecture

Serverless architectures often make use of microservices and **Function as a Service (FaaS)**. FaaS is a type of serverless computing that allows the execution of functions in response to events. AWS offers it as AWS Lambda.

Several other common types of serverless architectures facilitate various aspects of application development and deployment without the need for managing servers, such as **Backend as a Service (BaaS)**, storage, **Database as a Service (DBaaS)**, API gateway, streaming and event processing, and integration and workflow services.

Figure 1.8 shows some components of the cloud provider AWS for creating a serverless architecture.

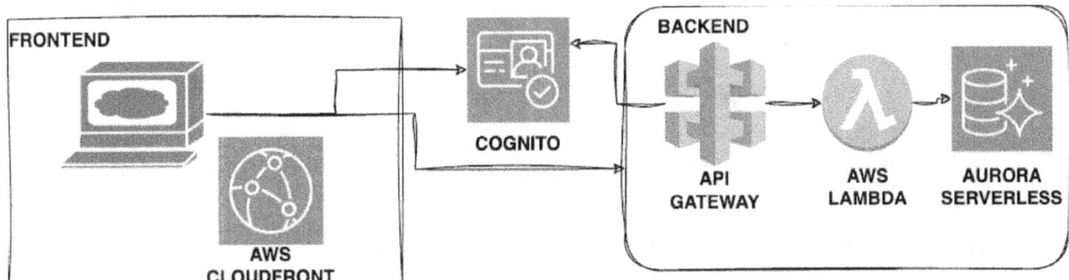

Figure 1.8: AWS serverless architecture

Serverless architecture revolutionizes application development by eliminating the burden of infrastructure management. Let's explore its benefits and drawbacks.

Benefits of serverless architecture

Serverless architecture offers significant benefits for businesses, emphasizing cost efficiency, scalability, productivity, quick deployments, and global distribution. It optimizes costs by charging only for consumed computing resources and scales applications automatically to match demand. This architecture reduces operational burdens, freeing developers to focus on coding and business logic. Deployment processes are streamlined, facilitating swift updates and feature releases. Additionally, the serverless architecture supports global distribution, improving application performance by minimizing latency.

Drawbacks of serverless architecture

Serverless architecture brings unique challenges, such as initial latency from cold starts, constrained control over the environment, risk of dependency on a single cloud provider, heightened security vulnerabilities, intricate state management, and obstacles in testing and debugging.

Pipe and filter architecture

The pipe and filter architecture consists of a series of processing units linked together, where the output from one unit serves as the input for the subsequent one. This pattern is characterized by its structure, which consists of a sequence of processing elements, known as filters, connected by pipes. The data flows through the pipes between filters, undergoing transformation or analysis at each step. This architectural style suits systems that process data in stages, allowing flexibility, reusability, and scalability.

Figure 1.9 illustrates the pipe and filter architecture.

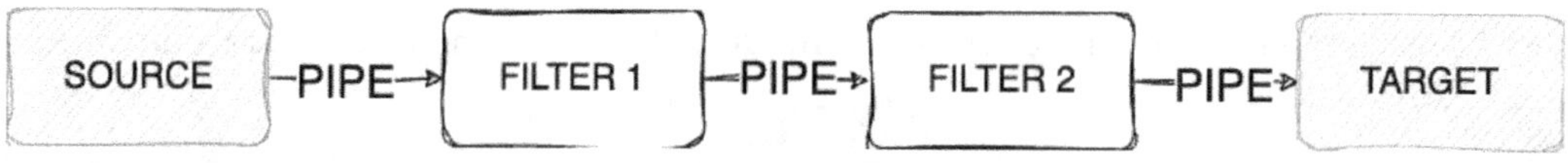

Figure 1.9: Pipe and server architecture

We can observe in the image the components of the pipe and filter architecture and how it works.

Explaining the core components

There are two core components of the pipe and filter architecture, the filter and the pipe, so let's learn more about them:

- **Filter**: Filters are the processing units that perform operations on the data. Each filter reads data from its input, processes it such as transforming, filtering, or aggregating it, and then writes the result to its output. Filters are designed to be independent from each other, focusing on a specific task.

- **Pipe**: Pipes act as connectors that carry data from one filter to the next. They are the pathways through which the processed data flows. Pipes can buffer data, allowing for asynchronous processing by different filters.

The pipe and filter architecture provides a robust framework for designing systems that process data in stages. It offers flexibility, modularity, and ease of maintenance. Its clear SoC and simplicity make it a popular choice for various applications.

Benefits of pipe and filter architecture

The pipe and filter architecture provides a flexible, loosely coupled framework that enables independent updates of filters without affecting others, supports parallel task execution, and allows filters to be treated as standalone entities, simplifying user interaction. This design promotes high reusability, facilitating the application of each filter across different contexts.

Drawbacks of pipe and filter architecture

While beneficial, the pipe and filter architecture faces limitations such as potential performance bottlenecks from managing multiple independent filters, a lack of suitability for interactive user applications, and inefficiency in handling extensive and continuous computations.

Selecting a database by architectural style

Selecting the proper database in alignment with an application's architectural style is crucial for optimizing performance, scalability, and reliability. This choice is influenced by the unique requirements of different architectural styles and necessitates a deep understanding of database technologies and their characteristics.

Types of databases

Databases can be categorized into various types based on their data model, architecture, and use cases. Here are the main types of databases.

Relational databases (RDBMSs)

These databases store data in tables, which are linked to each other through relationships, typically using SQL for data manipulation and queries. They are known for their **Atomicity, Consistency, Isolation, and Durability** (ACID) properties, ensuring reliable transactions. Examples include MySQL, PostgreSQL, Oracle, and Microsoft SQL Server.

NoSQL databases

NoSQL databases are recognized for their adaptability, ability to scale, and efficiency in managing extensive amounts of unstructured or semi-structured data. They may not strictly enforce ACID properties, opting instead for eventual consistency or other models to increase scalability and performance. They are designed to handle an array of data, which we will explore in the following sections:

- **Document databases**: Data is stored in documents using JSON, BSON, and XML. These databases are schemaless, meaning the data structure can vary from one document to another. They are well suited for storing, retrieving, and managing document-oriented information.

- **In-Memory Databases (IMDB)**: These databases store data in the main memory (RAM) to ensure faster access times compared to disk-based storage. They are ideal for applications requiring high throughput and low latency, such as caching, real-time analytics, and gaming.

- **Key-value stores**: The simplest form of database where each item contains keys and values.

- **Graph databases**: Specifically designed to handle data whose relationships are well represented as a graph and consist of nodes (entities) and edges (relationships). These databases are optimized for queries that involve navigating relationships, such as social networks, recommendation engines, and fraud detection. Examples include Neo4j and Amazon Neptune.

- **Wide-column stores**: Data is stored in tables, rows, and dynamic columns. They are optimized for queries over large datasets and are highly scalable. Wide-column stores are a NoSQL database that allows storing enormous amounts of data across many commodity servers.

- **Object-oriented databases**: They store data as objects, such as in object-oriented programming.

- **Time-series databases**: Optimized for storing and querying time-series data, which refers to data that is indexed by time (a timestamp). These databases are used extensively in financial services, monitoring, and IoT applications, where the need to record time-ordered events is critical.

- **NewSQL databases**: Aim to combine the scalability of NoSQL systems with the ACID guarantees of traditional relational databases.

Each database type offers unique features and is chosen based on the application's specific requirements, such as the nature of the data, the scale of the system, consistency requirements, and operational complexity.

Exploring the CAP theorem

The **CAP theorem**, or Brewer's theorem, is a fundamental principle that applies to distributed systems, particularly in the context of database systems and their design. It was formulated by Eric Brewer in 2000 during a keynote speech at the Symposium on **Principles of Distributed Computing (PODC)**. The theorem presents a choice between three guarantees in the presence of network partitions: consistency, availability, and partition tolerance.

However, the theorem posits that a distributed system can only guarantee two out of these three properties at any given time. Let's break down each component.

Consistency

All nodes see the same data at the same time. Consistency ensures that any read request to the system will return the most recent write for a specific data point across all nodes in the system. If a data item is written, subsequent accesses will always return the updated value.

Availability

Every request receives a (non-error) response, without guaranteeing it contains the most recent write. Availability means that the system remains operational and can handle requests even if some parts of the system are failing or inaccessible. The system is designed to avoid downtime.

Partition tolerance

The system maintains its operation even in the face of random partitioning caused by network outages. A partition-tolerant system can sustain any network failure that doesn't result in a complete system failure. In other words, the system can still function and uphold its guarantees even if communication breaks down between nodes.

Figure 1.10 presents the CAP theorem.

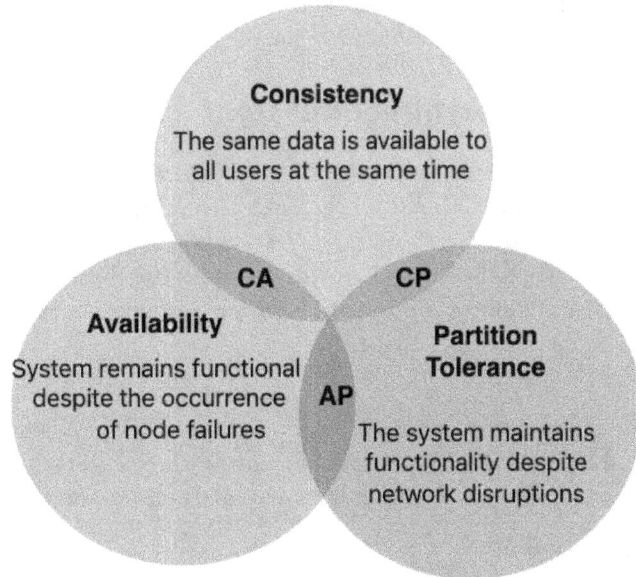

Figure 1.10: CAP theorem

The essence of the CAP theorem is a trade-off that distributed systems must make. The theorem categorizes distributed systems into three categories.

Consistency and Partition Tolerance (CP)

The system prioritizes consistency and partition tolerance over availability. In a network failure, the system might block operations to maintain consistency across partitions.

Availability and Partition Tolerance (AP)

The system prioritizes availability and partition tolerance over consistency. The system remains available during network failures, but the data may not be consistent across all nodes. Once the partition is resolved, the system can work to achieve consistency.

Consistency and Availability (CA)

Systems remain reliable and accessible when there is no network failure. This combination is not realistic in the context of the CAP theorem because it ignores the possibility of partitions in a distributed network. Real-world distributed systems must account for network failures, making partition tolerance a necessary consideration.

The CAP theorem has been foundational in the design and understanding of distributed systems, influencing the development of databases and storage systems and the architecture of various scalable services. It helps designers and engineers to make informed decisions about the trade-offs between consistency, availability, and partition tolerance when building distributed systems.

Selecting databases by architectural style

Now, we'll focus on choosing a database based solely on the architectural style, setting aside business needs to highlight the best-matched database for each architectural approach. Selecting an optimal database for a specific architectural style requires understanding the traits and needs of both the architecture and the database options. We will provide a summary of the mentioned architectural styles and the databases that align well with them, including explanations for each selection.

Monolithic architecture

Monolithic architectures often benefit from the strong consistency, ACID transactions, and relational data modeling capabilities of RDBMSs. These databases provide a robust and reliable foundation for applications where different components are tightly coupled and operate in a single process.

Client-server architecture

Client-server architectures, where clients interact with a central server that handles business logic and data storage, can use RDBMSs for their robustness and transactional integrity. However, for applications requiring more flexibility in data modeling or facing scalability demands, a document-oriented NoSQL database might be more appropriate due to its schema-less nature and ease of scaling.

Microservices architecture

In microservices architectures, applications are broken down into smaller, autonomous services that interact through network communication. NoSQL databases tend to be the favored choice in these scenarios for their horizontal scalability and capability to handle distributed data models, efficiently matching the distributed and scalable characteristics of microservices.

Event-driven architecture

EDAs can use event streaming platforms such as Apache Kafka as the backbone for managing event streams, providing durable storage, and facilitating real-time processing. Coupled with the NoSQL database for flexible data modeling or the NewSQL database for combining scalability with solid consistency, it supports event-driven systems' dynamic and asynchronous nature.

Serverless architecture

Serverless architecture allows the development and operation of applications and services without the necessity of overseeing infrastructure. Serverless databases, which automatically scale up and down to match application demand, are a natural fit. They offer cost-efficiency for unpredictable workloads and simplify operational management, aligning with the serverless principle of focusing on code rather than infrastructure.

Pipe and filter architecture

Pipe and filter architectures involve processing elements (filters) connected by data flows (pipes). IMDBs or stream processing systems can efficiently handle the transient and intermediate data between stages, offering the low latency and high throughput necessary for real-time data processing tasks.

It's important to note that these suggestions are starting points based on typical use cases and characteristics of the architectural styles and the databases. The optimal choice for a specific project can vary based on detailed requirements, including data access patterns, scalability needs, transactional requirements, and operational complexity. A thorough evaluation and a proof of concept are recommended before making a final decision.

Summary

In this chapter, we learned about the critical role of software architecture in successful software development. We saw that software architecture is more than just the blueprint for system design and implementation; it is the pivotal force that bridges the gap between intricate technical requirements and strategic business objectives. This foundational element ensures the delivery of high-quality, robust, and efficient software solutions, guiding strategic decisions throughout the software development life cycle, optimizing costs, and mitigating risks.

Then, we moved our discussion on to explaining the delineation between software architecture and design, exploring the key principles of software architecture. We were also introduced to prevalent architectural styles, highlighting the benefits and challenges posed by monolithic architecture, client-server architecture, microservices architecture, EDA, serverless architecture, and pipe and filter architecture.

Finally, we presented the types of databases and the CAP theorem and discussed how architectural styles influence the selection of the most suitable database for projects.

In *Chapter 2, Decision-Making Processes in Software Architecture*, we will gain an overview of the critical aspects of making architectural decisions in software development, emphasizing the importance of stakeholder involvement, understanding trade-offs, and aligning decisions with business goals.

Questions

1. What is the fundamental role of software architecture in software development?

2. How does software architecture differ from software design?

3. How do architectural decisions affect software quality attributes such as performance, security, and maintainability?

4. Why are principles such as low coupling and high cohesion important in software architecture?

5. What benefits and challenges does the microservices architecture offer?

6. What is the significance of the CAP theorem in the context of database selection?

Get This Book's PDF Version and Exclusive Extras

Scan the QR code (or go to packtpub.com/unlock). Search for this book by name, confirm the edition, and then follow the steps on the page.

Note: Keep your invoice handly. Purchase made directly from packt don't require one.

2

Decision-Making Processes in Software Architecture

This chapter provides a thorough examination of decision-making in software architecture, identifying it as fundamental to successful software development. It covers the nature of architectural decisions, the types encountered, and the processes for making these decisions. It presents the factors and trade-offs that influence architectural decisions and assesses the trade-offs through the **architecture trade-offs analysis method** (**ATAM**) alongside case studies to illustrate practical applications. The chapter stresses the need for aligning architectural decisions with business goals, detailing strategies for this alignment, and documenting decisions via **Architectural Decision Records** (**ADRs**) to ensure clarity and continuity. Overall, it serves as a guide for architects to make informed decisions that align with technical and business objectives, aiming for robust and scalable software solutions.

This chapter will cover the following topics:

- Unraveling decision-making processes

- Scrutinizing architectural factors

- Trade-offs in architectural decision-making

- Aligning architectural decisions with business goals

By the end of this chapter, you'll know about decision-making in software architecture, including defining decisions, types of architectural decisions, processes, and trade-offs, and assessing them using ATAM. The chapter also highlights the significance of aligning decisions with business goals and documenting them using ADRs. This chapter prepares you to confidently navigate the complexities of architectural decision-making and deliver robust software solutions aligned with business objectives.

Unraveling decision-making processes

Decision-making is the process of making choices about significant matters, particularly within a collective or organizational context.

This process serves as a guide to systematically making well-informed decisions. This is crucial since a wrong decision may lead to catastrophic situations, meaning time, money, and business loss. That said, what is a decision?

Before proceeding, think about and try to answer this question.

What is a decision?

If you look it up in a dictionary, you will find answers stating that a decision is a conclusion or resolution reached after considering the best or most appropriate option. To decide, we must have multiple options and a problem or need. If there is only one option, we don't have to decide; we have only one option available. However, when we have multiple options, choosing becomes more complicated, and we need something to assist us in selecting the best or most suitable option. This is where the decision-making process comes in. Now that we have clarified what constitutes a decision, let's explore some common software architectural decisions.

Software architectural decisions

Software architectural decisions are crucial choices that shape the structure and functionality of a software system. These decisions involve selecting appropriate strategies and technologies that facilitate the overall design and development of software, and they significantly impact its quality, performance, maintainability, and future growth. These decisions are made in the context of specific requirements, constraints, and goals and typically address the following areas:

- **Structural organization**: When designing software, it's essential to determine the high-level arrangement of the components and their interactions. This can involve choosing between architectural styles such as microservices, monolithic, event-driven, and service-oriented architectures.

- **Technology stack**: Selecting the appropriate programming languages, frameworks, databases, and tools to suit the project's needs.

- **Data management**: This involves making decisions related to data storage, access, and manipulation, including selecting between SQL and NoSQL databases, data modeling, and data distribution strategies.

- **Components communication**: This involves deciding on communication protocols between system components, such as REST APIs, message queues, and service buses.

- **Quantitative attributes**: Scalability, performance, availability, reliability, and resource usage are common requirements that necessitate decision-making. They can be measured and expressed numerically, making them objective in nature, which makes it easier to quantify, compare, and analyze them statistically. For example, regarding scalability and performance, we need to determine strategies for handling user growth, data volume, and transaction frequency without sacrificing performance. This includes making decisions about load balancing, caching, and distributed computing.

- **Quality attributes**: Requirements such as maintainability, usability, flexibility, portability, security, and testability should be addressed by selecting appropriate testing, monitoring, and logging strategies and tools. When it comes to security, ensuring system security requires making decisions on aspects such as authentication, authorization, data encryption, and compliance with security standards and regulations.

- **Deployment and infrastructure**: Decisions regarding software deployment, including cloud versus on-premises hosting, containerization, and orchestration tools.

- **Design principles and patterns**: By adopting standardized design principles and patterns, such as SOLID, **model-view-controller** (**MVC**), Factory, and Singleton, we can improve our code quality and reusability by solving common issues consistently.

The decisions related to software architecture are crucial because they can have long-lasting repercussions, are often expensive, and, once implemented, may be challenging to change. These decisions can significantly impact the success or failure of a software project. These decisions usually involve various stakeholders, such as architects, developers, project managers, and sometimes customers. This ensures that the decisions align with business goals, technical requirements, and constraints. Next, we will delve into the decision-making process and discuss how to apply it to software architecture.

Exploring decision-making processes

We saw that decision-making is the process of deciding about something important, especially in a group of people or in an organization. In software architecture, decision-making processes are the guiding framework, steering a project from conception to completion. These processes are not arbitrary choices but systematic approaches that navigate the complex terrain of technical considerations, business objectives, and stakeholder dynamics. It involves a structured approach to selecting, evaluating, and implementing critical design choices that define the system. They encompass thoroughly exploring available options, assessing their implications, and a conscious commitment to the chosen path.

The quality of decision-making in software architecture profoundly influences a software project's success.

Identifying different decision-making approaches

It's essential to know different approaches to decision-making. Decision-making in software architecture might involve choosing between one or more alternatives. Depending on the situation and resources available, more than one approach can be used.

Figure 2.1 presents the approaches to decision-making.

Figure 2.1: Decision-making approaches

Each decision-making approach has its unique characteristics and applications. Let's delve into them:

- **Rational**: Rational decision-making is a systematic and analytical process. It involves identifying requirements, generating alternatives, evaluating them based on criteria, and selecting the best solution. It assumes that the decision-maker has complete information and can objectively assess each option.

- **Incremental**: Incremental decision-making involves making small, manageable increments or steps. This is especially beneficial in intricate projects where predicting all requirements and challenges upfront is difficult. Decisions are made as the project evolves, allowing flexibility and adaptability to changing circumstances.

- **Satisficing**: Satisficing decision-making involves selecting the first option that meets the minimum requirements or criteria rather than searching for the best possible solution. It is helpful when time is limited or a good enough solution is sufficient for the project's needs. An excellent example of this type of decision-making is when we find a bug in the production environment and have to solve it quickly.

- **Intuitive**: This type of decision-making is based on the architect's or the decision-making team's experience, instincts, and personal insights. It is often used when rapid decisions are needed or when data is incomplete or too complex to analyze through rational methods.

- **Collaborative**: This involves including various stakeholders in the decision-making process. It recognizes the value of diverse perspectives and knowledge and aims to achieve a consensus or at least a decision that considers all the significant stakeholders' views.

- **Evidence-based**: This approach guides decisions using data, metrics, and empirical evidence. It involves collecting relevant data, analyzing it to draw conclusions, and basing the decision on these insights. It is particularly effective in reducing biases and assumptions in the decision-making process.

- **Strategic**: This type is focused on long-term impacts and alignment with overall business or project goals. It involves considering the broader implications of architectural decisions and requires a deep understanding of the project's vision, the competitive landscape, and future trends.

Indeed, we have all faced such decision-making situations in our projects, and we have likely employed more than one approach to arrive at a decision. Let's now explore the systematic and analytical measures involved.

Outlining the progression of decision-making steps

Navigating the complexity of architectural choices in sophisticated software systems can be likened to finding one's way through a labyrinth of options, each leading to varied consequences. A systematic, step-by-step approach assists experts in this journey, guaranteeing that their decisions are deliberate and consistent with business and technical goals.

Figure 2.2 illustrates the steps of the decision-making process.

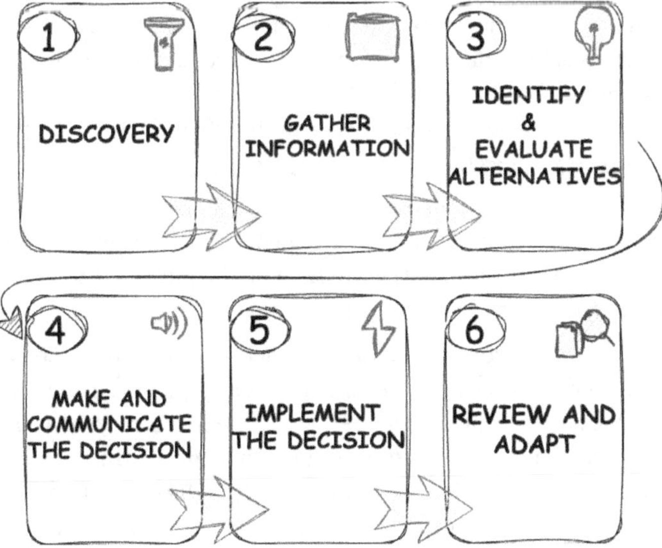

Figure 2.2: Steps of the decision-making process

Now, let's explore and understand each step carefully.

1. **Discovery**: The first step is crucial, and it involves recognizing the need or opportunity that requires a decision. It could be a need for a new system architecture, a technology stack update, or a response to changing business requirements. To do this, you need to ask the right questions to identify the issues that need to be resolved, the business objectives that need to be achieved, and the technical limitations that must be considered. Only then can you properly comprehend the necessity and move forward.

2. **Gather information**: Collect and analyze data that will influence the decision and its impact on the solution.

3. **Identify and evaluate alternatives**: During the information-gathering phase, you will likely discover multiple courses of action or choices. At this stage, the goal is to prioritize all viable and appealing options and assess each alternative against the project requirements, considering feasibility, risk, impact on existing systems, quantitative and qualitative attributes, and alignment with business objectives. This may involve prototyping, discussions with technical teams, or stakeholder consultations. This phase frequently includes analyzing trade-offs, and the ATAM technique can help us evaluate the trade-offs and decisions within a software system's architecture. We will discuss ATAM later in the *Trade-offs in architectural decision-making* section.

4. **Make and communicate the decision**: After considering all the information, you're prepared to pick the most suitable option for your needs. It's possible to opt for a blend of different choices. This decision should balance technical considerations with business needs and potential future requirements. The software architect often must justify the decision with stakeholders, highlighting the rationale and expected benefits. Ensure comprehensive decision documentation for clear understanding and future use while maintaining open and effective communication with everyone involved. Regarding the documentation, we can use the ADR document, a well-accepted document that records a significant architectural decision made along with its context and consequences. We will learn about it later in this chapter, in the *Aligning architectural decisions with business goals* section.

5. **Implement the decision**: At this point, you are set to initiate positive steps by implementing them. Work with the development team to implement the architectural decision. This involves detailed planning, defining architectural guidelines, and guaranteeing that the team comprehends and adheres to the selected path.

6. **Review and adapt**: In this concluding phase, reflect on the outcome of your decision to determine whether it has addressed the requirement you pinpointed in the phase of identifying the need. Should the decision fall short of meeting the identified need, revisiting specific stages of the process to arrive at a new decision could be beneficial. This may involve collecting more comprehensive or varied information or considering further options. For instance, after implementation, review the outcomes of the decision in the context of the system's performance, user feedback, and evolving project requirements. Be prepared to adapt the architecture as new information becomes available or the project needs to change.

This process emphasizes a thoughtful, informed approach to decision-making. It blends technical expertise with strategic thinking to guide software projects toward successful outcomes. Next, we'll delve into the factors influencing architectural decisions in software development.

Scrutinizing architectural factors

Many factors influence architectural decisions, including technical, business, and organizational aspects. Understanding these factors is essential for making an architecture that meets current requirements and can evolve over time. Let's start exploring the technical factors.

Technical factors

Technical factors lie at the heart of architectural decisions. These include the current state of the technology landscape, the specific requirements of the project, and the capabilities and limitations of different technologies and architectures. Key technical factors might involve the following:

- **Functional requirements**: These specify the behaviors, features, and functionalities a software system must offer to satisfy user needs, directly shaping the system's architecture. For example, in an online bookstore, functional requirements could include enabling users to search for books by title, author, or genre; providing detailed book information such as price, availability, and reviews; allowing users to create personal accounts for purchase management and order history; and supporting secure payment processing. Each requirement informs crucial architectural choices, such as implementing a robust database for search functionality and incorporating secure authentication services for user account management, ensuring the architecture adequately supports the system's functional demands.

- **Performance**: Performance is a critical factor in making architectural decisions. Everything from choosing algorithms to configuring hardware must prioritize system performance optimization. Factors such as caching mechanisms, data indexing, and parallel processing techniques become critical in achieving desired performance benchmarks.

- **Scalability**: Scalability is a critical aspect of software system architecture. It determines how well the system can manage growing volumes of data and user traffic while maintaining performance standards. Crucial decisions that impact scalability include database design, load balancing, and distributed architecture.

- **Reliability and availability**: Systems should be designed to function reliably in various conditions with minimal downtime and the ability to withstand faults.

- **Security**: In the digital world, it is crucial to guarantee that data is properly secured and complies with relevant laws and regulations. To protect against cyber threats, robust security measures must be integrated into the system's architecture. Decisions related to encryption methods, authentication mechanisms, and access controls significantly affect the system's ability to withstand cyber-attacks.

- **Maintainability**: Maintainability is a vital aspect to consider when developing a system. Various factors, such as modular design, code structure, and documentation, impact the ease with which a system can be maintained and evolved over time. Decisions prioritizing long-term maintainability include opting for well-established design patterns and adhering to coding standards.

- **Interoperability and integration**: Integration with third-party or existing enterprise systems can affect the architecture, particularly regarding interfaces, data exchange formats, and protocols. Therefore, it is essential to ensure the system can communicate and operate with other components.

- **Technology constraints**: Architectural choices can be influenced by existing technology stacks, compatibility with external systems, and available technology expertise within the team.

The technical factors presented are all essential considerations when making decisions about software architecture. In the next section, we will discuss how to approach the trade-offs involved in these factors. For now, let's examine the business factors that can also impact software architecture.

Business factors

Business factors relate to the strategic objectives, market positioning, and financial considerations of the organization the software aims to serve. These factors guide the software's purpose and scope to ensure alignment with business goals. Key business factors include the following:

- **Budget constraints**: Architectural decisions are significantly impacted by limited funds, which makes cost-effective solutions, essential features prioritization, open source technologies, optimized resource utilization, and cloud-based services important considerations.

- **Time constraints**: Constraints of time can significantly impact decision-making. Quick prototyping, automated testing, and modular development can help meet tight deadlines.

- **Regulatory requirements**: Compliance with regulatory standards is non-negotiable in many industries. Decisions related to data storage, privacy measures, and audit trails are pivotal to ensuring compliance.

- **Business goals and constraints**: The prioritization of certain architectural qualities is influenced by the organization's overall objectives, cost constraints, time-to-market requirements, and business strategy.

- **Evolution**: When making sustainable architectural decisions, it is vital to consider how a system might need to evolve in response to future requirements, technology changes, and business shifts.

- **Vendor lock-in**: Vendor lock-in arises when customers rely heavily on a single vendor's technologies. It presents challenges such as migration difficulties, which are technically challenging and costly, increased long-term costs due to proprietary technologies and potential vendor price hikes, and innovation constraints that limit access to advancements from other vendors, hindering growth and adaptability. Consequently, many opt for open standards, open source technologies, or multi-cloud strategies to prevent such dependency, aiming to secure more control and flexibility in their technological frameworks.

- **Internationalization and localization**: When making architectural decisions for global software, it's essential to consider **internationalization (i18n)** and **localization (l10n)** requirements. Internationalization involves designing software to support multiple languages and regions, addressing challenges such as character encoding, date and time formats, and cultural nuances. Localization tailors the software to specific locales by translating content and adapting features to meet regional preferences. Effective strategies for managing these factors include using Unicode for character encoding, externalizing text strings for easy translation, and designing flexible user interfaces that accommodate varying text lengths and formats. These considerations ensure the software is accessible and user-friendly for a global audience, enhancing usability and market reach.

- **Accessibility**: The requirement for software accessibility can shape architectural choices, particularly in the design of user interfaces and interactions. For instance, implementing alt-text for images ensures that visually impaired users can understand visual content through screen readers. Additionally, maintaining adequate color contrast helps those with color vision deficiencies to navigate and use the software effectively. These accessibility features are crucial considerations that can influence decision-making in software development to enhance usability for all users.

Last but not least, it is essential to consider organizational factors when making decisions about software architecture.

Organizational factors

Organizational factors focus on the organization's internal context in developing or deploying the software, including its culture, structure, and resources. These factors influence how software projects are managed and executed. Vital organizational factors include the following:

- **Team skills and experience**: The development team's expertise and knowledge can influence the choice of technologies and patterns in the architecture.

- **Stakeholder concerns**: Balancing different stakeholders' varying concerns and priorities is crucial in architectural decision-making. For example, while developers might prioritize ease of implementation, marketing teams could emphasize user experience and design features. Conflicts may arise when these priorities clash, influencing decisions to ensure all perspectives are considered and the architecture effectively supports diverse requirements. This process underscores the importance of integrating stakeholder feedback to create a well-rounded architectural strategy.

- **Architectural principles and guidelines**: Established principles and procedures within an organization or project can shape the decision-making process, promoting consistency and alignment with broader architectural goals.

- **Cultural and organizational dynamics**: The organization's culture and the dynamics of the development team, including communication patterns and decision-making processes, can influence the architectural direction.

- **DevOps practices and continuous delivery**: Adopting DevOps practices and the need for **continuous integration/continuous delivery (CI/CD)** can influence the architecture, particularly regarding automation, monitoring, and deployment strategies.

Understanding the distinctions between technical, business, and organizational factors is crucial in software architecture decision-making. We learned that technical factors focus on system construction and operation, business factors center on the external market and strategic objectives, and organizational factors relate to the internal capability for development and maintenance. Successfully balancing these factors ensures decisions align with strategic goals and organizational realities, leading to effective and sustainable software solutions.

Now, let's explore the trade-offs in architectural decision-making.

Trade-offs in architectural decision-making

Decision-making in software architecture is complex and involves a delicate balancing act among the factors we discussed, where trade-offs become the currency by which choices are measured. Now, we will explore the nuanced concept of trade-offs in software architecture, providing insights into their definition, typical examples, and strategies for practical evaluation and management.

Understanding trade-offs in software architecture

Trade-offs in software architecture refer to the inherent compromises made when selecting one architectural option over another. These compromises arise from conflicting goals, constraints, and requirements. In essence, making an advantageous decision in one aspect frequently comes at the expense of another. Recognizing and navigating these trade-offs is integral to strategic decision-making in software architecture.

Consider, for instance, the classic trade-off between technical factors: performance and maintainability. Opting for a highly optimized, performance-driven solution may result in intricate code that is harder to maintain. Conversely, prioritizing maintainability may involve abstractions and modular design, potentially impacting performance. The challenge lies in identifying the right balance that aligns with the project's goals. Let's explore other common trade-offs in architectural decisions:

- **Performance versus scalability**: A common trade-off often emerges between optimizing for immediate performance and designing for scalability. Implementing a highly performant, monolithic architecture may sacrifice scalability. Conversely, choosing a scalable microservices architecture may introduce latency, affecting immediate performance.

- **Scalability versus complexity**: Scalability refers to a system's ability to manage an increasing workload or its capacity to expand to support that workload. Achieving scalability might involve introducing load balancers, microservices, or distributed databases, which can increase the complexity of the system architecture and make it more challenging to implement, test, and manage.

- **Security versus usability**: Balancing security measures with user-friendly interfaces is another common trade-off. Stringent security protocols, such as multi-factor authentication, may enhance security but compromise the ease of use for end users.

- **Flexibility versus specificity**: Architectural decisions may involve trade-offs between building a highly flexible system that accommodates diverse requirements and crafting a solution tailored to specific needs. A generic, flexible solution might introduce complexities, while a specialized solution may need more adaptability to future changes.

- **Maintainability versus initial development speed**: Maintainability refers to the ease with which the system can be updated, modified, and extended over time. Prioritizing maintainability might involve adopting well-established design patterns, investing in documentation, and choosing technologies that emphasize long-term support. On the other hand, starting the development process to deliver features or products as quickly as possible might lead to choosing rapid development frameworks or compromising code quality or scalability that can impact maintainability.

- **Data redundancy versus data integrity**: Data redundancy increases fault tolerance and accessibility by duplicating data across multiple locations. While this can improve performance and availability, it might lead to challenges in maintaining data integrity and ensuring that all copies of the data are consistent and up to date.

- **Cost versus innovation**: Pursuing cutting-edge technologies and innovative solutions may clash with budget constraints. Adopting the latest technologies may incur higher initial costs, which can impact the overall project budget.

- **Innovation versus standardization**: Innovation encourages exploring new technologies, architectures, or methodologies to solve problems novelly, potentially offering competitive advantages. However, it carries risks associated with unproven technologies or approaches.

- **Standardization**: This focuses on using widely adopted technologies and practices, reducing risks, and ensuring compatibility, but possibly at the expense of missing out on innovative solutions that could offer better outcomes.

These are some common trade-offs in architectural decisions; however, an architect must tackle many others, such as interoperability versus optimal technology use, consistency versus availability, modularity versus performance, and so on. There is no ready answer; everything depends on the project's requirements and needs, and the architect must balance these factors to achieve the best possible solution. Now, we will learn about ATAM, a well-accepted and structured technique for evaluating and managing trade-offs effectively.

Evaluating the trade-offs

ATAM is a structured technique for evaluating the trade-offs and decisions within a software system's architecture. Developed by the **Software Engineering Institute (SEI)** at Carnegie Mellon University, it is designed to help assess the consequences of architectural choices against quality attributes requirements, such as performance, maintainability, and security. It provides a framework for identifying a software architecture's strengths and weaknesses in supporting the desired business goals and requirements.

The key objectives of ATAM are to identify architectural risks early, uncovering potential risks and vulnerabilities in the software architecture that could jeopardize the system's ability to meet its requirements. Evaluate architectural decisions, offering a systematic approach to assessing their impact on achieving quality attributes. In improving communication with stakeholders through its structured evaluation process, ATAM enhances communication among stakeholders by making explicit the trade-offs involved in architectural decisions.

Understanding the ATAM process

ATAM involves bringing stakeholders together to scrutinize the business motivations behind the system, including its functionalities, objectives, limitations, and desired non-functional qualities. From these motivations, quality attributes are identified and utilized to formulate scenarios. In collaboration with architectural strategies and decisions, these scenarios facilitate an evaluation of compromises, sensitivity points, and potential risks or non-risks. This evaluation can then be transformed into themes of risk and their consequences, allowing for iterative refinement. Each analysis cycle delves deeper, shifting from broader to more detailed inquiries based on findings from the preceding cycle. This iterative process continues until the architecture is optimized and all identified risk themes are adequately addressed.

Figure 2.3 illustrates the ATAM process, which is composed of nine steps.

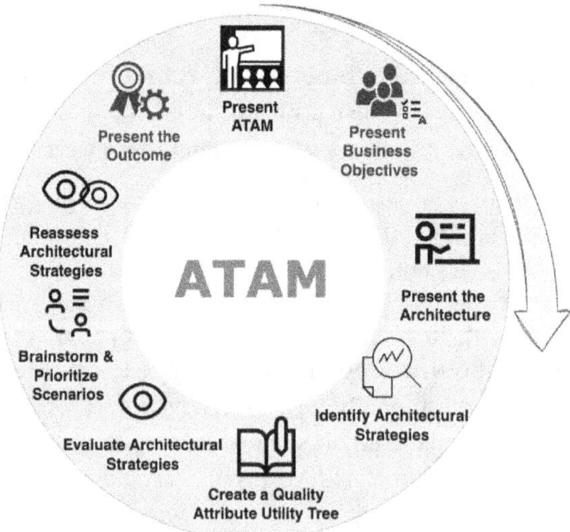

Figure 2.3: The ATAM process

Let's explore the nine steps of ATAM in more detail:

1. **Present ATAM**: Explain the ATAM methodology to stakeholders, clarifying any aspects of the process as needed.

2. **Present business objectives**: All participants share and assess the business objectives driving the system's development.

3. **Present the architecture**: The architect shares the overarching architecture with the team, ensuring the presentation is detailed enough for clear understanding.

4. **Identify architectural strategies**: The team presents and deliberates on various architectural plans for the system.

5. **Create a quality attribute utility tree**: Outline the primary business and technical requirements and link them to relevant architectural qualities. For each requirement, illustrate this connection through scenarios.

6. **Evaluate architectural strategies**: Assess each scenario based on its importance. Then, review the architecture's effectiveness in light of these scenarios.

7. **Brainstorm and prioritize scenarios**: With a broader group of stakeholders, share existing scenarios for expansion and prioritization.

8. **Reassess architectural strategies**: Reapply the steps of evaluating architectural strategies, utilizing insights gained from discussions with the broader stakeholder circle.

9. **Present outcomes**: Distribute all related documentation and findings to stakeholders.

These nine steps of ATAM can help us optimize and identify whether all risks are addressed. Next, let's check out the benefits of ATAM.

Benefits of ATAM

ATAM's proactive risk management enables teams to identify risks early, allowing them to tackle potential issues before they escalate into expensive problems. This approach leads to informed decision-making, as stakeholders acquire a more profound understanding of the outcomes stemming from architectural decisions, facilitating more knowledgeable choices. Moreover, ATAM promotes stakeholder alignment by fostering a shared comprehension of the trade-offs in architectural decisions, ensuring that business objectives harmonize with technical solutions. Additionally, emphasizing quality attributes guarantees that the architecture is more closely aligned with the system's long-term quality and performance targets.

Monitoring system – a case study

A technology company is developing a **health monitoring system** (**HMS**) to provide real-time health tracking for patients with chronic conditions. The system will collect data from wearable devices, allow healthcare professionals to monitor patient health remotely, and enable patients to access their health information via a web portal.

The first step to implementing the architecture trade-off analysis method is introducing ATAM to stakeholders. The purpose is to evaluate the HMS architecture to ensure it meets the system's goals. Then, following the method, we have to present and discuss the business objectives, such as the following examples:

- **Objective 1**: Ensure patient data is secure and private.

- **Objective 2**: Provide real-time health monitoring and alerts.

- **Objective 3**: Scale to accommodate an increasing number of users.

The next step is to present the proposed architecture, which focuses on data encryption for security, a microservices architecture for scalability, and a cloud-based solution for reliability and performance. Then, we will explore the architectural strategies, such as these examples:

- Use of encryption and secure data protocols for patient data.

- Adoption of a microservices architecture to facilitate scaling.

- Utilization of cloud services for data storage and computing power.

Now, we must create a quality attribute utility tree. It could be a document or even a diagram. *Figure 2.4* presents a quality attribute utility tree document.

QUALITY ATTRIBUTE UTILITY TREE FOR HMS

Root: Health Monitoring System

- Security
  - **Scenario 1:** Encrypt patient data in transit and at rest to prevent unauthorized access.
  - **Scenario 2:** Implement role-based access control for different user types (patients, doctors, administrators).

- Performance
  - **Scenario 1:** Process and display real-time health data within 2 seconds of receiving data from wearable devices.
  - **Scenario 2:** Generate health alerts and notifications within 5 seconds of identifying a potential health issue.

- Scalability
  - **Scenario 1:** Support concurrent use by up to 10,000 users without performance degradation.
  - **Scenario 2:** Dynamically scale cloud resources based on the number of active users to manage cost and performance efficiently.

- Reliability
  - **Scenario 1:** Achieve 99.99% uptime for the patient monitoring dashboard.

Figure 2.4: Quality attribute utility tree document

Architectural strategies are evaluated after the quality attribute utility tree document is created. Each scenario in the utility tree is discussed and rated by priority. The architecture is evaluated to determine how well it addresses these scenarios, focusing on trade-offs between security, performance, scalability, reliability, and usability.

We advance to scenario brainstorming and prioritization, where stakeholders brainstorm additional scenarios and prioritize them based on the system's goals and potential risks. Then, the architectural strategies are reassessed using the new information and scenarios, adjusting as necessary.

Finally, the final documentation, including the quality attribute utility tree and evaluations, is shared with all stakeholders.

Use case outcome

Through the ATAM process and the development of the quality attribute utility tree, the stakeholders understand the trade-offs involved in the HMS architecture. This process ensures that the architecture aligns with the business objectives and quality goals, mainly focusing on security and privacy concerns, real-time monitoring capability, and the system's ability to scale. This structured evaluation guides the decision-making process, highlighting areas for improvement and confirming the system's architectural direction.

In conclusion, trade-offs are integral to software architecture's decision-making landscape. Acknowledging their existence, understanding their implications, and employing strategic evaluation strategies are essential to successfully navigating the complexities of architectural decision-making. This section delved into these strategies, providing guidance on striking the right balance in the face of competing considerations.

Now, let's shift to understanding what business goals are and how to align expectations between architectural decisions and business goals.

Aligning architectural decisions with business goals

Aligning architectural decisions is essential at all levels, including business goals. Therefore, we must first answer the following question: What are business goals?

What are business goals?

Organizations have specific business goals to ensure growth, sustainability, and competitive advantage. These objectives may include increasing revenue, improving customer satisfaction, expanding market share, or ensuring regulatory compliance. Now that we know what business goals are, let's explore the role of architecture in achieving them.

The role of architecture in achieving business goals

Software architecture plays a pivotal role in achieving business goals by laying the foundational framework that allows companies to quickly adapt to market shifts, reduce operational costs, drive innovation, and secure a competitive advantage. This strategic alignment between architectural decisions and business objectives is critical for ensuring that technology investments deliver tangible business outcomes and support the organization's long-term vision.

Here, we present some key business goals that architecture helps to achieve:

- **Market agility**: In today's fast-paced business environment, adapting quickly to market and customer demands is crucial. A well-designed architecture enables faster deployment of new features, more accessible adaptation to changing business needs, and seamless integration with existing and emerging technologies.

- **Cost reduction**: A strategic architecture can reduce **capital expenditure (CapEx)** and **operational expenditure (OpEx)**. Optimize system design for efficiency and scalability to minimize hardware and infrastructure costs. Prioritize maintainability and modularity to lower long-term development and maintenance costs.

- **Innovation**: Architectures that support experimentation and iteration foster an innovation culture. Data exchange and analytics architectures provide insights to drive product and service innovation and exceed customer expectations.

- **Competitive advantage**: Flexible architecture is a competitive advantage that allows companies to provide exceptional customer experiences, simplify operations, and launch products faster. By using architecture to support strategic business goals, companies can stand out in the industry, attract and retain clients, and foster a more robust brand identity.

To achieve these benefits, architects and business stakeholders must collaborate closely, ensuring that the architecture is continuously aligned with the business's evolving goals and strategies. This involves regular communication, a shared understanding of objectives, and a commitment to aligning technology decisions with business priorities.

Impacts of aligned decisions

When architectural decisions align closely with business goals, they can profoundly positively impact the organization. This alignment results in a situation where technology supports the business and actively propels it forward. Such aligned architectural decisions can improve efficiency, productivity, and market responsiveness, fostering innovation and growth. This strategic alignment enhances risk management, reduces costs, and boosts customer satisfaction. It also strengthens business continuity and ensures that operations can withstand various challenges.

Impacts of misaligned decisions

Misalignment between architectural decisions and business goals can increase costs, reduce efficiency, and hinder scalability, impacting the organization's competitiveness. It may expose the system to security vulnerabilities, regulatory compliance issues, and customer dissatisfaction. Furthermore, it can result in missed market opportunities and compromised decision-making, necessitating ongoing communication and flexibility between business and IT leaders to realign strategies and operations.

Case studies of aligned and misaligned decisions

Let's examine two case studies that poignantly illustrate the tangible impact of aligned or misaligned architectural decisions on business outcomes. Examining instances where strategic alignment was achieved or missed provides invaluable insights into the correlation between architecture and success.

Case study 1 – seamless integration for enhanced customer experience

In a successful alignment scenario, a global e-commerce platform strategically redesigned its architecture to seamlessly integrate customer data across channels. This alignment significantly enhanced the overall customer experience, leading to increased satisfaction, retention, and improved revenue streams.

Case study 2 – misalignment causing operational friction conversely

A financial institution faced operational challenges due to misaligned architectural decisions. While technically sound, implementing a new system should have considered the intricacies of existing operational workflows. This misalignment resulted in operational friction, delays, and increased costs, underscoring the importance of strategic synchronization.

Case studies have shown that aligning architectural decisions with business goals is crucial for success. Strategic coupling between technology and business vision can lead to success, while misalignment can result in pitfalls.

Strategies for aligning architectural decisions

It's essential to take a strategic approach to ensure that your architectural decisions align with your business objectives. This should involve understanding your organizational goals comprehensively by engaging with stakeholders, understanding market dynamics, and keeping an eye on industry trends. You should also implement iterative feedback loops to ensure continuous alignment and use prioritization frameworks to focus on crucial business outcomes. Fostering cross-functional collaboration is essential to ensure that your decisions support your overall vision. Finally, applying agile methodologies will help you meet evolving business needs.

Now, let's discuss the significance of documenting architectural decisions and how we can effectively document them.

Documenting architectural decisions

Documenting architectural decisions is crucial and strategic because it provides a clear record of the rationale behind each decision. This ensures alignment with business objectives, facilitates stakeholder communication, and guides future development efforts. It also aids in maintaining system consistency, compliance, and efficiency over time.

Architecture decision records

Let's start by defining an **architectural decision record (ADR)**. An ADR is a document that records a significant **architectural decision (AD)**, its context, and its consequences.

ADRs are essential to any project, as they help document and track the decisions made during its life cycle. From creation to acceptance, an ADR goes through a series of states and, once accepted, it becomes immutable. If new insights require a different decision, a new ADR must be proposed and accepted to supersede the previous one.

The ADR process generates a collection of records that make up the decision log. This log provides valuable project context and detailed information on design and implementation choices.

Project members usually skim the headlines of each ADR to get an overview of the project context. However, they may also read the ADRs in detail to better understand specific implementation and design decisions.

The ADR process may face challenges such as contested decisions, requiring a clear conflict resolution mechanism such as a decision-making committee or mediator. While ADRs provide stability, they can become rigid, so it's important to remain adaptable with regular reviews and a process for updating decisions. Effective stakeholder engagement ensures well-rounded and widely accepted decisions.

No standard

There are no established standards for making this type of decision. A suitable ADR should be easy to write and maintain; otherwise, it risks becoming obsolete. It should be designed to be strategic, realistic, and measurable to promote sustainability and avoid unnecessary tasks. Clarity and objectivity are also essential to ensure that the ADR effectively communicates its purpose and rationale.

Structure

Typically, an ADR document should include the following sections:

- **Title**: Something declarative stating your purpose.
- **Date**: The day of the document.

- **Status**: The status of an ADR document varies based on the decision-making and implementation phases. The statuses range from *Proposed*, indicating that the decision is under review or discussion, to *Accepted*, where the decision is finalized for implementation. A *Rejected* status means the decision will not proceed, while *Deprecated* indicates that a previously accepted decision has become outdated. If a decision is marked as *Superseded*, it has been replaced by a more recent one due to new circumstances or better alternatives. Finally, *Implemented* signifies that the decision has been fully executed and is operational. These statuses are essential for monitoring the progression of decisions throughout a project, ensuring that all team members are informed and in sync.

- **Context**: The explanation of the fact and context in a rich, simple, and direct way.

- **Decision**: The conclusion is made based on the context. It is stated in complete sentences, using the active voice.

- **Consequences**: We must carefully weigh the trade-offs involved in making a decision. Thoroughly detailing all consequences is crucial, as architectural decisions are based on in-depth research and analysis. Emphasizing previous studies is essential.

Figure 2.5 illustrates an ADR document.

```
# Architectural Decision Record (ADR) Example
## Title
Replacing Synchronous REST Communication with Asynchronous
Messaging between Order and Payment Services

## Date
2024-03-21

## Status
Proposed

## Context
The current system uses synchronous REST calls for communication
between the Order Service and the Payment Service. This approach
has led to increased response times during peak loads,
affecting the overall user experience and system scalability.

## Decision
We will replace the synchronous REST communication with asynchronous, non-blocking
messaging. This change aims to decouple the Order Service from the Payment Service,
allowing for more scalable and resilient system architecture.

## Consequences
#### Positive:
 - Improved system scalability and ability to handle high volumes of
   transactions without significant delays.
#### Negative:
 - Requires the introduction of a message broker (such as RabbitMQ or Kafka),
   adding complexity to the infrastructure
```

Figure 2.5: ADR document

This is just an example of an ADR. You can add and remove sections according to your organization's needs. Another point is where to save your ADRs; I've seen some teams save them to Git repositories. However, some stakeholders, such as business stakeholders, don't have access to Git repositories, so I suggest storing them in a tool or network directory accessible to all stakeholders.

Summary

In this chapter, we learned about the importance of decision-making in software architecture. We discussed and scrutinized what a decision is and the kinds of software architectural decisions. We also explored the decision-making processes, identified different decision-making approaches, and outlined the progression of decision-making.

We delved into the architectural factors and learned about their categorization, such as technical, business, and organizational.

Then, we learned about the trade-offs in architectural decision-making, how to understand them, and how to evaluate them with ATAM. We also presented the ATAM process, its benefits, and a case study.

We approached the importance of aligning architectural decisions with business goals, clarifying the business goals, the role of architecture in achieving business goals, and the impact of aligned and misaligned decisions. We saw a case study for both, and we also presented strategies for aligning architectural decisions.

Finally, we presented the importance of documenting architectural decisions and how to make them through ADR documents.

The chapter delivered essential guidance that equipped you with the tools necessary to navigate decision-making in software architecture effectively. It presented a detailed approach to comprehending and implementing these processes and stressed the importance of harmonizing architectural choices with business aims. Furthermore, it introduced techniques such as ATAM for assessing trade-offs and ADR documents to document architectural decisions, thereby boosting your capacity to make knowledgeable decisions that contribute to developing robust and scalable software systems.

In *Chapter 3, Understanding the System Context*, we will explore system requirements gathering, emphasizing understanding the system context, stakeholders' engagement, and communication. We will delve into functional and non-functional requirements and elicit and document requirements techniques.

Questions

1. What are the primary categories of architectural factors?

2. Can you explain the concept of trade-offs in architectural decision-making?

3. What is ATAM?

4. How does aligning architectural decisions with business goals impact a project?

5. Describe a case study that illustrates the impact of architectural decision alignment with business goals.

6. Why is documenting architectural decisions important, and what method is recommended?

7. What strategies are recommended for aligning architectural decisions with business goals?

Get This Book's PDF Version and Exclusive Extras

Scan the QR code (or go to `packtpub.com/unlock`). Search for this book by name, confirm the edition, and then follow the steps on the page.

Note: Keep your invoice handly. Purchase made directly from packt don't require one.

3

Understanding the System Context

This chapter explores the role of **system context** in software architecture, which is essential for successful software development. It explains the difference between system context and software architecture and how to integrate it into architectural design. The chapter outlines the importance of stakeholder engagement and communication, identifying and categorizing system stakeholders, and offering effective engagement strategies. It also provides tools and techniques for communicating with stakeholders and strategies for overcoming common engagement challenges. The chapter also covers **functional requirements (FRs)** and **non-functional requirements (NFRs)**, best practices for collecting them, and challenges in managing them.

Finally, the chapter presents an overview of techniques for documenting and managing requirements and explains how to design the architecture using the **C4 model**, which stands for **context**, **container**, **component**, and **code**. This ensures that architectural documentation is straightforward and comprehensive.

This chapter will cover the following topics:

- Defining system context
- Stakeholder engagement and communication
- FRs and NFRs
- Documenting requirements and architecture

By the end of this chapter, you will comprehend the system context within software architecture, distinguishing it from other design aspects and integrating it efficiently. You will also learn effective stakeholder engagement strategies and the best practices for identifying and managing requirements. Furthermore, you will learn about techniques and tools for documenting requirements and fully immerse yourself in architecture using the C4 model. This will enable you to create clear and comprehensive architectural documentation.

Defining system context

The concept of system context is foundational in software architecture. It provides a lens through which architects and developers can view and understand the environment in which a software system operates. Let's delve into the definition of system context and how it differs from software architecture, its importance, and its primary factors for effective system design and implementation.

System context versus software architecture

System context defines a software system's environment and external interactions, including the relationships with users, other systems, and external interfaces. It establishes limits and external connections to understand how environmental factors affect the system. In contrast, software architecture focuses on the internal structure of the software system, detailing the architectural elements and their relationships. It involves making critical decisions to ensure the system meets technical requirements and optimizes performance and scalability. Essentially, while the system context looks outward to define how the system interacts with its surroundings, software architecture looks inward to design and organize the system's internal components and operations.

Understanding the system context

Understanding the system context involves recognizing and analyzing the myriad factors that interact with a software system. These factors can be broadly categorized into technical, operational, business, and environmental and social, as presented in *Figure 3.1*.

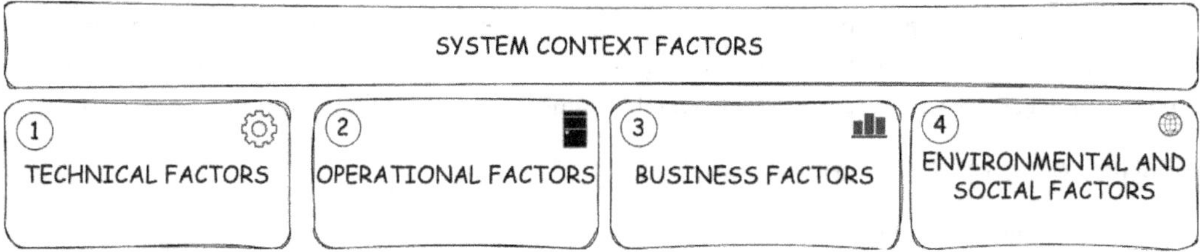

Figure 3.1: System context factor

Each factor's category encompasses various elements that can influence the system's design, development, and deployment processes:

- **Technical factors**: These encompass the hardware, software, networks, and technologies essential for supporting or interacting with a system. This includes physical devices such as servers, desktops, mobile devices, and IoT devices, which are vital for system operations. The software aspect covers systems, libraries, frameworks, or platforms that the system depends on or integrates with, including databases, middleware, and third-party **application programming interfaces (APIs)**. Additionally, the networking requirements entail internet connectivity, bandwidth, and network protocols that facilitate system functioning. Security is crucial, requiring adherence to protocols, encryption standards, and compliance mandates to safeguard data and ensure privacy. Lastly, interoperability is critical, with standards and protocols ensuring effective communication and operation with other systems.

- **Operational factors**: These are crucial components of the system context, focusing on the practical aspects of its day-to-day functionality within its designated environment. It involves strategies and methodologies for deploying, utilizing, managing, and maintaining the system to meet its operational goals and compliance standards. Key aspects include the deployment settings, which may be in cloud-based platforms, on-premises data centers, or hybrid environments. Maintenance and support encompass procedures and resources for system updates, issue resolution, and user support. Performance requirements specify the expected system behavior under average and peak loads, considering response times, throughput, and availability. The system's scalability and flexibility allow it to adjust to changing operational volumes and requirements without significant architectural changes. Additionally, disaster recovery and business continuity plans are critical for ensuring the system can recover from severe disruptions and maintain functionality in challenging situations.

- **Business factors**: These are essential elements related to the organization's goals, strategies, and processes, where the software system has a pivotal role. These factors encompass the business goals the system supports, such as increasing revenue, enhancing customer satisfaction, or optimizing operations. They also include market dynamics, such as trends, customer demands, and the competitive landscape, which can influence the system's features, usability, and innovation. Stakeholder requirements also play a crucial role, considering the needs, expectations, and constraints of all parties involved, such as customers, employees, partners, and suppliers. Additionally, cost constraints are significant, affecting technological, infrastructure, and development resource choices. Lastly, regulatory compliance is critical as the system must adhere to business-specific regulations and legal requirements to ensure legality and ethical operations.

- **Environmental and social factors**: These are critical in the system's context, encompassing physical and social environments. These factors include geographic distribution, which involves the physical locations of system users, data centers, and other infrastructure. This distribution impacts latency, data sovereignty, and localization needs. Cultural and social considerations also influence the design and use of a system. Cultural norms and social dynamics can affect **user interface (UI)** design, accessibility, and system usage patterns, requiring thoughtful integration to meet diverse user expectations effectively. Environmental sustainability is another critical factor, focusing on minimizing the system's environmental impact. This includes strategies to reduce energy consumption, optimize resource utilization, and decrease waste, reflecting a commitment to sustainable practices.

  Lastly, climatic conditions are crucial environmental variables significantly affecting hardware performance and reliability. These factors must be considered to ensure the system's robustness and continuous operation under various environmental conditions.

Software architects and developers must consider these key factors to ensure a robust system that can withstand challenges and meet internal and external requirements.

Integrating system context into architectural design

Once the system context is thoroughly understood, incorporating it into the architectural design process becomes crucial. This pivotal step ensures that the resulting software architecture aligns seamlessly with the external environment and the internal project goals. The integration process involves a multifaceted strategy, which is essential for developing resilient, adaptable systems that efficiently meet user needs and adhere to external requirements. Here are the main strategies:

- **Contextual analysis and documentation**: Start by thoroughly analyzing and documenting the system context, including all external entities, their interactions with the system, and any influential factors. Tools such as the **C4 model** can help visualize this information. We will approach it later in this chapter.

- **Stakeholder engagement**: Continuously interact with stakeholders to grasp their needs, expectations, and apprehensions. This ongoing engagement is essential for capturing evolving requirements and soliciting feedback. Based on this feedback, the architectural design would be modified to better align with stakeholder needs. For example, if stakeholders express concerns about system performance under heavy load, the architecture can be adjusted to include scalable microservices that handle increased traffic more efficiently. The project can better align with stakeholder needs and expectations by prioritizing continuous stakeholder engagement, incorporating feedback, considering a broad range of adjustments, utilizing specific interaction methods, and simplifying technical language. This approach enhances the architectural design and contributes to the overall success and satisfaction of all parties involved.

- **Adaptability and flexibility**: Design the architecture to be adaptable to changes in the system context. To design the architecture to be adaptable to changes in the system context, break down the system into smaller, independent modules that can be developed, tested, and maintained separately. This makes it easier to update or replace individual components without affecting the entire system.

- **Risk assessment**: Recognize and evaluate risks linked to external factors, such as reliance on third-party services or adherence to evolving regulations. Embed mitigation strategies directly into architectural design.

  Recognizing and mitigating risks ensures system stability and contributes to overall project success. Proactive risk management enhances stakeholder confidence, reduces the likelihood of unexpected disruptions, and ensures that the system remains aligned with business objectives and regulatory requirements.

- **Performance and scalability planning**: Consider the operational environment's impact on system performance and plan for scalability from the outset. This might include designing for load balancing, caching strategies, or distributed architectures.

- **Security and compliance**: Ensure the architecture incorporates necessary security measures and compliance with relevant regulations. This includes data encryption, secure communication channels, and privacy safeguards.

- **Prototype and feedback loops**: Use prototyping and early testing to validate architectural decisions against system context requirements. Establish feedback loops with stakeholders to refine the architecture based on real-world use and feedback.

Integrating system context into the architectural design is not a single occurrence but an ongoing process throughout the system's development life cycle. By continuously aligning the architecture with the external and internal factors that define the system context, we can ensure the creation of robust, responsive, and successful software systems. This alignment enhances the system's ability to meet current requirements and equips it to adapt to future challenges and opportunities, ensuring long-term relevance and value.

Next, we'll explore and learn how to engage and communicate with the stakeholders.

Stakeholder engagement and communication

Stakeholder engagement and communication are vital processes that ensure all parties interested in or impacted by a project are actively involved and informed throughout its life cycle. Effective engagement involves identifying and understanding stakeholders, establishing clear communication channels, and fostering collaboration and feedback. Tailoring messages to different audiences and maintaining transparency builds trust and consensus. Continuous engagement, active listening, and adapting to stakeholder feedback are vital practices that align project objectives with stakeholder expectations, ultimately contributing to the project's success.

Identifying the system's stakeholders

Identifying the system's stakeholders is a crucial initial step in any project, ensuring that all parties affected by or interested in the project are considered throughout its life cycle. *Figure 3.2* presents the main techniques for identifying stakeholders.

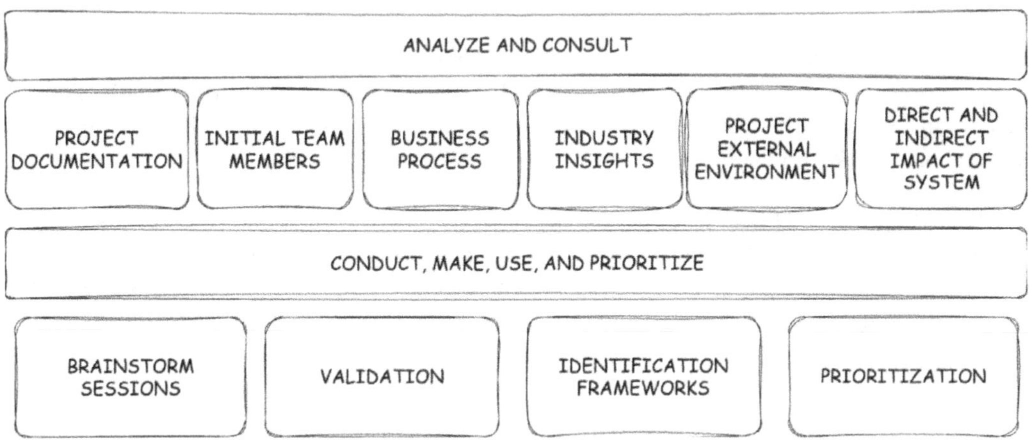

Figure 3.2: Techniques for identifying stakeholders

Start by reviewing existing project documentation, such as proposals and contracts, to gain initial insights into who might be affected by or have an interest in the project. Consult with initial project team members, including project managers, business analysts, and senior IT personnel, who can often pinpoint critical internal and external stakeholders.

Analyzing the business processes that the system will support or affect helps identify which departments, teams, or roles will be stakeholders. Utilizing stakeholder identification frameworks, such as the **responsible, accountable, consulted**, and **informed (RACI)** responsibilities, can systematically pinpoint stakeholders based on their involvement or impact on the project.

It is essential to consider both direct and indirect impacts. Direct stakeholders might include system users, while indirect stakeholders could encompass IT support teams or external partners reliant on the system's data. Examining the project's external environment is crucial to identifying external stakeholders such as regulatory bodies, suppliers, customers, and partners interested in the system's outcomes.

Conduct brainstorming sessions with project team members to ensure a broader perspective and identify any stakeholders that might have been overlooked. Also, understanding the wider industry context can help identify external stakeholders such as industry groups, regulatory agencies, and competitors.

After compiling a preliminary list of stakeholders, validate it with key team members and refine it based on feedback and further analysis. It is crucial to be inclusive at this stage and include all critical perspectives. Once stakeholders are identified, they should be prioritized based on their level of interest, influence, and impact on the project to focus engagement efforts where they are most needed.

Identifying stakeholders is an ongoing process that may require adjustments as the project evolves and new information emerges. Keeping the stakeholder list updated ensures that all relevant parties are engaged and their needs are considered throughout the project life cycle. With this understanding of identifying stakeholders, we can now categorize them.

Categorizing the stakeholders

Stakeholders can be broadly categorized into several types based on their interests, roles, and influence on the project. Understanding these categories helps in effectively managing their expectations and contributions. Here are the primary types of stakeholders, their interests and roles, and how an architect should work with them:

- **End users**: They are the individuals who will directly interact with the software. Their primary interest is in the system's usability, functionality, performance, and reliability. The architect should engage them through interviews, user surveys, and conducting usability tests to collect information on their requirements and expectations.

- **Business stakeholders**: This group includes clients, investors, and anyone with a financial or business interest in the project. They are concerned with the return on investment, market competitiveness, and the software's alignment with business objectives. They define business requirements and strategic goals. The architect should regularly communicate project progress, risks, and milestones and ensure the software architecture meets their business needs.

- **Project managers**: They oversee the project's development, ensuring it adheres to the planned schedule and budget constraints. They are interested in clear milestones, risk management, and resource allocation. The architect should maintain open communication regarding project requirements, restrictions, and changes and assist in aligning project objectives with architectural decisions.

- **Development team**: This team comprises developers, testers, UI / **user experience** (UX) designers, and anyone directly involved in creating the software. The architect should facilitate a collaborative environment, clearly communicate architectural decisions, and provide technical leadership and guidance.

- **System administrators and operations staff**: Focused on the system's deployment, operation, and maintenance. Their primary concerns include system stability, security, and operational costs. They manage the software's operational environment, ensure system performance, and handle upgrades and patches. The architect should work closely to understand operational requirements and constraints—design for maintainability, scalability, and ease of deployment.

- **Security experts**: They are in charge of integrating security considerations from the outset. The architect should collaborate with security experts to embed best practices and security measures into the software architecture.

- **External partners and vendors**: The architect should establish clear communication channels and partnership agreements with external partners and vendors. This benefits the architect by ensuring seamless collaboration and service integration, essential for project success. Cultivating relationships founded on trust and reciprocal advantages helps prevent misunderstandings, reduce risks, and enhance the efficiency and effectiveness of working with external entities. This proactive approach allows architects to manage dependencies better, align expectations, and achieve higher-quality project outcomes.

By recognizing the stakeholders and adopting stakeholder-specific strategies, software architects can effectively address the diverse needs and expectations within the project ecosystem, leading to more successful outcomes.

Strategies for effective engagement

Improving stakeholder engagement is a task that requires developing soft skills, such as empathy, active listening, emotional intelligence, and effective strategies.

Effective engagement strategies are essential for ensuring successful stakeholder interactions, fostering collaboration, and achieving project objectives. Several techniques can enhance stakeholder engagement, and some critical methods are presented in *Figure 3.3*:

Figure 3.3: Strategies for effective engagement

Establish clear, open, transparent, and consistent lines of communication. Avoid jargon to ensure everyone involved understands the ongoing processes and updates. This should be maintained over time, not just implemented sporadically. Show genuine interest in stakeholders' opinions and concerns through active listening, which can uncover valuable insights and build trust. It is also important to keep stakeholders informed about progress, changes, and decisions through regular updates, helping to manage expectations and maintain engagement.

Implementing mechanisms for collecting and responding to feedback shows that stakeholder input is valued and considered in decision-making processes. Ensure all stakeholder groups have opportunities to participate in relevant discussions and decisions to include diverse perspectives that can enrich project outcomes. Maintain transparency about how decisions are made and how stakeholder input will be used, as this fosters trust and accountability.

Recognize that different stakeholders may require different engagement approaches and tailor strategies to match their level of interest, influence, and preferred communication methods. Anticipate and address conflicts constructively by establishing clear procedures for resolving disagreements to maintain a positive engagement environment. Acknowledge contributions and celebrate successes to enhance stakeholders' commitment and support.

Regularly review and adapt engagement strategies based on feedback and outcomes to ensure continuous improvement, helping engagement efforts remain effective over time. By employing these strategies, architects can build strong relationships with stakeholders, ensuring their needs and concerns are addressed and their support is garnered for the project or initiative's success.

Having explored these strategies, let's now focus on overcoming challenges in stakeholder engagement.

Overcoming challenges in stakeholder engagement

When dealing with interests, we always face some challenges, and it's no different in projects. So, we need to recognize and learn how to overcome the obstacles. Overcoming challenges in stakeholder engagement involves strategic approaches and practical solutions to common barriers. Acknowledging and respecting the diversity of stakeholder interests and objectives is essential. Finding common ground and using negotiation and conflict resolution techniques can help address conflicting interests constructively.

To overcome communication barriers, it's essential to use clear, accessible language and employ various communication channels to ensure messages reach all stakeholders effectively. Tailoring communication strategies to suit the preferences and requirements of different stakeholder groups can enhance understanding and engagement.

Re-engaging disinterested stakeholders can be achieved by highlighting the project's relevance to their interests and using targeted communication to demonstrate the value of their participation and feedback. Building trust requires transparency, consistency, and reliability. Sharing information openly, fulfilling commitments, and actively listening will show stakeholders their opinions are valued and considered.

To avoid information overload, prioritize and streamline communication, focusing on key messages and using summaries or highlights to convey the most critical points. Addressing resource constraints involves prioritizing stakeholder engagement activities and seeking efficient methods of communication and interaction. Leveraging technology and collaborative tools can facilitate engagement with minimal resource expenditure.

Adapting to changing stakeholder dynamics requires regular reviews and updates of the stakeholder list and engagement strategies. It is vital to stay flexible and adjust engagement approaches as the project evolves and new stakeholders emerge.

With the advent of remote work, encountering global teams that navigate cultural and language barriers has become increasingly common. Bridging these differences requires employing culturally sensitive communication practices and, when necessary, using translation services.

Enhancing virtual engagement can be done using interactive tools and techniques, such as polls, breakout rooms, and interactive presentations to foster participation and interaction in online settings.

Finally, implementing mechanisms to measure the effectiveness of stakeholder engagement, such as feedback surveys, engagement metrics, and stakeholder interviews, can help refine and improve engagement strategies over time. By proactively addressing these challenges with thoughtful strategy and practices, meaningful and effective stakeholder engagement can be fostered, supporting project objectives and building strong, collaborative relationships with all stakeholders.

Tools and techniques for communication

Effective communication is the success of any project, initiative, or ongoing operation. Various tools and techniques are available to enhance clarity, ensure that messages are received and understood, and foster stakeholder collaboration. Each communication tool is designed for specific uses and offers varying levels of effectiveness. Email is the most appropriate method for formal communications, including agreements and detailed updates, due to its formal and documentable nature. For real-time conversations and quick updates, instant messaging platforms, such as Slack or Microsoft Teams, are more suitable because they allow immediate feedback and dynamic interaction.

Video conferencing tools, such as Zoom or Google Meet, are invaluable for face-to-face meetings and discussions, particularly with remote teams, helping to bridge the distance gap. Project management software, including platforms such as Trello, Asana, or Jira, is critical for integrating communication features with task tracking and progress updates, providing a comprehensive view of project statuses.

Collaborative document platforms, such as Google Docs or Microsoft Office Online, enable teams to collaborate on documents, spreadsheets, and presentations in real time, enhancing collaborative efforts. Online survey tools, such as SurveyMonkey or Google Forms, are effective for gathering extensive feedback and gauging opinions from various stakeholders. These tools ensure that a broad range of insights is considered in decision-making processes.

Social media platforms are excellent for broader community engagement, running awareness campaigns, and sharing informal updates, helping to keep a more comprehensive audience informed. Lastly, internal wikis and knowledge bases, such as Confluence, are central repositories for storing and sharing information, guidelines, and frequently asked questions, ensuring that vital knowledge is accessible to everyone involved.

Applying the strategies and these tools, we can ensure robust, effective, and adaptable communication that meets the needs of diverse audiences and project requirements.

We discussed the significance of engaging with stakeholders and effective communication methods. We outlined how to identify stakeholders, categorize them, and provide detailed strategies for engaging with them. Additionally, we discussed solutions to overcome challenges such as diverse interests, communication barriers, and stakeholder disengagement. The following section will delve into the system's FRs and NFRs.

FRs and NFRs

FRs and NFRs are two fundamental categories of specifications, and understanding the distinction between these two types of requirements is crucial for successful system development.

Understanding FRs

FRs specify what a system should do and how it interacts with its environment. They determine the system's behavior, inputs, processing, and output. These requirements are derived from user needs, system models, and business rules and are usually documented in use cases, user stories, or functional specification documents.

Clearly defined FRs offer clarity in development, acting as a blueprint for developers to understand precisely what needs to be built. This ensures that the development process is focused and efficient. Additionally, FRs play a crucial role in stakeholder communication, serving as a vital link between stakeholders and the development team to ensure a common understanding of the system's objectives. Furthermore, these requirements form the basis for testing, as they are used to create test cases for quality assurance, providing the criteria against which the system's functionality is verified and validated.

Let's present some FRs examples:

- A website must authenticate users before granting access to private information

- An e-commerce platform must calculate shipping costs based on the user's location and the package's weight

- A mobile app must refresh data whenever a user clicks on the screen

Next, we will move on to NFRs.

Understanding NFRs

Understanding **NFRs** is essential for ensuring that a system meets its functional objectives and achieves operational excellence and user satisfaction. It is one of the top items in software architecture that we architects are concerned about. Unlike FRs, which specify what a system should do, NFRs focus on how it performs these functions, significantly impacting its usability and effectiveness. These requirements encompass the system's performance, security, usability, and reliability, defining the operational standards and constraints crucial for its success.

The significance of NFRs extends across various key areas. They ensure the system is user-friendly and reliable, increasing user satisfaction. NFRs also address the system's scalability, responsiveness, and stability under varying loads, ensuring it performs well and remains operational under peak demands. Additionally, they define security protocols and data protection measures to safeguard against breaches and ensure compliance with legal and regulatory standards. Lastly, NFRs facilitate system updates, maintenance, and operation across different environments without significant changes, enhancing maintainability and portability.

We can set the NFRs into two categories: qualitative and quantitative.

- **Qualitative NFRs**: These are often subjective and involve the quality of UX or developers' maintainability. They require judgment and perception to assess and are typically improved through design and UX considerations.

- **Quantitative NFRs**: These are measurable and can be defined by specific numerical metrics that need to be achieved. These are often crucial for system performance and operational requirements and can be verified through testing and operational metrics.

Let's see some NFRs examples:

- The system should load the user dashboard within two seconds

- User data should be encrypted using AES-256 encryption

- The system should be available 99.9% of the time

- The application should be usable by people with a wide range of disabilities

After learning about FRs and NFRs, let's learn about the best practices for gathering them.

Best practices for gathering requirements

Gathering FRs and NFRs is a critical phase in the development process, demanding careful attention.

Best practices emphasize a structured and collaborative approach to gathering requirements, engaging stakeholders, utilizing diverse elicitation techniques, and maintaining flexibility to adapt to new insights and changes.

The process begins with stakeholder identification, recognizing all parties interested in the project's outcome. Engaging these stakeholders early and often is paramount to uncovering the full spectrum of requirements and expectations.

Effective communication is the backbone of successful requirements gathering. This involves not just talking but active listening, where the development team pays close attention to stakeholder inputs, asks clarifying questions, and encourages open discussions to dive deeper into the requirements. Techniques such as interviews, workshops, and surveys can be instrumental in this phase, each for gathering requirements" selected based on the project's context and stakeholders' preferences.

Documenting requirements accurately is equally crucial. Use cases, user stories, and functional specifications offer frameworks to capture FRs in a structured manner. Specify clear, measurable criteria for requirements to facilitate easier testing and validation. These documents should be accessible and understandable to technical team members and non-technical stakeholders, ensuring a shared understanding across the board. By leveraging use cases, user stories, and functional specifications and ensuring that documentation is clear, measurable, and accessible, development teams can create a solid foundation for building systems that meet user needs and achieve project goals.

As requirements are collected, prioritization becomes necessary to address time, budget, and resource constraints.

Validation and verification of requirements should occur continuously. Review sessions with stakeholders offer opportunities to confirm that the documented requirements align with their expectations and the project's goals. This iterative review process helps catch misunderstandings or missing requirements early when they are easier to address. Adopting an agile mindset can enhance flexibility and responsiveness to change. In situations where requirements might change over time, iterative development lets teams adapt their methods based on feedback and new learnings acquired throughout the project.

Lastly, a collaborative toolset can support the requirement-gathering process by facilitating documentation, communication, and tracking of changes. Tools that offer real-time collaboration, version control, and integration with other development tools can streamline workflows and keep everyone aligned.

Challenges in gathering and managing requirements

Navigating the complexities of gathering and managing requirements is fraught with pitfalls and challenges that can significantly impact a project's success.

One of the most common issues is dealing with vague or incomplete requirements. Stakeholders may have a clear, high-level vision of their needs but might not provide the detailed, actionable requirements necessary for precise development. This discrepancy can lead to misunderstandings, underestimations of the project scope, and gaps in the final product that fail to meet user expectations. Compounding this challenge is the fluid nature of requirements. As a project evolves, so can the vision and needs of stakeholders, which are influenced by changing market conditions, emerging competitive pressures, or new insights into user needs. These evolving requirements can disrupt carefully laid project plans, leading to overruns in both time and budget as teams scramble to adapt.

Communication, or the lack of it, is another critical hurdle. Miscommunication or insufficient communication among stakeholders, developers, and project managers can create a situation where requirements are not clearly understood or captured. This disconnect can result in a product that fails to meet the core needs it was intended to solve.

Another often overlooked aspect is the consideration of NFRs. These requirements, which detail how the system operates rather than what it does, are crucial for ensuring its viability and success in the real world. They often need more attention during the requirement-gathering process, leading to systems that may meet functional specifications but need more user satisfaction or operational efficiency.

Gold plating, adding features or enhancements without direct stakeholder request or straightforward value addition, can derail projects. This well-intentioned but misguided effort to exceed expectations can consume valuable resources, extend development timelines, and introduce complexity that complicates maintenance and future scalability.

> **Note**
>
> **Gold plating** refers to adding extra features, functionalities, or refinements to a software system that are not required by the project's specifications or requirements.

Lastly, scope creep presents a perennial challenge. The gradual expansion of a project's scope, often without increases in resources, time, and budget, can significantly strain a project, diluting focus and jeopardizing its successful completion. Through additional features, broader objectives, or more complex implementations, scope creep can transform a project from feasible to unmanageable.

These pitfalls and challenges highlight the critical importance of robust requirement-gathering and management practices. Addressing these problems requires a concerted effort to improve stakeholder communication, focus on FRs and NFRs, manage changes effectively, and guard against unnecessary feature creep. By recognizing and proactively managing these common challenges, project teams can enhance their chances of delivering successful, impactful solutions.

Agile methodology

Agile methodologies have significantly reshaped the software development landscape, particularly how teams approach and manage FRs and NFRs. Unlike traditional waterfall models, which treat requirement gathering as a phase that precedes design and implementation, agile methodologies advocate for a more iterative, collaborative, and flexible approach. This paradigm shift influences both the process and mindset with which teams handle requirements throughout the development life cycle.

At the core of agile methodologies is delivering value to the customer early and continuously. This is achieved by breaking down the project into manageable units of work, known as **iterations** or **sprints**, each resulting in a potentially shippable product increment. FRs and NFRs are gathered, prioritized, and refined just in time, aligning closely with this iterative cycle. Agile emphasizes the following principles:

- **Collaboration over documentation**: Agile methodologies emphasize direct communication and collaboration among cross-functional teams and with stakeholders. While comprehensive documentation, such as traditional **software requirements specification (SRS)** documents, is not disregarded, agile teams prefer working software over exhaustive paperwork. FRs and NFRs are often captured as user stories or features in a product backlog, a living document that changes and grows as the project progresses.

- **Continuous requirement elicitation**: In agile, requirement gathering is not a one-time activity but a continuous process. The product backlog is updated and refined as teams learn more about the user needs and the project's context. This adaptability allows for incorporating feedback from previous iterations, changing market conditions, or new technological opportunities, ensuring the product stays in line with what users need and the business wants to achieve.

- **Prioritization and flexibility**: Agile methodologies introduce a dynamic prioritization framework for managing requirements. Teams regularly prioritize the product backlog, ensuring the most valuable and urgent requirements are addressed first. This flexibility allows agile teams to respond to changes without derailing the project, contrasting the rigid scope management observed in traditional approaches.

- **Customer involvement**: Agile practices encourage frequent and early customer involvement in development. By engaging customers or end users in prioritization, review sessions, and feedback loops, teams can ensure that the FRs and NFRs align with actual user expectations and needs.

- **Incremental delivery and feedback**: Agile methodologies promote the incremental delivery of functional aspects of the project, allowing teams to gather input on real-world software. This approach validates the relevance and quality of the implemented requirements and helps identify any misunderstood, missing, or unnecessary requirements early in the development process.

Agile methodologies advocate for a more dynamic, collaborative, and user-centered approach to managing FRs and NFRs. By embracing change, prioritizing value delivery, and fostering continuous stakeholder engagement, agile teams can navigate the complexities of requirement management more effectively, leading to products that better meet user needs and adapt gracefully to changing environments.

Now that we are familiar with FRs and NFRs, we know how to gather and manage them, communicate effectively with stakeholders, and use best practices and strategies for engaging them. We are also aware of the challenges and pitfalls of gathering requirements, such as vague requirements, changing needs, miscommunication, and scope creep. Let's explore how to document requirements and architecture.

Documenting requirements and architecture

Documenting requirements and architecture is a foundational step in software development, ensuring clarity, alignment, and understanding among all project stakeholders. It systematically records a system's needs and specifications alongside its structural design to guide development, facilitate communication, and provide a basis for future maintenance and scalability. Adequate documentation serves as a blueprint, detailing what needs to be built and how to ensure the successful realization of the project's goals and objectives.

Additionally, it helps in risk management by identifying potential challenges early and providing a clear reference point for decision-making throughout the project life cycle.

Documenting and managing requirements

Documenting and managing requirements is a crucial aspect of software architecture, as it serves as the foundation for building systems that meet the needs of stakeholders. Effective requirement management ensures clarity, alignment, and traceability throughout the software development life cycle. This comprehensive process involves identifying, documenting, prioritizing, validating, and managing requirements from inception to delivery.

Let's delve into each aspect in detail:

- **Identifying**: To identify requirements effectively, it's crucial to recognize all software project stakeholders, including end users, customers, business analysts, developers, testers, and project managers. Subsequently, elicitation techniques, such as interviews, surveys, workshops, and observation aids were employed to gather stakeholder requirements. Moreover, distinguishing between FRs and NFRs is essential during this phase.

- **Documenting**: In the 2000s, **Unified Modeling Language** (**UML**) enjoyed widespread popularity, and the companies I consulted for or worked with relied on use case documents to document requirements. However, in contemporary times, agile methodologies have become prevalent in most companies. Consequently, user stories have emerged as the primary means of describing requirements in today's software development landscape.

- **Prioritizing**: Numerous techniques exist for prioritizing requirements, with three particularly noteworthy approaches. Firstly, considering their criticality and business value, the Moscow method categorizes requirements into must-have, should-have, could-have, and will-not-have segments. Secondly, the Kano model classifies requirements into essential, performance, and delighter categories, aiding in gauging their effect on customer satisfaction. Lastly, the cost-benefit analysis assesses the costs and benefits linked to each requirement, enabling informed prioritization decisions.

- **Validating**: To ensure thorough requirement validation and early feedback collection, it's essential to develop prototypes or mockups for stakeholder review in the initial stages of development. Additionally, conducting peer reviews and inspections of requirement documents aids in identifying inconsistencies, ambiguities, and omissions, promoting clarity and alignment among team members. Furthermore, defining clear acceptance criteria for each requirement facilitates objective validation and streamlines the acceptance testing process, ensuring that the final product meets stakeholder expectations effectively.

- **Managing**: To streamline requirement management, it's crucial to establish a formal process for handling changes, which involves capturing change requests, assessing their impact, and obtaining approval from relevant stakeholders. Implementing version control mechanisms for requirement documents enables tracking modifications and maintaining a comprehensive revision history. Continuously tracing requirements throughout the development life cycle ensures thorough consideration in the design, implementation, and testing phases. Effective stakeholder communication fosters a shared understanding of requirements and promotes collaborative efforts toward their fulfillment.

Tools are essential to support us in documenting and managing requirements, so let's approach them.

Tools for managing requirements

Harness specialized software tools, such as IBM Rational DOORS, Jama Connect, or Atlassian Jira, to streamline requirement elicitation, documentation, and management processes. Utilize collaboration platforms, such as Confluence or Microsoft SharePoint, to foster real-time collaboration and seamless document sharing among distributed teams. Implement version control systems, such as Git or Subversion, to effectively manage changes to requirement documents and maintain version control throughout the development life cycle.

Documenting and managing requirements requires careful attention to detail, effective communication, and stakeholder collaboration. Following a systematic approach to requirement management, we can ensure that the resulting systems meet stakeholders' needs and expectations while adhering to quality standards and project constraints. Now, let's explore how to document the architecture.

Documenting the architecture

Documenting the architecture of a software system is a crucial practice that involves creating detailed descriptions and diagrams to convey the system's structure, components, and design choices. This process ensures that all stakeholders understand the architecture, facilitates knowledge sharing, and aids in the system's future maintenance and evolution, ensuring consistency and reducing risks.

Additionally, well-documented architecture serves as a vital reference during system upgrades and migrations, ensuring consistency and reducing risks.

Documenting architecture with C4 model

The **C4 model** is a framework for visualizing software systems' architecture using hierarchical diagrams. It adopts an *abstraction-first* methodology for diagramming software architecture, using abstractions that mirror the thought processes and construction methods of software architects and developers. Software architect Simon Brown created it, focusing on simplifying the complex process of describing and communicating software architecture. It's called C4 because it encompasses four levels of architecture: context, containers, components, and code, each offering a different level of detail.

Abstractions

To effectively describe the static structure of a software system, we first need a shared set of abstractions to develop a ubiquitous language.

Figure 3.4 illustrates this set of abstractions.

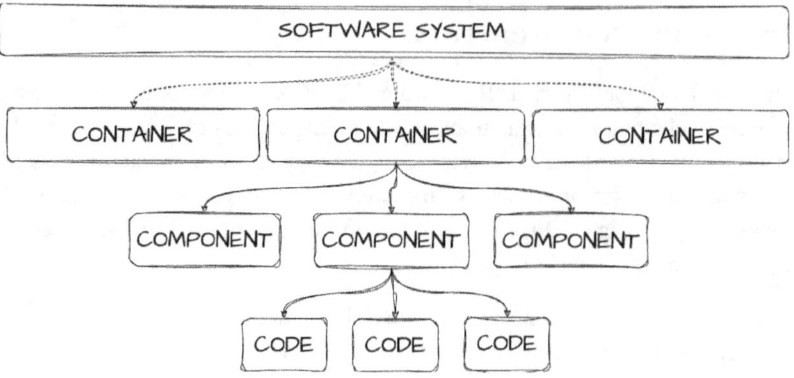

Figure 3.4: Abstractions

A software system that consists of one or more containers, such as applications and data stores, that house various components. These components are then implemented by one or more code elements, including classes, interfaces, objects, and functions. Additionally, people may utilize these software systems. Let's delve into each item:

- **Person**: The person represents one of the human users of your software system, such as actors, roles, personas, and other user categories.

- **Software system**: A software system represents the highest level of abstraction and is defined as something that delivers value to its users, whether human or not. It includes the system you are modeling and any others it depends on. Defining *software system* is challenging due to differences in terminology. Think of it as a project that a single team is in charge of building and maintaining with full access.

- **Container**: The term *container* refers not to Docker containers but to applications or data stores that must be operational for the software system to function effectively. A **container** is a runtime environment, such as web servers, applications, serverless applications, cloud storage, or databases.

- **Component**: A **component** is a set of implementation classes working behind a specific interface. It doesn't matter how they are physically packaged, such as in a jar or war artifact. Components operate in the same process space when placed inside a container, emphasizing their interdependence.

Levels of the C4 model

To get a comprehensive grasp of the C4 model, let's explore its four levels of architecture:

- **Context diagram**: This is the highest-level diagram showing the system's boundary, primary users, and interactions with other systems. It provides a high-level overview of how the system fits into the world around it, identifying the key stakeholders and external systems that interact with the solution.

- **Container diagram**: Zooming in from the context diagram, the container diagram shows the high-level technology choices, how the system is divided into containers (applications, data stores, microservices, etc.), and how those containers interact with each other. This diagram helps us understand the technology stack and the system's major parts.

- **Component diagram**: Further zooming in, the component diagram breaks down each container into its constituent components, showing how responsibilities are allocated among them. It highlights the internal structure of the containers, detailing how various parts of the system work together to process information and carry out operations.

- **Code diagram**: The most detailed diagram focuses on the implementation details of individual components, often represented as classes or interfaces. This level benefits developers looking to understand or modify the system at the code level.

Purpose and benefits

The **C4 model** describes system architecture through layers; its layered approach ensures that everyone, from developers to business executives, can grasp the key aspects of the system, fostering better collaboration and alignment across the project. Its simplicity and use of diagrams make it a practical approach for technical and non-technical stakeholders. The C4 model helps manage and mitigate the complexity of software architectures and provides a straightforward way to visualize and communicate architecture, making it easier for stakeholders to make informed decisions.

No need for a notation

The C4 model doesn't require specific notation or modeling language, particularly at the context level. You can use simple boxes and lines to represent a system, its users, and the other systems it interacts with. For more detailed model levels, consider using UML notation that consistently and accurately represents containers, components, and code using shapes and lines.

A case study using the C4 model

We'll apply the C4 model to an online auction system case study, focusing on creating the context and container diagrams. Due to space limitations and the specific scope of our project, we will not be developing the component and code diagrams at this stage. Please visit the official C4 model website at `https://c4model.com` for further details and examples. This approach allows us to tailor our architectural documentation to the needs of our project while ensuring a comprehensive grasp of the system's structure at both broad and detailed levels.

The system's requirements

We will consider these user stories when designing our architecture:

- As a seller, I want to list items for auction so that bidders can place bids on them.

- As a bidder, I want to view listed items to choose which items to bid on.

- As a bidder, I want to place bids on items I am interested in so that I can attempt to purchase them.

- As a winner, I want to make payments for items I win through a secure payment gateway to finalize my purchase.

- As the auction system, I want to send shipping details to the shipping service once an item is paid for so that the item can be delivered to the buyer.

System context diagram

Figure 3.5 depicts the system context diagram, which has been crafted based on the user stories.

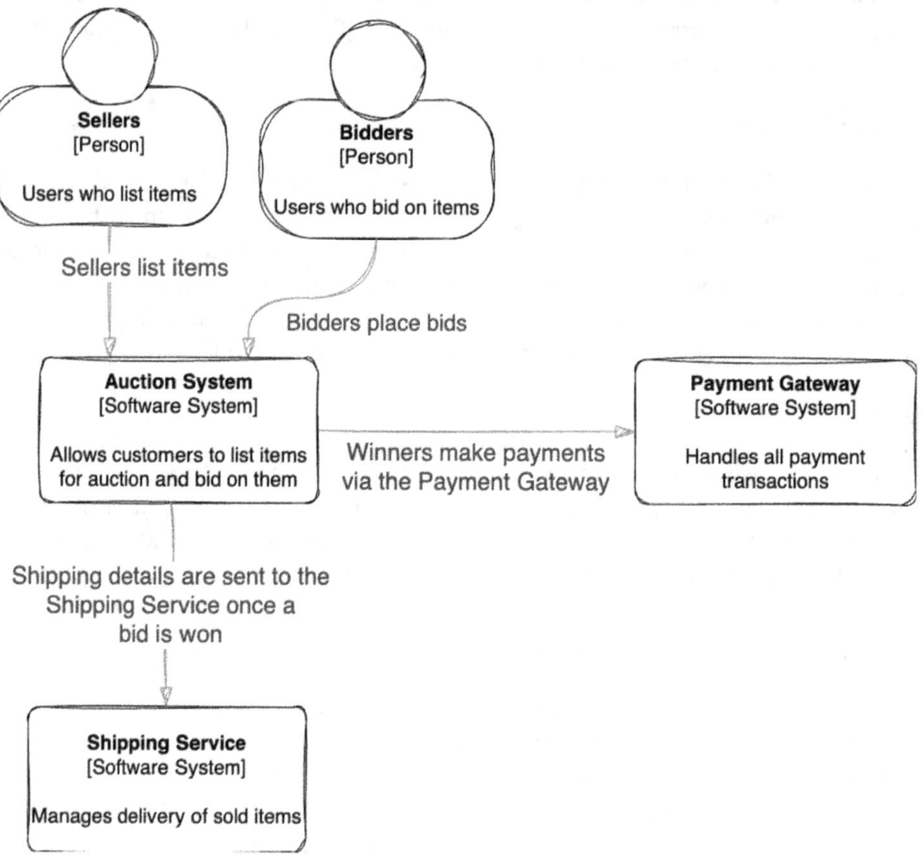

Figure 3.5: System context diagram

This diagram offers an overview of the system's interactions with its environment, showcasing how users and external systems connect and interact with the application. It is a foundational tool for understanding the system's high-level architecture, highlighting the critical external interfaces and user flows derived from the user stories.

Container diagram

Figure 3.6 depicts the container diagram, a zoom-in of the system context diagram.

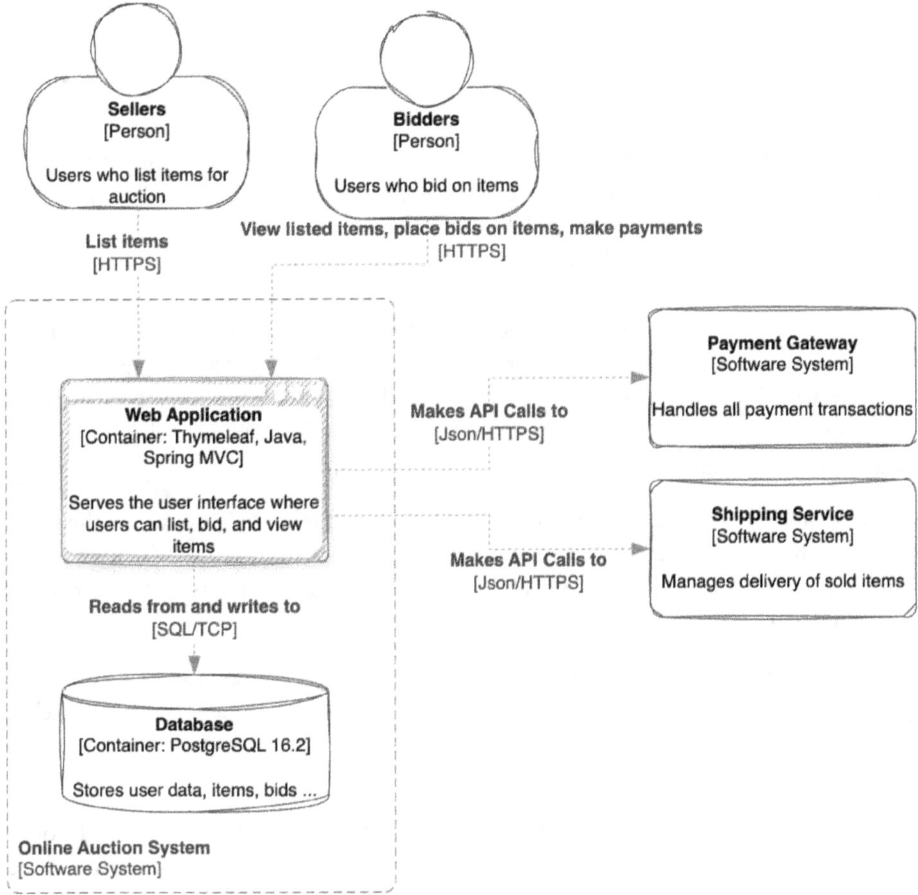

Figure 3.6: Container diagram

The container diagram delineates the comprehensive structure of the software architecture, showcasing the allocation of diverse responsibilities within it. It emphasizes the critical technological solutions utilized and delineates container communication pathways. This clear and technology-centric diagram is valuable for software developers and support or operations teams.

> **Note**
>
> It's essential to recognize that not all four levels of the diagram are necessary; for many software development teams, just the system context and container diagrams are sufficient.

Software development teams widely use the C4 model to ensure that all stakeholders, from technical developers to business managers, have a common understanding of how the system is structured. This approach helps clarify requirements and design and maintain system architecture throughout the software development life cycle.

Summary

In this chapter, we discussed the importance of system context in software architecture. We explained the difference between system context and software architecture and looked at different aspects of system context, such as technical, operational, business, environmental, and social factors. We also discussed how to incorporate system context into architectural design and the best strategies to use its influence effectively. Moreover, we covered stakeholder engagement and communication. We explained the processes for identifying and categorizing stakeholders, effective engagement strategies, overcoming engagement challenges, and tools for effective communication. Additionally, we examined FRs and NFRs, clarified their requirements, and discussed the best practices for gathering them. We also addressed the challenges in collecting and managing these requirements and discussed the agile methodology as a dynamic approach to requirement management.

Lastly, we explored the documentation of requirements and architecture. We outlined the steps for managing requirements, from identification to management, and discussed the documentation of architecture using the C4 model. We also explained its purpose and benefits and provided a case study to illustrate its application.

This chapter offered valuable information, providing a clear understanding of software architecture and its components. It included insights into technical, operational, and business factors, stakeholder engagement strategies, communication, agile methodology, and practical examples for documenting and managing architecture effectively.

In *Chapter 4, Monolithic Architecture*, we will explore monolithic architecture, detailing its optimal uses and limitations. The chapter outlines the **model-view-controller** (**MVC**) design pattern and its impact on modularity, maintainability, and scalability. It differentiates between stateful and stateless configurations and guides on building monolithic projects with Spring Boot, Spring MVC, and Spring Security with basic authentication. Security measures for data such as in transit and at rest are discussed, and the chapter concludes with an emphasis on the importance of testing, covering unit, integration, and end-to-end testing strategies.

Questions

1. What is the purpose of defining the system context in software architecture?

2. What is the difference between system context and software architecture?

3. What are functional requirements, and how are they captured?

4. How are non-functional requirements described in the text?

5. What best practices does the text recommend for managing requirements?

6. What does the text say about the C4 model's utility in documenting software architecture?

Get This Book's PDF Version and Exclusive Extras

UNLOCK NOW

Scan the QR code (or go to `packtpub.com/unlock`). Search for this book by name, confirm the edition, and then follow the steps on the page.

Note: Keep your invoice handly. Purchase made directly from packt don't require one.

Part 2: Exploring Architectural Styles

This part delves into the evolution of software architectures, guiding you through various architectural styles and their practical implementations. Starting from monolithic systems, you will progress through client-server and microservices architectures, learning about their unique characteristics, benefits, and trade-offs. The section also covers advanced patterns with Spring Cloud, event-driven architecture, and the integration of pipe-and-filter with serverless approaches, offering a comprehensive understanding of modern architectural paradigms.

This part has the following chapters:

- *Chapter 4, Monolithic Architecture*
- *Chapter 5, Client-Server Architecture*
- *Chapter 6, Microservices Architecture*
- *Chapter 7, Microservices Patterns with Spring Cloud*
- *Chapter 8, Event-Driven Architecture*
- *Chapter 9, Pipe-and-Filter and Serverless Architecture*

4

Monolithic Architecture

This chapter delves into monolithic architecture in software development, outlining its definition, pros and cons, and common patterns used within it, such as **layered architecture**, also known as **N-layer**, and the **Model-View-Controller (MVC)** pattern. It also covers stateful and stateless operations and when to use each approach.

We will demonstrate the implementation of a monolithic application using the Spring Framework. An online auction system is used as a case study to showcase appropriate architectural styles and technologies. We will cover setting up projects using **Spring Boot**, integrating **Spring Web MVC** with **Thymeleaf** for views, and implementing security measures with **Spring Security**.

This chapter covers automated testing, including unit, integration, and security testing. It guides setting up integration tests to verify the functionality of integrated components within a monolithic architecture.

This chapter will cover the following topics:

- Introduction to monolithic architecture
- Unpacking usual patterns in monolithic architectures
- Implementing a monolithic application
- Automated testing

By the end of this chapter, you will understand the role and configuration of monolithic architecture, how to engage common architectural patterns effectively, and how to implement robust and secure applications. Additionally, you will have gained insights into the best practices for automated testing, ensuring your monolithic applications are reliable and maintainable. This comprehensive understanding will equip you to create robust monolithic applications.

Technical requirements

All the code for this chapter can be found on GitHub at `https://github.com/PacktPublishing/ Software-Architecture-with-Spring/tree/main/ch4`. Ellipses in the code blocks indicate that parts of the code have been omitted, and the complete code is available on GitHub.

Introducing monolithic architecture

In *Chapter 1, Diving into Software Architecture*, we provided an overview of monolithic architecture. This chapter will delve deeper into this approach, its advantages and disadvantages, and how to implement a project in a monolithic architecture.

What is monolithic architecture?

Monolithic architecture is a traditional method for creating software applications. It involves building the application as a single unit, where all components and functionalities are closely integrated and deployed on a server as a single artifact. For example, a typical application consists of components such as a frontend, core application, services, and a database. When all these elements are integrated and installed on a server, it is referred to as a monolithic architecture characterized by closely intertwined services.

In the monolithic architecture, components such as the user interface, business logic, and data access operations are all contained within a single code base. This architectural style typically includes templates and follows the **MVC design pattern** or **N-layers**. *Figure 4.1* presents a traditional monolithic web application deployment.

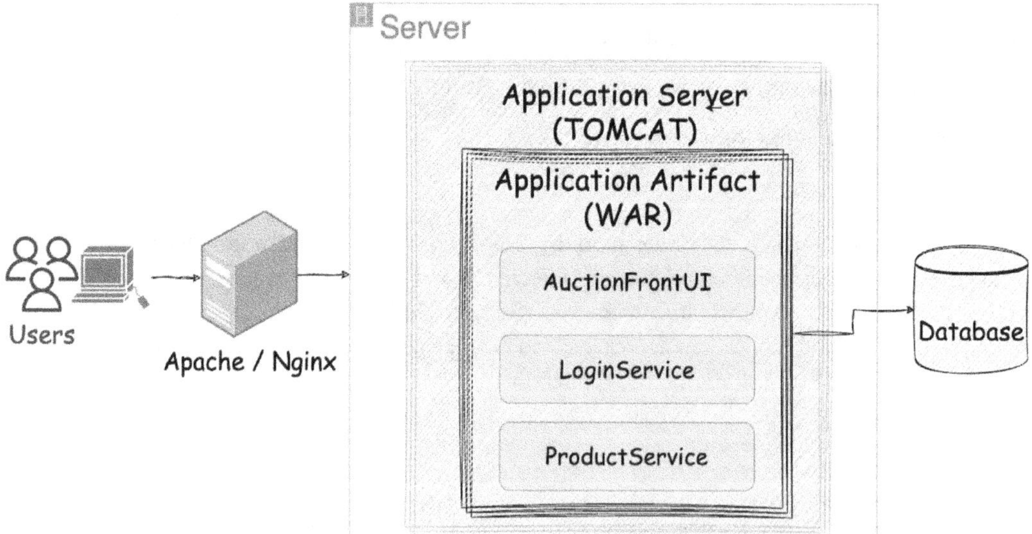

Figure 4.1: Monolithic web application deployment

The diagram depicts a standard monolithic web application deployment architecture using Apache Tomcat as the application server. It outlines how user requests travel through various system components. End users interact with the application via a web browser or client app, connecting through a web server—either Apache or Nginx—which serves as a conduit, forwarding requests to the application server and potentially handling static content, load balancing, and SSL termination. Within the central server environment, the application is deployed and managed as a **Web Application Archive (WAR)** file on Tomcat, which includes all necessary classes, libraries, and files. The application directly interacts with the database for data retrieval and management.

Benefits of monolithic architecture

Monolithic architecture offers several significant benefits, making it a suitable choice for many scenarios, particularly for small to medium-sized applications. Here are the key advantages:

- **Simplicity in development**: In a monolithic application, all components are part of a single software unit, simplifying the development process. Developers can easily manage the application because everything is in one place, making it straightforward to work on, test, and deploy.

- **Ease of deployment**: Deploying a monolithic application is typically straightforward because it involves a single executable or deployment unit. This simplicity reduces the complexity of managing multiple services and their dependencies, as seen in microservices architectures.

- **Performance**: Since all the components of a monolithic application run in the same process, communication between various components, such as function calls, is typically faster and more efficient than the network calls required in microservices. This can lead to better performance characteristics for applications where latency is critical.

- **Simplified debugging and testing**: Testing a monolithic application can be less complex than testing a distributed system. Since all components work within the same application, setting up integration tests and end-to-end testing environments is often more straightforward.

- **Reliability**: A monolithic architecture can offer more reliability in scenarios where all application parts must be closely aligned, for example, in real-time data processing applications. Changes in one module are less likely to unpredictably affect others since all modules are tightly coupled and tested together.

- **Simplified transaction management**: Handling transactions across multiple databases or services can be complex in distributed architectures. A monolithic application often accesses a single database, simplifying transaction management and ensuring data consistency more straightforwardly.

- **Cost-effectiveness for smaller applications**: A monolithic architecture is more cost-effective in terms of development and maintenance resources for small-scale applications. The overhead of managing multiple deployments, services, and databases typically associated with microservices might not be justified for smaller projects.

- **Ease of scaling**: Scaling a monolithic application can be straightforward if the load increases predictably and uniformly. Vertical scaling can be effectively utilized without the need to manage additional complexity.

- **Fewer cross-cutting concerns**: In a monolithic architecture, cross-cutting concerns such as logging, rate limiting, and security are implemented consistently throughout the application. This uniformity can help maintain consistency in handling these concerns across all parts of the application.

These benefits make monolithic architecture a good choice for projects where simplicity, ease of management, and initial development speed are more critical than flexibility and scalability. It's often used effectively in small to medium-sized applications, rapid prototyping, and businesses with well-defined, unchanging technological requirements.

Drawbacks of monolithic architecture

While monolithic architecture offers several advantages, particularly for small applications or projects with straightforward requirements, it also has significant drawbacks, especially as applications evolve. Here are the critical disadvantages associated with monolithic architecture:

- **Limited scalability**: As applications grow in size and complexity, monolithic architectures can become more challenging to scale efficiently. While vertical scaling is straightforward, horizontal scaling can be complex because the entire application needs to be replicated on each server rather than scaling only the components that require more resources.

- **Difficulties in managing large code bases**: A sizeable monolithic application can become difficult to understand and manage. As more features are added, the code base grows and becomes increasingly complex, slowing down development efforts and making it harder for new team members to get up to speed.

- **Impeded development velocity**: In a monolithic application, any changes, even minor ones, often require rebuilding and redeploying the entire application. This leads to slower development cycles and makes continuous delivery more challenging.

- **Risk of technology lock-in**: Monolithic applications often make adopting new technologies or frameworks difficult because introducing changes can affect the entire system. This can lead to technology lock-in, where an application must continue using outdated technologies because migrating to newer options is too disruptive or costly.

- **Availability issues**: In a monolithic architecture, the entire system could fail if one part of the application experiences a failure. This single point of failure makes it harder to ensure high availability and can lead to significant downtime.

- **Complicated scaling of individual components**: If only specific application components experience high demand, it is still necessary to scale the entire application, which is not resource efficient. This wastes resources and increases operational costs.

- **Challenges with continuous integration**: Continuous integration can become problematic, as every small change in any part of the application might require a full rebuild and redeployment. This can increase the risk of introducing bugs and simplify the integration process.

- **Complex refactoring**: Refactoring a monolithic application can be risky and complex. Changes in one part of the application can have unexpected effects on other parts, making it risky to improve or update sections of the code.

- **Overloaded IDEs and development tools**: As the application grows, the development environment can become slower and less responsive. **Integrated Development Environments (IDEs)** and other tools may need help to handle the large code base efficiently, impacting developer productivity.

These drawbacks often prompt organizations, especially those with large-scale, complex applications, to consider other architectural approaches, such as microservices, which can offer greater flexibility, scalability, and resilience. Now that we have learned about monolithic architecture and its advantages and drawbacks, let's unpack the usual patterns in monolithic architectures to boost maintainability, scalability, and development efficiency.

Unpacking usual patterns in monolithic architectures

How about we delve into the common patterns used in monolithic applications? By exploring these patterns, we can gain valuable insights into how these applications are designed and structured. Understanding these patterns can help us make informed decisions about designing our monolithic applications, making them more efficient and effective. Therefore, take the time to explore this topic and see what we can learn.

What is layered architecture?

Layered architecture, or **N-layer architecture**, is a software design pattern that organizes application components into a series of horizontal layers, each with distinct roles and responsibilities. It is the most typical architecture pattern used in software engineering. In this architecture, each layer only communicates with the adjacent layer and with a clear separation of concerns. This structure typically includes at least three layers, as shown in *Figure 4.2*:

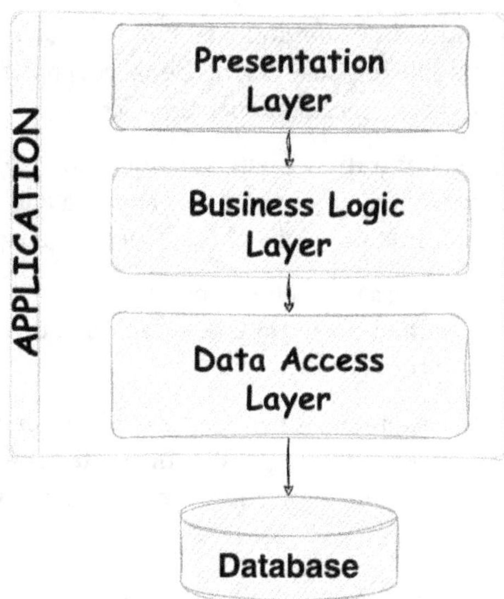

Figure 4.2: Layered (N-layer) architecture

Figure 4.2 illustrates the presentation, business, and data access layers. Let's examine these layers:

1. **Presentation layer**: Also known as the UI layer, this layer handles the user interface and user experience, including input and output.

2. **Business logic layer**: Also known as the service or domain layer, it contains business rules and logic specific to the application.

3. **Data access layer**: Also known as the persistence layer, it manages data persistence and retrieval from databases or other storage systems.

Additional layers can be added to monolithic applications to handle more specific processing or business logic.

The role of layered architecture in monolithic applications

Layered architecture is a systematic approach that enhances the organization and structure of monolithic applications. It boosts maintainability, scalability, and development efficiency. Although the components of such applications are tightly integrated, having distinct layers segregates responsibilities, streamlining development and maintenance.

The architecture splits a monolithic application into logical segments, such as the presentation, business logic, and data access layers. This division delineates each part's role, facilitating developers' more effective pinpointing and addressing specific functionalities or issues within the code base.

By isolating modifications to particular layers, the architecture minimizes their impact on the entire application. For instance, a change in the database schema primarily affects only the data access layer, leaving other parts of the application intact. This containment manages the application's complexity as it evolves, ensuring that updates or adjustments are more manageable.

While monolithic applications typically scale as a single entity, layered architecture introduces the possibility for more refined optimization strategies. For example, the presentation layer can be independently scaled from the business logic layer using techniques such as caching and load balancing, which separately manage user interface responsiveness and computational tasks.

Layered architecture also simplifies testing and debugging by permitting the independent testing of each layer. Developers can conduct unit tests on individual layers without activating the entire application, leading to faster detection and rectification of defects, thus enhancing the application's quality.

This architecture model supports developmental flexibility, allowing teams to work on different layers simultaneously without significant interference. Moreover, security measures can be tailored and implemented at different layers, creating a robust defense mechanism. For example, security protocols in the presentation layer can manage session operations, and those in the data access layer can oversee data validation and database access controls.

In conclusion, layered architecture is pivotal to the success of monolithic applications, providing a structured method that improves clarity, maintainability, scalability, and overall efficiency. This architectural style facilitates the systematic growth and adaptation of the application within the confines of a monolithic framework.

Model-View-Controller pattern

The MVC design pattern breaks down an application into three components: **model**, **view**, and **controller**. This pattern focuses mainly on the user interface side of an application, separating data and business logic from user input and presentation. The MVC pattern is commonly used in the presentation layer of the N-layer architecture.

Figure 4.3 shows the MVC pattern diagram.

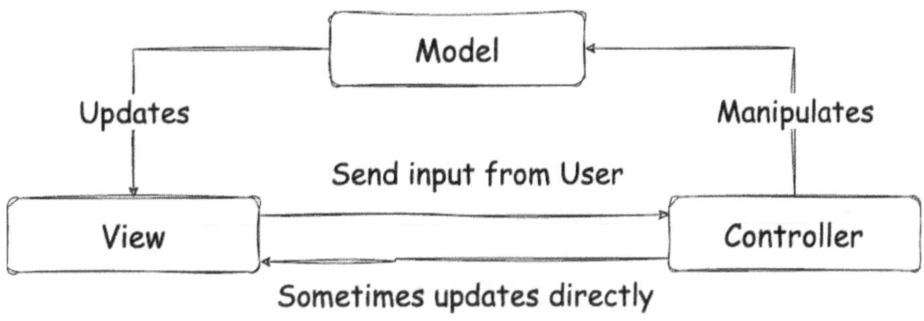

Figure 4.3: MVC pattern diagram

This figure illustrates the three components and their interactions. The model handles the application's data and business logic. It responds to requests for its state from the view and instructions to change it from the controller. The view presents the model's data in a user-friendly interface and interprets user actions for the controller. The controller manages all business logic, manipulates data using the model, and interacts with views to render the output. The separation of concerns principle is a compelling reason to use MVC. The MVC architecture facilitates dividing frontend and backend code into distinct components. This separation simplifies management and enhances the ease of modifying one side without disrupting the other.

MVC versus N-layer

MVC architecture primarily focuses on the user interface aspect of an application. It separates data and business logic from user input and presentation. On the other hand, N-layer architecture separates concerns across the entire application, including the data, business, and presentation layers. MVC can be utilized within the presentation layer of an N-layer architecture. This combination allows developers to organize the presentation layer effectively while maintaining a clean separation between the business logic and data access layers. By leveraging the strengths of both architectural patterns, this hybrid approach promotes clean code organization and scalability, making it a practical solution for many applications. *Figure 4.4* illustrates the use of an MVC pattern with an N-layer architecture.

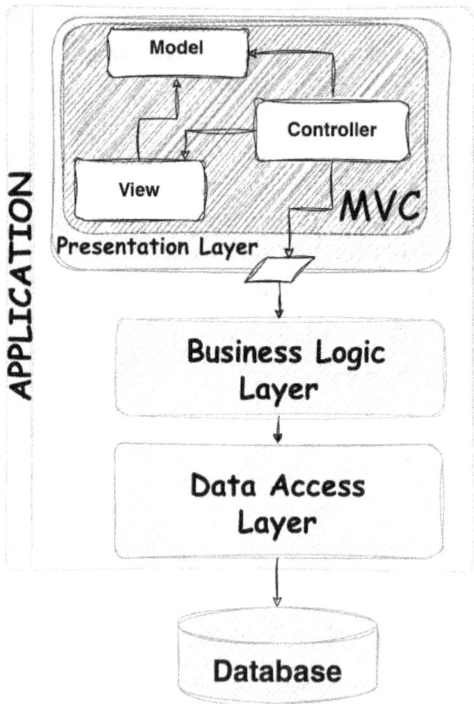

Figure 4.4: MVC within N-layer

In *Figure 4.4*, we can see that the MVC pattern is utilized within the presentation layer of the N-layer architecture.

Stateful versus stateless

Understanding the difference between stateful and stateless architectures is essential for designing and implementing software systems, particularly in the context of web services, applications, and network protocols.

Stateful

A **stateful system** refers to a system that retains information across several interactions or sessions. It stores and references data with every user interaction or transaction, allowing it to recollect past actions and adjust its behavior based on previous interactions. The most common method for managing state is through an *HTTP session*, which creates a unique session ID stored in a cookie on the client's browser. Other state management methods include *local storage*, *session storage*, and *cookies*. For more secure storage, session data can be stored in a database. Java EE application servers have built-in support for session management and clustering.

However, maintaining this state requires significant resources, including extra storage and maintenance. Moreover, scaling stateful systems can be challenging as it demands ensuring state consistency across different instances or components of the system.

Monolithic systems are generally implemented using a stateful approach. Many traditional banking systems are designed as monolithic applications where all the core functionalities, such as account management, transaction processing, customer service, and reporting, are integrated into a single code base. These systems often maintain stateful information about user sessions and transactions.

Stateless

A **stateless system** doesn't retain any memory of past interactions. It processes each request as an isolated event without considering past requests. Stateless systems treat every transaction as a standalone occurrence without referencing past activities.

The main characteristics of stateless systems are their simplicity and predictability. Earlier interactions do not influence them, so outcomes are more consistent. They're also easier to scale because any part of the system can process each request independently without requiring previous context. Additionally, stateless systems are more resource efficient because they don't need to maintain state information between transactions.

Stateless architectures are particularly well-suited for applications that handle a large number of users, such as public APIs. They also excel in services where each request is independent. These architectures facilitate load balancing and redundancy, bolstering the system's overall strength. A prime example is the *stateless RESTful service*, where each API call includes all the necessary information for the server to process.

> **Note**
>
> For developers and architects, grasping the distinction between stateful and stateless systems is crucial. This understanding is critical to selecting the correct design pattern that aligns with the system's operational requirements and challenges. Such a decision can profoundly impact the system's performance, scalability, and complexity.

We've previously explored the monolithic, N-layer, and MVC patterns, and now we'll apply our knowledge with Spring to code a monolith application.

Implementing a monolithic application

It's time to code, the best part for us solution lovers. It's exciting to code solutions, see things start taking form while the project advances, and learn a new technology or another way to solve a problem. So, we will save time and discuss why we should use **Spring**.

Why you should use Spring

Spring is a user-friendly framework for Java application development that simplifies everyday tasks such as database integration, transaction management, security, and messaging. Its core feature is **dependency injection**, which makes dependency management and separation of concerns easier and improves maintainability and testability.

Spring Boot, a time-saving boon, simplifies Spring dependency management by providing auto-configuration to Spring and third-party libraries whenever possible. This reduces development time and supports embedded servers for easier deployment and testing, sparking excitement among software engineers about the increased efficiency in their development process.

Spring MVC, a versatile web framework, supports REST APIs and centers on the DispatcherServlet. It manages HTTP interactions and facilitates clear separation of model, view, and controller. On the other hand, **Spring Security** provides a customizable framework for authentication and access control, protecting against threats such as session fixation and **cross-site request forgery** (CSRF). There are many other components, such as **Spring Cloud**, which simplifies the development of distributed systems, **Spring Batch** for building batch applications, and many more.

Designed for scalability and integration with **J2EE** technologies, Spring supports various deployment environments, making it ideal for enterprises of any size. In conclusion, the Spring Framework is a complete, modular, and configurable solution that can adapt to the needs of almost any application development project.

Online auction case study

Due to its limited budget, *WX-Auction*, a hypothetical company, seeks to develop an online auction system swiftly and cost-effectively. The company aims to rapidly deploy this system to evaluate its market viability and gather early user feedback without significant financial investment.

System definition and mission

The online auction system facilitates online auctions involving sellers and bidders. The stakeholders want a system that can be accessed online, that is, via a web browser, and that provides a login page that identifies who is logged in. Logged users can register and list their products.

Selecting the architectural style and technologies

After evaluating the functional and non-functional requirements with stakeholders, we determined that a monolithic architectural style suits our application. We chose this approach primarily because it facilitates quicker development, testing, and deployment for a relatively small **minimum viable product (MVP)**. Additionally, a monolithic architecture helps reduce costs related to cloud or on-premises resources and lowers the number of professionals required for maintenance. Moreover, it simplifies scaling up server capabilities should user demand exceed initial expectations.

As the application grows or requires more granular scaling, a monolithic architecture's limitations could outweigh its benefits, making other architectures more appealing.

Regarding the technology stack, we will use Java 21, Maven, and the Spring Framework components, such as Spring Boot, Spring Security, Spring Web MVC, and Spring Data, and take advantage of their facilities.

Creating projects using Spring Boot

Spring Boot simplifies creating standalone production-grade applications with minimal setup. It provides auto-configuration, starter dependencies, built-in monitoring, and embedded servers, allowing developers to focus on application logic. The **Spring Initializr** tool quickly creates a new Spring Boot project by selecting the project type, programming language, Spring Boot version, and metadata. It is accessible at `https://start.spring.io/`. *Figure 4.5* presents the configuration of our initial project.

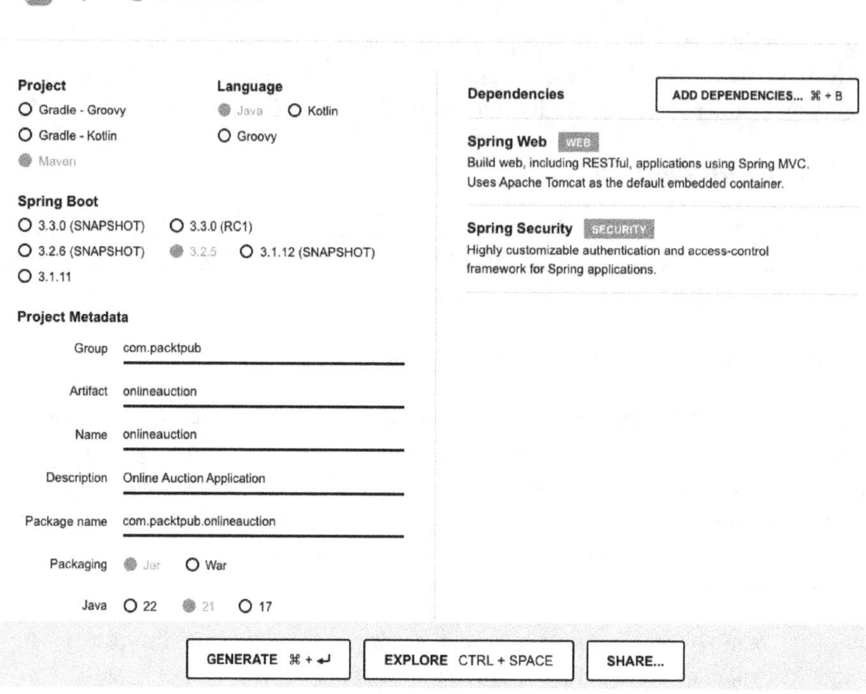

Figure 4.5: Spring Initializr

Spring Initializr creates a project structure that includes a build file for either Maven or Gradle, the Spring Boot app class, and other necessary files in a ZIP file.

Understanding and implementing MVC

Let's implement the MVC pattern in our project using Spring MVC and the server-side template Thymeleaf.

Figure 4.6 illustrates the components and the flow of a typical Spring MVC application.

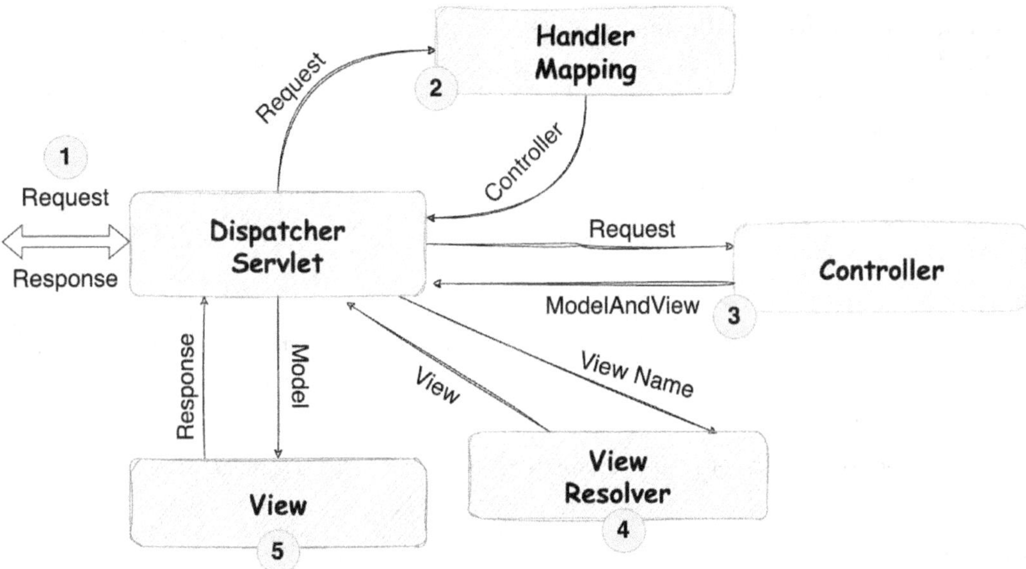

Figure 4.6: Spring Web MVC components and flow

The flow typically starts with a request to the dispatcher servlet, the central coordinator of Spring MVC, which then uses the handler mapping to forward the request to the appropriate controller. The controller processes the request, populates the model, and returns it with the view name to the dispatcher servlet. The view resolver then picks up the view name and resolves it to a specific view template, and the view renders the response that is sent back to the client. This architecture effectively separates the roles and responsibilities within the application, making it easier to manage and scale.

To utilize Spring MVC, we must include the following dependency:

```
<dependency>
    <groupId>org.springframework.boot</groupId>
    <artifactId>spring-boot-starter-web</artifactId>
</dependency>
```

We can create a controller using Spring with the @Controller annotation over the class name. The @RequestMapping annotation is optional, and it specifies the base URL path (/products) for all request-handling methods in the controller. It serves as a prefix for all the request mappings within this controller. So, any request to paths starting with /products will be routed to this controller:

```
@Controller
@RequestMapping("products")
public class ProductController {

...
```

The following code defines a method to handle GET requests to the `/login` endpoint using the `@GetMapping(value="/login")` annotation. The method returns the `"login"` string as the logical view name to render. The view resolver resolves this by locating the corresponding view template file named `login.html`:

```java
@GetMapping(value="/login")
public String login() {
    return "login";

...
```

The Spring `ViewResolvers` model object facilitates data transfer from the controller to the view and vice versa. It enables different data usage within views and captures user input to execute necessary logic by controllers.

The following code snippet demonstrates a request-handling method to transmit data from controller to view:

```java
@GetMapping("/{id}")
public String listProducts(Model model, @PathVariable("id") Integer
id) {
  model.addAttribute("product",
                        productService.getProductById(id));
  return "product-item";
}
```

The `Model` object's `addAttribute` method takes two parameters: a string attribute name and an object to pass to the view. The view templates can access controller-provided attributes using the expression language `${...}` syntax:

```html
<body> ${product.name} </body>
```

The product name is printed using the `${product.name}` code passed through the product attribute in the `product-list` view.

The following code snippet is a view example for passing data from the view to the controller:

```html
<form th:action="@{/products/add}" th:object="${product}"
method="post">
<input type="text" id="name" th:field="*{name}">
```

The Thymeleaf `th:action="@{/products/add"` attribute sets the form action to `/products/add`. The @ symbol denotes a **spring expression language** (**SpEL**) expression, and `@{...}` is a Thymeleaf URL expression used for generating URLs.

The `th:object="${product}"` attribute binds the form to the `product` object. If they exist, Thymeleaf will automatically populate form fields with values from the `product` object.

The `th:field="*{name}"` attribute binds the input field to the name property of the `product` object. The `"*{...}"` syntax is a Thymeleaf expression for binding form fields to object properties.

The code snippet of the controller is as follows:

```
@PostMapping("/add")
public String saveProduct(@ModelAttribute Product product) {
  productService.saveProduct(product);
  ...
```

The `@ModelAttribute` annotation binds form data to the `Product` object, allowing access to the submitted data.

Implementing the view with Thymeleaf

We've covered implementing controllers and Thymeleaf. Thymeleaf is often used with Spring and has native support in Spring Boot, making development more straightforward. It allows dynamic data to be inserted into static content to create views, with a clear HTML-like syntax and powerful expression language. This combination streamlines the creation of dynamic web applications using integrated Java development practices.

To add Thymeleaf to our project, we need to add the following dependency:

```
<dependency>
  <groupId>org.springframework.boot</groupId>
  <artifactId>spring-boot-starter-thymeleaf</artifactId> </dependency>
```

Let's add the Thymeleaf Layout Dialect as a dependency. This dialect lets us create layouts and reusable templates for improved code reuse:

```
<dependency>
  <groupId>nz.net.ultraq.thymeleaf</groupId>
  <artifactId>thymeleaf-layout-dialect</artifactId>
</dependency>
```

After adding the dependency, let's learn where to add our templates.

Where should we add the templates to our project?

The project has a `resources` folder containing two main folders created by Spring Boot by default: `templates` and `static` folders. The `templates` folder is where we can add our templates, while the `static` folder is where we can add static resources such as images and CSS files. You can refer to *Figure 4.7* to see the project folder structure.

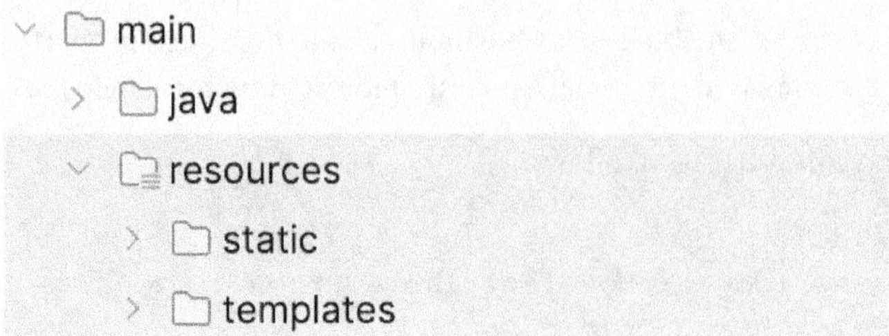

Figure 4.7: Project folder structure

Our first template is `layout.html`, the base for other templates to add code:

```
<html xmlns:layout="http://www.ultraq.net.nz/web/thymeleaf/layout">
..
  <section layout:fragment="content"> </section>
```

Thymeleaf's layout dialect uses `xmlns:layout="http://www.ultraq.net.nz/web/thymeleaf/layout"` to define layout attributes. The `<section>` tag element is marked with `layout:fragment="content"`, identifying it as a reusable fragment. It can be included in other templates by referring to it as content.

The following code snippet shows the `home.html` content:

```
<html xmlns:layout="http://www.ultraq.net.nz/thymeleaf/layout"
layout:decorate="~{layout.html}">
<body>
  <section layout:fragment="content">
...
```

The `layout:decorate="~{layout.html}"` attribute tells Thymeleaf to apply a layout template to the current page. `~{layout.html}` indicates that the template file named `layout.html` should be used as the base layout.

Figure 4.8 shows the `home.html` content using the layout; the header is inside `layout.html`.

Figure 4.8: Layout with home.html content

Figure 4.9 shows the `products.html` content using the same layout; the header is inside `layout.html`.

Figure 4.9: Layout with the products.html content

The web page's layout is based on `layout.html`, which contains the header section. The content of `layout.html` was replaced by `home.html` and later by `products.html`, but we reused the header section. With the MVC model implemented, let's now focus on security.

Implementing security with Spring Security

Security is vital in any project to protect data, ensure compliance, and prevent financial losses. **Spring Security** is a robust framework for Java apps that offers authentication, authorization, session management, security headers, and CSRF protection. It integrates with various authentication mechanisms, including LDAP, OAuth, and JDBC-based user stores, and works seamlessly with Spring Boot.

Basic authentication overview

Basic authentication is a straightforward method for verifying a user's identity when accessing a web server. It sends the user's credentials, such as a username and password, encoded in base64 format as part of the HTTP request header. While easy to implement, basic authentication is not secure over unencrypted connections such as HTTP because the credentials can be easily intercepted and decoded. That's why it's essential to use it with HTTPS, which encrypts the connection, ensuring the credentials remain confidential and secure during transmission.

Implementing basic authentication with Spring Security

Spring Security offers robust support for implementing basic authentication in Spring Boot apps. First, we need to add the required dependencies to the project:

```
<dependency>
   <groupId>org.springframework.boot</groupId>
   <artifactId>spring-boot-starter-security</artifactId>
</dependency>
```

Once the dependency is added, we can configure Spring Security.

Configuring Spring Security

Spring Security 6 has some changes and improvements compared to its previous versions. One significant change is the new way of setting up security configurations. The use of security configuration with `WebSecurityConfigurerAdapter` has been deprecated in favor of component-based security configurations. This change promotes a more modular and flexible approach to security configurations.

Moreover, Spring Boot 3 has also brought changes in expressing security configurations, especially with the adoption of Spring Security 6. If you encounter issues with the `antMatchers()` method not being recognized, it may be due to the new lambda-oriented style. Let's delve into the implementation of Spring Security 6 configuration:

```
@Bean
public SecurityFilterChain filterChain(HttpSecurity http) throws
Exception {
  http
    .authorizeHttpRequests(authorize -> authorize
      .requestMatchers("/home", "/login",
      "/register").permitAll().anyRequest().authenticated())
    .formLogin(form -> form.loginPage("/login")
                    .defaultSuccessUrl("/products", true))
    .logout(logout -> logout.logoutSuccessUrl("/home"))
    .csrf(csrf -> csrf.csrfTokenRepository(new
                    CookieCsrfTokenRepository()))
    .httpBasic(Customizer.withDefaults());
    return http.build();
}
```

Configure HTTP security using the `SecurityFilterChain` bean instead of the deprecated `WebSecurityConfigurerAdapter`. The `authorizeHttpRequests()` method now incorporates a lambda expression for request authorization and works with `requestMatchers()` to set specific authorization policies for various paths. The `.formLogin(...)` method facilitates form-based authentication and changes the login URL to `/login`, replacing the default Spring Security login page and directing users to /products after a successful login. The .logout(...) method manages logout features and establishes the /home page as the redirection point after logout. The .csrf(...) method activates and configures CSRF protection, essential for blocking unauthorized commands from trusted users, and stores CSRF tokens in a cookie—ideal for single-page applications that require CSRF tokens on the client side for subsequent requests. Lastly, the .httpBasic(...) method initiates HTTP Basic Authentication, a straightforward scheme supported by the HTTP protocol, with the Customizer.withDefaults() method setting the default configurations that prompt clients for credentials using the standard HTTP header.

Implementing the authentication process

Storing passwords in databases, also known as **at rest**, in plain text form is highly insecure. In a data breach, attackers can immediately use plain text passwords. By using BCryptPasswordEncoder, passwords are hashed before they are stored. Each hashed password is unique due to the salting process, even if two users have the same password. The following code snippet returns an instance of BCryptPasswordEncoder, a PasswordEncoder implementation that uses the BCrypt hashing solid function:

```
@Bean
public PasswordEncoder passwordEncoder() {
  return new BCryptPasswordEncoder();
}
```

Then, the following code snippet uses the passwordEncoder method in the filterChain method to hash the password:

```
public SecurityFilterChain filterChain(HttpSecurity http)
                                        throws Exception {
  AuthenticationManagerBuilder builder =
    http.getSharedObject(AuthenticationManagerBuilder.class);

  builder.userDetailsService(userDetailsService())
                  .passwordEncoder(passwordEncoder());

  ...
```

AuthenticationManagerBuilder is a builder object essential for constructing AuthenticationManager, the main Spring Security component responsible for managing authentication. It is configured with UserDetailsService to load user data and PasswordEncoder for hashing and verifying passwords.

The Spring Security framework utilizes the UserDetailsService interface to obtain personalized user data during authentication. This interface provides flexibility in integrating various data sources and follows the single responsibility principle by separating user data retrieval from authentication mechanisms. By implementing your own UserDetailsService, you can customize and extend the user loading process to include additional user properties. One widespread use case is creating a custom implementation with **Spring Data JPA** to interact with a database. The following code snippet presents the implementation of `UserDetailsService` by the `UserDetailsCustomService` class:

```java
@Service
public class UserDetailsCustomService implements UserDetailsService {
  @Autowired
  private UserRepository userRepository;

  @Override
  public UserDetails loadUserByUsername(String username)
                       throws UsernameNotFoundException {

    User user = userRepository.findByUsername(username)
            .orElseThrow(() -> newUsernameNotFoundException(
          "User not found with username: " + username));

    return new UserDetailsCustom(
            user.getUsername(),
            user.getPassword(),
            user.getRoles().stream()
                .map(r -> new
                SimpleGrantedAuthority(r.getName()))
                    .collect(Collectors.toList()),
            user.isEnabled()
    ...
```

The `CustomUserDetailsService` class implements the `UserDetailsService` interface and overrides the `UserDetails loadUserByUsername(String username)` method. `UserRepository` is a JPA repository that handles data operations on the user entity. When `loadUserByUsername` is called, it tries to fetch a user by the given username. If successful, it converts the user entity into a Spring Security `UserDetails` object, which includes roles or authorities. `UserDetails` is an interface that provides user information and is implemented by the `UserDetailsCustom` class. `SimpleGrantedAuthority` is the basic concrete implementation of `GrantedAuthority`. It stores a string representation of an authority granted to the `Authentication` object; in this case, it gets the user's roles through the `r.getName()` attribute from the `Role` entity.

By integrating `UserDetailsService` in this way, Spring Security can handle a wide range of authentication scenarios, making it a powerful and flexible choice for securing Spring applications.

Figure 4.10 shows our login page. Now, we can try to log into our application.

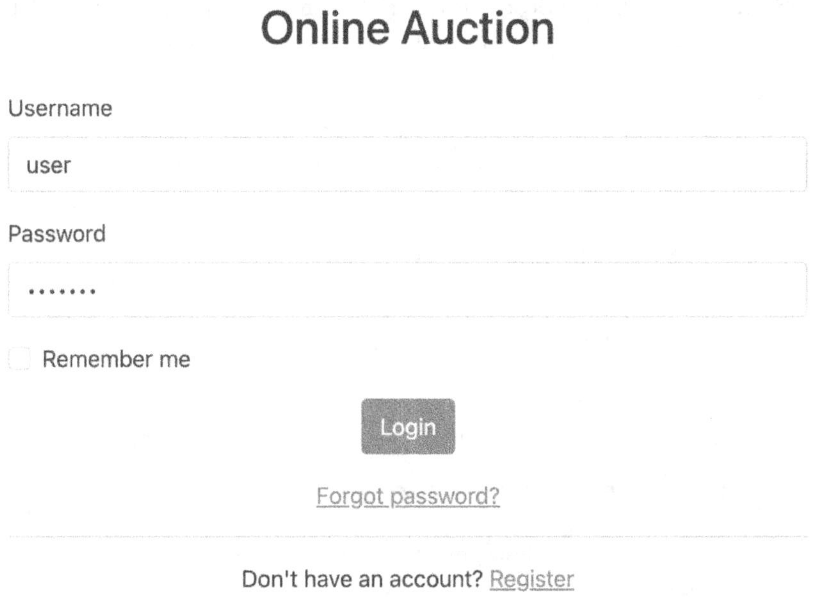

Figure 4.10: Login page

If we have successfully logged in, we can access the product page. However, if we try to access the product page without logging in, we are redirected to the login page. *Figure 4.11* presents the **Products** page.

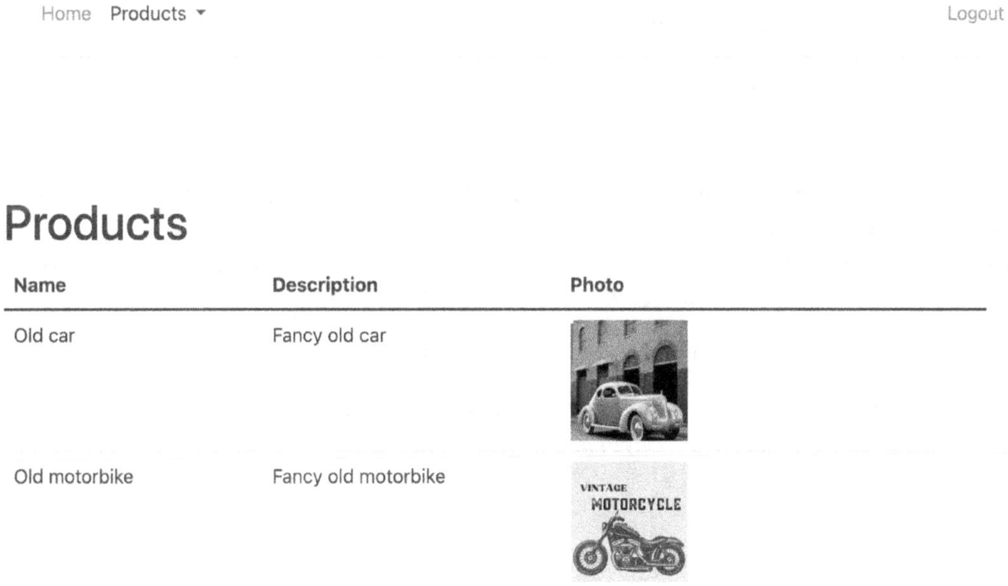

Figure 4.11: Products page

Only logged-in users can access the **Products** page. Now, let's learn some expressions that allow views to adapt based on the application's security context. The following code snippet shows the dependency on the Spring Security integration modules that must be added to the project:

```
<dependency>
  <groupId>org.thymeleaf.extras</groupId>
    <artifactId>thymeleaf-extras-springsecurity6</artifactId>
</dependency>
```

The following code snippet shows the namespace to `layout.html`:

```
<html …
        xmlns:sec="http://www.thymeleaf.org/thymeleaf-extras-
        springsecurity6"
```

Access to the admin menu can be restricted to users with the ROLE_ADMIN role:

```
<li sec:authorize="hasRole('ROLE_ADMIN')">
```

The `sec:authorize` attribute lets you use Spring Security expressions directly within the Thymeleaf template, such as `hasRole`.

We can use a similar approach to verify the user is logged in:

```
<li sec:authorize="isAuthenticated()">
```

The `sec:authorize` attribute lets you use the Spring Security `isAuthenticated()` expression to show content only if the user is logged in.

Now, let's discuss the security of data transmission.

Implementing security in transit

Ensuring security during data transmission is of utmost importance. The **Secure Sockets Layer (SSL)** is a widely accepted security protocol that helps establish encrypted links between web servers and browsers during online communication. SSL technology guarantees that all data transmitted between browsers and servers is encrypted and secure.

To implement SSL in a Spring Boot 3 application using Spring Security 6, follow these steps:

1. **Obtain an SSL certificate**: Purchase a certificate from a **certificate authority (CA)** or generate a self-signed certificate for development purposes using tools such as OpenSSL.

2. **Configure HTTPS in the application**: Place your SSL certificate in your Spring Boot application, typically in the `src/main/resources` directory, and add the following properties to your `application.properties` or `application.yml` file:

```
server.port=8443
server.ssl.key-store=classpath:keystore.jks
server.ssl.key-store-password=yourpassword
server.ssl.keyStoreType=JKS
server.ssl.keyAlias=tomcat
```

Here, `server.port` specifies port `8443`, which is a common choice for HTTPS to avoid conflicts with the default HTTP port `8080` and the default HTTPS port `443`. `server.ssl.key-store` refers to the path of your keystore file containing the server certificate and private key. `key-store-password` relates to the password and `server.ssl.keyStoreType` specifies the key store type that contains the server's SSL certificate. JKS is a Java Key Store, but there are other types, such as PKCS12, JCEKS, and BKS. Lastly, `server.ssl.keyAlias` is the alias of the digital certificate.

Ensuring that data transmitted between your server and clients is secure is essential for protecting sensitive data and maintaining your users' trust.

Creating a JKS certificate

Creating a JKS certificate involves using the **keytool** utility, which is included with the **Java Development Kit (JDK)**. Here's an example of creating it using the command line in a terminal:

```
keytool -genkeypair -alias myappkey -keyalg RSA -keysize 2048
 -keystore mykeystore.jks -validity 365
```

You will be prompted to enter some information, and then the `mykeystone.jks` file is created. Now, let's explore another vital theme in software development: automated testing.

Automated testing

Automated testing plays a vital role in software development. It ensures that certain software satisfies its intended requirements and operates correctly in various scenarios. Automated tests act as a protective barrier, preventing new changes from disrupting the existing functionality. They also help in early issue detection, reducing the cost and time required to address bugs that may otherwise be found after release. When changes are made to the application, automated tests can be rerun to confirm that no new errors have been introduced and that previously resolved issues have not re-surfaced.

Automated tests execute quickly and can be run more frequently than manual tests. This is essential in a monolithic architecture where changes in one section of the system could affect others. Furthermore, automated tests provide documented evidence of the system's intended behavior, which is extremely helpful in orienting new team members or reviewing previously developed features.

Overall, having a robust suite of automated tests instills confidence in developers and teams, ensuring that software works as intended and meets its specified requirements.

Types of automated tests

Some of the leading automation tests are as follows:

- **Unit tests**: Java frameworks such as JUnit and Mockito are commonly used to facilitate unit testing, which involves testing individual components or functions in isolation from the rest of the application.

- **Integration tests**: These tests aim to verify that different components within the application interact as expected, such as the interaction between the database layer and the business logic layer.

- **Functional tests**: These tests are run against the fully integrated system to ensure the application functions as expected from an end-user perspective. Automation tools such as Selenium or TestComplete can be used to test the user interface.

- **Performance tests**: Tools such as JMeter and Gatling are used to simulate multiple users or high loads, which is essential for ensuring that the application performs well under expected load conditions.

- **Security tests**: Automated security testing tools such as ZAP, formerly known as OWASP ZAP, and Fortify can scan for vulnerabilities and ensure the effectiveness of security measures.

- **End-to-end tests**: These tests ensure the entire application functions correctly in a realistic environment simulating user scenarios.

We will discuss each type in *Chapter 12, Testing*; for now, let's implement an integration test in our monolithic application.

Implementing integration tests

When creating integration tests for a login page in a Spring Boot 3 application using Spring Security 6, it is necessary to set up a test environment that imitates the login mechanism's real-world behavior. The first step is setting up the dependencies:

```
<dependency>
  <groupId>org.springframework.boot</groupId>
    <artifactId>spring-boot-starter-test</artifactId>
    <scope>test</scope>
</dependency>
```

`spring-boot-starter-test` includes JUnit, MockMvc, AssertJ, Mockito, Hamcrest, and JsonPath libraries for testing applications. JUnit is an excellent Java framework for unit testing with annotations and assertions. Spring Test and Spring Boot Test offer enhanced integration testing capabilities. AssertJ provides a library with fluent assertion methods. Mockito generates mock objects and verifies object interactions. Hamcrest crafts matcher objects, enabling sophisticated assertion logic. MockMvc tests controllers without launching an entire HTTP server. JsonPath makes assertions and extracts elements from a JSON document during testing.

Creating the integration test class

The `@SpringBootTest` annotation is used in the Spring Boot framework, primarily in writing integration tests. It plays an essential role in the testing phase of application development by providing a comprehensive environment that simulates the application's runtime. Let's create an integration test class to test our application's login:

```
@SpringBootTest(webEnvironment = SpringBootTest.WebEnvironment.RANDOM_
PORT)
@AutoConfigureMockMvc
public class LoginIntegrationTests {
    @Autowired
    private MockMvc mockMvc;
...
```

The `@SpringBootTest` annotation loads the entire application context for integration testing with Spring Boot. For web layer testing, the `webEnvironment` parameter is set to `SpringBootTest.WebEnvironment.RANDOM_PORT`. This sets up the embedded web server on a random port, preventing port conflicts and making HTTP communication with the application possible.

The `@AutoConfigureMockMvc` annotation sets up `MockMvc`, a Spring MVC framework that allows HTTP requests to be sent to the DispatcherServlet and responses to be evaluated without launching an HTTP server. The annotation is helpful for testing controllers and Spring MVC components, streamlining configuration, and enhancing test sustainability.

Writing test cases

Now, we will write a test case that uses MockMvc to perform requests against the login endpoint and validate the results:

```
@Test
public void testSuccessfulLogin() throws Exception {
    mockMvc.perform(formLogin("/login")
        .user("user").password("test123"))
        .andExpect(redirectedUrl("/home"));
...
```

The `mockMvc.perform(formLogin("/login"))` instruction sends a request with MockMvc to simulate a form login on a specified URL, /login. `.user("user").password("test123")` sets the username and password to be submitted with the form, and `.andExpect(redirectedUrl("/home"))` tests whether the response includes a redirect to a specific URL, /home, upon successful login.

Testing security

For more complex scenarios, such as testing different roles and privileges, we can use the `@WithMockUser` annotation to simulate login as different users. Still, first, we need to add the `spring-security-test` dependency:

```
<dependency>
   <groupId>org.springframework.security</groupId>
   <artifactId>spring-security-test</artifactId>
   <scope>test</scope>
</dependency>
```

`spring-security-test` is an extension of the Spring Security framework that supports testing security configurations and components in Spring applications. It provides utilities for testing secured endpoints, building security-aware mock requests, and simulating authenticated users with specified roles and authorities. The following code snippet shows a controller's method that will be executed only if the user has the ADMIN role:

```
@PreAuthorize("hasRole('ADMIN')")
@GetMapping("/admin")
public String admin() {
   return "admin";
}
```

To test the controller that permits access only to users with specific roles, we must add the `@WithMockUser` annotation to our tests:

```
@Test
@WithMockUser(username="admin", roles={"USER", "ADMIN"})
public void testAdminAccess() throws Exception {
 mockMvc.perform(get("/admin")).andExpect(status().isOk());
 ...
```

The `@WithMockUser` annotation in the Spring Security Test framework allows us to simulate a test under the security context of a user with designated attributes, eliminating the need for actual user authentication. In the code, the `username` attribute is set to `admin`, and the `roles` attribute is set to USER and ADMIN, granting access permissions to different application sections based on the authenticated user's level of authority.

Summary

This chapter explored monolithic architecture, a unified software development model in which components such as the user interface, business logic, and data access are integrated into a single program. We examined its benefits, including ease of development, testing, and deployment, alongside challenges such as scalability issues.

We discussed common patterns within monolithic systems, such as layered architecture and the MVC pattern. We highlighted their roles in organizing complex systems and distinguishing between stateful and stateless operations to guide their appropriate use.

A hypothetical online auction system case study detailed the implementation of monolithic applications using the Spring Framework, specifically Spring Boot, Spring MVC, and Spring Security, besides integrating it with the server-side template Thymeleaf. This example demonstrated the effectiveness of selecting architectural styles and technologies and incorporating security features.

The chapter concluded with an overview of automated tests, focusing on integration tests essential for verifying the functionality of integrated components within monolithic architectures.

This chapter provided a comprehensive understanding of monolithic architectures, covering architectural patterns, practical implementation examples using Java and Spring, and discussions on security and testing. It has prepared you to tackle real-world software development challenges.

In *Chapter 5, Client-Server Architecture*, we will explore client-server architecture and uncover its foundational concepts, components, communication protocols, and models. We will then implement an application using Java and Spring within a client-server architecture, applying the main cross-cutting concerns regarding this architectural style.

Questions

1. What is monolithic architecture?

2. How is a layered architecture typically organized in a monolithic application?

3. What is the **model-view-controller** (**MVC**) pattern, and how is it used in monolithic architectures?

4. What is the difference between stateful and stateless systems in the context of monolithic architectures?

5. How does the Spring Framework facilitate the development of monolithic applications?

6. What role does Spring Security play in a monolithic application?

7. Why is automated testing important in monolithic architectures, and what types of tests are typically involved?

Get This Book's PDF Version and Exclusive Extras

Scan the QR code (or go to `packtpub.com/unlock`). Search for this book by name, confirm the edition, and then follow the steps on the page.

Note: Keep your invoice handly. Purchase made directly from packt don't require one.

5

Client-Server Architecture

This chapter discusses client-server architecture in software development, covering its definition, key components, advantages, and drawbacks. It highlights design principles for applications based on this model and common communication protocols, including **Representational State Transfer (REST)** principles and best practices for developing RESTful APIs.

The chapter also covers implementing a client-server application using the Spring framework, focusing on token-based authentication with **JSON Web Tokens (JWTs)**. It includes API documentation with OpenAPI and code coverage testing using the JaCoCo library. These practical skills are essential for building robust and secure modern software solutions.

This chapter will cover the following topic:

- Introducing client-server architecture
- Exploring the client-server architecture types
- Client-server communication protocols
- Implementing a client-server application
- Code coverage testing

By the end of this chapter, you will understand client-server architecture, its components, and communication protocols. You'll learn to implement secure applications and gain insights into best practices for documenting APIs and conducting code coverage testing, ensuring your applications are reliable and maintainable.

Technical requirements

All the code for this chapter can be found on GitHub at `https://github.com/PacktPublishing/Software-Architecture-with-Spring/tree/main/ch5`. Ellipses in the code blocks indicate that parts of the code have been omitted, and the complete code is available on GitHub.

Introducing client-server architecture

Let's delve deeper into the definition of client-server architecture and learn about its main components, advantages, and disadvantages, as well as approach an application design of this architecture. Let's start exploring what it is.

What is client-server architecture?

Client-server architecture forms the backbone of modern distributed computing. It elegantly partitions tasks between two distinct entities: **clients** and **servers**. Clients (the user-facing applications on personal computers, smartphones, or web browsers) initiate requests and interact with the system. On the other hand, servers (typically powerful machines) handle the heavy lifting. They manage databases, store and serve files, and execute complex applications. This division of labor allows clients to remain lightweight and responsive while servers can focus on data management and intensive computations. The beauty of this architecture lies in connecting multiple clients to a single server, either on a local network or across the vast expanse of the internet. This centralized access to resources ensures efficient data management and simplifies software updates as changes are deployed on the server, automatically affecting all connected clients. *Figure 5.1* presents a typical client-server architecture.

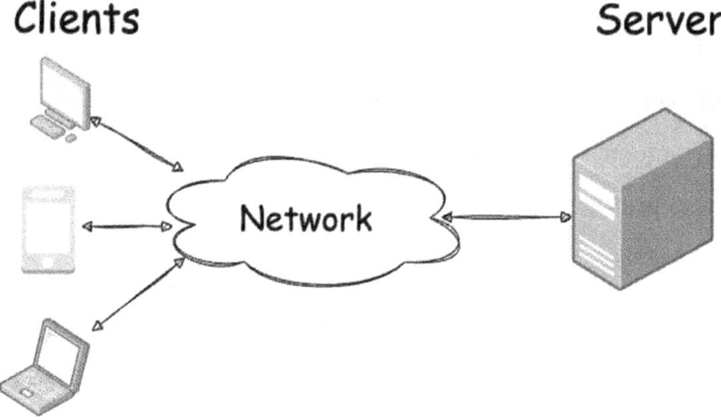

Figure 5.1: Client-server architecture

The figure presents the essential components of client-server architecture: the client or clients, the server, and the network that connects them. To know more about them, you can go through the following:

- **Client**: The client acts as the user interface, sending requests and presenting server responses in an accessible format. Clients vary in complexity, and there are thick or thin clients:

  - **Thick client**: In a client-server architecture, a thick or fat client performs significant processing independently of the server. Thick clients execute business logic, manage data locally, and can operate in disconnected mode. Examples include desktop applications and traditional software installations such as Salesforce Classic, a desktop application.

  - **Thin client**: In a client-server architecture, a thin client relies heavily on the server for processing and data storage. The server performs most of the processing tasks, while the client functions as an interface for input and output. Data is primarily stored on the server, with minimal storage local to the client. Thin clients require a continuous network connection to the server. Examples of thin clients include web browsers accessing applications such as Salesforce Sales Cloud, Zoho CRM, and HubSpot CRM. Many **Internet of Things** (**IoT**) devices also function as thin clients, collecting data and sending it to a centralized server for processing.

Choosing between a thick or thin client setup in a client-server architecture depends on several factors, including application requirements, network reliability, security considerations, and the need for mobility and remote access:

- **Server**: Servers handle client requests and execute data processing, storage, and management tasks. It is designed to be robust and scalable, efficiently managing resources to serve multiple clients concurrently.

- **Network**: The network is the medium that facilitates communication between clients and servers. It can be a **local area network** (**LAN**), a **wide area network** (**WAN**), or the internet. The network ensures that requests and responses are transmitted between clients and servers efficiently and securely. It can involve hardware components such as routers, switches, and communication protocols that govern the interaction between clients and servers.

Client-server architecture is the backbone of modern distributed computing and deserves special attention. So, let's explore it further and design a client-server application architecture.

Designing the architecture of a client-server application

A client-server architecture will separate the presentation layer from the core application, creating distinct client applications. These clients could be HTML web pages, mobile applications, desktop software, or any other interface communicating with a server via a network. Consequently, the server-side application would house the business logic and data access services in a thin client model or house only the data access services in a fat client model. *Figure 5.2* illustrates the architectural design of a client-server application.

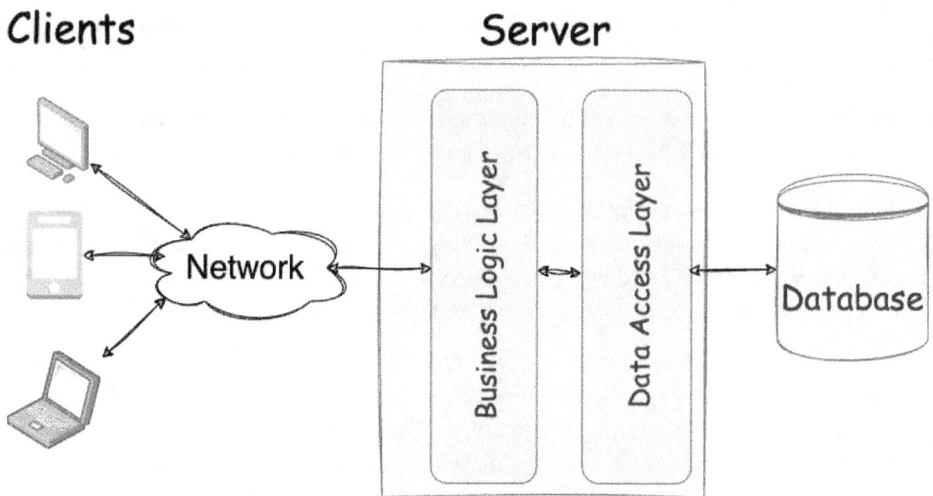

Figure 5.2: Architectural design of a client-server application

In a client-server architecture, the process follows a structured sequence:

1. The client sends a request to the server.

2. The server forwards the request to the business logic layer, which processes the request using necessary business rules and logic.

3. If needed, it communicates with the data access layer to retrieve or modify information in the database.

4. The database executes the operations and returns the results to the data access layer, which sends the data back to the business logic layer.

5. The business logic layer prepares a response, which the server sends back to the client.

6. The client presents the information to the user through the user interface.

Now the client-server architecture process has been explained, let's examine the benefits of it.

Benefits of client-server architecture

Client-server architecture is a widely adopted computing framework that offers numerous benefits, making it suitable for various applications and environments. Let's explore some crucial benefits of client-server architecture:

- **Centralized management**: A significant benefit of client-server architecture is centralized management. In this model, resources, data, and services are centralized on servers, simplifying administration and maintenance. System administrators can perform updates, security patches, and backups on the server side, reducing the need to manage individual client devices. This centralization also facilitates better control over data security and integrity, as sensitive information is stored and managed in a single location, enabling robust security measures and access controls to be implemented effectively.

- **Data consistency and integrity**: A single centralized database server typically manages all data transactions in client-server architectures. This centralization ensures that all data manipulations are controlled and managed consistently, preserving data integrity.

- **Scalability**: Scalability is another crucial advantage of client-server architecture. Servers can be upgraded with more powerful hardware or added to a load-balanced cluster to handle increased loads. This flexibility allows the system to grow with the users' demands, ensuring that performance remains optimal even as the number of clients or the amount of data increases.

- **Performance optimization**: In terms of performance, client-server architecture allows for specialized hardware and software configurations on the server side to handle intensive tasks and large volumes of data. This capability enables the server to process requests quickly and efficiently, providing clients with fast and reliable responses. The division of labor, where clients handle the user interface and servers manage data processing, ensures that tasks are performed by the most suitable components of the system.

- **Resource sharing**: Resource sharing is efficiently managed in a client-server model. Multiple clients can access shared resources on the server, such as files, applications, and databases. This setup reduces redundancy, as resources do not need to be duplicated across multiple devices, lowering overall costs. It also ensures that all clients can access the most up-to-date information and services, as the server makes updates and changes centrally.

- **Reliability**: The client-server model also enhances reliability and uptime. Servers can be configured with redundancy and failover mechanisms to ensure continuous operation even during hardware failures. Regular maintenance and monitoring can be performed without significantly impacting clients, as servers can be taken offline for repairs or upgrades while a backup server takes over.

In short, client-server architecture provides centralized management, ensuring data consistency and integrity, scalability, resource sharing, and improved performance. It's best for applications needing centralized control and secure, consistent data access. Despite these benefits, client-server architecture has drawbacks, which we'll discuss next.

Drawbacks of client-server architecture

While highly beneficial in many contexts, client-server architecture has drawbacks that can make it less suitable for some applications. Recognizing these limitations is vital for making informed architectural decisions and avoiding pitfalls.

- **Single point of failure**: One major drawback of client-server architecture is the potential for a single point of failure. Since the server is the central hub for resources and services, the entire system can become inaccessible to all clients if it goes down. This dependency on the server's availability necessitates robust failover and redundancy mechanisms, which can be complex and costly to implement and maintain. In environments where high availability is critical, the risk of server downtime can pose significant challenges.

- **Performance bottlenecks**: The server can become a performance bottleneck if an excessive number of clients access it simultaneously, which results in slow response times and reduced performance.

- **Scalability limitations**: While servers can be scaled to handle more clients, this scalability has physical and practical limits. As the number of clients grows, the server can become a bottleneck, leading to performance degradation. Load balancing and horizontal scaling can mitigate this, but these solutions add complexity and cost. The client-server model might not be a good choice for applications with highly variable or unpredictable loads, such as social media platforms or large-scale streaming services.

- **Latency**: Latency is another concern in client-server architecture. The physical distance between clients and servers can introduce latency, affecting the application's performance. Even minor delays can be unacceptable in real-time applications such as financial trading platforms or online gaming. Ensuring low-latency connections might require distributed servers and edge computing solutions, adding further complexity and cost.

- **Security vulnerabilities**: Centralized servers are attractive targets for cyber-attacks. If a server is compromised, it can expose sensitive data and disrupt services for all clients.

- **Maintenance**: Maintenance and updates can become cumbersome in a client-server setup. While centralized management simplifies some aspects, it also means that any server maintenance or downtime affects all clients. Scheduled downtimes must be carefully planned to minimize disruption, which can be challenging in a global environment where clients may operate in different time zones.

By carefully evaluating these advantages and drawbacks, we can conclude whether or not client-server architecture is the most suitable for our application. Adding another piece of knowledge to support this evaluation, we will explore and compare three other client-architecture types.

Exploring the client-server architecture types

Several types of client-server architecture are designed to meet different requirements and constraints. We will discuss the primary types, including two-tier, three-tier, and n-tier architectures. Although not specifically a client-server architecture, n-tier extends the concept of three-tier architecture by adding more tiers. Each type varies in complexity, scalability, performance, security, maintainability, reusability, and use cases.

> **Note**
>
> It's essential to understand the difference between a tier and a layer. While a layer denotes the logical separation of components, a tier physically separates a layer into different running machines.

Two-tier architecture

The two-tier architecture is a client-server model where the client directly interacts with the server to request services and retrieve data. *Figure 5.3* presents a two-tier architecture.

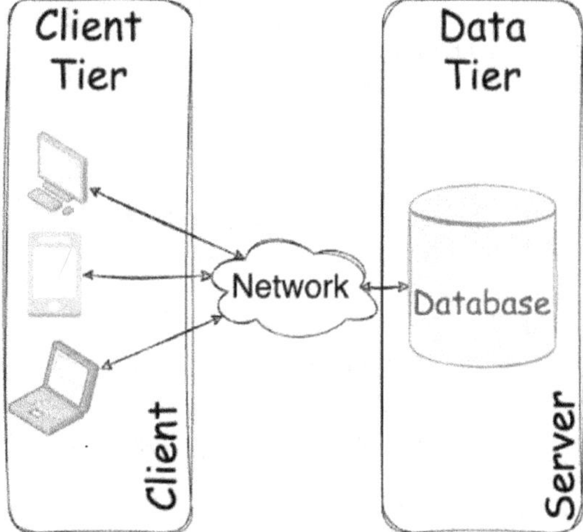

Figure 5.3: Two-tier architecture

The two-tier architecture typically consists of the following tiers:

- **Client tier**: Also known as the application tier, it holds the user interface or client application where users interact with the application. It can be a web application, mobile application, or desktop application. The client tier handles user inputs and outputs and communicates directly with the data tier.

- **Data tier**: The data tier, or database tier, is the data storage layer, usually consisting of a **database management system** (**DBMS**) such as MySQL. It manages data storage, retrieval, and management. The client tier directly interacts with this tier to perform database operations.

The client and server layers can be adjusted to create a fat client or thin client setup. In a fat client architecture, the client tier is responsible for the user interface and business logic, while the data tier mainly handles data storage. Conversely, in a thin client architecture, the client tier focuses solely on the user interface, and the server tier manages business logic and data storage.

Three-tier architecture

The three-tier architecture is an advanced client-server model that introduces an additional layer between the client and the server. This middle layer, or application server, manages the application's business logic, allowing for better organization, scalability, and maintenance. *Figure 5.4* presents the three-tier architecture.

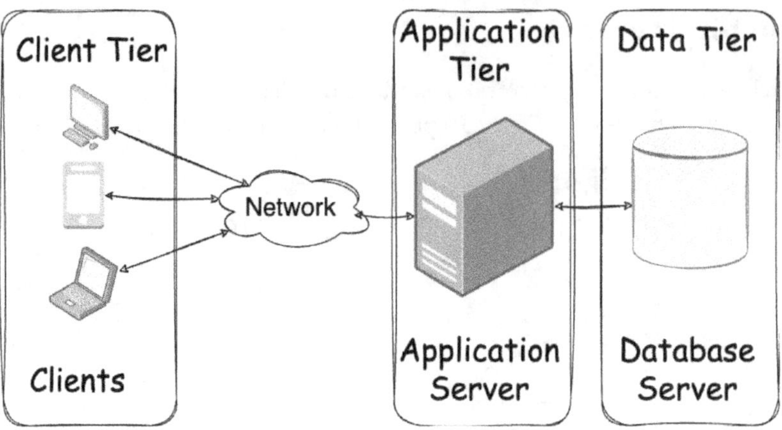

Figure 5.4: Three-tier architecture

The three-tier architecture typically consists of the following tiers:

- **Client tier (presentation layer)**: This tier presents information to the user and gathers their input. It can be a desktop application, web browser, or mobile app. The client tier interacts with the application server to request services and display data.

- **Application tier (business/logic layer)**: This middle tier handles the application's core functionality, processing client requests, performing calculations, and making logical decisions. The application server acts as an intermediary, receiving requests from the client tier, processing them, and then interacting with the database tier to retrieve or update data.

- **Data tier (data layer)**: This tier is responsible for storing, retrieving, and managing data using a DBMS.

The three-tier architecture is commonly used in web applications, enterprise applications, and other large-scale systems where scalability and maintainability are critical.

N-tier architecture

The N-tier architecture, also known as multi-tier architecture, extends the concept of the three-tier architecture by adding more tiers. Each tier has a specific responsibility, which can be distributed across multiple servers. Besides the client tier, application tier, and data tier seen previously in the three-tier architecture, it may include additional servers such as the following:

- **Web services tier**: Manages external service integrations, such as APIs or third-party services.

- **Security tier**: Implements security protocols and access controls to protect the application and its data.

- **Caching tier**: Improves performance by temporarily storing frequently accessed data.

The N-tier architecture is a versatile and robust solution that divides an application into multiple layers, each responsible for a specific function. This approach enhances scalability, maintainability, and security, making it suitable for complex and large-scale applications despite its increased complexity and cost.

Contrasting two-tier, three-tier, and n-tier architectures

Now that we know about the two-tier, three-tier, and N-tier architectures, let's contrast them according to their scalability, performance, maintainability, reusability, and security:

- **Scalability**: A two-tier architecture is limited, making it suitable for small to medium-sized applications. On the other hand, a three-tier architecture offers better scalability because the middle tier can handle business logic, thus reducing the load on clients and the database. N-tier architectures are highly scalable, as each tier can be independently scaled based on load and specific requirements.

- **Performance**: Two-tier architectures typically provide faster performance for small-scale applications due to having fewer tiers and direct data access. On the other hand, three-tier architectures offer balanced performance by separating concerns and allowing optimization of the middle tier, which can improve overall performance. N-tier architectures can optimize performance at each tier, introducing additional tiers may also introduce latency.

- **Maintainability**: Initially, two-tier architectures are a breeze to maintain. However, as the application grows, the ease diminishes, and the architecture may become a hindrance. The three-tier architecture, with its separation of concerns, steps up the game, making updates and management more effortless, even as the application expands. With their clear separation of responsibilities, N-tier architectures offer a high level of maintainability, ensuring straightforward updates and changes, regardless of the application's size.

- **Reusability**: In a two-tier architecture, reusability is limited because business logic is usually embedded within the client. On the other hand, three-tier architectures improve reusability by encapsulating business logic in the middle tier, making it reusable across multiple clients. N-tier architectures provide the highest level of reusability, as services and components in each layer can be reused across different parts of the application or even in other applications.

- **Security**: Security in a two-tier architecture is essential, as direct database access by clients can pose significant risks. In a three-tier architecture, security is improved because the middle tier can enforce security policies and limit direct database access. N-tier architectures provide the highest level of security, with multiple layers implementing robust security measures, including authentication, authorization, and data encryption.

The choice of a two-tier, three-tier, or N-tier architecture depends on the application's specific requirements. Two-tier architectures are best for small applications with low complexity and limited scalability needs. Three-tier architectures are suitable for medium-sized applications that need a balance of performance, maintainability, and scalability. N-tier architectures are best for large-scale, complex applications that require high scalability, maintainability, reusability, and security. Now, let's approach the client-server communication protocols.

Client-server communication protocols

Client-server communication protocols enable effective and secure data exchange between clients and servers. These protocols establish the rules and conventions for communication, ensuring that requests and responses are transmitted reliably and correctly. Recognizing and applying the appropriate protocol involves understanding the application's requirements, including performance, security, and data integrity needs. Here are some common protocols:

- **Hypertext Transfer Protocol** (**HTTP**): This is a high-level protocol used primarily for transmitting hypertext documents on the World Wide Web. It operates on a request-response model; the client starts sending a request to the server, and the server replies with the requested resources or an error message. HTTP is stateless, meaning each request is processed independently and does not retain information from prior interactions. Its secure version is **Hypertext Transfer Protocol Secure** (**HTTPS**), which utilizes the **Secure Sockets Layer** (**SSL**) and **Transport Layer Security** (**TLS**) to encrypt data transferred between the client and server, ensuring confidentiality and integrity.

- **WebSocket**: This is a specialized protocol for full-duplex communication channels over a single **Transmission Control Protocol** (**TCP**) connection. It enables full-duplex communication, maintaining a persistent connection for real-time interaction. This protocol reduces the overhead of HTTP headers, making it more efficient for frequent data exchanges. Additionally, it is supported by most modern web browsers and servers. WebSockets are particularly useful for web applications that require real-time data exchange.

- **Advanced Message Queuing Protocol** (**AMQP**): This enables applications to communicate through a message broker. Applications send and receive messages through a message broker such as RabbitMQ and Apache ActiveMQ. AMQP supports reliable, asynchronous, and decoupled communication between distributed systems. It ensures that messages are delivered securely and timely, even during network failures.

- **Simple Object Access Protocol** (**SOAP**): This is a protocol for exchanging information between applications in a distributed environment. It uses **Extensible Markup Language** (**XML**) for message formatting and relies on HTTP for transmission. SOAP ensures interoperability across different systems and platforms. SOAP messages are XML documents with four parts: envelope, header, body, and fault sections. Despite offering platform independence, extensibility, reliability, and security, SOAP messages can be complex and large, affecting performance. SOAP is commonly found in legacy systems but has gradually been replaced by RESTful APIs. RESTful APIs are more straightforward, lightweight, accessible to develop and use, and better suited for modern web applications and mobile devices.

These protocols ensure reliable, secure, and efficient communication between clients and servers, enabling a wide range of Internet applications and services. Although several other communication protocols exist, we have stayed focused on the most common ones when developing applications. Now, let's explore another standard method of communication over a network between a client and a server: REST.

REST

REST is an architectural style for designing applications that communicate over a network. It depends on a stateless, client-server, and cacheable communication protocol, typically HTTP. REST consists of a set of guidelines and principles rather than being a formal standard or protocol. In *Architectural Styles and the Design of Network-based Software Architectures*, Roy Fielding's doctoral dissertation introduced and defined REST and its principles as follows:

- **Statelessness**: A request from a client to a server must include all the information the server requires to process and fulfill the request. The server must not store any state of the client session.

- **Client-server architecture**: Both the client and server should be able to evolve independently. The server provides resources, and the client accesses and manipulates these resources.

- **Cacheability**: Responses must be implicitly or explicitly marked as cacheable or non-cacheable to prevent clients from reusing stale or inappropriate data.

- **Layered system**: A client typically cannot discern whether it is connected directly to the end server or through an intermediary.

- **Uniform interface**: REST relies on a uniform interface between components to simplify and decouple the architecture, which enables each part to evolve independently. This interface is typically HTTP-based.

REST is a set of architectural principles, so let's learn how it is implemented.

RESTful APIs

RESTful refers to web services implementing REST principles. If a web service adheres to REST principles, it is often called RESTful. Here are the main characteristics of RESTful web services:

- **Resources and URIs**: Resources are identified by **uniform resource identifiers** (**URIs**). For example, in a URI such as `https://my-app-services/products/123`, `products` identifies a product resource, and `123` is the resource's identification.

- **HTTP methods**: RESTful services use standard HTTP methods such as `GET`, `POST`, `PUT`, `DELETE`, and `PATCH` to perform representation operations on resources:

  - `GET`: Retrieve a resource

  - `POST`: Create a new resource

  - `PUT`: Update an existing resource

  - `DELETE`: Remove a resource

  - `PATCH`: Update partially an existing resource

- **Representation**: Resources can be represented in various formats, such as JSON, XML, text, or HTML. Clients interact with these representations rather than the actual resource itself.

- **Stateless communication**: According to REST principles, each client-server interaction must be stateless, meaning the server does not store client context between requests.

- **Status codes**: RESTful APIs utilize standard HTTP status codes to communicate the result of an API request. For instance, a `200 (OK)` status indicates that the request was successful, a `404 (Not Found)` status indicates that the resource was not found, and a `500 (Internal Server Error)` status indicates a server-side error.

These are the characteristics of RESTful. Now, let's look at the best practices for designing one.

Designing RESTful APIs

Designing a RESTful API involves several best practices; let's check the main ones:

- **Use meaningful URIs**: URIs should be readable, convey the resource's identity, and be plural. For example, `/api/products/123` is preferable to `/api/getProduct?id=123`.

- **Versioning**: Include versioning in the URI to maintain backward compatibility as the API evolves – for example, `/api/v1/products`.

- **Statelessness**: Ensure that each request from a client to a server possesses all the information needed to understand and process the request. Avoid server-side sessions.

- **Use HTTP methods correctly**: Adhere to the standard use of HTTP methods. For example, use `GET` for reading data, `POST` for creating data, `PUT` for updating data, `DELETE` for deleting data, and `PATCH` for partially updating the data.

- **Provide functional responses**: Always return helpful and informative responses. Include relevant status codes and error messages to help clients understand the result of their requests.

- **Secure your API**: Implement authentication and authorization mechanisms to protect your API from unauthorized access. Encrypt data for transmission between the client and server using HTTPS.

In summary, REST is a concept or architecture, while RESTful refers to web services that adhere to its principles. The **Richardson Maturity Model** is a way to classify and evaluate RESTful APIs based on their adherence to REST principles. It was introduced by Leonard Richardson, a thought leader in the API space, and it provides a structured approach to assessing the maturity and quality of a RESTful API. I recommend looking it up on the internet and studying it. Now, let's proceed to implement our client-server application.

Implementing a client-server application

Now, it's time to code. When we learn something new, this is always the expected part of the book. We want to see what we have learned applied, how it works in code, and how we can use it to provide a solution. Then, let's examine the current situation of our case study: imagine yourself at a large round table with the stakeholders. They will present to you and your team the results of the project that was issued in the market. In real life, at this time, we sometimes have butterflies in our stomachs, and we are anxious to listen to them.

Online auction case study

The stakeholders start the presentation. The hypothetical *WX-Auction* company is pleased with the success of our online auction application. It was a tremendous success; the number of users registered to the application and the number of transactions made in it surpassed the company's expectations. The stakeholders want to expand these statistics; they believe the number of users using the application would double if we had a mobile application version since everyone has a cell phone. They warned us that budget is a barrier and that the time to market for launching the mobile application is crucial.

System definition and mission

Our technical team is currently discussing our mission: to create a mobile application version of our online auction system. We face two significant constraints: a limited budget and a tight timeline.

After extensive discussions, the team concluded that developing a new web and mobile application would be more efficient than refactoring the current web application to work on mobile devices. Refactoring the user interface would likely result in a subpar user experience. The team agreed to leverage the existing monolithic application as much as possible, providing a web user interface and a mobile application to access the already established business logic. A client-server architecture was deemed appropriate to align with our budget constraints. However, creating separate mobile applications for Android and iOS and a web application would require more time and effort.

Therefore, the team decided to develop the web application using **React** and the mobile application using **React Native**. This approach allows for a single development process that works seamlessly across all devices, optimizing our time and resources.

A client-server architecture will also scale better than our monolithic application if we need it, as the number of users is expected to grow.

> **Note**
>
> It is outside the scope of this book to present the client's code and explain React and React Native. However, the source code and instructions for executing it are provided in the GitHub repository. To learn more about React, access the official website: `https://react.dev`.

Next, let's start implementing our server application.

Implementing the server

Our previous monolithic application was well developed using the MVC and N-tier architecture, so it will be easy to refactor it to become a client-server application. *Figure 5.5* presents our application's new architecture.

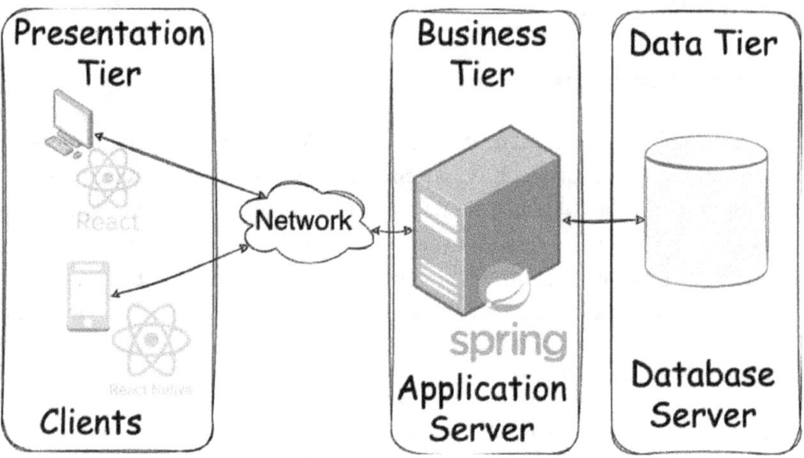

Figure 5.5: System architecture

Let's create our new application using a client-server architecture and a three-tier model. Communication will use RESTful web services.

Removing the Thymeleaf artifacts

Since we will remove the presentation from the server side, we must remove the Thymeleaf artifacts and libraries from our project. We remove the *templates* and *static* folders and their contents, then remove the following Thymeleaf libraries: `spring-boot-starter-thymeleaf`, `thymeleaf-layout-dialect`, and `thymeleaf-extras-springsecurity6`.

Refactoring the controllers

As we evolve our project to a client-server architecture, we must replace `@Controller` with the `@RestController` annotation in our controllers. The `@RestController` annotation is a specific version of `@Controller` used to create RESTful web services. It is used when the controller's methods need to return data such as JSON and XML rather than views. Regarding the response handling, it combines `@Controller` and `@ResponseBody`. This means that the return value of methods in `@RestController` is written directly to the HTTP response body as JSON or XML, eliminating the need for `@ResponseBody` on each method.

The following code snippet shows the `ProductController` class previously used, but it now replaces the `@Controller` annotation with the `@RestController` annotation:

```
@RestController
@RequestMapping("products")
public class ProductController{
```

The `listProducts` method has been updated. We removed the `Model` object, previously used to pass data to the view. Now, we use the `ResponseEntity` object to encapsulate the product list, improving the clarity and adaptability of the Spring-based RESTful web services. This enables you to define custom HTTP status codes, include custom headers, and manage the response body, offering flexibility in handling errors and maintaining consistent, standardized responses. The method will be returned with `HttpStatus.OK` – that is, a status code of `200` when products are available. If there are no products to return, `HttpStatus.NOT_FOUND` (status code of `404`) will be returned. The following code snippet presents the `listProducts` method:

```
@GetMapping
public ResponseEntity<List<Product>> listProducts() {
    Optional<List<Product>> products = productService.getAllProducts();
    return products.isPresent() ? new
        ResponseEntity<>(products.get(), HttpStatus.OK) :
        new ResponseEntity<>(HttpStatus.NOT_FOUND);
```

Since we created the monolithic project with a well-designed MVC and N-tier architecture, we don't need to refactor the business and data layers. Now, let's secure our REST API with token-based authentication.

Securing API with token-based authentication

In the previous monolithic project, we utilized basic authentication, a simple HTTP protocol method. However, it has limited security since the credentials are not encrypted and must be sent with every request. Token-based authentication is more suitable for our new client-server architecture project. The detailed flow of token-based authentication is illustrated in *Figure 5.6*.

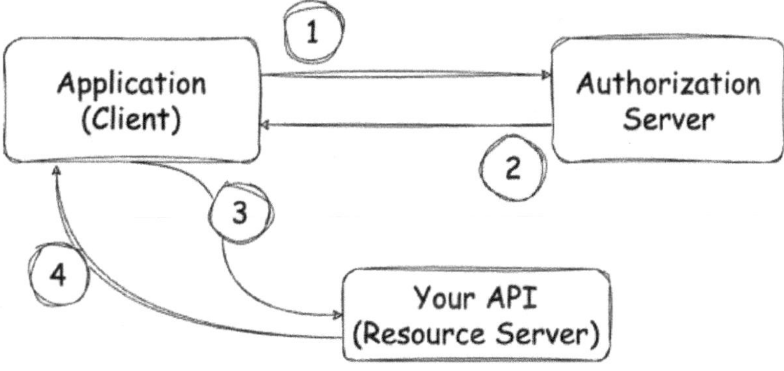

Figure 5.6: Flow of a token-based authentication

Let's detail the steps:

1. The client calls the authorization server through an endpoint, such as `/api/auth`, passing the credentials to the authorization server.

2. Upon authorization, the server issues an access token to the client application.

3. The client application calls the protected resources by including the `Authorization: Bearer <access token>` key-value pair in the header.

4. The resource server validates the token; if it is valid, it grants access to the requested resources.

We will use JWT, an open standard (*RFC 7519*), to implement token-based authentication. A JWT consists of three parts: a header, a payload, and a signature. It is compact and URL-safe. *Figure 5.7* presents an example of a JWT generated in our application being decoded using the website `https://jwt.io/`.

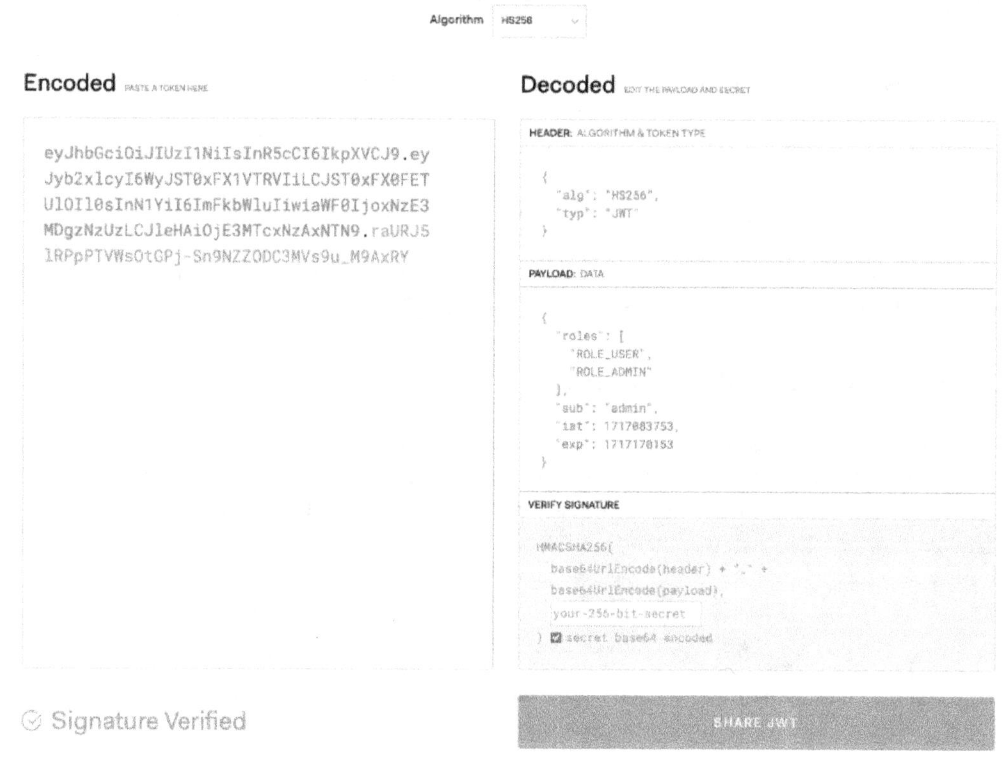

Figure 5.7: JWT

The JWT generated by the authorization server is in the left pane. In contrast, the right-hand side contains the **HEADER** pane with the token type (JWT) and the signing algorithm, such as the cryptographic HS256. The **PAYLOAD** pane holds claims, which are statements about the user, such as user ID, roles, and expiration time. The **VERIFY SIGNATURE** pane is used to verify the token's integrity and ensure it hasn't been tampered with. Now, let's implement the code to generate the token.

Implementing JWT

The following dependency must be added to our project to create and validate the JWT:

```
<dependency>
  <groupId>io.jsonwebtoken</groupId>
  <artifactId>jjwt</artifactId>
  <version>0.12.5</version>
</dependency>
```

The `application.properties` file includes `security.jwt.secret-key`, which is used for computing the **hash-based message authentication code** (**HMAC**) and can be generated using the online tool available at `https://appdevtools.com/hmac-generator`. It also includes `spring.security.jwt.expiration`, which indicates the token's expiration time in milliseconds:

```
security.jwt.secret-key= replace_with_jwt_secret_generated
security.jwt.expiration-time=86400000
```

The following code snippet is the `JwtService` class that handles all matters related to the token, such as creating and validating it:

```
@Service
public class JwtService {
  @Value("${security.jwt.secret-key}")
  private String secretKey;

  public String generateToken(UserDetails userDetails) {
    Map<String, Object> claims = new HashMap<>();
    List<String> roles = new ArrayList<>();
    userDetails.getAuthorities().forEach(n ->
                        roles.add(n.getAuthority()));
    claims.put("roles", roles);
    return createToken(claims, userDetails.getUsername());
  }
  private String createToken(Map<String, Object> claims,
                                  String subject) {
```

```
return Jwts.builder()
        .setClaims(claims).setSubject(subject)
        .setIssuedAt(new
          Date(System.currentTimeMillis()))
          .setExpiration(new
            Date(System.currentTimeMillis() +
                 jwtExpiration))
          .signWith(SignatureAlgorithm.HS256,
            secretKey).compact();
```

The `secretKey` attribute is assigned the `security.jwt.secret-key` value, which was previously defined in the `application.properties` file.

Within the `generateToken` method, a claims map is initialized to store the JWT's claims, such as roles extracted from the `userDetails` object. Once the claims map is populated, the `createToken` method utilizes it and the username to generate the JWT.

In the `createToken` method, a map of claims and a subject (which here represents the username) are taken as parameters. `Jwt.builder()` is used to configure the token's claims, subject, issue date, and expiration date. This method signs the token employing the HS256 algorithm and a secret key. Finally, the `createToken` method returns the compact JWT.

The following snippet of code is the `JwtAuthenticationFilter` class:

```
public class JwtAuthenticationFilter extends OncePerRequestFilter {
```

`JwtAuthenticationFilter` is a filter responsible for retrieving the JWT from the `Authorization` header and authenticating it for every incoming request. If the token is found invalid, the request will be rejected. However, if the token is deemed valid, the procedure involves extracting the username from the token, locating the corresponding user in the database, and establishing the user details in the authentication context. This enables the user information to be accessible across different application layers.

Next, the following code snippet is the `SecurityConfiguration` class, configuring the security settings:

```
@Configuration
public class SecurityConfiguration {

@Bean
  public SecurityFilterChain securityFilterChain
                  (HttpSecurity http) throws Exception{
    http
      .csrf(csrf -> csrf.disable())
      .cors(cors -> corsFilter())
```

```
        .authorizeHttpRequests(authorize -> authorize
            .requestMatchers("/api/auth").permitAll()
            .anyRequest().authenticated())
    .sessionManagement(session -> session
    .sessionCreationPolicy(
        SessionCreationPolicy.STATELESS))
    .authenticationProvider(authenticationProvider())
    .addFilterBefore(jwtAuthenticationFilter,
        UsernamePasswordAuthenticationFilter.class);
return http.build();
```

CSRF protection is disabled by calling `csrf().disable()` since it's not needed for stateless applications. Setting up CORS configuration for cross-origin resource sharing involves calling `cors().addFilter(corsFilter)`.

The `authorize.requestMatchers("/api/auth").permitAll()` code grants permission to all users without authentication for requests to the `"/api/auth"` endpoint.

The `authenticationProvider` method configures the authentication provider, which should return an implementation of the `AuthenticationProvider` interface for processing authentication requests.

To ensure that JWT validation happens before the default authentication processing, add `JwtAuthenticationFilter` to the security filter chain by calling `addFilterBefore(jwtAuthenticationFilter, UsernamePasswordAuthenticationFilter.class)`.

The following code snippet illustrates the `authenticationProvider` method within the `SecurityConfiguration` class:

```
@Bean
  public AuthenticationProvider authenticationProvider() {

    DaoAuthenticationProvider authProvider = new
        DaoAuthenticationProvider();
    authProvider.setUserDetailsService(userDetailsService);
    authProvider.setPasswordEncoder(passwordEncoder());
    return authProvider;
```

`DaoAuthenticationProvider` is an in-built implementation of `AuthenticationProvider`. It retrieves user details from `UserDetailsService` and validates the password using `PasswordEncoder`. To set `UserDetailsService`, you need to call `authProvider.setUserDetailsService(userDetailsService)`, where `userDetailsService` is a custom implementation of `UserDetailsService` responsible for loading user-specific data. After that, you can set the password encoder for `authProvider` by calling `authProvider.`

`setPasswordEncoder(passwordEncoder())`. The `passwordEncoder` method returns an instance of `PasswordEncoder` used to encode and decode passwords. Finally, the method returns the configured `authProvider`. The Spring Security framework then uses this provider to authenticate users by comparing the provided credentials against those stored in the database. `DaoAuthenticationProvider` ensures that the application can securely handle user authentication by leveraging the configured user details service and password encoder.

The following code snippet is the implementation of the authentication controller:

```java
@RestController
@RequestMapping("/api/auth")
public class AuthenticationController {
  @PostMapping
  public AuthenticationResponse createAuthenticationToken(
        @RequestBody AuthenticationRequest
        authenticationRequest) throws Exception {
    authenticationManager.authenticate(new
      UsernamePasswordAuthenticationToken(
          authenticationRequest.getUsername(),
          authenticationRequest.getPassword()));
    final UserDetails userDetails =
        userDetailsService.loadUserByUsername(
          authenticationRequest.getUsername());
    final String token = jwtService.generateToken
        (userDetails);
    return new AuthenticationResponse(token);
```

The `AuthenticationController` class is a controller, and the `createAuthenticationToken` method generates the token. It utilizes `authenticationManager` to verify the user's credentials. This is achieved by creating a `UsernamePasswordAuthenticationToken` token with the username and password provided in `AuthenticationRequest`.

Upon successful authentication, the method retrieves the user details using `userDetailsService` by invoking `userDetailsService.loadUserByUsername(authenticationRequest.getUsername())`. This retrieves a `UserDetails` object for the authenticated user.

Subsequently, the method generates a JWT for the authenticated user by calling `jwtService.generateToken(userDetails)`. This token is created based on the user details.

Finally, the method returns an `AuthenticationResponse` object containing the generated token. This response is sent back to the client, providing the JWT that will be used for subsequent authenticated requests.

Calling the authentication service

Let's call our authentication service to create a token. *Figure 5.8* illustrates the authentication endpoint being accessed via the Postman tool.

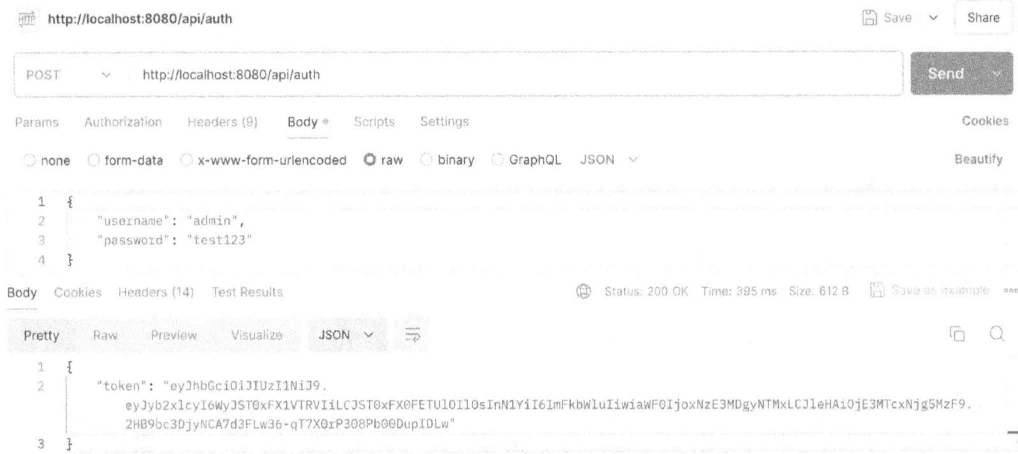

Figure 5.8: Authentication service

Once we provide the credentials, including the username and password in the body, and they are validated, we obtain a valid token. At this point, we can call the /products endpoint by including the access token received from the authorization endpoint. *Figure 5.9* depicts the process of calling the /products endpoint.

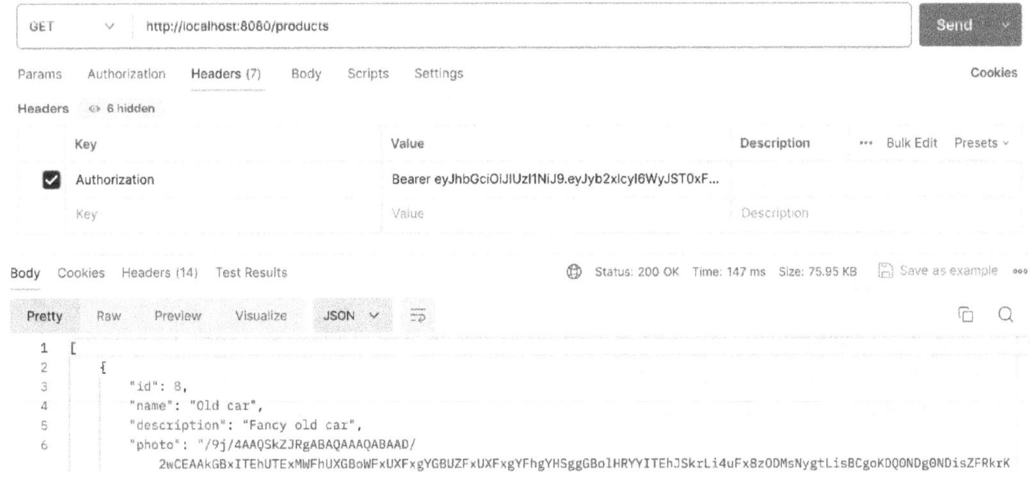

Figure 5.9: Calling the /products endpoint with a valid token

We can observe that the service returned a list of products and 200 as the status code using a valid token. *Figure 5.10* presents the calling of the /products endpoint without a token.

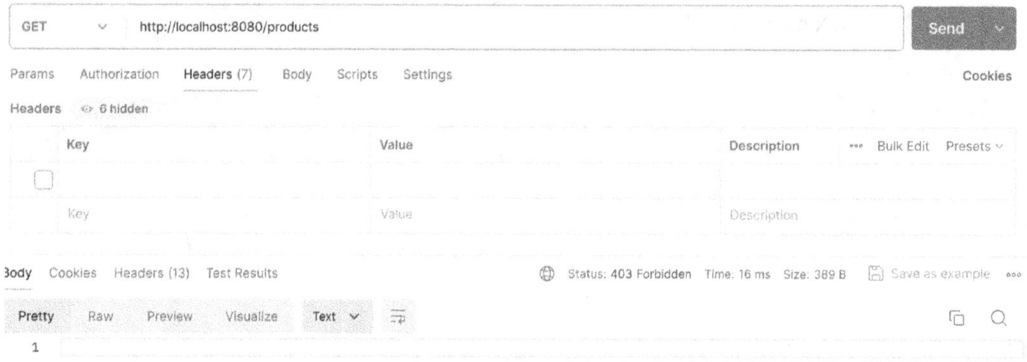

Figure 5.10: Calling the endpoint without a valid token

Using an invalid token, the service does not return the list of products and returns 403 as a status code instead of 200. *Figure 5.11* shows that the admin user can access the /admin endpoint because it has the admin role inside the token.

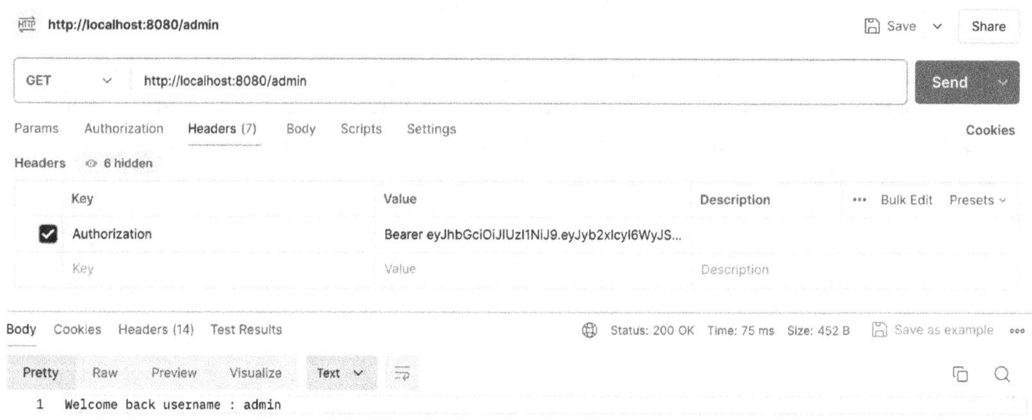

Figure 5.11: Calling the /admin endpoint

If the user does not have the ROLE_ADMIN role, it will get an error and won't be able to execute the /admin endpoint. Now that we have successfully implemented security in our server application, let's approach the documentation of our APIs, which is another significant theme.

Documenting a Spring Rest API with OpenAPI

Documentation is crucial to developing REST APIs. To document an API using OpenAPI in a Spring application, you can use the SpringDoc OpenAPI library, which integrates seamlessly with Spring Boot. By the way, OpenAPI is a specification for defining APIs. It establishes a standard, language-independent interface for RESTful APIs, enabling humans and computers to discover and understand a service's capabilities without needing access to the source code, documentation, or network traffic inspection.

The following dependency, `springdoc-openapi-starter-webmvc-ui`, needs to be added to the project:

```
<dependency>
  <groupId>org.springdoc</groupId>
  <artifactId>springdoc-openapi-starter-webmvc-ui
  </artifactId>
  <version>2.5.0</version>
</dependency>
```

The following code snippet presents the `OpenApiConfiguration` class:

```
@Configuration
@OpenAPIDefinition(info = @Info(title = "API Documentation - Online
    Auction", version = "1.0"), security = @SecurityRequirement(
        name = "bearerAuth"))
@SecurityScheme(name = "bearerAuth", type = SecuritySchemeType.HTTP,
    scheme = "bearer", bearerFormat = "JWT")
public class OpenApiConfiguration {
```

The `OpenApiConfiguration` class configures OpenAPI documentation for a Spring Boot application. It uses the `@OpenAPIDefinition` annotation to set the API documentation's title and version. The `@SecurityRequirement` and `@SecurityScheme` annotations define the API's security, such that to call the endpoints, the user needs to pass a JWT. *Figure 5.12* presents the Swagger documentation called using `http://localhost:8080/swagger-ui/index.html`.

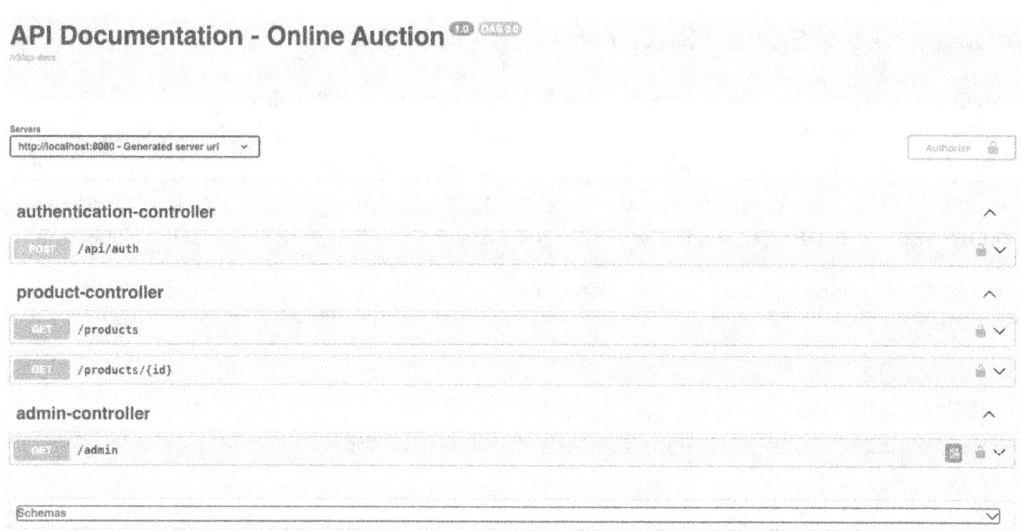

Figure 5.12: Swagger documentation

The documentation presents our endpoints separated by their controllers. The Schema session describes the request and response structure. We can configure the controller's name, add comments to the endpoints, execute the endpoints, and much more. To go even deeper into the documentation, the library provides many annotations, such as `@Operation` and `@Responses`, to document our endpoints' requests, responses, and errors. We won't approach them here, but I recommend you look up the online documentation at `https://springdoc.org`. We will now proceed with code coverage testing to ensure that our code is thoroughly tested by identifying untested parts of the code base, thus enhancing the reliability of our application.

Code coverage testing

We previously implemented integration tests in our project, but we need to know whether they are enough or how much of our code they test. Now, we will learn about code coverage testing.

What is code coverage testing?

Code coverage testing is a metric used in software testing to measure how much of the source code is executed during testing. The purpose of code coverage testing is to identify untested parts of the code base and ensure that as much code as possible is covered by tests.

Implementing code coverage testing

We can use a library such as JaCoCo to implement code coverage testing in our project. JaCoCo integrates well with building tools such as Maven. Let's add the JaCoCo plugin to the pom.xml file:

```xml
<plugin>
    <groupId>org.jacoco</groupId>
    <artifactId>jacoco-maven-plugin</artifactId>
    <version>0.8.12</version>
    <executions>
      <execution>
        <goals>
          <goal>prepare-agent</goal>
        </goals>
      </execution>
      <execution>
        <id>report</id>
        <phase>verify</phase>
        <goals>
          <goal>report</goal>
        </goals>
      </execution>
    </executions>
</plugin>
```

After adding the plugin, we can run the Maven command line:

```
mvn clean verify
```

Then, the code coverage testing report is generated in target/site/jacoco. *Figure 5.13* presents the project's code coverage testing report.

← → C   ⓘ localhost:63342/onlineauction-server/ch5/onlineauction-server/target/site/jacoco/index.html?_ijt=fmdts58pr5mcnqm3nqkgdpmc3q&_ij_reload=RELOAD_ON_SAVE

onlineauction

onlineauction

Element	Missed Instructions	Cov.	Missed Branches	Cov.	Missed	Cxty	Missed	Lines	Missed	Methods	Missed	Classes
com.packtpub.onlineauction.entity		1%		0%	97	100	19	22	43	46	0	3
com.packtpub.onlineauction.service.security		1%		0%	58	60	45	47	33	35	1	3
com.packtpub.onlineauction.exception		0%		0%	62	63	42	43	31	32	3	4
com.packtpub.onlineauction.dto.request		0%		0%	20	20	3	3	9	9	1	1
com.packtpub.onlineauction.service.security.filters		26%		25%	8	10	15	21	0	2	0	1
com.packtpub.onlineauction.controller		21%		0%	7	13	11	17	5	11	0	4
com.packtpub.onlineauction.service.impl		13%		n/a	3	4	5	6	3	4	0	1
com.packtpub.onlineauction.dto.response		0%		n/a	2	2	4	4	2	2	1	1
com.packtpub.onlineauction.config		96%		n/a	1	14	2	33	1	14	0	3
com.packtpub.onlineauction		37%		n/a	1	2	2	3	1	2	0	1
Total	1,841 of 2,057	10%	254 of 258	1%	259	288	148	199	128	157	6	22

Figure 5.13: Report of project's coverage testing

The report is the `index.html` document, and displays code coverage statistics for our project, explicitly showing metrics for different packages and classes within the project. It includes the following key metrics:

- **Missed Instructions**: The number of instructions of basic blocks of code not covered by tests and the percentage of instructions covered by tests

- **Missed Branches**: The number of branches, decision points such as `if/else` not covered by tests, and the percentage of branches covered by tests

- **Missed Cxty**: The complexity (cyclomatic complexity) of the code that is not covered by tests

- **Missed Lines**: The number of lines of code not covered by tests

- **Missed Methods**: The number of methods not covered by tests

- **Missed Classes**: The number of classes not covered by tests

To achieve meaningful coverage, it's essential to ensure that tests comprehensively validate the code's behavior, including edge cases and error handling. Code coverage should be integrated into a broader testing strategy, including unit, integration, functional, and manual tests. Regularly reviewing and analyzing coverage reports helps identify gaps and improve the effectiveness of tests.

Summary

This chapter explored client-server architecture in software development, detailing its components (client, server, and network) and highlighting its advantages, such as centralized management, data consistency, scalability, performance optimization, resource sharing, and reliability. It also acknowledged the drawbacks, including single points of failure, performance bottlenecks, scalability limitations, latency issues, and security vulnerabilities. The chapter introduced various client-server architectures, including two-tier, three-tier, and n-tier models, contrasting their scalability, performance, maintainability, reusability, and security to understand their real-world implications clearly.

The chapter also covered a range of client-server communication protocols, such as HTTP, WebSocket, AMQP, and SOAP, and delved into the principles and best practices for designing RESTful APIs. A detailed case study of an online auction system illustrated the practical application of these concepts, emphasizing the importance of aligning with budget constraints and ensuring scalability using a client-server architecture. This case study involved implementing a client-server application using the Spring framework, replacing Thymeleaf with RESTful web services, and securing the API with token-based authentication using JWTs. Additionally, the chapter discussed documenting APIs with OpenAPI and conducting code coverage testing with the JaCoCo library to ensure thorough testing of the code base, equipping you with the knowledge to create robust, scalable, and secure client-server applications.

In *Chapter 6, Microservices Architecture*, we will explore the microservices architecture, uncovering its foundational concepts, synchronous communication, monitoring, and management using Spring Actuator, and add our microservices to containers.

Questions

1. What is a client-server architecture?

2. How do thick and thin clients differ in a client-server architecture?

3. In what scenarios might a two-tier architecture be preferred over more complex models?

4. How was token-based authentication implemented in the case study?

5. What tool was recommended for API documentation?

6. Why is code coverage testing important?

7. What is REST, and why is it important in client-server communication?

Get This Book's PDF Version and Exclusive Extras

Scan the QR code (or go to packtpub.com/unlock). Search for this book by name, confirm the edition, and then follow the steps on the page.

Note: Keep your invoice handly. Purchase made directly from packt don't require one.

6

Microservices Architecture

This chapter explores microservices architecture, highlighting its key characteristics, such as autonomy and specialization, and presenting its benefits and challenges.

The chapter transitions the online auction client-server project into a microservices architecture, using it as a case study. It discusses strategies for identifying the boundaries of the domains through the bounded contexts of the **domain-driven design (DDD)**, refactoring, and selecting the appropriate databases based on the **CAP theorem**.

Additionally, this chapter discusses implementing clean architecture within a microservices context. The chapter offers detailed guidance on designing and implementing microservices, including synchronous communication using the **RestClient** and monitoring and management with **Spring Boot Actuator**.

The chapter ends with practical steps for containerizing microservices using **Docker** and **Docker Compose** and emphasizes the benefits of containerization for development and deployment.

This chapter will cover the following topics:

- Introducing microservices architecture
- Transitioning the application to microservices
- Synchronous communication
- Monitoring and managing the microservices
- Adding our microservices into containers

By the end of this chapter, you will have a strong understanding of microservices architecture and how to apply the clean architecture guidelines and have gained practical guidance on transitioning a project to microservices. This knowledge will empower you to develop resilient, adaptable, and easily maintainable applications based on microservices.

Technical requirements

All the code for this chapter can be found on GitHub at `https://github.com/PacktPublishing/ Software-Architecture-with-Spring/tree/main/ch6`. Ellipses in the code blocks indicate that parts of the code have been omitted, and the complete code is available on GitHub.

Introducing microservices architecture

Microservices architecture is an approach where applications are composed of small, autonomous services. Each service is designed to fulfill a specific business capability, allowing it to be developed, deployed, and scaled independently. This architecture contrasts with traditional monolithic architectures, where all components are interconnected and run as a single unit. *Figure 6.1* illustrates a microservices architecture.

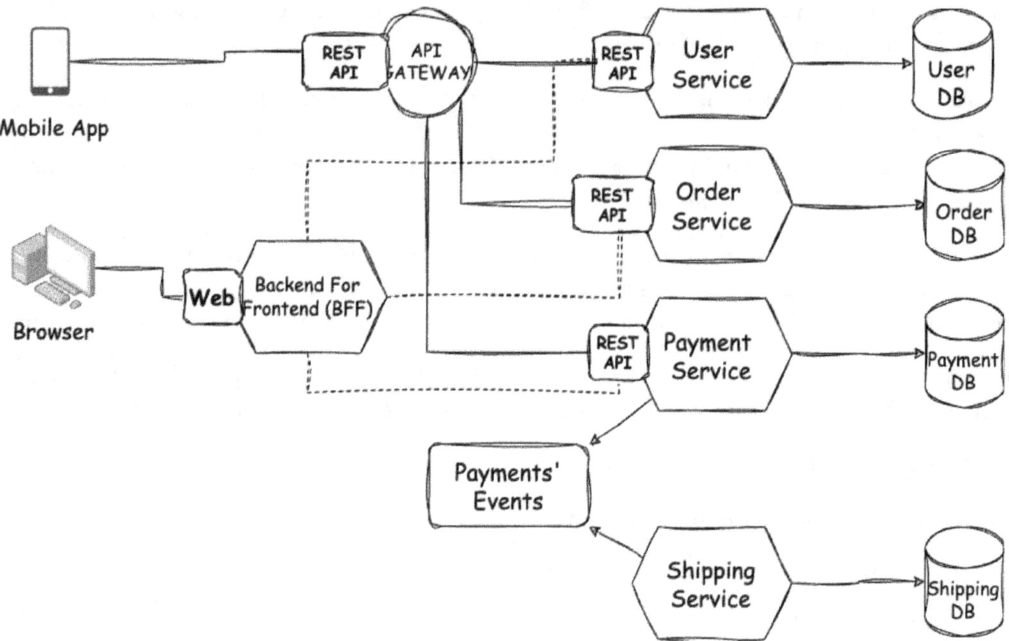

Figure 6.1: Microservices architecture

The microservices architecture consists of individual services serving specific business functions, such as user management, order processing, payment handling, and shipping operations. These services must be independent, with well-defined boundaries and separate databases. Microservices should conceal their internal workings and offer endpoints for operations. Consumers can interact with microservices via RESTful APIs or by consuming messages through message queues. Well-defined boundaries between microservices contribute to a system with low coupling and high cohesion. Two other essential components in a microservices architecture are the **API gateway** and the **backend for frontend (BFF)**.

An API gateway is a server that serves as an API frontend, receiving requests from clients and directing them to the appropriate backend services. A BFF is a service that caters to a particular frontend application or user experience. Now, let's unveil two crucial characteristics of microservices.

Unveiling crucial characteristics of microservices

When developing microservices, keep these two words in mind: *autonomy* and *specialization*. Write these words on a sticky note and stick them where they are always in your vision.

Autonomy in a microservices context refers to the ability of a microservice to operate independently of other services. A specialized microservice is designed to handle a specific business capability or functionality. **Specialization** ensures that each microservice is highly focused on a particular aspect of the application.

But how do we build autonomous and specialized microservices? Let's learn how to achieve that.

Building autonomous and specialized microservices

Let's examine the primary techniques to build autonomous and specialized microservices:

- **Single responsibility principle (SRP)**: SRP states that a class or module should have only one reason to change, meaning it should have only one job or responsibility. When applied to microservices, SRP ensures that each service focuses on a specific business capability or function, making development more straightforward and the system more maintainable, reliable, and scalable.

- **Domain-driven design (DDD)**: DDD can help us define bounded contexts within our business domain and design microservices around these contexts. Each service should handle a specific aspect of the business, aligning closely with business processes.

- **Separate code bases**: Maintain separate code bases for each microservice to ensure independent development and deployment.

- **Separate data stores**: Assign each microservice its database to ensure data independence. This prevents direct data access between services and avoids tight coupling.

- **Specialized operations**: Create coarse-grained APIs with specialized operations aligned with each service's responsibility, handling all business rules related to its specific function. While it is generally recommended to avoid thin-grained microservices focused solely on CRUD operations, lightweight CRUD-based services can benefit simpler systems. They provide straightforward, maintainable solutions without added complexity. Choose the approach based on the system's size and specific needs, balancing simplicity and maintainability.

- **Continuous integration and deployment**: Employ CI/CD pipelines for every microservice using tools such as Jenkins to automate testing and deployment. Containerize the microservices to ensure consistency across environments and manage deployments.

Benefits of microservices architecture

Microservices architecture offers numerous benefits. Let's examine the main ones:

- **Technology independence**: A benefit of microservice architecture is the flexibility to choose the best-suited technology for each service. This allows teams to select languages, frameworks, and tools most appropriate for specific tasks or performance requirements, optimizing development efficiency, enhancing service performance, and facilitating innovation. Additionally, it enables the gradual adoption of new technologies without requiring a complete system overhaul.

- **Maintainability**: The microservices architecture improves maintainability by breaking a complex system into more minor, self-contained services, which allows for independent updates and concurrent development by multiple teams, enhancing efficiency and flexibility.

- **Robustness**: Each service is isolated and independently deployable. This minimizes the impact of a failure in one service on other services, improving overall system resilience.

- **Scalability**: Microservices enable independent scaling of services based on demand, allowing efficient resource allocation and improving the system's ability to handle varying loads.

- **Easy deployment**: In a microservices architecture, deployment is simplified because each service is self-contained and can be deployed independently. This allows for updates, bug fixes, and new features without requiring a complete system redeployment. Tools such as Docker and Kubernetes automate service deployment, scaling, and management, reducing downtime and enabling continuous delivery.

- **Addition of new services**: A microservices architecture allows for the easy addition of new services as each service operates independently with well-defined APIs. This enables seamless integration of new components to the system while supporting rapid iteration and scaling as business needs evolve.

- **Faster time-to-market**: Smaller, independent teams can work on different services simultaneously, accelerating development and deployment processes.

Despite these benefits, microservices architecture has some drawbacks, which we'll explore next.

Drawbacks of microservices architecture

While highly advantageous in various scenarios, microservices architecture has drawbacks that may render it less suitable for specific applications. Recognizing these limitations is crucial for making well-informed architectural decisions and avoiding pitfalls:

- **Data management**: Maintaining data consistency across distributed services can be challenging and often requires complex strategies such as distributed transactions. Developers must usually implement eventual consistency and other patterns, such as **SAGA** and **Two-Phase Commit** (**2PC**), to manage data integrity effectively.

- **Deployment complexity**: Managing the deployment and maintenance of multiple independent services can be challenging. Every service requires individual deployment, monitoring, and maintenance, adding to the operational workload and requiring strong DevOps practices to ensure smooth and efficient operations.

- **Inter-service communication**: Network latency and reliability become critical as services communicate over the network, which can introduce performance bottlenecks. Implementing strategies such as circuit breakers, retries, and timeouts is essential to handle these challenges effectively. Asynchronous communication methods such as message queues can help decouple services and improve system resilience.

- **Cost**: Building a microservices architecture has cost challenges. These include increased resource requirements, operational complexities, higher networking overhead, more significant development and maintenance efforts, data management expenses, security, compliance, and additional training. Although microservices offer scalability, flexibility, and resilience benefits, they also come with associated costs. It's vital to carefully consider these factors and implement cost-management strategies to ensure that the advantages of adopting a microservices architecture outweigh the expenses.

- **Reports**: Creating reports in a microservices architecture presents challenges, including data consistency issues, complex data aggregation, potential performance slowdowns, and ensuring report accuracy and security. This requires robust error handling, consistent security policies, comprehensive logging, advanced tools, and effective management planning.

- **Monitoring, logging, and tracing**: Monitoring, logging, and tracing in microservices architecture pose challenges due to the need to manage and correlate data across multiple independent services, handle increased data volume, and use sophisticated tools to aggregate, analyze, and visualize the data effectively. Overcoming these challenges requires careful planning, the right tools, and adherence to best observability practices.

- **Debugging and troubleshooting**: Debugging microservices is challenging due to their distributed architecture, where multiple independent services interact over a network. This complexity makes it challenging to trace issues across service boundaries, manage inconsistent logs, and correlate events effectively. Additionally, each service may be developed in different languages and run on separate environments, complicating the debugging process further.

By understanding microservices' advantages and drawbacks, developers and architects can design robust and efficient systems that align with modern software development practices. Having understood the benefits and disadvantages of microservices, let's transition our client-server application to incorporate a microservices architecture.

Transitioning the application to microservices

Microservices is a modern approach to software development that many companies are adopting. However, transitioning an existing system takes more work. Many variables are involved, such as the microservices' parallel development and the current system's maintenance. We must decide whether to overhaul the entire system or gradually replace or rewrite it with a new one (*Strangler Fig pattern* by Martin Fowler). Should we start transitioning the code or the database? It is a hard decision with many options. We need to select the best one that fits our needs and situation. To explore this topic further, I recommend reading *Monolith to Microservices: Evolutionary Patterns to Transform Your Monolith* by Sam Newman.

For learning purposes, we will transition the entire system at once. It will give a glimpse of the transition process. Then, let's move on to our case study. The stakeholders want to talk to us; we are becoming famous and vital to the company's success.

Online auction case study

The WX-Auction company is currently enjoying the success of our online auction application. The client-server version has significantly increased our user base, especially with the success of the mobile application. Users actively engage in more trades, marking a significant milestone in our journey.

With the influx of new investments, the stakeholders are now keen on preparing our system for a global launch. This is crucial to ensure our system's performance remains unaffected, even with a growing user base. They want the system to be easy to add new services to in the future, such as online trade transactions, payment, and shipping.

System definition and mission

After extensive discussions, the team concluded that a microservice architecture would be a good fit since it provides scalability according to necessity and simplifies the composition of new services.

> **Attention**
>
> The adoption of microservices must be well analyzed, including the pros and cons and whether it is essential for your case. With many clients, I've seen simple projects built as microservices using Kubernetes: unnecessary complexity and expensive maintenance costs. The case study presented here is a simple case for us to follow for learning.

Starting the transition process

Breaking down the current application into distinct business capabilities or domains is a good place to start. This helps you understand the functional areas and their boundaries within the application. How can we define the business capabilities? DDD can help us complete this step successfully. It can significantly aid in transitioning from a monolithic or client-server application to a microservices architecture by providing a structured approach to decomposing the system into well-defined, business-aligned services. Let's learn about the main concepts of DDD.

Comprehending the basics of domain-driven design

Here, I'll introduce the basics of DDD, which will be sufficient to continue our transition. For a more profound comprehension of DDD, I suggest the book *Domain-Driven Design: Tackling Complexity in the Heart of Software* by Eric Evans:

- **Bounded contexts**: A bounded context defines a clear boundary within which a particular model is described and applicable. Each bounded context aligns with a specific business capability and can be mapped to a microservice. Identifying bounded contexts helps break down the monolith into smaller, manageable pieces that reflect the business domains.

- **Entities and value objects**: Entities are objects that possess a unique identity that persists over time, while value objects are immutable and do not have a different identity. By modeling entities and value objects, you can understand the core data structures and relationships within each bounded context, facilitating the transition to microservices.

- **Aggregates**: An aggregate is a group of related entities and value objects treated as a single unit for data changes. Each aggregate has a root entity known as the aggregate root. Defining aggregates helps maintain data consistency within each microservice and manage transactions effectively.

- **Domain events**: Domain events represent significant business events within a bounded context. They can communicate changes and coordinate activities across different microservices, supporting eventual consistency and decoupling between microservices.

- **Repositories**: Repositories allow access to aggregates and other entities from a data store. Designing repositories around aggregates ensures that microservices can handle their data independently and maintain data integrity.

Designing the bounded context of the online auction application

We must identify the application's business contexts and domain events (their relationship). Identifying bounded contexts will help to break down the application into smaller, manageable pieces that reflect the business domains. *Figure 6.2* presents the bounded context of the current online auction application.

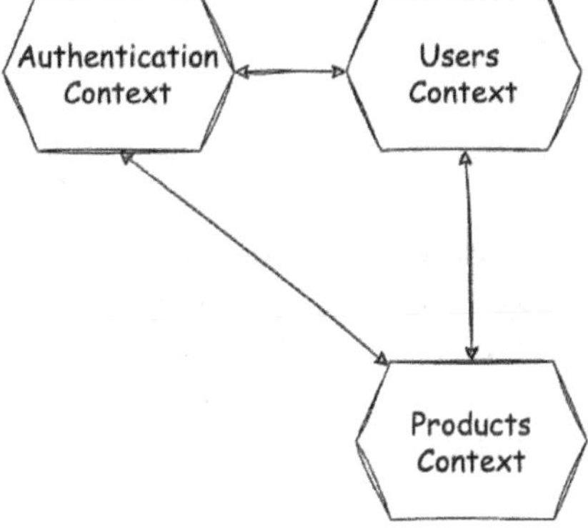

Figure 6.2: The bounded context of the current online auction application

The figure presents the bounded contexts of the online auction application that we must evolve into microservices. Let's explore each context:

- **User context**: This manages users and related data and interacts with the authentication context to verify user credentials and handle authentication.

- **Authentication context**: This handles user authentication and authorization and interacts with the user context to manage authentication details and administrative permissions.

- **Products context**: This manages the product catalog and related operations.

Identifying bounded contexts helps break down the monolith into smaller, manageable pieces that reflect the business domains. Now that we have our bounded contexts, let's present the current database model. We must break the database into many databases, one for each microservice.

The online auction application's database

We need to analyze our database since we are evolving our current project, a client-server, to microservices. *Figure 6.3* presents the current database model that we will have to refactor.

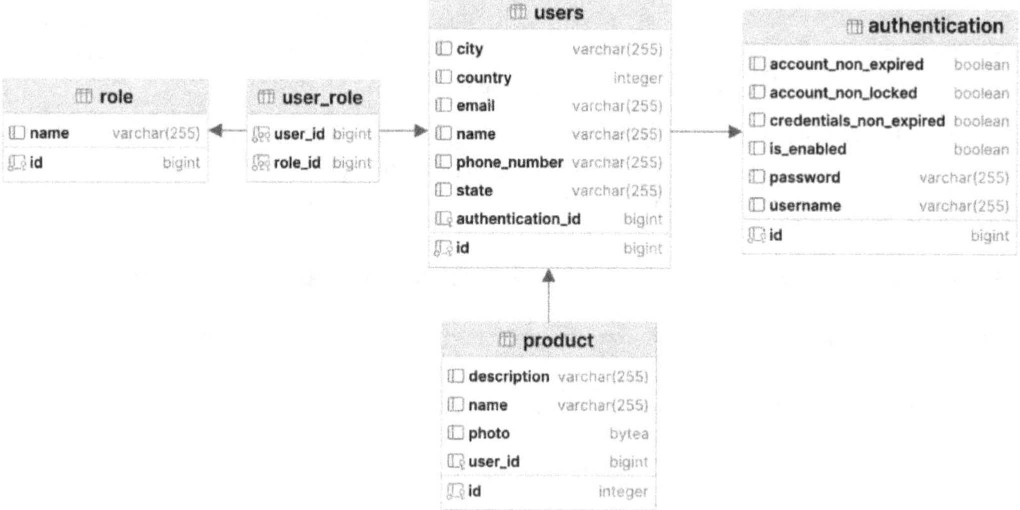

Figure 6.3: Current client-server's database model

The database model comprises five tables: authentication, users, user_role, role, and product. A user can possess multiple roles, and each user can have various products associated with them. Each user has an authentication record in the authentication table. This model supports a system where users can have different roles, authenticate through various means, and have multiple products associated with their accounts. *Figure 6.4* illustrates the microservices with their tables after refactoring.

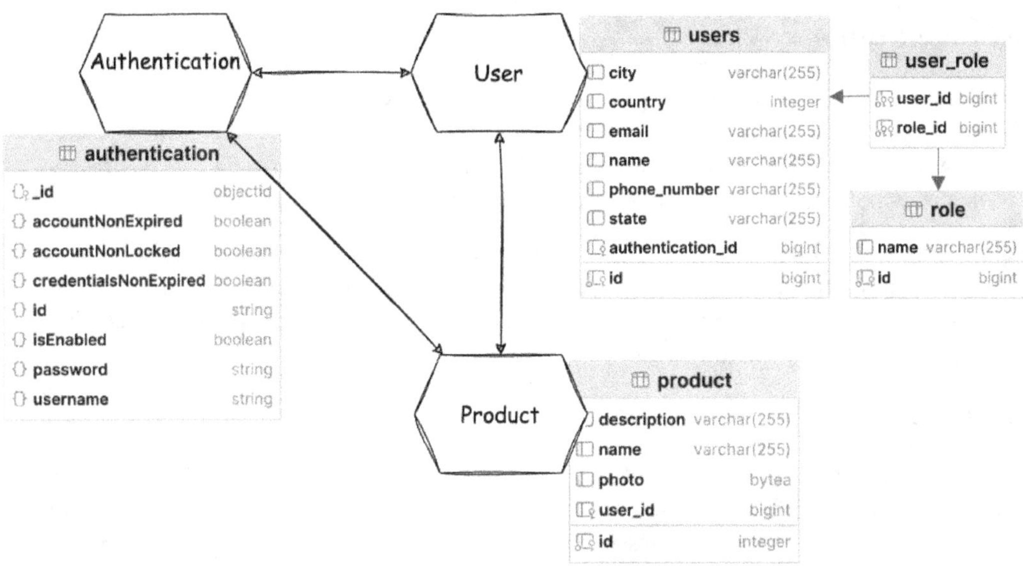

Figure 6.4: Microservices with their tables

Transitioning to microservices splits the database model; each microservice will have its own database. As we always think about performance, scalability, and a robust application, now is the time to consider the type of database we should use in the microservices.

Selecting the proper database

To select the proper database, we need to analyze what is expected from it, its business capabilities, and the **Consistency, Availability, and Partition (CAP)** theorem to support our decision.

Choosing the proper database for each microservice based on the CAP theorem involves balancing consistency, availability, and partition tolerance according to each service's specific needs and characteristics. Let's analyze each microservice – authorization, user, and product.

The user service

The user service typically requires strong consistency to ensure accurate user profile data. High availability is also desirable for efficiently handling user queries. While there is moderate read and write traffic, consistency remains the top priority.

Based on the CAP theorem, the user microservice prioritizes **consistency and partition tolerance (CP)** as its key objectives. A relational database is the recommended database type for user microservices, as it provides strong consistency and supports transactional integrity, both of which are essential for managing user profiles effectively. NewSQL databases are also a viable option, combining the scalability of NoSQL with the **Atomicity, Consistency, Isolation, and Durability (ACID)** properties of traditional relational databases.

The authentication service

The authentication service requires high availability to ensure users can always authenticate. Consistency is essential, but it can be eventually consistent for some aspects, such as logging out users. It typically involves, low to moderate write traffic with a high read traffic pattern. Then, based on the CAP theorem, the authentication microservice priorities are **availability and partition tolerance (AP)**.

A NoSQL database is the recommended database type for authentication microservices. These databases provide high availability and partition tolerance, crucial for reliably handling authentication and token management across distributed systems. In-memory databases may help store session data and tokens, providing high availability and low latency.

The product service

The product microservice requires consistency to ensure accurate product information is displayed to users. While high availability is desirable to handle potentially high traffic from users browsing products, consistency must take precedence to maintain data integrity. The service typically experiences moderate to high read traffic with moderate write traffic.

Based on the CAP theorem, the product microservice prioritizes consistency and partition tolerance (CP) as its core principles. A relational database is the recommended database type for product microservices, as it provides strong consistency and supports complex queries needed for accurate product information. As with user service, NewSQL databases are also a viable option in this context.

Figure 6.5 presents the database type of each microservice of our system.

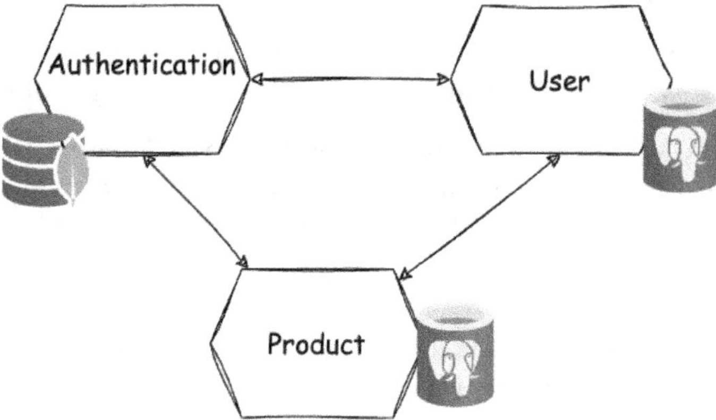

Figure 6.5: Microservices with their type of database

Selecting the appropriate database types based on the CAP theorem and the specific requirements of each microservice can help us ensure that the system is well-optimized for performance, reliability, and scalability. Evolving the system to microservices in some way will force us to change how we work, that is, the team structure and approach. Let's explore the vertical team approach.

Vertical team approach in microservices architecture

Traditional organizations often employ a horizontal team structure. This structure divides responsibilities by technical layer, with distinct teams managing the frontend, backend, and database layers. *Figure 6.6* illustrates this horizontal team structure.

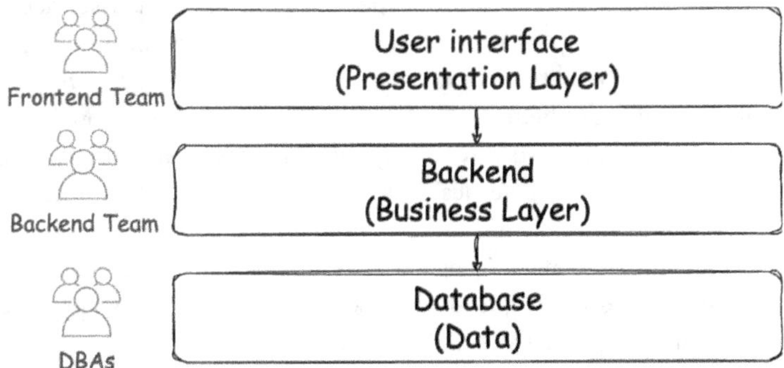

Figure 6.6: Horizontal team structure

The primary drawback of a horizontal architecture is the involvement of multiple teams in planning and implementing each feature. This can lead to tight coupling between teams, potentially causing friction in schedules and deadlines. Some detailed challenges include the complex planning and coordination required among teams, tight coupling of workflows, scheduling friction due to different team timelines and priorities, inconsistent prioritization, and increased communication overhead. These challenges can hinder development progress and lead to misunderstandings and conflicts among team members, complicating the overall process.

However, a vertical team structure becomes more advantageous as organizations adopt a microservices architecture. This approach organizes teams around specific business capabilities, such as user management, payments, orders, and shipping, with each team responsible for all technical layers within their domain. *Figure 6.7* presents a vertical team structure.

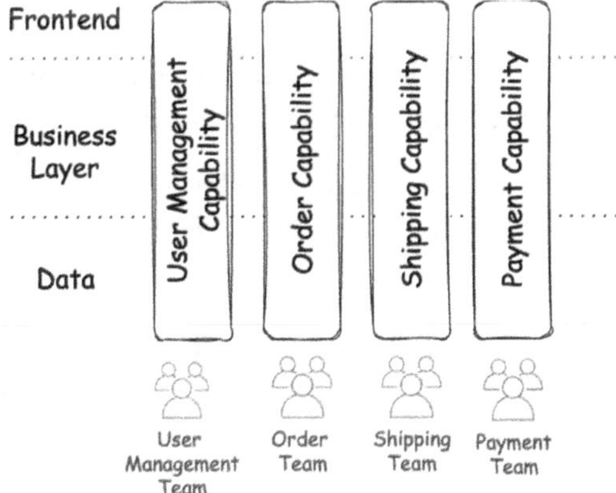

Figure 6.7: Vertical team structure

The primary reason for adopting a vertical team structure in a microservices architecture is to align teams more closely with business goals and outcomes. Each team becomes a cross-functional unit capable of independently developing, deploying, and maintaining a complete service. This alignment fosters greater agility, faster delivery, and improved ownership and accountability.

Vertical teams are essential for boosting agility and speed. They oversee their services from start to finish, enabling faster decision-making and implementation of changes while reducing dependencies and eliminating bottlenecks. Vertical teams gain deep insights and expertise when focusing on a specific business capability, leading to better feature development and innovation. By aligning teams with business capabilities, technical efforts directly support organizational objectives, increasing the strategic impact of development activities. Vertical teams are responsible for the entire lifecycle of their services, from development to deployment and maintenance, fostering a strong sense of accountability and encouraging higher-quality outcomes. As business needs change, vertical teams offer scalability and flexibility, allowing organizations to adjust the composition or number of teams based on specific business capabilities without disrupting the entire system.

The vertical team approach in microservices architecture offers significant agility, focus, alignment, ownership, and scalability benefits. However, it also introduces challenges such as resource duplication, knowledge silos, integration complexity, variability in standards, and management overhead. Organizations must thoughtfully consider these pros and cons and implement strategies to mitigate the challenges while maximizing the benefits. By doing so, they can effectively leverage the potential of microservices architecture to drive business success. Now that we have a picture of our application built using a microservices architecture, let's explore one more topic before implementing the authorization service: clean architecture.

Clean architecture

So far, in our projects, we have used N-layer architecture, which, while modular, doesn't consistently achieve the same level of separation as clean architecture. This can potentially complicate the testing process, and it often becomes tightly coupled with the frameworks and tools it uses, making changes more challenging.

With this in mind, clean architecture is a guideline for creating highly maintainable code that focuses on business and is independent of technologies such as frameworks and databases.

Clean Architecture combines various design principles and patterns, such as SOLID principles. Its core idea is to organize the system into layers based on business value. *Figure 6.8* presents the clean architecture layers.

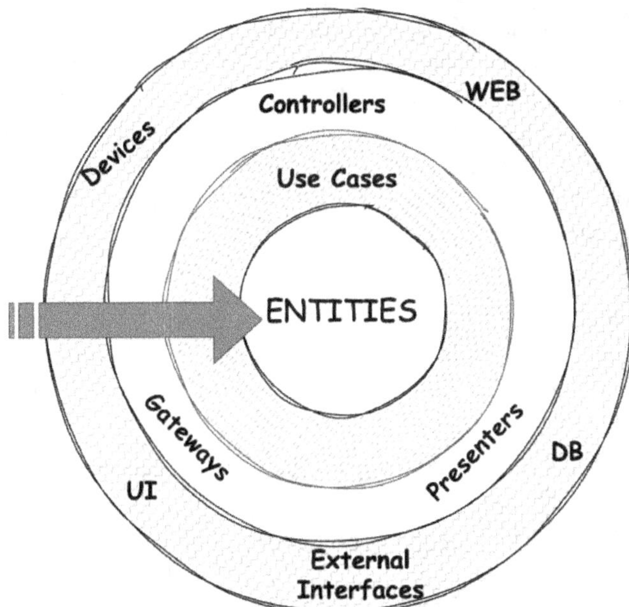

Figure 6.8: Clean architecture layers

The highest layer (**Entities**) contains business rules, while each subsequent layer moves closer to devices.

In this layered approach, the inner layers correspond to higher levels of abstraction, encompassing business logic and rules. In contrast, the outer layers handle more concrete operations, such as user interface and data access.

This structure allows for flexibility and scalability, as we can define as many layers as necessary for our business needs. However, adhering to the dependency rule is crucial: higher-level layers should never depend on lower-level ones. This ensures that the core business logic remains isolated from external changes, enhancing the system's adaptability and maintainability.

Clean architecture embodies the following essential characteristics:

- **Testability**: The business rules can be rigorously tested in isolation; that is, we can test the business rules independently of technologies.

- **Independent of external elements**: The clean architecture ensures that business rules and core logic are decoupled from specific frameworks, user interfaces, database technologies, and any external components. This enables flexibility and ease of modification without affecting the core functionality.

Clean architecture emphasizes the separation of concerns, ensuring that different aspects of the system are isolated and independent.

While clean architecture brings numerous benefits, it is important to acknowledge that adopting it can introduce challenges. One of the main complexities is the increased overhead in setting up the different layers, particularly in smaller projects where this level of abstraction may seem excessive. Additionally, there is often a learning curve for teams unfamiliar with the approach, requiring a deeper understanding of design principles and discipline in adhering to the architectural boundaries. These factors can initially slow down development, but the long-term gains in maintainability and flexibility often outweigh the initial investment.

> **The dependency rule**
>
> Remember that higher-level layers must never depend on lower-level ones. The entity layer must not know use cases, which in turn must not know controllers, and so on.

Let's investigate clean architecture by analyzing and implementing the authentication service.

Implementing the authentication service

Let's implement our authentication service, which will be developed using clean architecture. Before delving into the code and responsibility of each class, *Figure 6.9* illustrates the new authentication service structure using the clean architecture approach.

Figure 6.9: The project's structure

In our authentication service, the main folders are `internal`, `adapter`, and `config`.

Exploring the internal folder

The `internal` folder is responsible for business rules and encapsulates entities and use case layers. Framework annotations, database libraries, and external object references are not allowed here. Three folders are inside the `internal` folder: `entities`, `usecases`, and `repositories`.

- `entities`: Entities are the core business rules that apply across the entire enterprise. They can be implemented as objects with methods or as a collection of data structures and functions. Entities are `plain old Java objects (POJOs)`. Frameworks and libraries such as Lombok or JPA annotations are prohibited here.

- `usecases`: Use cases are the active business rules that manage data flow between entities and external interfaces, representing user-system interactions. They define the system's responses to specific inputs, ensuring controlled operations. As intermediaries between core business logic (entities) and outer layers (such as interfaces and frameworks), use cases ensure consistent application of business rules and isolation from implementation details.

- `repositories`: Repositories are interfaces for accessing and managing entities. They provide methods for interacting with data sources, enabling the retrieval of individual entities or lists of entities. By abstracting data access logic, repositories ensure a consistent API and separate business logic from data storage mechanisms.

There may be other folders inside the `internal` folder as long as they don't violate the clean architecture with code that contains external components.

Exploring the adapter folder

The `adapter` folder represents the interface adapters layer. It contains adapters that convert data formats between use cases, entities, and external systems such as databases or web interfaces. It has two main folders: `datasources` and `transportlayers`:

- `datasources`: Data sources act as adapters for various storage systems, interfacing with SQL databases, REST APIs, and Elasticsearch. They implement the repository interfaces to handle data retrieval and storage, separating business logic from storage details.

- `transportlayers`: The transport layer is an input mechanism that triggers use cases to execute business logic. It can be RESTful APIs with controllers handling incoming requests, events, cron jobs, and so on. Isolating business logic within use cases decouples the system from any specific transport layer or controller implementation.

Exploring the config folder

The config folder contains configurations for security, OpenAPI, and other settings. The main focus for clean architecture is the `usecases` folder, which includes a `UsecasesConfiguration` class responsible for injecting data sources that implement the repositories into the use cases using the dependency inversion principle.

Now, let's explore each layer of the clean architecture and its objects through the flow of token generation to understand the clean architecture.

Entity layer

The following code snippet shows the `Authentication` class in the entities layer represented by the `internal.entities` folder:

```
public class Authentication {
    private Long id;
    private String username;
    private String password;
    ...
```

It's a simple POJO without external annotation, such as Lombok.

Use case layer

The following code snippet presents the `GenerateTokenUseCase` class in the use case layer inside the `internal.usecases` package:

```
package com.packtpub.authenticationservices.internal.usecase;


public class GenerateTokenUseCase {
 private final AuthenticationManagerRepository
                      authenticationManagerRepository;
 private final UserRepository userRepository;
 private final TokenRepository tokenRepository;
 public GenerateTokenUseCase(
      AuthenticationManagerRepository
          authenticationManagerRepository,
      UserRepository userRepository,
       TokenRepository tokenRepository) {
```

The `AuthenticationManagerRepository`, `UserRepository`, and `TokenRepository` interfaces are repositories implemented by data source classes. The repositories separate the internal business rules from the external objects.

The `GenerateTokenUseCase` class has only one method: `execute`. One method per class has pros, such as focusing on a single responsibility, simplicity, and reusability, and cons, such as class proliferation.

The following snippet code presents the `execute` method from the `GenerateTokenUseCase` class:

```
public Optional<String> execute(String username, String
                                password) {
...
   if (authentication.isPresent()) {
       authentication.get().setRoles(
          userRepository.getRolesByUsername(username));
```

The `userRepository.getRolesByUsername(username)` procedure executes a call to user services to get the user roles. In the internal context, it does not know if it is a RESTful API or a database; it does not matter for the business rules. It just needs to know that it will get the user's roles to generate the token.

The flow without violating the dependency rule

Consider a scenario where a use case needs to interact with data sources, such as a JPA repository or a RESTful API. We must avoid direct calls to the data source to adhere to the dependency rule, which states that no inner circle – in this case, the use case layer – should know about the outer circle (the interface adapter). Instead, we utilize an interface (`repositories`) within the inner circle. The data sources that reside in the outer circle implement the `repositories` interface. This approach ensures that all dependencies flow inward, maintaining the independence of the inner layers. We use dynamic polymorphism to invert the dependencies, allowing us to uphold the dependency rule regardless of the control flow direction.

The following code snippet presents the `UseCaseConfiguration` class that is inside the `config.usecases` package. It has a bean that injects the `UserRestApi`, `AuthenticationManager`, and `TokenJwt` data sources into the `GenerateTokenUseCase` class:

```
package com.packtpub.authenticationservices.config.usecases;
@Configuration
public class UseCaseConfiguration {
  @Bean
  public GenerateTokenUseCase generateTokenUseCase
            (UserRestApi userRestApiGateway,
             AuthenticationManager authenticationManager,
             TokenJwt tokenJwt) {
```

The following code snippet presents `UserRestApi`, the data source, which implements the `UserRepository` interface:

```
@Service
public class UserRestApi implements UserRepository {
```

Through the **dependency inversion** principle, it does not violate the dependency rule. Now, let's explore the interface adapters.

The interface adapters

This layer's software includes adapters that convert data between the preferred formats for use cases and entities and those needed for external systems such as databases, web services, or message queues. It also manages data conversion from the format used by entities and use cases to the format required by the persistence framework, such as a database. It handles all external data interactions, keeping the core application logic separate from external dependencies.

The following snippet of code presents the `AuthenticationController` class. It starts the flow by calling `generateTokenUseCase.execute`:

```java
public class AuthenticationController {
   private final GenerateTokenUseCase generateTokenUseCase;

   @PostMapping
   public ResponseEntity<AuthenticationResponse>
         createAuthenticationToken(@RequestBody
         AuthenticationRequest authenticationRequest) throws
         Exception {
         final Optional<String> token =
               generateTokenUseCase.execute
               (authenticationRequest.getUsername(),
                authenticationRequest.getPassword());
```

The adapters are responsible for isolating frameworks and libraries, such as those that transform requests and responses from APIs and using **object-relational mapping (ORM)** to map entities from and to the database from the core business application.

Frameworks and Drivers Layer

We don't code here; this layer contains the details of data storage, such as database drivers and other technical information. It is at the outermost level and should depend on the inner layers, not vice versa.

Now that we have learned about clean architecture and implemented the authorization service using clean architecture, let's delve into microservices communication.

Synchronous communication

Microservices communicate in various ways, each serving different needs based on the system's architecture and requirements. Here, we will explore synchronous communication, a foundational aspect of microservices architecture, where services interact directly and expect an immediate response.

It is characterized by its request-response nature, making it suitable for scenarios requiring instant feedback and **real-time** data exchange.

Synchronous communication often leads to tighter coupling between services. Each service needs to know the endpoint of the service it communicates with, creating a direct dependency.

A key advantage of synchronous communication is the ability to provide immediate feedback. This is crucial for operations requiring real-time confirmation or data retrieval.

RESTful APIs and GraphQL are typical examples of synchronous communication with microservices. GraphQL allows clients to request specific data, which is suitable for cases where frontend developers need more flexible data retrieval.

Benefits of synchronous communication

The main benefits of synchronous communication are simplicity, real-time interaction, and a predictable workflow between the microservices:

- **Simplicity**: Synchronous communication is effortless to implement and comprehend, particularly for developers well-versed in web-based client-server interactions

- **Real-time interaction**: Immediate responses make synchronous communication ideal for use cases that require real-time interaction, such as user authentication

- **Predictable workflow**: The request-response model provides a predictable workflow, making handling errors and managing service dependencies easier.

Challenges of synchronous communication

The main challenges of synchronous communication are latency, scalability, and fault tolerance:

- **Latency**: Network latency can significantly impact performance, particularly in high-load environments or when services are distributed across different geographic locations.

- **Scalability**: Synchronous communication can become a bottleneck as services and interactions grow. Each request ties up resources until a response is received, potentially leading to higher resource consumption.

- **Fault tolerance**: If a service fails or becomes unavailable, it can disrupt the entire request chain, leading to cascading failures. This requires robust error handling and fallback mechanisms.

Synchronous communication enables real-time interaction but presents challenges such as latency and scalability. As microservices architecture evolves, it is crucial to balance its benefits with the need for efficient and resilient systems.

Coupling between microservices

Coupling describes the level of interdependence between microservices. In microservices communication, different types of coupling can significantly impact the system's flexibility, maintainability, and scalability. Here are the main types of coupling in microservices communication:

- **Temporal coupling**: Temporal coupling occurs when microservices depend on the availability and timing of other services. It often arises in synchronous communication scenarios but can happen in asynchronous systems if timing is critical. If service A must wait for a response from service B to proceed, they are temporally coupled. This dependency can cause cascading failures or delays. Distributed transactions require multiple services to complete operations coordinated, leading to temporal coupling.

- **Shared databases coupling**: When multiple microservices directly access and manipulate the same schema, they become tightly coupled. Changes in the database structure can necessitate changes in all dependent services.

- **Deployment coupling**: This occurs when microservices must be deployed or scaled together due to interdependencies. Services are deployed together because they are tightly integrated, making it difficult to deploy or scale them independently.

As a consultant, I've encountered the three types of coupling, and when we don't tackle them at the beginning of the project, it's tough to tackle them later. Since the project is in production, it involves many teams, and the refactoring is not so simple because we need to coordinate all the pieces. As some friends say, change the tires while driving. Now, let's learn how to reduce the coupling between microservices.

Reducing coupling in microservices

To achieve a loosely coupled microservices architecture, consider the following strategies:

- **Embrace domain-driven design**: Embracing DDD is crucial, as it aligns microservices with bounded contexts to minimize interdependencies and promote autonomy.

- **Define clear contracts**: Defining clear contracts with well-defined API specifications and versioning is essential to reduce the impact of changes and maintain consistency across services. For example, consider an API for a user service. Versioning can be implemented by including the version number in the API endpoint, such as `/api/v1/users` for version 1 and `/api/v2/users` for version 2. The well-defined contract might specify the request and response formats, including required fields, data types, and potential error codes. If a new field is added to the user data in version 2, the old version can still be maintained to ensure backward compatibility.

- **Use asynchronous communication**: Asynchronous communication is highly effective in temporally decoupling services. Message queues, such as RabbitMQ or Apache Kafka, can buffer and relay messages between services, ensuring each service can operate independently and process messages at its own pace.

- **Implement service discovery**: Use a service registry to discover services, avoiding hard-coded dependencies dynamically. Service discovery uses a centralized registry to track and locate services dynamically, avoiding hard-coded dependencies. This reduces coupling by allowing services to connect based on real-time registry information, enabling flexibility, scalability, and fault tolerance as services can be updated or scaled without disrupting consumers. We delve into its details in *Chapter 7, Microservices Patterns with Spring Cloud*.

- **Ensure data independence**: Services should be designed to own their data, preventing direct access by other services. Data replication can share necessary data between services without tightly coupling them.

The other type of microservices communication is asynchronous communication, which we will discuss and delve into in *Chapter 8, Event-Driven Architecture*. Now, let's implement synchronous communication between our microservices using the RestClient.

Using the RestClient for synchronous communication

When implementing calling using synchronous communication, we have some options, such as RestTemplate, Spring Cloud OpenFeign, and RestClient. While writing this book, the Spring Framework team suggested on their page to use RestClient since it offers a more modern API for synchronous HTTP access.

The RestClient is instantiated through one of the static create methods, or we can use `builder()` to obtain a builder that offers additional configuration options. Once the RestClient is created or built, it is thread-safe and can be utilized concurrently by multiple threads. The following snippet of code presents how to create a `RestClient` instance:

```
RestClient restClient = RestClient.create();
```

After creating the instance, we make a call using it. The following code snippet presents the code that calls the user services to get the user's roles:

```
RoleResponse result = restClient
    .get()
    .uri(userServiceUrl + "/v1/users/{username}/roles",
                                            username)
    .retrieve()
    .body(RoleResponse.class);
```

The `get` method sets up a request and specifies the URL through the `uri` method. The `{username}` denotes that the data of the `username` parameter will replace it. The `retrieve` method gets the response, and the body converts the response into the `RoleResponse` class.

Performing a post using RestClient is simple; the following code snippet presents it:

```
ResponseEntity<Void> response = restClient.post()
  .uri("/v1/users")
  .contentType(APPLICATION_JSON)
  .body(user)
  .retrieve()
  .toBodilessEntity();
```

The post method sets up a request, and contentType sets the content-type header to application/ JSON. Then, the user object is passed as a body parameter, and toBodilessEntity converts the response into a response entity without a body.

Handling exceptions using RestClient is simple and is presented in the following code snippet:

```
Boolean result = restClient.get()
    .uri(authenticationServiceUrl +
          "/v1/api/auth/validate?token={token}", token)
    .retrieve()
    .onStatus(HttpStatusCode::is5xxServerError, (request,
          response) -> {
              throw new MyCustomException(
                  response.getStatusCode().toString(),
                  response.getStatusText());
    })
    .body(Boolean.class);
```

Using the onStatus, we can define a custom exception, MyCustomException, according to the HttpStatusCode.

The RestClient offers many enhanced and modern features, making it a strong choice for synchronous communication. It provides an abstraction over HTTP libraries, enabling seamless transformation of Java objects into HTTP requests and creating Java objects from HTTP responses. The Spring Framework team recommends it over the other options. The next time you need a synchronous communication library, the RestClient is the right option. Now, let's explore another important subject when working with microservices architecture: monitoring.

Monitoring and managing the microservices

The shift to microservices architecture introduces new challenges, making monitoring essential for system reliability, performance, and security. Monitoring helps detect issues, optimize performance, facilitate debugging, enhance security, scale resources efficiently, improve development processes, and gain business insights. Investing in robust monitoring solutions is indispensable for achieving operational excellence and delivering high-quality software in a microservices environment. In our favor, we have Spring Boot Actuator to support us in monitoring and managing our microservices.

What is Spring Boot Actuator?

Spring Boot Actuator is an integral part of the Spring Boot framework. It offers tools for monitoring and managing applications. The built-in endpoints give insights into the application's health, performance metrics, and environmental data. For different monitoring and management needs, these endpoints can be accessed through HTTP, JMX, or custom protocols.

Adding Spring Boot Actuator to the microservices

We must add the following dependency to add Spring Boot Actuator to our project:

```xml
<dependency>
    <groupId>org.springframework.boot</groupId>
    <artifactId>spring-boot-starter-actuator</artifactId>
</dependency>
```

Since our project is secured with Spring Security, we must also enable access to actuator endpoints in the `SecurityConfiguration` class:

```java
.authorizeHttpRequests(authorize -> authorize
    .requestMatchers("/api/auth", "/swagger-ui/**",
    "/v3/apidocs/**", "/actuator/**").permitAll()
```

Adding the `"/actuator/**"` will enable all endpoints from the Spring Boot Actuator. *Figure 6.10* shows the endpoint health from the Spring Boot Actuator executed.

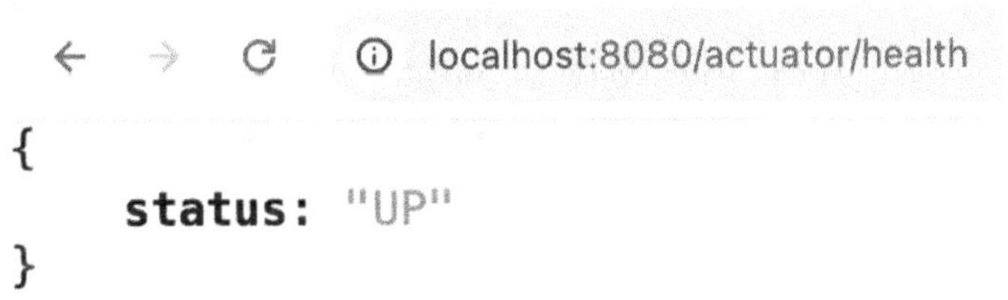

Figure 6.10: Spring Boot Actuator's health endpoint

After calling the **/actuator/health** endpoint, our application's status was returned; it is up. Spring Boot Actuator provides several built-in endpoints for monitoring and managing your application. Here are the primary Spring Boot Actuator endpoints and their purposes:

- **/actuator/health**: This provides health information about the application. It typically shows whether the application is up and can include additional health indicators such as database status if configured.

- **/actuator/info**: This displays arbitrary application information. It can be configured to include details such as application name, description, version, and more.

- **/actuator/metrics**: This provides metrics on the application's current state, including memory usage, garbage collection, and other performance-related metrics.

- **/actuator/loggers**: This allows viewing and configuring the logging levels of the application at runtime.

- **/actuator/threaddump**: This provides a thread dump of the JVM, which helps diagnose thread-related issues.

- **/actuator/httptrace**: This endpoint displays trace information for HTTP requests. It helps debug and monitor HTTP traffic.

- **/actuator/env**: This shows properties from the Spring Environment, including system properties, environment variables, and configuration properties.

- **/actuator/beans**: This command lists all Spring beans in your application context, including their dependencies.

- **/actuator/mappings**: This provides a detailed view of all `@RequestMapping` paths.

- **/actuator/auditevents**: This shows audit events such as authentication and authorization events.

- **/actuator/scheduledtasks**: This displays the scheduled tasks in the application.

- **/actuator/caches**: This provides information about available caches and their current state.

- **/actuator/configprops**: This displays a list of all `@ConfigurationProperties`.

I suggest you play with these endpoints to learn about and explore each one more and how they can be helpful in your applications.

In the `application.properties` file, you can configure which endpoints are exposed using the `management.endpoints.web.exposure.include` property. The following code snippet enables `health` and `metrics`:

```
management.endpoints.web.exposure.include = health,metrics
```

You can expose all endpoints using the * character instead of the endpoint's name.

Securing the Spring Boot Actuator endpoints

Regarding security, it's not recommended that you leave all the Spring Boot Actuator endpoints accessible to everyone. As presented in the following code snippet, let's change the `SecurityConfiguration` class to allow only users with the `ADMIN` role to access the endpoints:

```
.authorizeHttpRequests(authorize -> authorize
    .requestMatchers("/api/auth", "/swagger-ui/**",
                     "/v3/api-docs/**").permitAll()
    .requestMatchers("/actuator/**").hasRole("ADMIN")
    .anyRequest().authenticated())
```

A new `requestMatchers` was added for the `"/actuator/**"` path. The `.hasRole("ADMIN")` instruction guarantees that only those with the `ADMIN` role can access the Spring Boot Actuator endpoints.

Spring Boot Actuator is a valuable component offering essential tools for maintaining, monitoring, and managing Spring Boot applications efficiently. Let's shift gears and cover another vital subject: adding microservices to containers.

Adding the microservices into containers

Containerization is a pivotal innovation in contemporary software development's transformative journey. Let's explore the practical steps and strategic insights needed to containerize microservices effectively.

Introduction to containers

Containers, particularly those managed by Docker, offer numerous advantages in a microservices architecture. They provide isolated environments for each microservice, ensuring consistent behavior across development and deployment stages. This isolation enhances security and makes scaling individual services straightforward.

To containerize your microservices, you need Docker installed on your development machine. If it's not installed, follow the instructions on Docker's official website.

Containerizing the authentication microservice

To containerize our authentication microservice, we must create a Dockerfile in the project. The following code snippet presents the content of the Dockerfile:

```
FROM openjdk:21-jdk-slim
COPY target/authorization-service.jar authorization-service.jar
ENTRYPOINT ["java", "-jar", "authorization-service.jar"]
```

To get authentication-service running, proceed with the following steps:

1. Inside the root project, we can build the project using this command:

    ```
    docker build -t auth-service:latest .
    ```

2. Run the container:

    ```
    docker run -d -p 8080:8080 auth-service:latest
    ```

For the other services, follow the same steps but change the port number. Although creating these steps is simple, they are tedious and laborious. The good news is that we can set up and run simultaneously with Docker Compose, but first, let's learn what a multi-stage build is.

Multi-stage builds

A multi-stage build is a Docker feature that permits you to use multiple FROM statements in your Dockerfile, each representing a different stage of the build process. This feature is handy for creating lean, production-ready Docker images by separating the build and runtime environments. Here are the key benefits of multi-stage builds:

- **Reduced image size**: Using multi-stage builds, you can include all the necessary build tools and dependencies in the build stage but exclude them from the final image. This results in smaller, more efficient Docker images.

- **Improved security**: Smaller images with fewer tools and dependencies reduce the attack surface, enhancing security.

- **Optimized layer caching**: Multi-stage builds help optimize Docker layer caching, making the build process faster and more efficient by reusing unchanged layers.

The following code snippet presents a Dockerfile using a multi-stage build:

```
# Stage 1: Build Stage
FROM maven:3.9.7-eclipse-temurin-21-alpine AS builder
WORKDIR /app
COPY pom.xml .
COPY src ./src
RUN mvn clean package
## Stage 2: Runtime Stage
FROM openjdk:21-jdk-slim
WORKDIR /app
COPY --from=builder /app/target/authentication-services*.jar ./
authentication-services.jar
EXPOSE 8080
ENTRYPOINT ["java", "-jar", "authentication-services.jar"]
```

In this multi-stage Dockerfile, we begin with the build stage. The FROM maven:3.9.7-eclipse-temurin-21-alpine AS builder line specifies that the base image for this stage is a Maven image with Java 21. This stage will compile and generate the jar application through Maven.

The next step is the runtime stage. It starts with FROM openjdk:21-jdk-slim, specifying a smaller base image containing only the JDK runtime, making it lighter. The COPY --from=builder command copies the built JAR file from the builder stage into the current working directory of the runtime container. This approach ensures that the final Docker image is minimal, containing only what is necessary to run the application.

This approach improves efficiency and security, making the final image more suitable for production deployment.

Managing multi-container applications

Docker Compose simplifies the management of multi-container applications using a single `docker-compose.yml` file. It automates network creation for enhanced security and reduces configuration overhead. This tool is beneficial for developing, testing, CI/CD pipelines, and microservices architecture, especially for local distributed application development. Here's an example of a `docker-compose.yml` file:

```
version: "3.8"
services:
  authentication-services:
    build: ../authentication-services
    ports:
      - "8080:8080"
    environment:
      DATABASE_URL: PATH_TO_DATABASE
      USER_SERVICE_URL: http://user-services:8081
    depends_on:
      - postgresql
  user-services:
    ...
  product-services:
    ...
  postgresql:
    ...
```

The complete version of the `docker-compose` file is in the source code repository. The `services` section defines our services, such as microservices, databases, and event streaming platforms such as Kafka.

The `authentication-services`, `user-services`, and `product-services` are our microservices, and `postgresql` is the database for our microservices.

The `build` is the relative path to the project's Dockerfile, and `ports` specifies the ports of the service and the host; in this case, both are `8080`.

`DATABASE_URL` and `USER_SERVICE_URL` are environment variables. The former determines the database URL, and the latter defines the URL for connecting to the user services at `http://user-services:8081`.

This Docker Compose setup ensures the defined services are correctly built, configured, and linked, enabling seamless communication and reliable startup order management.

Now, let's run and test our microservices project. I suppose you already cloned it from GitHub, then go to the `ch6/docker` folder, open a terminal, and run this command:

```
docker-compose up -d
```

The database and services containers will be created and running. *Figure 6.12* presents a screenshot of the successful creation of the containers.

```
✓ Network docker_default                               Created
✓ Container postgres_db                                Started
✓ Container docker-authentication-services-1           Started
✓ Container docker-user-services-1                     Started
✓ Container docker-product-services-1                  Started
```

Figure 6.11: Containers created

To certify that it is all up and running, run this command:

```
docker ps
```

The result will be the three services and the database running.

The following instruction inside the `docker-compose.yml` provided us with a complete database – all tables created and populated:

```
- ./postgres/init.sql:/docker-entrypoint-initdb.d/init.sql
```

Now that we have everything running, it's time to test our services to check whether everything is working.

Calling the services

Let's call the authentication microservice running on port `8080` to generate a token. The result of the call is presented in *Figure 6.13*.

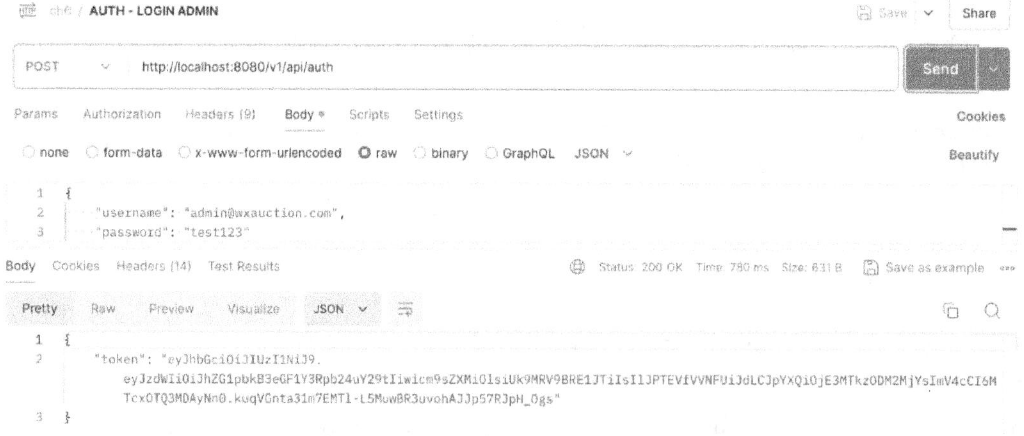

Figure 6.12: Generating a token through the authentication microservice

Now, let's check whether the token is valid or invalid. *Figure 6.14* shows that the token is valid.

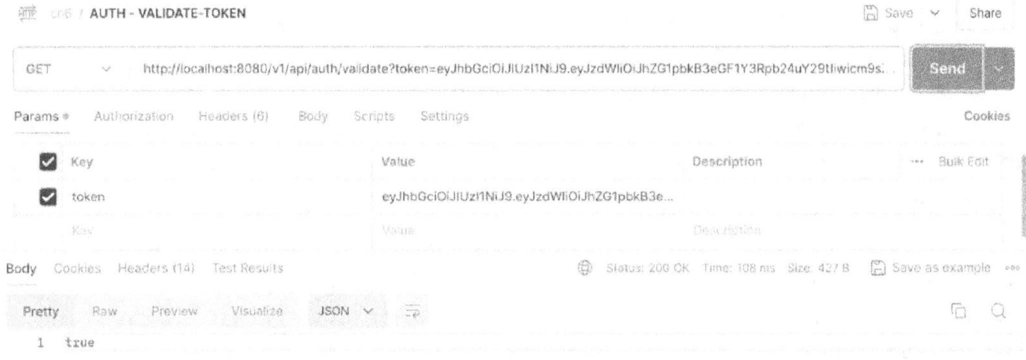

Figure 6.13: Validating the token

Let's use the token to call the list of products. *Figure 6.15* illustrates the successful call.

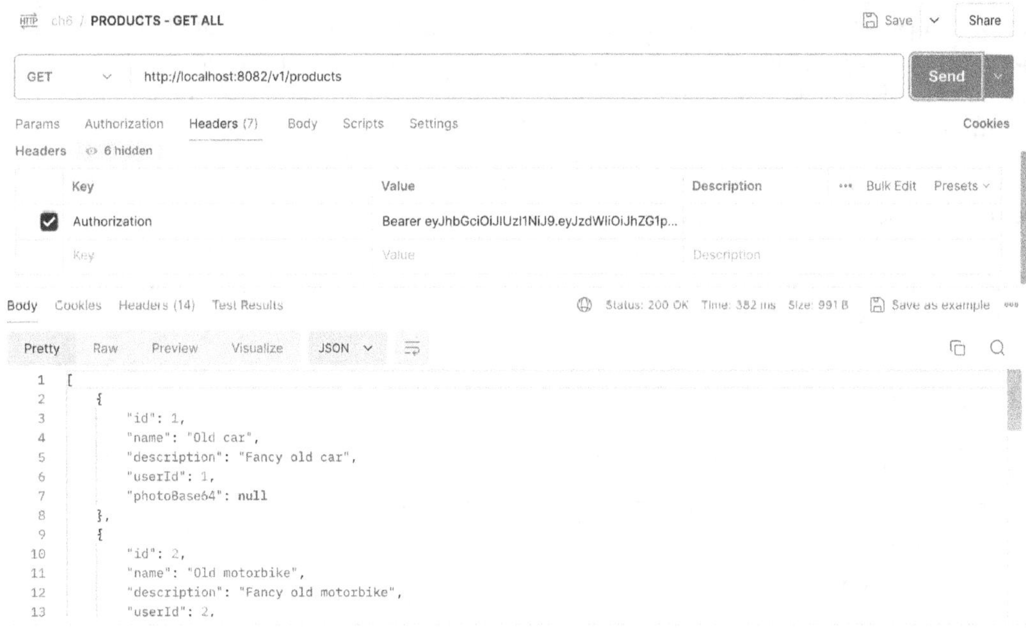

Figure 6.14: Calling product microservices with a valid token

Docker enhances the development and deployment of microservices by providing isolation, scalability, and efficiency. It allows for rapid deployment and smooth transitions between development, testing, and production environments. Following the outlined steps, you can effectively containerize your microservices, leveraging Docker's full potential for a robust architecture.

Summary

This chapter explored microservices architecture in depth, its core characteristics, such as autonomy and specialization, and its benefits and drawbacks. It also presented the transition of the previous client-server application to a microservices architecture using domain-driven design principles. It identified the bounded contexts, refactored the database, and selected appropriate databases based on the CAP theorem. Additionally, implementing a microservice highlighted the importance of clean architecture to maintain the separation of concerns and ensure flexibility and testability.

The chapter also covered synchronous communication using RestClient, demonstrating how to implement inter-service communication efficiently. It also emphasized the significance of monitoring and managing microservices with Spring Boot Actuator, providing insights into monitoring, health checks, and diagnostics.

Finally, the chapter detailed the process of containerizing microservices using Docker and Docker Compose, illustrating how containerization enhances development and deployment efficiency.

The chapter equipped you with comprehensive knowledge of microservices architecture, including practical strategies for transitioning to microservices architecture, best practices for designing and implementing microservices, tools for monitoring and managing microservices effectively, and an understanding of the benefits of containerization. This information is invaluable for creating robust, scalable, and maintainable microservices-based applications.

In *Chapter 7, Microservices Patterns with Spring Cloud*, we will explore essential microservices patterns facilitated by Spring Cloud, such as resilient microservices with Resilience4j, centralized configuration management with Spring Cloud Config, service discovery with Eureka, efficient load balancing strategies with Spring Cloud LoadBalancer, and managing and securing microservices with Spring Cloud Gateway.

Questions

1. What are the core principles of microservices architecture, and why are they important?

2. How does domain-driven design facilitate the transition from a monolithic architecture to microservices?

3. How does clean architecture benefit microservices development?

4. What role does Spring Actuator play in managing microservices?

5. What are the benefits and challenges of using synchronous communication in microservices?

6. What are the benefits of using Docker and Docker Compose for microservices?

7

Microservices Patterns with Spring Cloud

This chapter explores microservices patterns with Spring Cloud, starting with service discovery and highlighting its roles in achieving scalability, resilience, and flexibility using Eureka, a service registry from Spring Cloud Netflix.

We then cover load balancing, which is crucial for effectively distributing network traffic among servers and enhancing performance and reliability. We focus on implementing client-side load balancing using Spring Cloud LoadBalancer.

After that, we explain and implement a gateway pattern using Spring Cloud Gateway to centralize routes, and also cover managing configurations with Spring Cloud Config, emphasizing centralized configuration management for distributed systems.

Finally, this chapter covers implementing resilience patterns using Resilience4J and the key resilience patterns, such as circuit breaker, retry, rate limiter, bulkhead, and fallback.

This chapter will cover the following topics:

- Discovering and registering services with Eureka
- Balancing the load with Spring Cloud LoadBalancer
- Routing with Spring Cloud Gateway
- Managing configuration with Spring Cloud Config
- Applying resilience with Resilience4J

By the end of this chapter, you will know how to implement service discovery, load balancing, gateways, configuration management, and resilience patterns in a microservices architecture. These patterns are crucial for developing robust, resilient, and scalable microservices applications and will empower you to apply them.

Technical requirements

All the code for this chapter can be found on GitHub at `https://github.com/PacktPublishing/Software-Architecture-with-Spring/tree/main/ch7`. Ellipses in the code blocks indicate that parts of the code have been omitted, and the complete code is available on GitHub.

Discovering and registering services with Eureka

So far, we've used the typical fixed URIs method for communication between services, where the address of the target service is hardcoded in the client service's configuration. While simple, this approach can lead to inflexibility and does not support load balancing. This is where service discovery comes into play; it is a vital concept in microservices architecture that addresses the limitations of fixed URI service calls. It allows services to dynamically find and communicate with each other without relying on static configurations. This dynamic mechanism is crucial for building scalable, resilient, and flexible microservices. *Figure 7.1* illustrates the service discovery architecture.

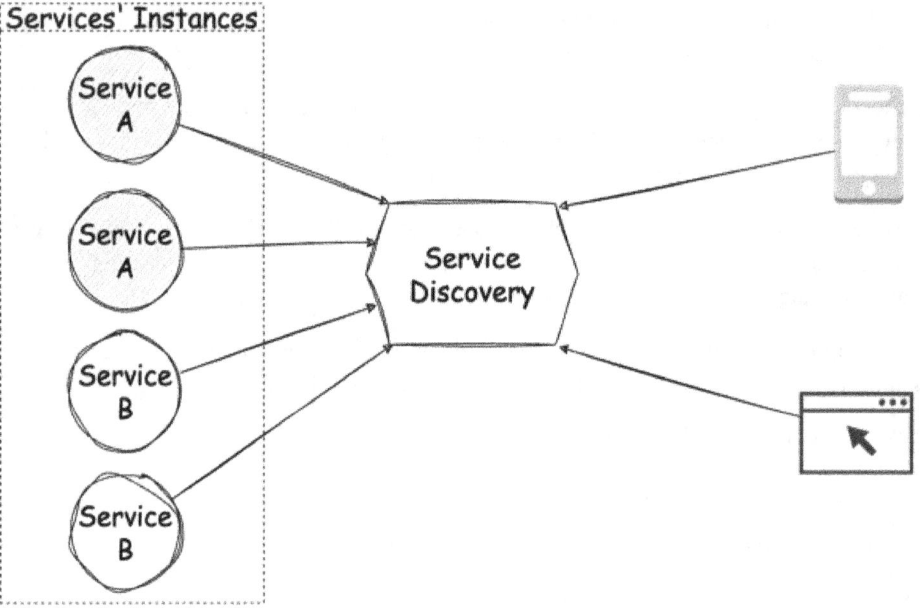

Figure 7.1: Service discovery architecture

When services start, they initiate the process by registering themselves with the service discovery. They send their details, such as IP address, port, and health status, to the service discovery registry. The service discovery component then takes over, maintaining a registry of all available service instances and their health status. It uses health checks to ensure that only healthy instances are listed and available for discovery.

When client applications need to communicate with service A or B, they don't directly call a fixed IP address or URL. Instead, they query service discovery to find the current, healthy instances of the required service. Service discovery can return multiple instances of a service.

If service A needs to communicate with service B, it follows the same process. If a service goes down, the service discovery removes the IP address of the non-functioning instance from its registry.

Now, let's check out the benefits and drawbacks of service discovery.

Benefits

Let's learn the main benefits of service discovery in a microservices architecture:

- **Dynamic scalability**: Services can scale up and down dynamically, and new instances can register themselves, making them available for discovery immediately.

- **Fault tolerance**: Service discovery helps to manage failures gracefully. If a service instance fails, it is removed from the registry, and requests are rerouted to available instances.

- **Load balancing**: Service discovery can integrate with load balancers to distribute requests evenly across service instances, enhancing performance and reliability.

- **Network resilience**: Services can be discovered by their logical names, so they adapt to network changes, such as IP address changes or service relocations, without manual intervention.

Besides the benefits, service discovery also has some drawbacks.

Drawbacks

The main drawbacks of service discovery are as follows:

- **Single point of failure**: If the service registry is not managed correctly and is replicated, it can become a single point of failure. If the central registry fails, the entire service discovery mechanism could be disrupted, potentially leading to downtime or communication failures among services. To minimize the risk of the service registry becoming a single point of failure, deploy multiple instances with load balancing, enable replication for data synchronization, implement backups, failover mechanisms, and monitoring with alerts. Integration with a service mesh can provide additional resiliency and intelligent traffic routing.

- **Complexity and inconsistency**: Adding service discovery mechanisms increases system complexity by requiring additional components such as the service registry and discovery agents. The service registry may have delays or inconsistencies, leading to outdated or inaccurate service information for reasons such as network latency or replication lag between registry nodes. During this time, services querying the registry might receive obsolete information. To address consistency, robust mechanisms such as retry logic and health checks are essential for handling stale data.

In a microservices architecture, service discovery offers benefits such as dynamic scalability, fault tolerance, load balancing, and network resilience. However, it also presents challenges such as single points of failure, complexity, and inconsistency. Proper management, including deploying multiple instances, load balancing, replication, and robust monitoring, is essential to overcome these drawbacks and maximize the advantages of service discovery.

Implementing the service discovery with Eureka

The industry has several widely used service discovery tools, each with unique features and advantages, such as Etcd, Consul, Zookeeper, and Eureka.

We'll implement service discovery using Spring Cloud Netflix. It includes Eureka, a service registry for dynamic communication between services without fixed configuration. Integrated with Spring Cloud, Eureka allows easy registration and discovery of microservices using simple annotations and properties in Spring Boot applications.

We'll create a dedicated microservice to manage service discovery, offering advantages such as centralized management, scalability, fault tolerance, simplified maintenance, consistent discovery across environments, and enhanced security.

We can use the Spring Initializr tool to create the new service, `service-discovery-services`, and add the Spring Web MVC, Spring Boot Actuator, and Eureka Server libraries.

The following code snippet shows the Eureka Server dependency, `spring-cloud-starter-netflix-eureka-server`, added to the `pom.xml` file:

```xml
<dependency>
    <groupId>org.springframework.cloud</groupId>
    <artifactId>spring-cloud-starter-netflix-eureka-server
    </artifactId>
</dependency>
```

It also added the **Spring Cloud BOM (Bill of Materials)** to the `dependencyManagement` section of your `pom.xml` file, ensuring consistent and compatible versions of Spring Cloud dependencies:

```xml
<dependencyManagement>
  <dependencies>
    <dependency>
      <groupId>org.springframework.cloud</groupId>
      <artifactId>spring-cloud-dependencies</artifactId>
      <version>${spring-cloud.version}</version>
      <type>pom</type>
      <scope>import</scope>
    </dependency>
  </dependencies>
</dependencyManagement>
```

The following configuration snippet presents the properties added to `application.properties`:

```
spring.application.name=service-discovery-services
server.port=8761
eureka.client.register-with-eureka=false
eureka.client.fetch-registry=false
```

The `spring.application.name` property sets the application name to `service-discovery-services`. The `server.port` property sets the port to `8761`, the default port for Eureka Server. When set to `false`, the `eureka.client.register-with-eureka` and `eureka.client.fetch-registry` configure a standalone Eureka server. It won't register itself and fetch the registry from Eureka.

To enable the Eureka server, we only need to add the `@EnableEurekaServer` annotation to the `main` Spring Boot class, as shown in the following code snippet:

```
@EnableEurekaServer
@SpringBootApplication
public class ServiceDiscoveryServicesApplication {
```

The `@EnableEurekaServer` annotation activates the Eureka Server functionality, ensuring necessary configurations and beans are available, and enables component scanning for Eureka-related components.

After running the application, the Eureka server will be available at `http//:localhost:8761`. *Figure 7.2* illustrates the Eureka server console:

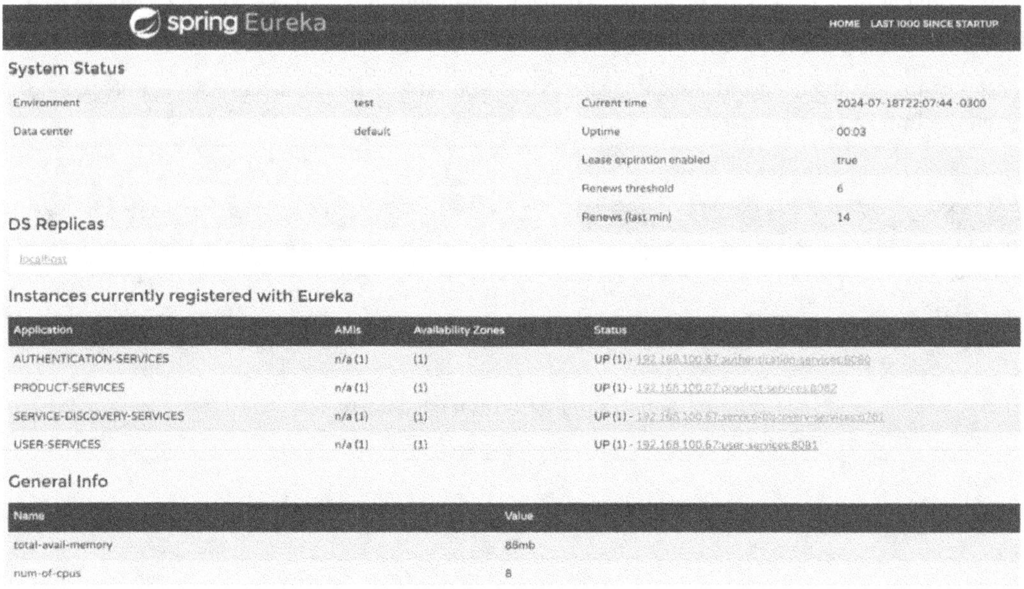

Figure 7.2: Eureka server console

The Eureka server console overviews the server's status and configuration, including system status, renewal metrics, replicas, and instances sections. With our service discovery up and running, it's time to set up the services to register in the Eureka server.

Registering the services

Registering the services in the Eureka server is easy. Simply add the `spring-cloud-starter-netflix-eureka-client` dependency and the Spring Cloud BOM mentioned in the *Implementing the service discovery with Eureka* section:

```
<dependency>
  <groupId>org.springframework.cloud</groupId>
  <artifactId>spring-cloud-starter-netflix-eureka-client
  </artifactId>
</dependency>
```

The following configuration snippet is needed to configure Eureka as well:

```
eureka.client.serviceUrl.defaultZone=http://localhost:8761/eureka
eureka.instance.preferIpAddress=true
```

The `eureka.client.serviceUrl.defaultZone` property specifies the default Eureka server URL where the client will register itself and fetch the registry. The `eureka.instance.preferIpAddress` property indicates that the Eureka client should register its IP address rather than its hostname. It is particularly beneficial in dynamic environments, such as cloud and containerized deployments, where IP addresses consistently and directly address service instances.

After successfully configuring and launching all services, you can see the registered services in *Figure 7.3* through the Eureka server console:

Instances currently registered with Eureka

Application	AMIs	Availability Zones	Status
AUTHENTICATION-SERVICES	n/a (1)	(1)	UP (1) - 192.168.100.67:authentication-services:8080
PRODUCT-SERVICES	n/a (1)	(1)	UP (1) - 192.168.100.67:product-services:8082
SERVICE-DISCOVERY-SERVICES	n/a (1)	(1)	UP (1) - 192.168.100.67:service-discovery-services:8761
USER-SERVICES	n/a (1)	(1)	UP (1) - 192.168.100.67:user-services:8081

Figure 7.3: Services registered in the Eureka server

If you turn off some service, its status will be turned down. Now that the service is registered, how do the services communicate? The following code snippet presents the refactor of the `UserRestApi` class from authentication services:

```java
public class UserRestApi implements UserRepository {
  private final RestClient restClient;
  private final DiscoveryClient discoveryClient;
  @Override
  public List<String> getRolesByUsername(String username) {
  ServiceInstance serviceInstance =
    discoveryClient.getInstances("USER-SERVICES").get(0);
  RoleResponse result = restClient.get()
    .uri(serviceInstance.getUri() +
    "/v1/users/{username}/roles", username)
              .retrieve()
              .body(RoleResponse.class);
```

The `UserRestApi` class was refactored to use `DiscoveryClient`, a Spring Cloud interface, to interact with a service registry.

`discoveryClient.getInstances` retrieves a list of instances for the user services, where `USER-SERVICES` is the application's name.

It then uses `serviceInstance.getUri()` in the REST call to dynamically build the REST call using the discovered service instance's URI. It's important to note that we only retrieve the first instance through the `discoveryClient.getInstances("USER-SERVICES").get(0)` instruction. What happens if there is more than one instance of `USER-SERVICES`? This is a trade-off of the `discoveryClient` interface, as each service must handle the logic of managing multiple instances and failover scenarios. However, there's no need to worry. Spring Cloud provides another tool, the Spring Cloud LoadBalancer, which we will explore next.

Balancing the load with Spring Cloud LoadBalancer

Load balancing spreads network traffic across multiple servers to prevent any single server from becoming overwhelmed, improving responsiveness and availability. Load balancers sit between client devices and backend servers, routing client requests to available servers based on predefined algorithms. These algorithms can be as simple as a round-robin that distributes requests sequentially or as complex as considering the current server load and health checks.

Figure 7.4 illustrates how a load balancer works.

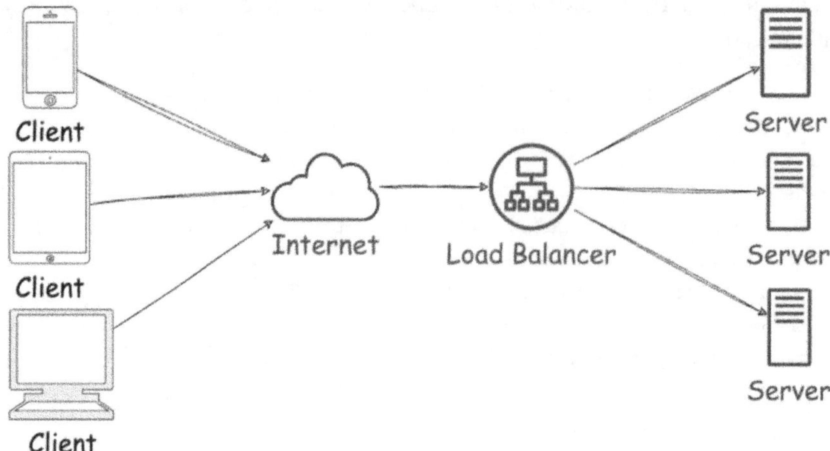

Figure 7.4: Load balancer

When clients send requests to the server, it creates traffic. A load balancer, either hardware or software, intercepts these requests and routes them to the most suitable server node, which processes them and delivers the response to the client. The load balancer repeats this process for each request, using various techniques to decide which server will handle each request.

Client-side load balancing

Traditional server-side load balancing uses a centralized load balancer to route client requests to the server. This may introduce a bottleneck and additional latency due to the extra hop. On the other hand, client-side load balancing involves distributing the load at the client level rather than using a central load balancer. The client maintains a list of available servers and decides which server to send each request to. Our project will utilize the Spring Cloud LoadBalancer as client-side load balancing. It offers customizable load-balancing strategies and seamless integration with service discovery, simplifies load-balancing configuration, and dynamically manages service instances, reducing the need for custom implementations. *Figure 7.5* presents the authentication and user services with Spring Cloud LoadBalancer.

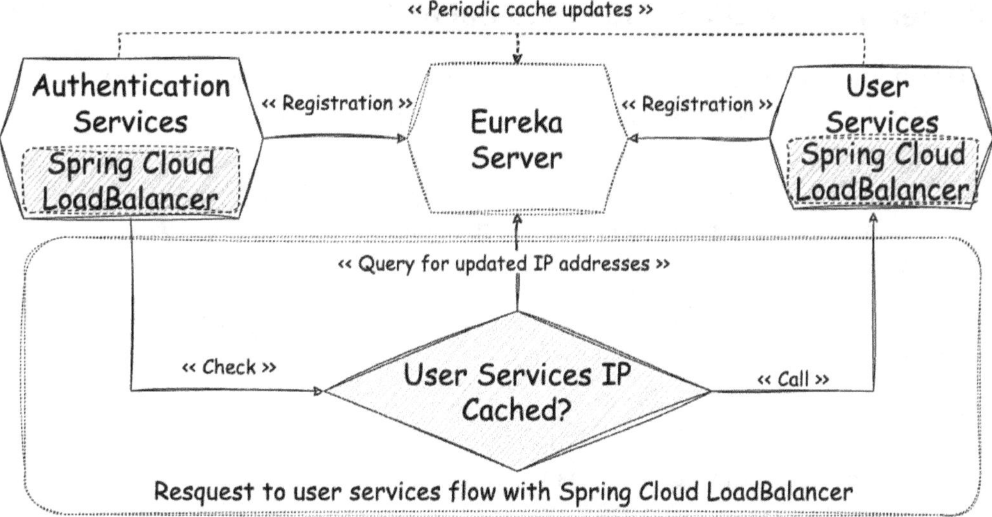

Figure 7.5: Spring Cloud LoadBalancer added to the services

Let's scrutinize how it works:

- **Registration**: Both authentication and user services register their instances and IP addresses with the Eureka server during startup. This allows Eureka to maintain a registry of available services and their locations.

- **Periodic cache updates**: The Spring Cloud LoadBalancer keeps the cache up to date by periodically refreshing the IP addresses in the Eureka server. This ensures that the cached data remains consistent with the service registry.

- **Request to user services flow with Spring Cloud LoadBalancer**: When authentication services need to request user services, the following flow is performed:

- **Check**: When authentication services need to call user services, they first consult the Spring Cloud LoadBalancer, which checks its local cache for the IP addresses of the user services.

- **User services IP addresses are cached**: If the cache contains the user services IP addresses, the authentication services proceed to call the user services directly.

- **Query Eureka for updated IP addresses**: If the IP addresses are not cached, the Spring Cloud LoadBalancer queries the Eureka server to fetch the list of IP addresses for the user services. Once they have been obtained, the authentication services call the user services.

When Spring Cloud LoadBalancer is added to the services, the load of the Eureka server is lessened since the services cache the service's IP addresses locally and refresh them periodically. Let's now implement client-side load balancing.

Implementing the client-side load balancing

To implement load balancing in our services with Spring Cloud LoadBalancer, we must add the `spring-cloud-starter-loadbalancer` dependency:

```
<dependency>
  <groupId>org.springframework.cloud</groupId>
  <artifactId>spring-cloud-starter-loadbalancer</artifactId>
</dependency>
```

In the `BeansConfiguration` class, let's set up the `RestClient` to utilize the load balancer in every call with the `@LoadBalanced` annotation:

```
@LoadBalanced
@Bean
public RestClient.Builder restClient() {
    return RestClient.builder();
}
```

Now, we only have to refactor the code where we make the calls. Let's take, for example, the code to get the user's roles inside the `UserRestApi` class from authentication services:

```
RoleResponse result = restClient.build()
    .get()
    .uri(URI.create("http://USER-SERVICES/v1/users/" + username + "/
        roles"))
    .retrieve()
    .body(RoleResponse.class);
```

The code replaces the previous instruction, `.uri(serviceInstance.getUri() + "/v1/users/{username}/roles", username)`, with `.uri(URI.create("http://USER-SERVICES/v1/users/" + username + "/roles"))`. It replaced the previous call that uses DiscoveryClient and has no ability by default to rotate the calls.

When using load balancing, the RestClient processes the URL using the virtual hostname USER-SERVICES to request a service instance from the load balancer instead of the physical address, hiding the actual service location and port from the client service.

The Spring Cloud LoadBalancer evenly distributes requests among available service instances in a round-robin fashion. Let's test the load balancing and check that it works as expected.

Checking the load balancing

To check that the load balancing is working, let's make some changes in our authentication services to log the path of the service that the load-balancing client calls.

> **Attention**
>
> The following changes in the code are only to check that the load balancing is working.

The following code snippet is a custom interceptor that implements another `ClientHttpRequestInterceptor` and overrides the `intercept` method to log the path and port number of the user services it calls:

```java
@Component
public class CustomLoadBalancerInterceptor implements
    ClientHttpRequestInterceptor {


private final LoadBalancerClient loadBalancerClient;


@Override
public ClientHttpResponse intercept(HttpRequest request,
    byte[] body, ClientHttpRequestExecution
    execution) throws IOException {
ServiceInstance instance = loadBalancerClient.choose(
    "USER-SERVICES");
if (instance != null){
  log.info("Calling service instance: host={},
        port={}, path={}", instance.getHost(),
        instance.getPort(), request.getURI().getPath());

...
```

It will intercept all requests and logs the user services' host, port, and path. The `ServiceInstance instance = loadBalancerClient.choose("USER-SERVICES")` instruction uses `loadBalancerClient` to get the service's instance of a service to which a request will be routed. Then, in the `BeansConfiguration` class, we refactor the `restClient` method:

```java
public RestClient.Builder restClient(
    CustomLoadBalancerInterceptor
    customLoadBalancerInterceptor) {
        return RestClient.builder()
        .requestInterceptor(customLoadBalancerInterceptor);
```

We must add the `CustomLoadBalancerInterceptor` class as a parameter to the `restClient` method to be injected and add `.requestInterceptor(customLoadBalancerInterceptor)`, which will intercept every call.

Once everything is configured, let's test it. First, start up `service-discovery-services` followed by `authentication-services` and `user-services`. Run the following command five times for `user-services` inside the `root` folder, changing the port number each time:

```
mvn spring-boot:run -Dspring-boot.run.arguments="--server.port=8086"
```

In the example, the user services have started using ports 8081, 8084, 8085, 8086, and 8087, as illustrated in *Figure 7.6*.

Figure 7.6: User services instances

Run the following `curl` command a couple of times or use the Postman collection provided in the repository:

```
curl --location 'http://localhost:8080/v1/api/auth' \
--header 'Content-Type: application/json' \
--data-raw '{
    "username": "user@wxauction.com",
    "password": "test123"}'
```

Figure 7.7 shows the authentication services console after some calls using the previous `curl` command:

Figure 7.7: Load balancing the user services call

Look at the user's service port number; it rotates among the available user service instances. The first instance was in port 8081, and after calling all the instances, it started again calling 8081. Now that we have covered load balancing, let's move on to Spring Cloud Gateway.

Routing with Spring Cloud Gateway

A gateway acts as an entry point for client requests, routing them to the appropriate services within a network. In a microservices architecture, the gateway functions as a reverse proxy that routes client requests to the appropriate microservice based on the request's path, headers, or other criteria. It simplifies client interactions by providing a single access point. It can enforce security, manage traffic, and perform other essential tasks to ensure efficient and secure communication between clients and services.

Benefits of using a gateway

We can get the following benefits when implementing a gateway in a microservices architecture:

- **Centralized routing**: Simplifies client interactions by providing a single endpoint, such as `http://localhost:8072`, for accessing various services.

- **Security**: A gateway can enhance security by centrally managing authentication and authorization, ensuring only verified and permitted users can access the system's resources. It can also monitor and log all access requests, providing a comprehensive audit trail that helps you identify and respond to suspicious activities in real time. Furthermore, the gateway can protect against common security threats such as **SQL injection**, **cross-site scripting** (**XSS**), and **distributed denial-of-service** (**DDoS**) attacks by filtering and validating incoming requests before they reach the backend services.

- **Load balancing**: A gateway can apply load balancing functionality by distributing incoming requests evenly across multiple instances of a service, thereby improving availability and performance.

- **Rate limiting**: A gateway can limit the number of requests in a given timeframe by controlling the rate of incoming requests to prevent overloading services. This helps mitigate the risk of service degradation or outages due to sudden traffic spikes.

- **Monitoring and analytics**: A gateway enhances monitoring and analytics by collecting comprehensive metrics and logs from all incoming and outgoing traffic, providing a centralized point for monitoring and analysis. This centralized approach enables the aggregation of detailed performance data across all services, such as request and response times, error rates, and throughput. Doing so helps to identify performance bottlenecks, optimize resource utilization, and tune the system for better efficiency.

When using a gateway, paying attention to two key issues that can negatively impact our microservices architecture is essential. One concern is that if the gateway is not designed for high availability, it can become a bottleneck or a single point of failure. It is essential to analyze and implement strategies such as load balancing, horizontal scaling, redundancy across multiple geographic regions, health monitoring, self-healing mechanisms, rate limiting, and DDoS protection to ensure high availability and prevent any single point of failure.

Another issue is latency, as each request must pass through an additional hop, potentially introducing delays. Knowing what a gateway is and the benefits and drawbacks of having one in a microservices architecture, let's delve into the Spring Cloud Gateway.

Implementing a gateway with Spring Cloud Gateway

Spring Cloud Gateway is the Spring Cloud project library for building and deploying API gateways within a microservices architecture using Spring WebFlux or Spring Web MVC. It provides some key features such as routing, predicates, and filters.

Routing directs requests to specific services and can be static and dynamic. Static routes are predefined in the application's configuration file, while dynamic routes are configured at runtime using mechanisms such as Eureka. Each route can be customized with predicates and filters to tailor the routing logic. Predicates are conditions that determine whether a request should be routed, while filters can modify incoming and outgoing requests and responses.

Let's move forward to the gateway implementation and delve into these features. *Figure 7.8* illustrates the online auction microservices architecture with the gateway services.

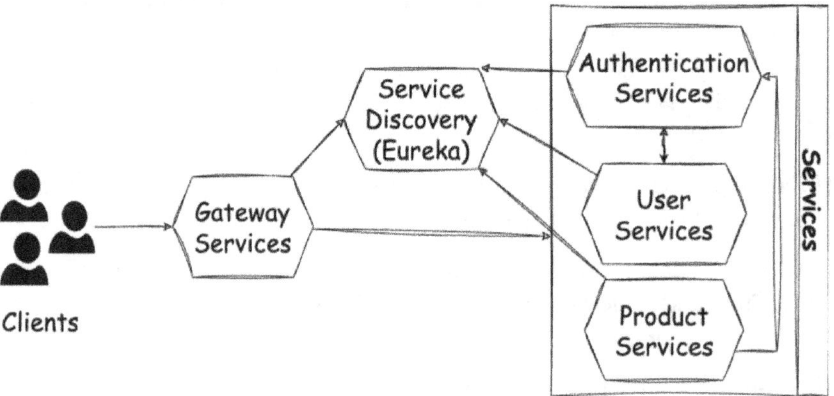

Figure 7.8: Online auction microservices architecture with a gateway

The gateway services are the entry point to our online auction application. Any client's call to any service will obligatorily pass through the gateway services. As the gateway gets the service addresses from service discovery, it redirects the call to the appropriate service. The communication of the services behind the gateway is kept straight; that is, they communicate with each other directly without passing through the gateway.

The gateway will be a new service, `gateway-services`, that can be created using Spring Initializr. *Figure 7.9* illustrates the dependencies that need to be added to the project:

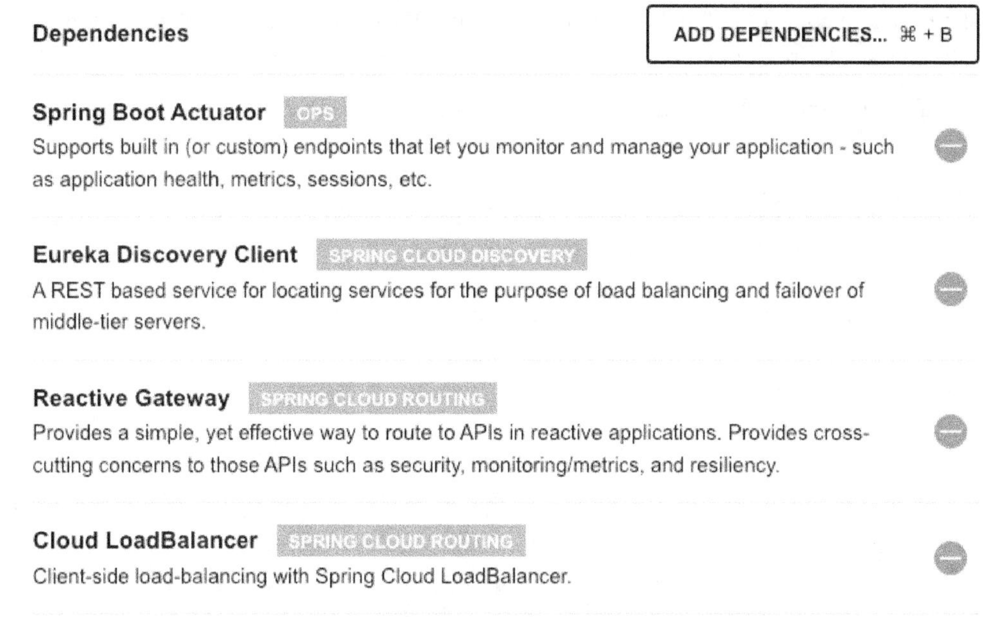

Dependencies

ADD DEPENDENCIES... ⌘ + B

Spring Boot Actuator `OPS`
Supports built in (or custom) endpoints that let you monitor and manage your application - such as application health, metrics, sessions, etc.

Eureka Discovery Client `SPRING CLOUD DISCOVERY`
A REST based service for locating services for the purpose of load balancing and failover of middle-tier servers.

Reactive Gateway `SPRING CLOUD ROUTING`
Provides a simple, yet effective way to route to APIs in reactive applications. Provides cross-cutting concerns to those APIs such as security, monitoring/metrics, and resiliency.

Cloud LoadBalancer `SPRING CLOUD ROUTING`
Client-side load-balancing with Spring Cloud LoadBalancer.

Figure 7.9: Gateway services' dependencies

The reactive gateway dependency adds gateway functionalities. The Eureka Discovery Client connects the gateway to the service discovery to obtain the service addresses and connect itself. The Spring Boot Actuator provides functional endpoints to monitor the gateway. So, let's configure the gateway to connect to the discovery services.

Connecting the gateway to the discovery services

Once the project has been created, the following configuration is needed to connect the gateway to the service discovery:

```
spring:
  cloud:
    gateway:
      discovery.locator:
        enabled: true
        lower-case-service-id: true
```

`spring.cloud.gateway.discovery.locator.enable` configured to `true` allows the gateway to create the routes based on the services registered with service discovery, and `lower-case-service-id` will permit us to call the services using lowercase in the URL.

The configuration to connect to Eureka is omitted since it is the same as what was discussed in the services discovery section. Now, let's call the authentication services.

Figure 7.10 illustrates the call to authentication services through the gateway.

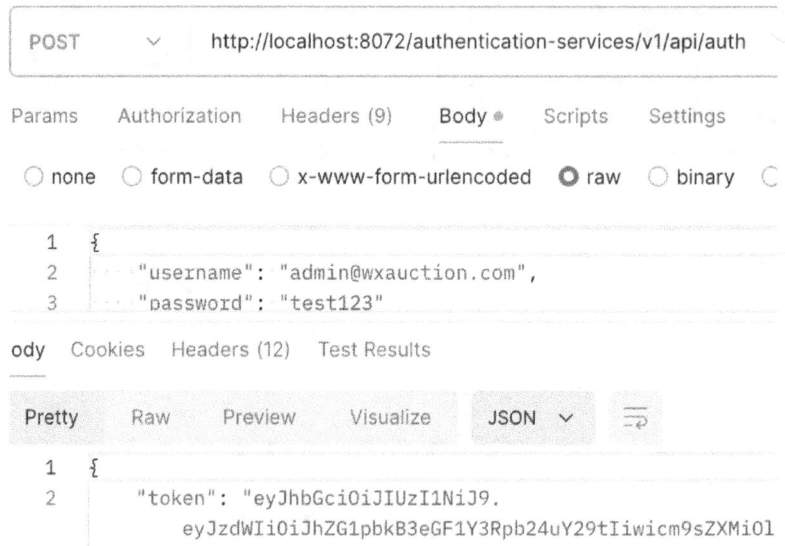

Figure 7.10: Calling authentication services through the gateway

It uses the gateway address `http://localhost:8072` to access the authentication services endpoint. Clients will use the same address to call user and product services as well. Spring Boot Actuator provides endpoints to visualize the routes and configurations managed by the gateway, as presented in *Figure 7.11*.

```
- {
    predicate: "Paths: [/authentication-services/**], match trailing slash: true",
  - metadata: {
        management.port: "8080"
    },
    route_id: "ReactiveCompositeDiscoveryClient_AUTHENTICATION-SERVICES",
  - filters: [
        "[[RewritePath /authentication-services/?(?<remaining>.*) = '/${remaining}'], order = 1]"
    ],
    uri: "lb://AUTHENTICATION-SERVICES",
    order: 0
},
```

Figure 7.11: Routes and configurations managed by the gateway

If we call `http://localhost:8072/actuator/gateway/routes`, we can see the routes managed by the Spring Cloud Gateway. Now, let's learn about predicates and filters.

Predicates and filters

In Spring Cloud Gateway, predicates and filters are essential components that manage and manipulate incoming HTTP requests and outgoing responses. They play distinct yet complementary roles in the request-processing pipeline, allowing sophisticated routing and processing logic.

Predicates

Predicates define the conditions that must be met for an incoming request to be routed to a specific backend service. They act as the criteria or rules determining whether a particular route should handle a request. It evaluates various attributes of the incoming request, such as the URL path, headers, query parameters, HTTP methods, and more.

Built-in predicates

Spring Cloud Gateway provides several built-in predicates, including the following:

- **After / Before / Between**: Matches requests after or before a specific date and time, or between two dates and times.

- **Header**: Matches requests based on the presence of a header with a particular name and value.

- **Method**: Matches requests based on the HTTP method, such as GET or POST.

- **Path**: Matches requests based on the URL path.

- **Query**: Matches requests based on the presence of a query parameter with a specific name and value.

Built-in predicates in Spring Cloud Gateway provide a powerful way to define routing rules based on various attributes of incoming requests.

Filters

Filters are powerful features that allow you to modify incoming HTTP requests and outgoing HTTP responses. Filters can be applied globally or to individual routes, and they play a crucial role in the processing pipeline by enabling cross-cutting concerns such as authentication, logging, metrics, and throttling.

Built-in filters

Spring Cloud Gateway provides a rich set of built-in filters that can readily handle common scenarios. The main ones are as follows:

- **AddRequestHeader**: Adds a header to the request

- **AddResponseHeader**: Adds a header to the response

- **AddRequestParameter**: Adds a query parameter to the request

- **RewritePath**: Rewrite the request path using a regular expression

- **ModifyRequestBody**: Modifies the request body

It's time to delve into predicates and filters through an example.

Using predicates and filters to modify a URL

Let's use a predicate and a filter to shorten the URL of the authentication services. The calls will use `authentication` instead of `authentication-services`, as presented in the following address: `http://localhost:8072/authentication/v1/api/auth`. The following configuration snippet makes this work:

```
routes:
  - id: auth
    uri: lb://authentication-services
    predicates:
      - Path=/authentication/**
    filters:
      - RewritePath=/authentication/(?<path>.*), /$\{path}
```

This configuration creates a gateway route that directs traffic to the `authentication-services` service using load balancing, specifically via the URI `uri: lb://authentication-services`.

The `Path` predicate dictates that any incoming request with a URL path starting with `/authentication/` will be directed to `authentication-services`.

The `RewritePath` filter utilizes a regular expression to modify the URL path of the request before it is forwarded to the destination service.

In addition to the built-in predicates and filters, we can also create very powerful custom filters.

Custom filters

Custom filters allow you to modify and enhance request and response processing beyond built-in capabilities. They implement cross-cutting concerns such as authentication, logging, rate limiting, and data transformation. Custom filters provide more control over traffic flow, can be applied globally or to individual routes, and are categorized into pre-filters and post-filters based on their execution phase:

- **Pre-filters**: These filters are executed before the request is forwarded to the downstream service.

- **Post-filters**: These filters are executed after the response is received from the downstream service but before it is returned to the client.

The following code snippet checks for the `x-correlation-id` attribute in the header request. If it does not exist, it creates one, sends it to downstream services, and then returns it to the client:

```java
@Component
public class CustomGlobalFilter implements GlobalFilter {
  @Override
  public Mono<Void> filter(ServerWebExchange exchange,
              GatewayFilterChain chain) {
    if (correlationId == null) {
      correlationId = UUID.randomUUID().toString();
      exchange.getRequest().mutate().header(
        "x-correlation-id", correlationId ).build();
    }
    String finalCorrelationId = correlationId;
    return chain.filter(exchange).then
        (Mono.fromRunnable(() -> {
            exchange.getResponse().getHeaders().add(
              "x-correlation-id", finalCorrelationId);
...
```

To create a custom filter, the `CustomGlobalFilter` class implements the `GlobalFilter` interface of Spring Cloud Gateway. The `GlobalFilter` interface contains a single-method filter with the `ServerWebExchange` parameter, which represents the current HTTP request and response, and `GatewayFilterChain`, which represents the chain of filters the request will pass through. After the method signature, the following code is the pre-filter logic implementation, the instruction `exchange.getRequest().mutate().header(CORRELATION_ID, correlationId).build()` adds the header `x-correlation-id` attribute to send to the downstream service, and the post-filter is executed inside the functional programming instruction `chain.filter(exchange).then(Mono.fromRunnable(() -> {`. The instruction `exchange.getResponse().getHeaders().add( CORRELATION_ID, finalCorrelationId)` adds the header `x-correlation-id` attribute to the response header.

Figure 7.12 shows it returned to the client.

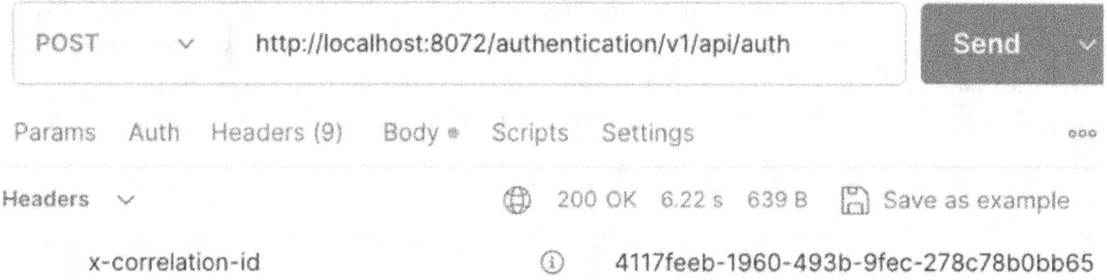

Figure 7.12: The attribute header x-correlation-id returned to the client

The gateway services returned the `x-correlation-id` attribute header to the client.

Spring Cloud Gateway effectively manages and routes requests, offering predicates, filters, and service registry integration features. These capabilities enhance flexibility, security, and performance. While it may introduce some latency, the centralized routing, security, and monitoring make it essential for developing and managing a robust, scalable, and efficient microservice architecture.

Managing configuration with Spring Cloud Config

In a microservice architecture, managing configuration is crucial as applications scale and the number of services increases. Managing configuration locally through the application's configuration presents significant problems, particularly regarding security, such as database passwords and redeployment when a property's value changes. While simple and suitable for small projects, managing configurations locally can become cumbersome and error-prone as an application grows.

The configuration manager service provides a centralized approach to managing configurations across multiple applications and environments. This service externalizes configuration management, enabling dynamic updates and centralized control. *Figure 7.13* illustrates the architecture of microservices, with the addition of a configuration management service.

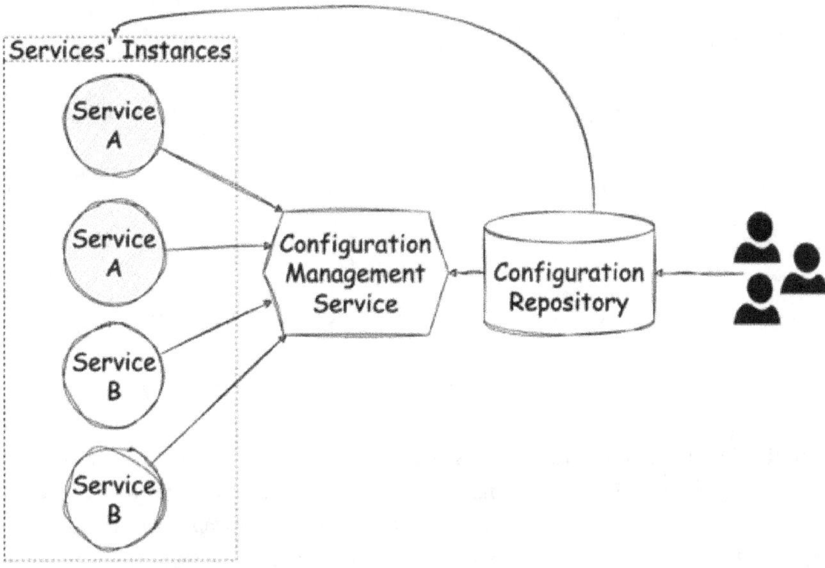

Figure 7.13: Configuration management service

When the services start, they call the configuration management service to obtain the configuration information. The configuration data is in a repository, which can be filed under source control, such as GitHub, a key-value data store, or a database. The team can add or change the values, and the running services must be notified of these changes.

Implementing configuration management with Spring Cloud Config

Spring Cloud Config is a solution for managing configurations, enabling centralized storage, and managing configuration properties for distributed systems. It supports various backend storage options, including Git, SVN, HashiCorp Consul, and Vault, allowing versioned and audited configuration changes. By externalizing configuration from application code, Spring Cloud Config promotes a clear separation of concerns and facilitates managing and updating configurations without redeploying applications. It consists of a server acting as a configuration server and a client library for fetching configurations, supporting dynamic updates, and ensuring consistency across environments in microservices architectures.

The project uses a public GitHub repository to store the configuration files at `https://github.com/wandersonxs/online-auction-configuration.git`. Let's upload the project's properties and YAML configuration files to the repository. *Figure 7.14* shows the repository with the files uploaded.

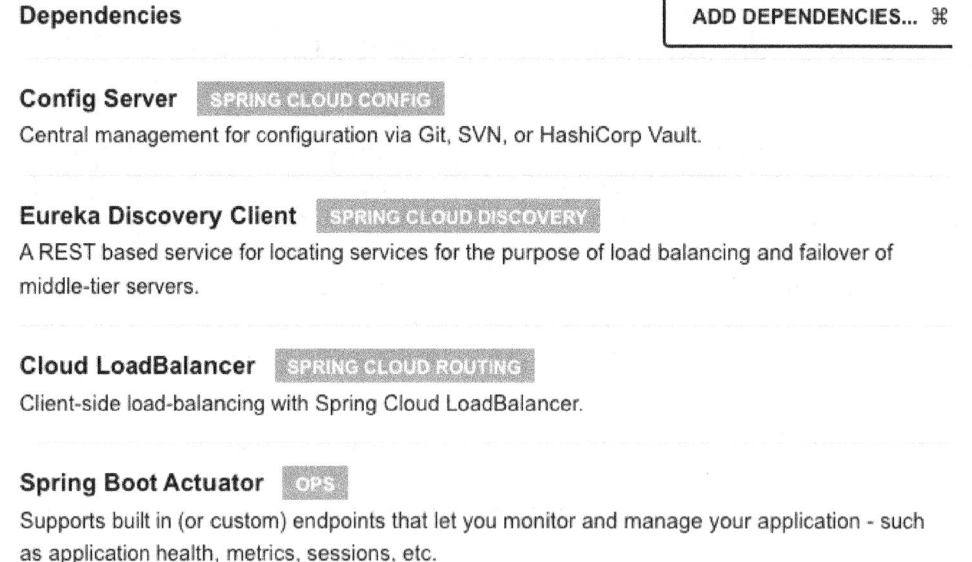

Figure 7.14: Project's configuration files into GitHub repository

You may have noticed that the configuration files' names are not `application.properties` or `application.yaml`. The Spring Cloud Config Server expects the project's name to identify the correct configuration for the service. The filename pattern is *applicationname.properties* or *applicationname-profile.properties*, such as `authentication-services.properties`, `authentication-services-dev.properties`, and `authentication-services-prod.properties`. Here, we will use the default pattern, *applicationname.properties*, without specifying the profile.

Once the repository has been created and the files have been uploaded, let's create the configuration server; our service will be named `configuration-services`.

Figure 7.15 illustrates the project's dependencies.

Dependencies   ADD DEPENDENCIES... ⌘

Config Server   SPRING CLOUD CONFIG
Central management for configuration via Git, SVN, or HashiCorp Vault.

Eureka Discovery Client   SPRING CLOUD DISCOVERY
A REST based service for locating services for the purpose of load balancing and failover of middle-tier servers.

Cloud LoadBalancer   SPRING CLOUD ROUTING
Client-side load-balancing with Spring Cloud LoadBalancer.

Spring Boot Actuator   OPS
Supports built in (or custom) endpoints that let you monitor and manage your application - such as application health, metrics, sessions, etc.

Figure 7.15: The project's dependencies

Spring Cloud Config enables central management. Eureka Discovery Clients connects the configuration service to service discovery and client load balancing. Spring Boot Actuator provides valuable endpoints to manage the configuration server.

The following code snippet presents the main Spring Boot class with the @ EnableConfigServer annotation:

```
@EnableConfigServer
@SpringBootApplication
public class ConfigurationServicesApplication {
```

The @EnableConfigServer annotation enables the Spring Cloud Config Server, and the following configuration snippet refines its configuration:

```
spring.cloud.config.server.git.uri= https://github.com/wandersonxs/
online-auction-configuration.git
spring.cloud.config.server.git.default-label=main
```

The spring.cloud.config.server.git.uri property sets the GitHub repository address where the configuration files are, and spring.cloud.config.server.git.default-label sets the branch to get the files from, in this case, the main branch.

Once the configuration server is running, we can access the configuration files data at http://localhost:8888/authentication-services.yml, where authentication-services is the service name. We can use .yml to get the result as yml or .properties to get the result as properties, as illustrated in *Figure 7.16*.

```
spring.application.name: authentication-services
server.port: 8080
eureka.client.serviceUrl.defaultZone: http://local
eureka.instance.preferIpAddress: true
spring.data.mongodb.uri: mongodb://auction_app:auc
management.endpoints.web.exposure.include: *
security.jwt.secret-key: db839c04439bf54361bea3985
security.jwt.expiration-time: 86400000
```

Figure 7.16: authentication-services configuration

The configuration data for authentication-services is presented as properties. If we change the path to user-services.yml, the user services' configuration data will result as a YAML file. Let's adapt the services to connect to the configuration server to get the data.

Adapting the services to connect to the configuration server

Let's get the authentication services and set it up to connect to the configuration services. The process is the same for all other services.

Add the following dependencies to the service:

```xml
<dependency>
  <groupId>org.springframework.cloud</groupId>
  <artifactId>spring-cloud-starter-config</artifactId>
</dependency>
<dependency>
    <groupId>org.springframework.cloud</groupId>
    <artifactId>spring-cloud-starter-bootstrap</artifactId>
</dependency>
```

`spring-cloud-starter-config` is the client that enables the connection to the configuration server. `spring-cloud-starter-bootstrap` ensures that the configuration properties from the Spring Cloud Config Server are loaded before the main application context is initialized. In other words, without it, the application would try to inject a property before getting it from the configuration server, and the application would crash.

The following configuration snippet presents the new properties:

```
spring.application.name=authentication-services
server.port=8080
spring.config.import=optional:configserver:${CONFIG_SERVER_URI:http://
localhost:8888}
```

The application name and port configuration should be specified locally in the project because these settings are essential for the Spring Boot application's initial startup and bootstrapping. The `spring.config.import=optional:configserver:${CONFIG_SERVER_URI:http://localhost:8888}` property instructs Spring Boot to retrieve configuration from configuration services. The `CONFIG_SERVER_URI` environment variable specifies the URL for the service, defaulting to `http://localhost:8888` if it is not set. The `optional:` prefix ensures that the application can start even if the configuration services are unavailable.

That is it! When the authentication services are started, they will look up the configuration in the configuration server. And if we update a property's value while the services are already running, the changes will automatically be picked up without requiring a restart.

What happens if properties' values change?

If we update a value's property in the GitHub repository for an application, the configuration server will serve the latest value's property version. However, if the application is running, Spring Boot won't update the value's property for the application running. So, we can restart the application or use an annotation provided by the Spring Boot Actuator, `@RefreshScope`. The following code snippet shows this:

```
@RefreshScope
@SpringBootApplication
public class AuthenticationServicesApplication {
```

The `@RefreshScope` annotation has been added to the main Spring Boot application class. Then, Spring Boot Actuator provides us with the `/actuator/refresh` endpoint to get the newest values from the configuration server. The following `curl` command can be executed to achieve this refresh:

```
curl -X POST http://localhost:8080/actuator/refresh
```

Externalizing configurations to a configuration server and using a Git repository simplifies configuration management, ensuring consistency and ease of updates across multiple environments and services. Let's now learn how to apply resilience to our services using Resilience4J.

Applying resilience with Resilience4J

Resilience is crucial for maintaining system stability and reliability in a microservices architecture. Resilience refers to the system's ability to gracefully handle and recover from failures. Unlike monolithic architectures, where a failure in one component can cause the entire system to become unavailable, microservices can be designed to isolate failures and continue to function smoothly. This is where resilience patterns and tools such as Resilience4J come into play. We will explore the five key client-side resilience patterns: circuit breaker, retry, rate limiter, bulkhead, and fallback.

Client-side resilience patterns are strategies and techniques applied at the client level to handle failures and ensure smooth operation in a distributed system, mainly when communicating with microservices. These patterns help clients cope with potential service unavailability, latency issues, and other failures, improving the overall reliability and user experience. Let's start with the circuit breaker pattern.

Circuit breaker

The circuit breaker pattern prevents a client from repeatedly invoking a failing service. It monitors the number of recent failures, and if a threshold is reached, it breaks the circuit and stops sending requests for a predefined period, giving the failing service time to recover. The circuit breaker has three states: open, half-open, and closed. *Figure 7.17* illustrates the circuit breaker states and flow.

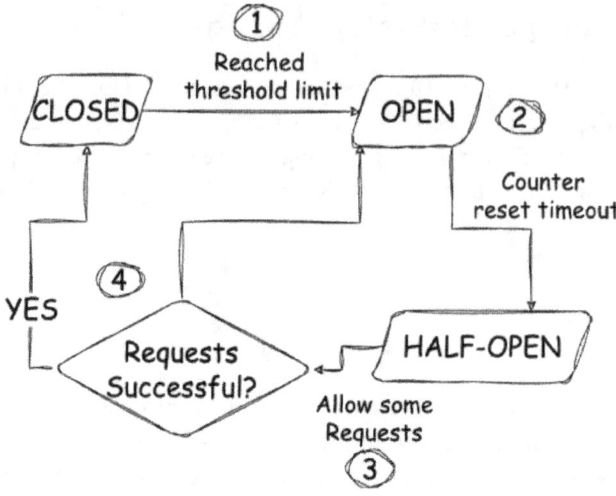

Figure 7.17: Circuit breaker states and flow

The circuit breaker flow is as follows:

1. Requests typically pass through in the closed state, but if failures exceed a threshold, the circuit breaker transitions to an open state.

2. In the open state, requests are blocked to prevent further failures. After a timeout, it moves to a half-open state.

3. In the half-open state, a limited number of test requests are allowed.

4. If successful, the state transitions back to closed; if not, it returns to open.

Now that we know how the circuit breaker works, let's implement it. The authentication service calls the user service to get the roles, so let's get this case to implement the circuit breaker pattern using Resilience4J.

The following dependencies must be added to authentication services to enable the circuit breaker resilience pattern:

```xml
<dependency>
    <groupId>io.github.resilience4j</groupId>
    <artifactId>resilience4j-spring-boot3</artifactId>
</dependency>
    <groupId>org.springframework.boot</groupId>
    <artifactId>spring-boot-starter-aop</artifactId>
</dependency>
```

`resilience4j-spring-boot3` makes managing circuit breakers in a Spring Boot application easier by integrating Resilience4J with Spring Cloud. The `spring-boot-starter-aop` dependency is needed for using Resilience4J's annotations in a Spring Boot application, as these annotations rely on Spring AOP to apply circuit breaker logic and other cross-cutting concerns.

Now, in authentication services, let's enable the circuit breaker while calling the user services to get the user roles:

```
public class UserRestApi implements UserRepository {
  @CircuitBreaker(name = "userServices")
  @Override
  public List<String> getRolesByUsername(String username){…
```

The `@CircuitBreaker` annotation activates the circuit breaker for the `getRolesByUserName` method, which retrieves user roles. `userServices` is used for circuit breaker configuration as an instance, as presented in the following configuration snippet:

```
resilience4j.circuitbreaker:
  instances:
    userServices:
      register-health-indicator: true
      wait-duration-in-open-state: 10s
      failure-rate-threshold: 10
      slow-call-rate-threshold: 10
      slow-call-duration-threshold: 1s
      minimum-number-of-calls: 5
      automatic-transition-from-open-to-half-open-enabled: true
```

Under `instances`, we define individual circuit breakers for different services, such as `userServices` or any other needed services.

When set to `true`, `register-health-indicator` enables the circuit breaker's health indicator. This allows monitoring of the circuit breaker via Spring Boot Actuator endpoints, providing health status information about the circuit breaker. This information helps understand the breaker's current state (closed, open, half-open) and overall health.

`wait-duration-in-open-state` specifies how long the circuit breaker remains open before transitioning to the half-open state. For example, if the circuit breaker trips to the open state due to exceeding the failure rate or slow call rate threshold, it will wait for 10 seconds before moving to the half-open state to test if the external service has recovered.

`failure-rate-threshold` sets the threshold for the failure rate as a percentage. If the percentage of failed calls exceeds 10%, the circuit breaker will trip to the open state.

`slow-call-rate-threshold` sets the threshold for the rate of slow calls as a percentage. If the percentage of slow calls exceeds 10%, the circuit breaker will consider this a factor in tripping to the open state.

`slow-call-duration-threshold` defines how long it takes before a call is considered slow. Any call taking at most 1 second is regarded as a slow call. This threshold is used with `slow-call-rate-threshold` to determine whether the circuit breaker should trip to the open state.

The `minimum-number-of-calls` parameter specifies the minimum number of calls required before the failure and slow call rates are calculated. The circuit breaker will only consider tripping to the open state when at least five calls have been made.

`automatic-transition-from-open-to-half-open-enabled` set to `true` will automatically transition from open to half-open.

Let's test our circuit breaker implementation.

Testing the circuit breaker

Once the circuit breaker is set up, run all services except user services. Do not run user services.

Now, let's call the authentication services endpoint, `http://localhost:8080/v1/api/auth`, a couple of times. *Figure 7.17* shows the result of this.

```
Body   Cookies   Headers (13)   Test Results

Pretty    Raw    Preview    Visualize    JSON  v

1   {
2       "type": "about:blank",
3       "title": "Internal Server Error",
4       "status": 500,
5       "detail": "CircuitBreaker 'userServices' is OPEN and does not permit further calls",
6       "instance": "/v1/api/auth",
7       "description": "Unknown internal server error."
8   }
```

Figure 7.18: Circuit breaker in open state

This indicates that the user service is open and does not permit further calls until it is closed again, and *Figure 7.19* presents the metrics for it.

```
{
  - circuitBreakers: {
     - userServices: {
          failureRate: "80.0%",
          slowCallRate: "0.0%",
          failureRateThreshold: "10.0%",
          slowCallRateThreshold: "10.0%",
          bufferedCalls: 5,
          failedCalls: 4,
          slowCalls: 0,
          slowFailedCalls: 0,
          notPermittedCalls: 3,
          state: "OPEN"
        }
     }
}
```

Figure 7.19: Circuit breaker metrics for userServices

The metrics have been obtained through the Spring Boot Actuator endpoint, `http://localhost:8080/actuator/circuitbreakers`, which presents the failure rate, slow call rate, not permitted calls, circuit breaker state, and so on.

There are many more parameters to refine our configuration, and it is worth exploring the Spring Cloud Resilience4J documentation. Now, let's check the fallback pattern.

Fallback

The fallback pattern provides an alternative response or behavior when a request for a service fails. This could be a default value, a cached response, or a call to a different service.

We only need to specify `fallbackMethod` in the `@CircuitBreaker` annotation to implement the fallback in our code:

```
@CircuitBreaker(name = "userServices",
    fallbackMethod = "getRolesFromCache")
public List<String> getRolesByUsername(String username){
```

We need to create the `getRolesFromCache` method using the following code snippet:

```
public List<String> getRolesFromCache(String username, Throwable t){
  return List.of("ROLE_GUEST");
}
```

`fallbackMethod` must obey the same return and parameters as the original method, plus the `Throwable` parameter, which is the last parameter.

Do not run the user services to test the fallback. After returning the token, check it at `https://jwt.io`. It contains the `ROLE_GUEST` that was returned by the fallback. Now, let's move on to the retry pattern.

Retry

The retry pattern allows the client to automatically retry a failed request a certain number of times before giving up. This is useful for transient errors such as network timeout, rate limiting, and service unavailability that might be resolved with a subsequent attempt.

Implementing the retry using Resilience4J is simple. The following code snippet is added above the `getRolesByUsername` function, which was made to enable the circuit breaker:

```
@Retry(name = "userServicesRetry",
    fallbackMethod = "getRolesFromCache")
```

The `@Retry` annotation enables the retry pattern, and the following configuration snippet sets up the retry mechanism:

```
resilience4j.retry:
  instances:
    userServicesRetry:
      max-attempts: 3
      wait-duration: 1s
  metrics:
    enabled: true
```

It defines retry settings for the `userServicesRetry` instance. The `max-attempts` parameter specifies a maximum of three retry attempts with a one-second pause between each attempt through the `wait-duration` parameter. The `metrics` block enables the collection of metrics to monitor the retry behavior. This setup helps handle transient failures by retrying the operation and provides visibility into the retry process through metrics.

Do not run the user services to test the retry. If you debug the code, you will see that after three retries, it calls the `getRolesFromCache` fallback, returning the `ROLE_GUEST` role. The next pattern we will explore is the rate limiter.

Rate limiter

The rate limiter pattern controls the rate of requests sent to a service to prevent it from being overwhelmed. It limits the number of requests within a given timeframe.

To implement the rate limit, the following dependency must be added:

```xml
<dependency>
  <groupId>io.github.resilience4j</groupId>
  <artifactId>resilience4j-ratelimiter</artifactId>
</dependency>
```

Add the `@RateLimiter` annotation above the method to implement the rate limiter, as shown in the following code snippet:

```java
@RateLimiter(name = "userServicesRateLimiter")
public List<String> getRolesByUsername(String username) {
```

Then, we need to specify the rate limiter configuration, as presented in the following configuration snippet:

```yaml
resilience4j:
  ratelimiter:
    metrics:
      enabled: true
    instances:
      userServicesRateLimiter:
        register-health-indicator: true
        limit-for-period: 5
        limit-refresh-period: 60s
```

The instances section defines individual rate limiter settings for `userServicesRateLimiter`. `register-health-indicator` enables the health indicator for the rate limiter, allowing it to be monitored via Spring Boot Actuator endpoints. `limit-for-period` specifies that a maximum of five calls are allowed within each refresh period, `limit-refresh-period`, which is 60 seconds here.

This setup helps control the rate of requests to a service, prevent overload, ensure fair usage, and provide visibility into the rate limiter's behavior through metrics and health indicators.

To test it, start all services and call the authentication endpoint, `http://localhost:8080/v1/api/auth`, a couple of times. *Figure 7.20* shows the result when a rate limiter is reached.

```
Body    Cookies   Headers (13)   Test Results

Pretty    Raw    Preview    Visualize    JSON  v

1  {
2      "type": "about:blank",
3      "title": "Internal Server Error",
4      "status": 500,
5      "detail": "RateLimiter 'userServicesRateLimiter' does not permit further calls",
6      "instance": "/v1/api/auth",
7      "description": "Unknown internal server error."
8  }
```

Figure 7.20: Rate limiter result

When the rate limiter is reached, further calls are permitted only when a new timeframe is established. Let's explore our last pattern, the bulkhead pattern.

Bulkhead

The bulkhead pattern isolates different parts of the system to prevent a failure in one component from cascading to others, such as heavy traffic to user services cascading to product services. This can be achieved by allocating separate resources, such as thread pools, for different services or functionalities. Resilience4j provides two bulkhead types: **SEMAPHORE**, which limits concurrent calls, which is ideal for lightweight, non-blocking operations within a single JVM, and **TREADPOOL**, which uses a bounded queue and thread pool to handle requests, making it suitable for blocking calls or I/O operations by managing concurrent threads and queuing excess requests.

The following code snippet implements the bulkhead pattern:

```
@Bulkhead(name = "userServicesBulkhead", type = Bulkhead.Type.
SEMAPHORE)
public List<String> getRolesByUsername(String username) {
```

Using Resilience4J, we only need to add the `@Bulkhead` annotation above the method and define its `type`, such as `SEMAPHORE`.

The following configuration snippet provides the configuration for the bulkhead pattern:

```
resilience4j:
  bulkhead:
    instances:
      userServicesBulkhead:
        max-concurrent-calls: 3
        max-wait-duration: 1s
    metrics:
      enabled: true
```

Within the `instances` section, the configuration specifies individual bulkhead settings for `userServicesBulkhead`. The `max-concurrent-calls` setting allows a maximum of three concurrent calls. The `max-wait-duration` setting sets the maximum wait duration to one second, meaning that if the bulkhead is full, a thread will wait up to one second for permission before failing. The `metrics` block enables the collection and exposure of metrics related to the bulkhead. This setup helps control the number of concurrent calls to a service.

To test it, add the following code to the `UserController` class at the beginning of the `getUserRoles` method:

```
Thread.sleep(20000);
```

Start all services and call the authentication endpoint `http://localhost:8080/v1/api/auth` a couple of times. *Figure 7.21* presents the return of the bulkhead.

```
Body   Cookies   Headers (13)   Test Results

Pretty     Raw      Preview      Visualize      JSON  v     ⇛

1  {
2      "type": "about:blank",
3      "title": "Internal Server Error",
4      "status": 500,
5      "detail": "Bulkhead 'userServicesBulkhead' is full and does not permit further calls",
6      "instance": "/v1/api/auth",
7      "description": "Unknown internal server error."
8  }
```

Figure 7.21: Bulkhead result

When the limit of three concurrent calls was reached, the fourth call was not permitted because the bulkhead was full.

The difference between a rate limiter and a bulkhead is that while the former limits the total calls within a timeframe, the latter limits the number of concurrent calls.

Presenting the application in a microservices architecture

Now that the online auction application has been completely implemented in a microservices architecture, its architecture is presented in *Figure 7.22*.

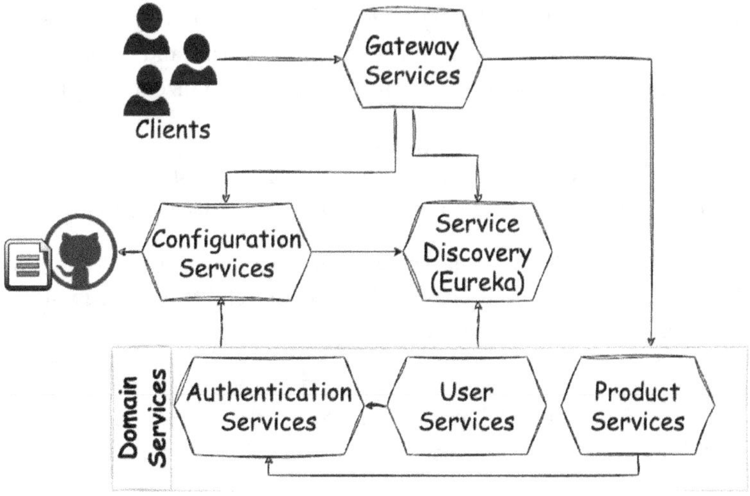

Figure 7.22: Online auction application in a microservices architecture

The figure illustrates our final online auction application, built using a microservices architecture. In this setup, clients send requests to gateway services, which then route those requests to the appropriate domain services such as authentication, users, and product services. All services are registered with a service discovery tool (Eureka) that allows dynamic lookup and communication.

Configuration services handle centralized configuration management. They retrieve settings from GitHub and apply them across all services. The implementation of client-side load-balancing and resilience patterns such as circuit breaker, fallback, retry, rate limiter, and bulkhead further enhances the architecture by ensuring service stability and reliability, even under high load or partial system failure.

This architecture demonstrates several key features: it supports scalability by allowing microservices to scale independently, enables dynamic service discovery through Eureka, maintains consistent, centralized configuration via the configuration services, and promotes loose coupling by minimizing dependencies through interactions via the gateway.

Summary

In this chapter, we explored microservices patterns with Spring Cloud. We focused on the service discovery, load balancing, gateway, configuration management, and resilience patterns.

We discussed service discovery in detail, emphasizing the dynamic mechanisms that enable seamless communication between services. We used Eureka as a case study for this discussion.

Next, we covered the importance of load balancing in distributing network traffic across multiple servers to enhance performance and reliability. We provided practical steps for implementing client-side load balancing using Spring Cloud LoadBalancer and highlighted its role in improving system robustness.

Additionally, we delved into gateway implementation with Spring Cloud Gateway, explaining how gateways act as reverse proxies to centralize routing, enhance security, and manage HTTP requests effectively. We also discussed the use of predicates and filters to customize routing logic.

The chapter also explored configuration management using Spring Cloud Config, illustrating the benefits of centralized configuration management for distributed systems. We explained how to externalize configuration properties and adapt microservices to connect to a configuration server.

Finally, we introduced resilience patterns using Resilience4J, such as circuit breaker, retry, rate limiter, bulkhead, and fallback. These patterns are essential for system stability and reliability by gracefully handling failures and ensuring seamless operation.

Overall, this chapter has equipped you with comprehensive knowledge of service discovery, load balancing, gateway, configuration management, and resilience patterns in a microservices architecture. This information is invaluable for creating robust, scalable, and maintainable microservices-based applications.

In *Chapter 8, Event-Driven Architecture*, we will explore the core principles and practical applications of event-driven architecture using Spring Cloud Stream.

Questions

1. How does Eureka facilitate dynamic communication between microservices?

2. How does client-side load balancing improve system performance in microservices?

3. What are some of the key features provided by Spring Cloud Gateway to manage API requests in microservices?

4. What is the purpose of predicates and filters in Spring Cloud Gateway, and how do they work together?

5. Why is centralized configuration management important in microservices, and how does Spring Cloud Config facilitate this?

6. What is the purpose of the circuit breaker pattern in Resilience4J, and how does it enhance system resilience?

Get This Book's PDF Version and Exclusive Extras

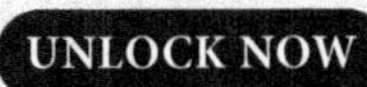

Scan the QR code (or go to `packtpub.com/unlock`). Search for this book by name, confirm the edition, and then follow the steps on the page.

Note: Keep your invoice handly. Purchase made directly from packt don't require one.

8

Event-Driven Architecture

This chapter covers event-driven architecture, which is crucial for modern software development, especially with microservices. It explains the asynchronous nature of this architecture and its benefits, such as system scalability and real-time processing capabilities. It also discusses the core components, advantages, and challenges of implementing event-driven architecture.

The chapter also approaches fundamental event concepts, discusses service interactions and workflows, and covers common event-driven patterns such as publish-subscribe, event notification, event-carried state transfer, message inbox and outbox, and the Saga pattern.

The chapter concludes by exploring and implementing an event-driven architecture in the online auction application using **Spring for Apache Kafka** with **Apache Kafka**.

This chapter will cover the following topics:

- Introducing event-driven architecture
- Understanding the fundamentals of events
- Exploring event-driven architecture patterns
- Building event-driven services with Apache Kafka

By the end of this chapter, you will have a strong grasp of the principles, patterns, and practical implementations of event-driven architecture, empowering you to design and construct scalable, resilient, and efficient event-driven systems using Spring Kafka with Apache Kafka.

Technical requirements

All the code for this chapter can be found on GitHub at `https://github.com/PacktPublishing/Software-Architecture-with-Spring/tree/main/ch8`. Ellipses in the code blocks indicate that parts of the code have been omitted, and the complete code is available on GitHub.

Introducing event-driven architecture

Event-driven architecture is a paradigm that relies on events to initiate and facilitate communication among loosely coupled services. It is a prevalent approach in applications developed using microservices.

Because of its asynchronous characteristic, event-driven architecture decouples event production from event consumption and robustly handles asynchronous data flows.

An event is a significant change in state or an occurrence that necessitates awareness and response from other parts of the system.

Asynchronous communication

In the context of event-driven architecture, asynchronous communication refers to a method of interaction where microservices exchange information without requiring both parties to be available and active simultaneously. Asynchronous communication can decouple services and allow them to communicate by sending messages that can be processed later rather than waiting for an immediate response, as in synchronous request-response communication. This is typically achieved using event brokers, queues, or streams that act as intermediaries to store and forward messages between services.

The core components of event-driven architecture

The core components of event-driven architecture are producers, events, an event broker (channel), and consumers. Let's look into these components in detail:

- **Producers**: Producers are the sources that generate events. These can be applications, services, devices, or any system component that detects a state change and emits an event to signal that change. Examples include user actions such as clicking a button, system alerts, data updates, and IoT device signals.

- **Events**: The central element of event-driven architecture represents a noteworthy change in the system or an occurrence that triggers a response.

- **Event broker (channel)**: The event broker or channel is the communication medium through which events are transmitted from producers to consumers. It can be implemented using various messaging technologies, including message brokers such as Apache Kafka and RabbitMQ, service buses, or streaming platforms.

- **Consumers**: Consumers are the components that receive and process events. They perform actions based on the events they consume, such as updating a database, triggering other processes, or communicating with other systems. Consumers can be applications, microservices, or even other event producers.

Figure 8.1 presents an event-driven architecture with its components: producers, events, an event broker, and consumers.

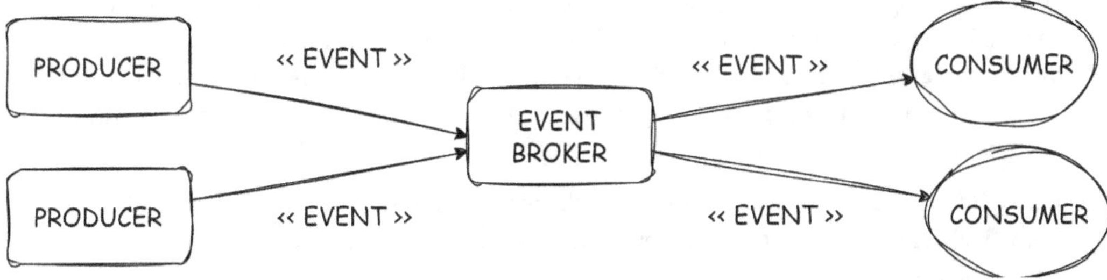

Figure 8.1: Event-driven architecture

The figure illustrates the asynchronous communication between producers and consumers through an event broker. Producers generate events, and the event broker acts as an intermediary that receives events from the producers and sends them to consumers. This diagram demonstrates how an event broker enables asynchronous communication, decoupling producers and consumers and enabling them to operate independently.

When designing and implementing such systems, it's important to understand the advantages, such as scalability, enhanced system flexibility, and resilience, and be aware of the challenges, such as ensuring message delivery reliability and managing eventual consistency. Awareness of these factors helps you make informed decisions when adopting this architecture. Now, let's explore in more detail the benefits and challenges of event-driven architecture.

Benefits of event-driven architecture

Modern software development widely uses event-driven architecture to build scalable and responsive systems. Here are some benefits and challenges of using it:

- **Scalability**: Event-driven architecture allows systems to handle many events simultaneously. It is particularly effective for distributed systems where components must operate independently and scale horizontally.

- **Loose coupling**: In an event-driven architecture system, components are decoupled, permitting them to be developed, deployed, and scaled independently. These components or services communicate through events rather than relying on direct interactions, such as those used in RESTful API calls. This decoupling results in a more robust, adaptable, and maintainable system. However, it's important to note that services remain logically coupled by the event structure and semantics. This means that any changes to the formats or meanings of events require coordination between the producers and consumers.

- **Real-time processing and responsiveness**: Event-driven architecture enables real-time or near-real-time data processing by allowing components to communicate through events, capturing and responding to changes immediately. An event broker routes events from producers to consumers, ensuring asynchronous, low-latency interactions. Technologies such as message queues and event streams support efficient event handling and scalability, making it ideal for applications needing immediate responses, such as financial trading systems, monitoring systems, and IoT applications.

- **Resilience**: Event-driven architecture can enhance system resilience by isolating failures from individual components. If one component fails, others can continue to operate, reducing the risk of total system failure.

- **Simplified integration**: Event-driven architecture facilitates integration between heterogeneous systems and services through an event bus or messaging system, making it easier to integrate new services without significantly changing existing ones.

As everything has trade-offs, let's check out the challenges of using an event-driven architecture.

Challenges of event-driven architecture

Alongside the advantages of event-driven architecture, there are challenges that we must be aware of:

- **Complexity**: Designing and implementing event-driven systems demands careful planning to manage event flows, service dependencies, and potential race conditions, where multiple services process events in parallel, and the outcome depends on the order in which those events are handled. Proper event flow management is essential to ensure the correct processing order and to prevent message loss or duplication.

- **Debugging and monitoring**: Event-driven systems can pose significant management challenges due to their asynchronous nature. Tracing the flow of events and identifying the source of issues requires advanced monitoring and logging tools. To address debugging and monitoring challenges in event-driven architecture, utilize advanced monitoring tools such as Prometheus and Grafana for real-time insights and centralized logging solutions such as the **Elasticsearch, Logstash, and Kibana (ELK)** stack for aggregating logs. Employ distributed tracing tools such as Zipkin and Jaeger to visualize event flows and set up alerting systems for real-time issue detection. Maintain detailed documentation and use visualization tools to map out event flows, aiding in understanding and debugging the system.

- **Consistency**: Maintaining data consistency in an event-driven architecture can be challenging due to out-of-order event arrivals or variations in processing times. Consistency can be achieved through event sourcing, distributed transaction patterns such as the message inbox and outbox pattern and the Saga pattern, and designing for eventual consistency, which ensures that while data may be temporarily inconsistent, it will eventually converge to a correct state. Additionally, idempotent event handlers prevent unintended side effects by ensuring that reprocessing the same event multiple times has the same result as processing it once.

- **Event overload**: Excessive event generation can strain the event broker, increasing storage needs and processing latencies. Effective event filtering and prioritization help ensure that only meaningful events are produced and consumed efficiently.

- **Data duplication**: In an event-driven architecture, data duplication across services can lead to synchronization challenges. To address data duplication, use unique event identifiers, idempotent operations, and eventual consistency models. A centralized event store can also help synchronize data and reduce inconsistencies.

- **Latency**: In an event-driven architecture, managing latency is crucial. Strategies include optimizing network communication, using efficient event processing, employing asynchronous processing, and implementing load balancing and scaling to distribute the workload.

- **Transaction management**: Implementing transactions across multiple services in an event-driven system can be complex. Traditional **two-phase commit** (**2PC**) protocols ensure atomicity by making all participants agree to commit or roll back changes. However, 2PC introduces tight coupling, blocking behavior, and coordination overhead, making it less suitable for distributed, highly scalable architectures where services must remain independent and loosely coupled. Instead, alternative patterns such as the Saga pattern are preferred. The Saga pattern divides a transaction into smaller, independent steps with compensating actions in case of failure, ensuring eventual consistency rather than immediate consistency. This makes Saga suitable for long-running business processes where strict atomicity is not required. Other alternatives include idempotent event processing, where duplicate events do not cause unintended side effects, and transactional outbox patterns, which ensure that events are reliably published alongside database changes without requiring distributed transactions.

Event-driven architecture offers significant benefits in scalability, real-time processing, responsiveness capabilities, resilience, flexibility, and simplified integration. However, it also introduces complexity, consistency, difficulties in debugging and monitoring, and transaction management challenges. Now that we have looked into event-driven architecture, let's explore events.

Understanding the fundamentals of events

Event-driven architecture revolves around events. Understanding the fundamentals of events is crucial for designing and implementing robust event-driven architecture systems. This section explores events' core aspects, characteristics, types, and how they fit into the overall architecture.

What is an event?

An event is a significant change in state or occurrence within a system that interests other system components. It represents an action or condition triggering a response or processing by other system parts. Events are fundamental communication units in event-driven architecture, allowing systems to react to changes in real time.

Characteristics of events

Events have characteristics that define their nature and how they are handled within an event-driven architecture system:

- **Immutable**: Events must be immutable, meaning they cannot be altered after publication. This ensures consistency across distributed systems. If a correction is needed, a new compensating event should be emitted instead of updating an existing one.

- **Temporal**: Events occur at a specific point in time. They often include timestamps to indicate when the event took place.

- **Descriptive**: Events carry information about what happened and may include relevant data or metadata. This data helps consumers understand and process the event.

- **Asynchronous**: Events are typically processed asynchronously, allowing for decoupled and independent operations between producers and consumers.

Events can be classified into some types; let's explore them.

Acknowledging the types of events

Events can be categorized based on their nature and purpose:

- **Simple events**: Basic occurrences that do not involve complex logic or multiple conditions are known as simple events. They usually involve a straightforward action or change in state and typically carry minimal information. These events are often used in systems where real-time processing is crucial. For example, a temperature sensor reading in an IoT system might generate simple events every time a new reading is available.

- **Composite events**: Composite events are complex events composed of multiple simple events, often representing a higher-level condition or pattern. They involve the correlation of multiple simple events and are used for detecting patterns or aggregating information across events. In a security monitoring system, for example, detecting a security breach might involve combining multiple events, such as failed login attempts and suspicious access patterns.

- **Domain events**: Domain events are significant occurrences within the business domain that reflect a state change or condition that the domain experts care about. They represent essential milestones within the domain, such as *Order Placed* or *Customer Registered*. Domain events often carry business-specific data and notify other parts of the system about changes that might affect their behavior. In an e-commerce system, for example, when a customer places an order, a domain event might be generated to initiate processes such as payment and inventory checks.

- **System events**: System events are related to the internal workings or infrastructure of the system, such as resource availability, performance metrics, or system failures. They are often generated by the system and used for monitoring, management, or maintenance purposes. For example, an event indicating that a server's CPU usage has exceeded a certain threshold is a system event that might trigger scaling operations.

Events define a schema and contracts between producers and consumers independent of the event type. Let's understand what event schemas and contracts are.

Event schemas and contracts

Events are defined using schemas or contracts to ensure consistent communication between producers and consumers. An event schema specifies the structure and format of the event data, including required fields, data types, and any optional metadata. Typical formats for defining event schemas include JSON, Avro, and Protocol Buffers.

Event contracts are agreements between producers and consumers on events' expected structure and behavior. They provide a shared understanding of how events should be created, transmitted, and processed, reducing the risk of miscommunication and errors.

Fetching data models

In event-driven architecture, the push and pull models are the two fundamental approaches to managing event distribution and processing.

Push model

In the push model, events are actively sent (pushed) to consumers by the event source or an intermediary, such as an event broker. *Figure 8.2* illustrates the push model.

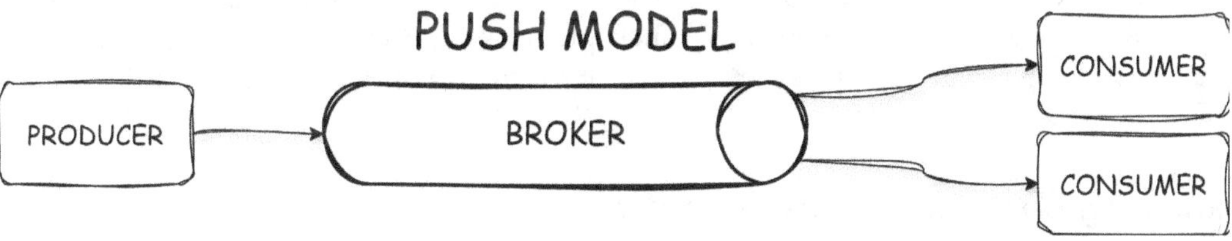

Figure 8.2: Push model

When an event occurs, it is immediately dispatched to all subscribed consumers, who then process it in real time. This model is often used in scenarios where low latency is crucial, and events must be processed as soon as they occur. For example, the push model ensures that users receive updates instantly in a real-time notification system.

Message brokers and cloud services implementing the push model include RabbitMQ and AWS **Simple Notification Service (SNS)**.

Pull model

In the pull model, consumers actively request (pull) events from an event source or intermediary at their own pace. *Figure 8.3* illustrates the pull model.

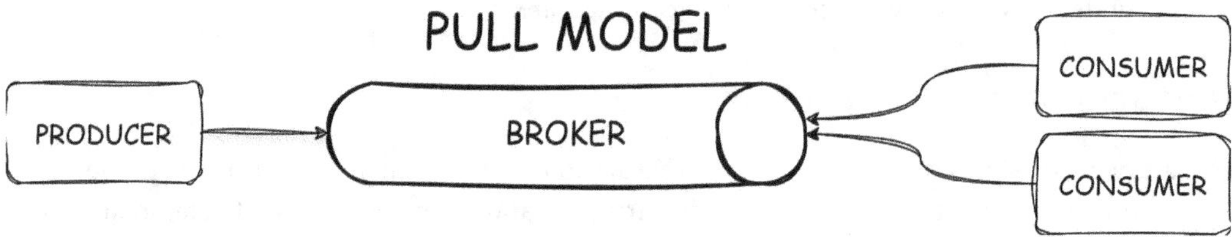

Figure 8.3: Pull model

Instead of being pushed to consumers, events are stored in a queue or topic, and consumers poll this storage periodically to retrieve and process events. This model is helpful in scenarios where consumers must control the event or batch processing rate. For instance, a data analytics pipeline might use the pull model to fetch and process data in manageable chunks.

Message brokers that implement the pull model include Apache Kafka and **AWS Simple Queue Service (SQS)**.

The choice between push and pull models depends on the system's requirements. The push model is ideal for applications requiring immediate event processing and low latency, but it can lead to issues if the consumer cannot keep up with the event rate. On the other hand, the pull model provides greater flexibility and control over event processing rates, but it can introduce latency due to the polling interval.

In an event-driven architecture system, a combination of both models might be employed to balance real-time processing needs with the ability to handle varying workloads effectively. Now, let's learn about two common architectural styles for managing interactions and controlling the flow between the services.

Managing interactions and workflow

Event-driven architecture usually employs two common architectural styles to manage and control workflow between services: orchestration and choreography. They are two distinct approaches to managing interactions and workflows in distributed systems. Both methods aim to coordinate the activities of multiple services to achieve a specific business goal, but they differ significantly in their control mechanisms and design philosophies.

Orchestration

Orchestration refers to a centralized approach where a central controller, often called an **orchestrator**, manages and directs the interactions between services. The orchestrator coordinates the sequence of service invocations and ensures that the overall workflow progresses according to a predefined plan. The following are the main characteristics of orchestration:

- **Centralized control**: A single orchestrator controls the flow of operations, deciding which services to call and in what order

- **Explicit workflow definition**: The workflow logic is explicitly defined within the orchestrator

- **Ease of management**: Centralized control makes managing and monitoring the overall workflow easier, as the orchestrator coordinates all interactions

- **Error handling**: The orchestrator can implement complex error handling and compensation logic, ensuring the workflow can recover from failures

Figure 8.4 presents the flow of e-commerce using an orchestrator architectural style.

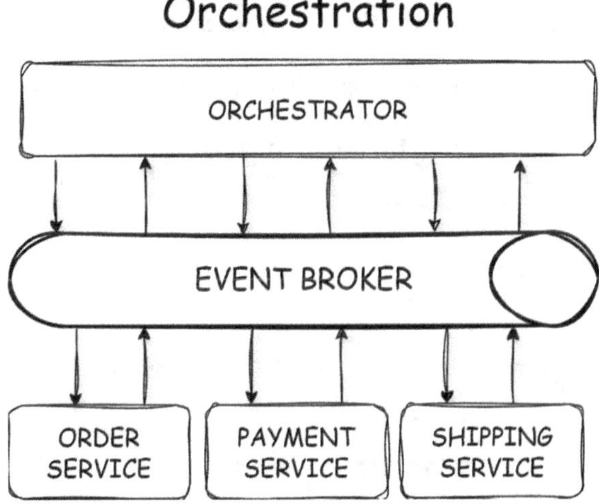

Figure 8.4: Orchestration architectural style

In the orchestration architectural style, a central orchestrator service controls the sequence of operations and interactions between services via a message broker. When a customer places an order, the order service processes it and sends an event to the orchestrator through the event broker. The orchestrator then sends an event to the payment service via the event broker. Once the payment service completes the payment, it sends an event back to the orchestrator through the event broker, which then sends an event to the shipping service. The orchestrator manages the communication between services to ensure each step is executed in the correct order.

Now, let's learn about another architectural style for managing and controlling workflow between services: choreography.

Choreography

Choreography refers to a decentralized approach where each service independently decides when and how to interact with other services based on events. There is no central controller; instead, services communicate directly with each other, reacting to events and making autonomous decisions. The main characteristics of choreography are as follows:

- **Decentralized control**: Each service has autonomy and makes decisions based on the events it receives, leading to a more loosely coupled system

- **Implicit workflow definition**: The workflow emerges from the interactions between services rather than being explicitly defined in a central location

- **Scalability and flexibility**: The decentralized nature of choreography can lead to better scalability and flexibility, as services can be added or modified without changing a central controller

- **Complexity in coordination**: Managing the overall workflow can become complex, as there is no single point of control to oversee the entire process

Figure 8.5 presents the flow of e-commerce using a choreography architectural style.

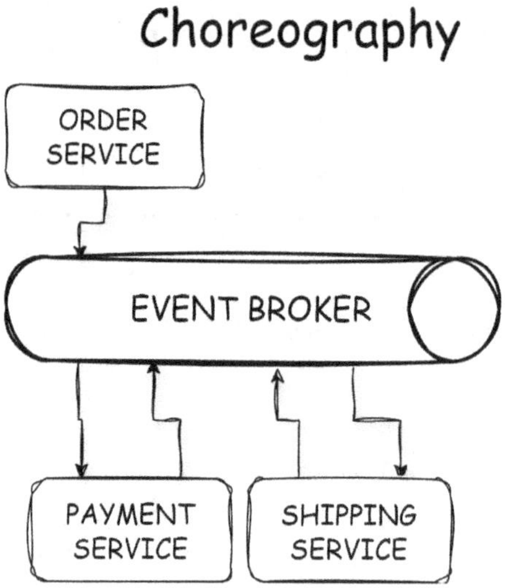

Figure 8.5: Choreography architectural style

In choreography architecture, services communicate by reacting to events from other services without a central coordinator. When a customer places an order, the order service processes it and notifies the payment service. The payment service processes the payment and notifies the shipping service. Each service operates independently, enhancing scalability and allowing independent evolution.

Another fundamental difference lies in the type of messages exchanged in each style. In orchestration, messages are typically commands—explicit instructions sent by the orchestrator to tell a service what action to perform next. The orchestrator determines the flow and actively directs the involved services. In contrast, choreography relies on events, representing facts about things that have already happened. Services react to these events and decide independently what action to take in response. This distinction reinforces the centralized nature of orchestration, where control flows through command messages, and the decentralized nature of choreography, where control emerges from the event stream.

Both orchestration and choreography have their advantages and use cases. Orchestration suits scenarios where central control and explicit workflow definition are beneficial, making managing and monitoring complex workflows easier. On the other hand, choreography is ideal for systems requiring high scalability and flexibility, where services must operate autonomously and respond to events dynamically.

Choosing between orchestration and choreography depends on the system's requirements, including the complexity of workflows, flexibility, and the desired level of control over service interactions. In many cases, a hybrid use of orchestration and choreography can provide the best balance, leveraging the advantages of each technique to accomplish the desired system behavior.

We have now explored and grasped event-driven architecture. Next, let's explore important and commonly used event-driven patterns in an event-driven architecture.

Exploring event-driven architecture patterns

Event-driven architecture leverages various design patterns to effectively handle events and ensure robust, scalable, and maintainable systems. These patterns help manage event generation, transmission, processing, and storage complexities. We will present some commonly used patterns in event-driven architecture.

Publish-subscribe

The **publish-subscribe pattern** in event-driven architecture involves producers sending events to a broker, which distributes the events to multiple consumers. Messages are pushed to consumers, and consumers can be added or removed without affecting the producer. A durable subscription allows inactive consumers to receive missed events upon reconnection.

An example is a social media platform where users subscribe to updates from other users. When a user posts a new update, it is published to all subscribers.

Event notification

Event notification is a simple pattern where the producer emits an event to inform consumers that a change or action has occurred. These events carry minimal information, so consumers may need to fetch additional data if required. While this approach reduces event size and is easy to implement, it can increase latency and create tighter coupling by requiring follow-up requests.

The following JSON snippet illustrates an example of a user placing a bid on an item in the auction system:

```
{
    "userId": "1",
    "productId": "2",
    "bidAmount": 150.00
}


WITH:


{
    "eventType": "BidAdded",
    "userId": "1",
    "productId": "2",
    "bidAmount": 150.00
}
```

Note that the event notification pattern only includes the user and product IDs, so the event contains minimal information for other services. *Figure 8.6* illustrates service interactions using an event notification pattern.

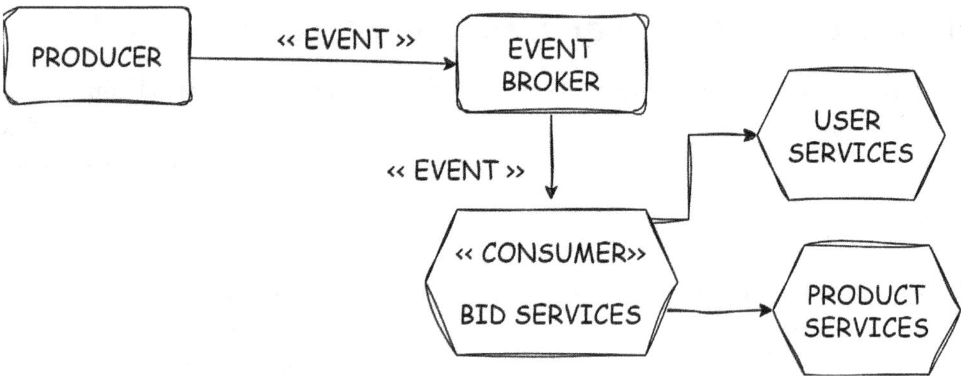

Figure 8.6: Service interaction using the event notification pattern

If the consumer needs more user or product data, additional service requests are required, creating a coupling between services. This can cause delays, lower system performance, and create dependencies that make the system harder to manage and maintain. Possible solutions to minimize the tight coupling between services would be implementing a shared cache or using the pattern event-carried state transfer.

Event-carried state transfer

In the **event-carried state transfer pattern**, events contain all the information consumers need to process, eliminating the need to fetch additional data.

The following code snippet presents an example of the previous JSON with complete user and item data:

```
{
  "user": {
    "id": "112233",
    "name": "Wanderson Xesquevixos"
  },
  "product": {
    "id": "98765",
    "description": "Sport Car 1977"
  },
  "bidAmount": 150.00
}
```

This reduces latency by providing all necessary data within the event and simplifies consumer logic. However, events can become large and may contain redundant information.

Message outbox pattern

The message outbox pattern ensures reliable event publishing in distributed systems while preserving data consistency. Before sending a message, the service saves it to a database outbox table within the same transaction that updates the business data. A background process then reads from this table and publishes the event to the broker. This approach prevents message loss if the service crashes after committing the transaction but before sending the event, ensuring that every persisted change is eventually reflected in the event stream. An example is an e-commerce application that saves an order in the database while simultaneously storing an `OrderPlaced` event in the outbox table. This event is later published to notify other services, maintaining a consistent view between the internal data state and external event consumers.

Message inbox pattern

The message inbox pattern consumes and processes messages reliably in distributed systems while preserving data consistency. When a service receives an event, it first stores the message in a dedicated inbox table before executing any business logic. This approach helps prevent duplicate processing and enables exactly-once or idempotent execution, even in crashes or retries. By persisting the message before processing, the system ensures that operations are only applied once, maintaining consistency between the event stream and the service's internal state. For example, a billing service receiving a `PaymentConfirmed` event writes the message to its inbox table and checks whether it has already been processed. Only then does it apply the payment logic, avoiding double charging and ensuring a consistent transactional outcome.

Saga pattern

The **Saga pattern** manages long-running transactions and ensures data consistency across multiple services by breaking a transaction into smaller steps, each of which can be compensated if it fails. It represents a single business process, as illustrated in *Figure 8.7*.

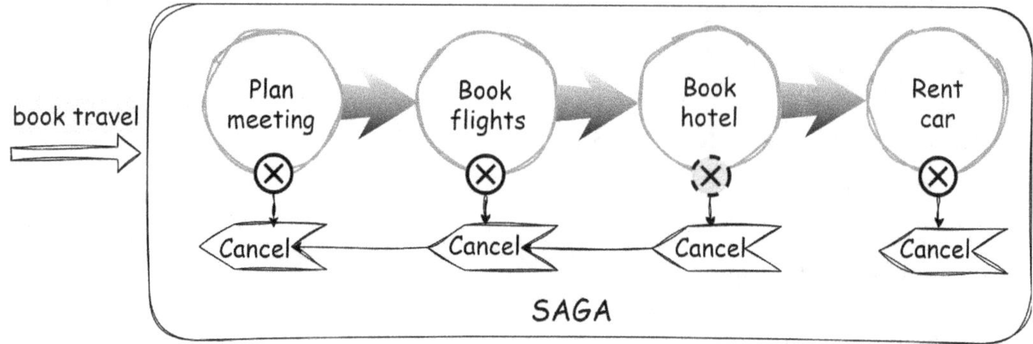

Figure 8.7: The Saga pattern process

In a travel booking system, a saga coordinates the booking of flights, hotels, and vehicle rentals. If any step fails, the saga triggers compensating actions to cancel the already completed bookings.

The Saga pattern ensures data consistency and handles long-running transactions. However, it is complex to implement and manage compensating transactions.

We've learned many new concepts; now, let's move on to the next section and apply them by implementing event-driven services in our online auction application.

Building event-driven services with Apache Kafka

Now, it's time to start coding and put what we've learned into practice. I'm excited about event-driven architecture because it is scalable, flexible, and responsive and introduces techniques and tools that enhance performance and resilience. Let's explore the powerful possibilities event-driven architecture brings in our online auction case study.

Online auction case study

Since we switched our online auction to a microservices architecture and incorporated features such as gateway, load balancing, distributed configuration, and applying resilience, our system has become more reliable and efficient. Users are now enjoying the improved performance, and issues with the application have been minimal.

The stakeholders have requested an important new feature for the system: the ability for users to place bids on products in auctions. An essential requirement is that the user must have an account with enough funds to approve the bid at the auction.

System definition and mission

Our technical team is committed to providing a reliable bidding experience. We will use an event-driven architecture to connect our auction and escrow services to achieve this goal. This approach allows the auction service to initiate bids while the escrow service verifies fund availability, enabling both systems to operate independently and scale as needed.

Additionally, we will use Kafka as the backbone for event delivery, supporting reliable coordination between services and enabling patterns such as Saga to maintain eventual consistency in distributed transactions.

Let's begin by setting up our event-driven environment, exploring and configuring Apache Kafka, also known as Kafka.

Introduction to Kafka

Apache Kafka is a distributed platform designed for event streaming and can process trillions of events daily. Originally developed by LinkedIn, Kafka has become a vital component of modern data architectures, serving as a backbone for real-time data streaming applications.

Kafka's primary role is to provide a reliable, scalable, and durable mechanism for asynchronous message exchange between different components of an application. It acts as a publish-subscribe messaging system, where producers publish events to topics, and consumers subscribe to these topics to consume events in real time.

Kafka's ability to process and transmit data at high throughput makes it a popular choice for use cases ranging from logging and monitoring to complex data pipelines, stream processing, and microservices architectures.

The main characteristics of Kafka

Apache Kafka boasts several characteristics that set it apart as a robust and versatile event streaming platform:

- **Distributed architecture**: Kafka's architecture includes brokers, producers, consumers, and topics. Thanks to its distributed architecture, Kafka can manage vast amounts of data across several nodes, providing high availability and fault tolerance.

- **Topic-based organization**: Data in Kafka is organized into topics. Each topic can have multiple partitions that can be independently consumed. This enables concurrent processing and load balancing.

An example is a topic with three partitions:

- If there is only one service instance, then it will handle all three partitions

- If there are two instances, one instance will handle two partitions, and the other will handle the other partition

- Each partition will be allocated to one service instance if there are three instances

- If there are four instances, three instances will each handle one partition, and one instance will be idle

- **Offsets**: In Kafka, the position of a consumer within a partition is tracked using offsets. Each message in a partition has a unique offset, and consumers must commit their current offset to Kafka. This ensures that consumers can resume from where they stopped in case of failure, ensuring reliable message processing. It also allows for the flexibility to replay messages by resetting the offset.

- **Consumer groups**: Kafka enables consumers to be organized into groups. Each consumer in a group processes messages from a subset of partitions, allowing for parallel consumption and load distribution. Only one consumer processes each message from a partition within the group.

- **Commit log storage**: Kafka's storage model is based on a commit log, where messages are stored in the order they are produced. This immutable log ensures data integrity and provides a reliable audit trail of events.

- **Exactly once semantics**: Kafka ensures messages are delivered precisely once, preventing loss or duplication. This is critical for maintaining data accuracy and consistency in complex processing scenarios.

Figure 8.8 illustrates a simplified architecture of Apache Kafka.

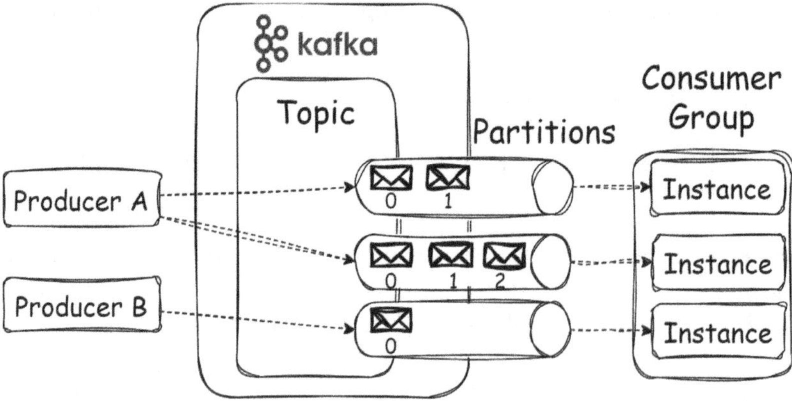

Figure 8.8: Simplified Apache Kafka architecture

The diagram provides a simplified overview of the Apache Kafka architecture, highlighting the interaction between producers, topics, partitions, and consumer instances. The topic has three partitions: partitions 0, 1, and 2. Each partition maintains an ordered sequence of messages, with offsets starting from zero.

When producers send a message without specifying a partition, Kafka automatically determines the partition using a built-in strategy. If a key is provided, Kafka assigns messages with the same key to the same partition, maintaining order. If no key is provided, Kafka uses a round-robin approach to distribute messages across partitions evenly. Additionally, Kafka allows for custom partitioning logic if needed. This approach ensures load balancing and message order consistency where required.

A consumer group is a set of service instances that share the same group ID. Within a consumer group, each topic partition is allocated to exactly one consumer instance. If you have three service instances in the same consumer group and three partitions, each instance will be assigned to one partition, ensuring that each message in a partition is consumed by only one instance. If one of the instances goes down, Kafka will automatically reassign the partitions that were allocated to that instance to the remaining operational instances within the group, ensuring continued processing without duplication.

Now that we understand what Kafka is, let's explore Spring for Apache Kafka.

Exploring Spring for Apache Kafka

Spring for Apache Kafka is a Spring project that seamlessly integrates Spring applications and Apache Kafka. It builds on the familiar Spring programming model, offering abstractions and configurations that simplify Kafka producer and consumer development. With Spring for Apache Kafka, we can easily create, configure, and manage Kafka-based messaging within a Spring Boot application, using annotations such as `@KafkaListener` for consuming messages and `KafkaTemplate` for producing them.

The framework also integrates with other Spring modules, such as Spring Retry, Spring Transaction, and Spring Boot Actuator, enabling robust features such as error handling, retries, message conversions, and metrics collection. By leveraging dependency injection, declarative configuration, and consistent APIs, Spring for Apache Kafka helps us to focus on business logic while reducing boilerplate code and ensuring clean separation of concerns in event-driven architectures.

Designing the new functionalities

Before implementing the new features, let's design the architecture of our online auction application. *Figure 8.9* illustrates the architecture of the online auction application, including the newly added auction and escrow services.

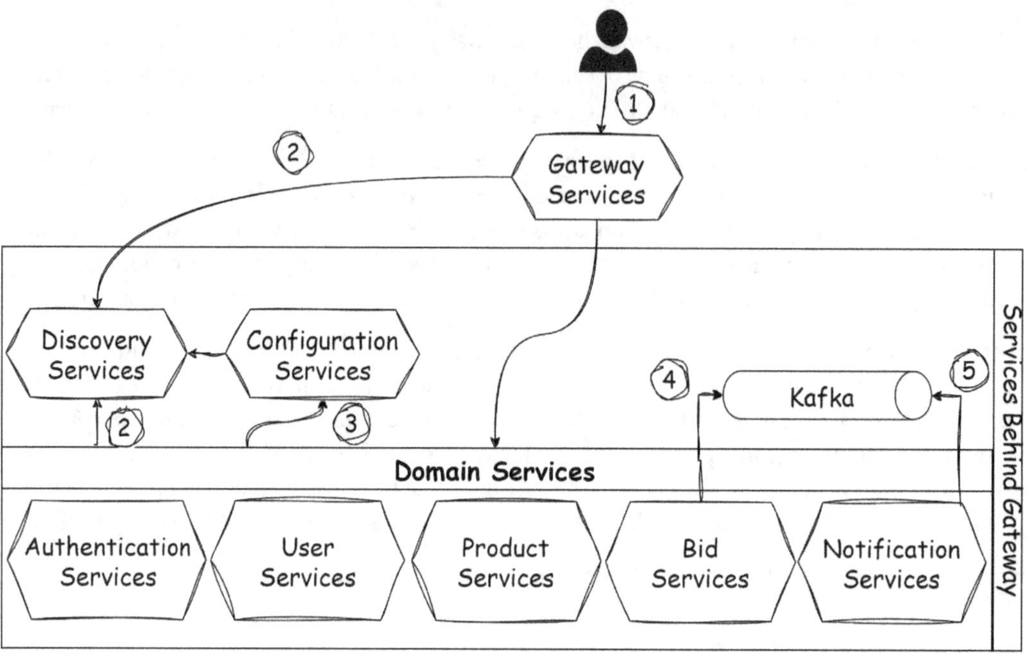

Figure 8.9: Online auction architecture

Let's outline the architecture of our online auction application:

- Clients interact exclusively with the gateway services, which act as the single entry point and route incoming requests to the appropriate downstream services

- When starting up, the services are registered in the discovery services (Eureka)

- Services retrieve their configuration from configuration services

- Auction services handles the bids and communicates with escrow services through messages via Kafka, the message broker

With the architecture of our online auction application defined, we can now turn our attention to the bidding flow. *Figure 8.10* illustrates the end-to-end process when a user places a bid.

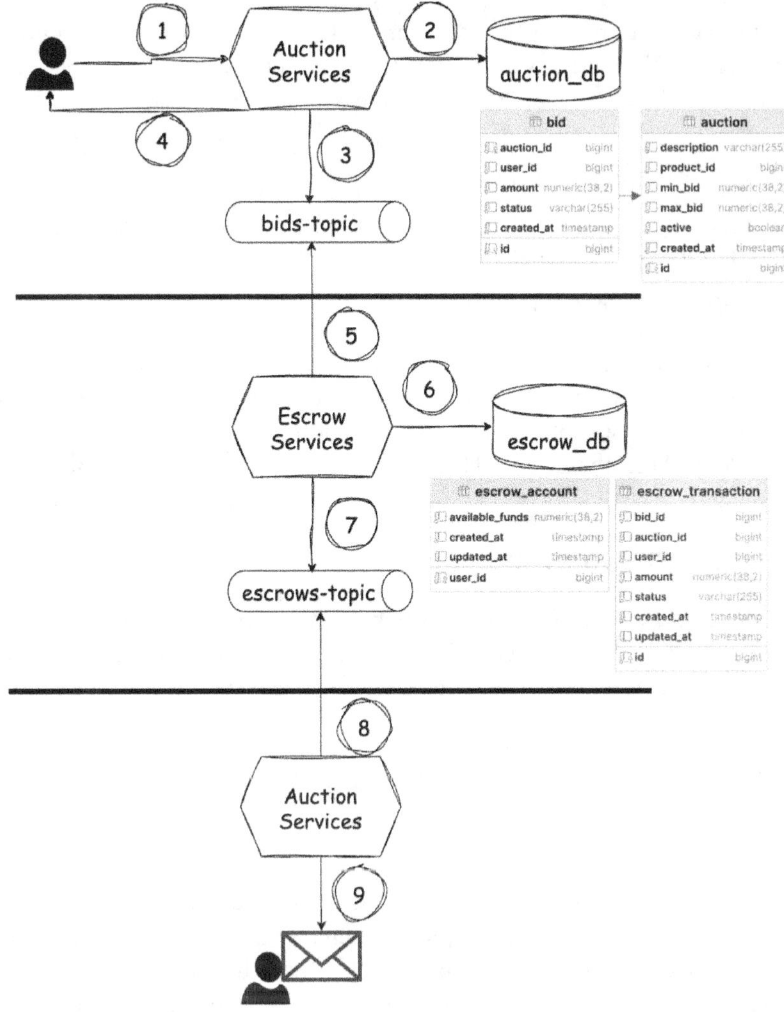

Figure 8.10: End-to-end process of placing a bid

Let's review the process of placing a bid from end to end:

1. The user adds a bid in an auction via the auction services API.

2. The auction services API saves the bid with the status as `PENDING` in the database.

3. The auction services API publishes an event to the Kafka topic named `bids-topic`. This message contains `bidId`, `userId`, `auctionId`, `amount`, and `createdAt`.

4. The auction services API returns to the user, informing them that their bid was placed.

5. The escrow services API listens to the `bids-topic` Kafka topic. When a new message arrives, it checks whether the user has sufficient funds in their escrow account.

6. The escrow services API reviews the user's fund balance alongside the total amount of bids they have reserved. The bid is accepted if the total amount of reserved bids, plus the current bid amount, is less than or equal to the user's fund balance. Otherwise, it is rejected.

7. The escrow services API then emits a new event to the `escrows-topic` Kafka topic. This event includes a status indicating whether the bid was accepted or rejected.

8. The auction services API listens to the `escrows-topic` Kafka topic. Upon receiving a message, the bid status is updated in the bid table.

9. The auction services API notifies the user.

With this detailed design in place, we are well-prepared to transition from planning to execution. It's time to start coding the new services, ensuring we adhere to the architectural guidelines and leverage best practices to build scalable, reliable, and efficient solutions. This coding phase will bring the architecture to life, enabling the enhanced features that will drive value for our users and support the platform's ongoing success.

Implementing the auction services

To create the auction services, we can use **Spring Initializr**. The dependencies for the auction services API are the same as those for other projects, such as the user services API. The only difference is that we must include the Spring for Apache Kafka dependency, as shown in the following code snippet:

```xml
<dependency>
  <groupId>org.springframework.kafka</groupId>
  <artifactId>spring-kafka</artifactId>
</dependency>
```

The `spring-kafka` dependency enables seamless integration between Spring applications and Apache Kafka. It provides support for producing and consuming Kafka messages, along with features such as serialization, deserialization, listener containers, and error handling, making it essential for implementing event-driven communication between services in the online auction application.

The following code snippet presents our controller for handling the bid placement:

```java
@RequestMapping("/v1/bids")
public class BidController {
  @PostMapping
  public BidResponse create(
    @RequestBody BidRequest bidRequest) {

    Bid bid = BidMapper.INSTANCE.map(bidRequest);
    bidRequest.setCreatedAt(bidRequest.getCreatedAt());
    Bid bid1 = createBidUseCase.execute(bid);
    return BidMapper.INSTANCE.map(bid1);

}
```

To receive bid requests, the `BidController` class exposes a REST endpoint under `/v1/bids` through a `POST` operation. It serves as the entry point for users to place bids. The method delegates the bid creation logic to `createBidUseCase.execute`, which initiates the process of placing the bid.

The following code snippet defines the `BidDatasource` class, which implements the `BidRepository` interface:

```java
public class BidDatasource implements BidRepository {
  private final BidProducer bidProducer;
  @Override
  public Bid save(Bid bid) {
    BidEntity bidentity = BidMapper.INSTANCE.toEntity(bid);
    bidentity.setStatus(BidStatus.PENDING.name());
    Bid bidSaved = BidMapper.INSTANCE.map(
      bidJpaRepository.save(bidentity));
    bidProducer.placeBid(bidSaved);
    return bidSaved;
  }
}
```

The `save` method of the `BidDatasource` class orchestrates the bid-related business logic. It persists the bid with a `PENDING` status and publishes the event through `BidProducer`, initiating the asynchronous bidding flow. The following code snippet presents the `BidProducer` class:

```java
@Slf4j
@Component
public class BidProducer {
  private final KafkaTemplate<String, Bid> kafkaTemplate;
  private static final String BIDS_TOPIC = "bids-topic";
  private static final String KEY_BIDS_TOPIC = "key-bids";
  ...
  public void placeBid(Bid bid) {
    log.info("Place bid: {}", bid);
    kafkaTemplate.send(BIDS_TOPIC, KEY_BIDS_TOPIC, bid);
    log.info("Bid {} sent to bids topic to validate user
      funds!", bid.getId());
  }
}
```

The `BidProducer` class is responsible for publishing bid-related events to Kafka, allowing asynchronous processing by other services, such as the escrow service. It acts as the event producer in the auction service, sending bid messages to the `bids-topic` Kafka topic.

`KafkaTemplate<K, V>` is a high-level abstraction for interacting with Kafka, where `K` is the message key type and `V` is the message value type—in this case, `String` for the key and a `Bid` object for the payload. It handles serialization, partitioning, retries, and error handling, simplifying Kafka operations.

In the `placeBid` method, the `kafkaTemplate.send` function is used to dispatch the `bid` message to the `bids-topic` Kafka topic using the `key-bids` key. It is asynchronous, which means the message is sent to the Kafka broker in a non-blocking manner. It does not wait for any consumer to process the message. This decoupled messaging approach enables services to remain isolated and independently scalable while participating in a larger, event-driven workflow.

The following code snippet is the Kafka properties configuration for the producer in `application. properties`:

```
spring.kafka.bootstrap-servers = localhost:9092
spring.kafka.producer.key-serializer = org.apache.kafka.common.
serialization.StringSerializer
spring.kafka.producer.value-serializer = org.springframework.kafka.
support.serializer.JsonSerializer
spring.kafka.producer.properties.spring.json.add.type.headers = false
```

The `spring.kafka.bootstrap-servers` property specifies the Kafka broker(s) to which the producer will connect.

The `spring.kafka.producer.key-serializer` property defines the serializer class for the message key. Since Kafka messages consist of a key and a value, this setting ensures that keys are serialized as UTF-8 encoded strings. This is necessary because Kafka expects bytes, and this property tells the producer how to convert a `String` key into byte format.

The `spring.kafka.producer.value-serializer` property specifies the serializer class for the message value. In this case, `JsonSerializer` provided by Spring Apache for Kafka converts Java objects into JSON format before sending them to Kafka. This allows for interoperability and easier consumption by other services.

The `spring.kafka.producer.properties.spring.json.add.type.headers` property disables adding Java class type information (`__TypeId__`) in Kafka message headers. By default, `JsonSerializer` includes this metadata to help consumers deserialize the object. However, setting it to `false` avoids potential deserialization issues in consumers, making the message format cleaner and more interoperable.

Now, let's implement the escrow services API, focusing on handling and processing incoming messages from Kafka as consumers.

Implementing the escrow services

To set up the escrow services project, we can use Spring Initializr. Its structure and dependencies mirror those of the auction services API, including the `spring-Kafka` dependency for message consumption.

The following code snippet is the `BidConsumer` class, which is in charge of listening to `Bid`:

```
@Component
public class BidConsumer {
  private final EscrowProducer escrowProducer;
  private final GetUserEscrowBalanceUseCase
    getUserEscrowBalanceUseCase;
  private final GetUserEscrowReservationsUseCase
    getUserEscrowReservationsUseCase;
  private final CreateEscrowTransationUseCase
    createEscrowTransationUseCase;
  @KafkaListener(topics = "bids-topic", groupId = "escrow-
    group")
  public void bidConsumer(BidEvent bidEvent) {
    BigDecimal balance =
      getUserEscrowBalanceUseCase.execute(
        bidEvent.getUserId());
    BigDecimal totalFundReserved =
      getUserEscrowReservationsUseCase.execute(
        bidEvent.getUserId());

    EscrowTransaction escrowTransaction = new
      EscrowTransaction( null, bidEvent.getAuctionId(),
        bidEvent.getId(),bidEvent.getUserId(),
        bidEvent.getAmount(), null,
        bidEvent.getCreatedAt());
    if(balance.compareTo(totalFundReserved.add(
      bidEvent.getAmount()))) >= 0){
        bidEvent.setStatus(BidStatus.ACCEPTED.name());
        escrowTransaction.setStatus(
          EscrowStatus.RESERVED.name());
    } else{
      bidEvent.setStatus(BidStatus.REJECTED.name());
      escrowTransaction.setStatus(
        EscrowStatus.REJECTED.name());
    }
```

```
        createEscrowTransationUseCase.execute(
          EscrowTransactionMapper.INSTANCE.map(escrowEvent));

        escrowProducer.placeEscrow(escrowEvent);
    }
}
```

The `BidConsumer` class is responsible for processing incoming Kafka messages related to bid events. It leverages Spring for Apache Kafka's `@KafkaListener` annotation to define a consumer method, enabling seamless integration with Kafka topics.

The `@KafkaListener` annotation subscribes the `bidConsumer` method to the `bids-topic` Kafka topic under the `escrow-group` consumer group. A consumer group allows multiple instances of the escrow service to consume messages from the topic in parallel while ensuring that each message is processed only once by one instance. Kafka manages message distribution among the consumers within the same group, enabling horizontal scalability and fault tolerance. If one consumer instance goes down, Kafka will automatically reassign its partitions to other active consumers in the group, maintaining continuous processing. Whenever a message is published to this topic, Spring Apache for Kafka automatically deserializes the message payload into a `BidEvent` object and invokes the method.

Upon receiving a `BidEvent` object, the method first retrieves the user's financial data by invoking `GetUserEscrowBalanceUseCase` to obtain the available balance and `GetUserEscrowReservationsUseCase` to calculate the total amount already reserved in escrow. It then performs the fund validation logic by comparing the available balance against the sum of current reservations and the new bid amount. If the user has sufficient funds, the bid is accepted; otherwise, it is rejected. The result of this validation—either ACCEPTED or REJECTED—is encapsulated in `EscrowEvent`, which is then mapped to the `EscrowTransaction` domain entity and persisted using `CreateEscrowTransationUseCase`. Finally, the method uses `EscrowProducer` to publish `EscrowEvent` back to the `escrows-topic` Kafka topic, allowing the auction service to process the outcome accordingly.

Now, let's review the necessary configuration for the Kafka consumer. The following snippet outlines the required settings in `application.properties`:

```
spring.kafka.consumer.group-id = escrow-group
spring.kafka.consumer.key-deserializer = org.apache.kafka.common.
serialization.StringDeserializer
spring.kafka.consumer.value-deserializer = org.springframework.kafka.
support.serializer.ErrorHandlingDeserializer
spring.kafka.consumer.properties.spring.deserializer.value.delegate.
class = org.springframework.kafka.support.serializer.JsonDeserializer
spring.kafka.consumer.properties.spring.json.value.default.type = com.
packtpub.escrowservices.adapter.transportlayers.restapi.dto.event.
BidEvent
spring.kafka.consumer.properties.spring.json.trusted.packages = *
```

The configuration block uses Spring Apache for Kafka to set up the Kafka consumer in the escrow services API.

The `spring.kafka.consumer.group-id` property defines the consumer group ID. All instances sharing this ID form a group and coordinate message consumption, ensuring each message is processed only once per group.

The `spring.kafka.consumer.key-deserializer` property specifies that the key of the Kafka message will be deserialized as a `String` type.

The `spring.kafka.consumer.value-deserializer` property defines a wrapper deserializer for better error handling. It catches deserialization exceptions and redirects them to a recoverable mechanism instead of failing the entire listener container.

The `spring.kafka.consumer.properties.spring.deserializer.value.delegate.class` property indicates that the actual deserialization should be delegated to `JsonDeserializer`, which converts the JSON payload into a Java object.

The `spring.kafka.consumer.properties.spring.json.value.default.type` property sets the target class type for deserializing the JSON payload. In this case, Kafka will deserialize the incoming messages to the `BidEvent` class.

The `spring.kafka.consumer.properties.spring.json.trusted.packages` property allows the deserialization of classes from any package. This is required for security reasons since Spring Apache for Kafka restricts deserialization by default. The wildcard (`*`) means all packages are trusted.

These properties configure a robust Kafka consumer that listens to messages, gracefully handles deserialization errors, and ensures type-safe message consumption using `BidEvent`.

Since `BidProducer` in the auction services API and `BidConsumer` in the escrow services API cover the core aspects of messaging in this architecture—demonstrating how to produce and consume events using Spring Kafka—we will not get into the implementation details of `EscrowProducer` in the escrow services API or `EscrowConsumer` in the auction services API. These components follow the same event-driven messaging principles already explained, and their structure and configuration mirror what we have already covered.

Now that our new services are in place, it's time to test the implementation and validate that the communication and business logic are working as expected.

Executing tests for bid placement

With our application's new features in place, we can proceed with the steps to test the implementation:

1. Execute the Dockerfile in `ch8/docker-resources/database` and `ch8/docker-resources/kafka` to set up the databases and Kafka.

2. Run the services in the following order: `service-discovery-services`, `configuration-services`, `gateway-services`, `authentication-services`, `user-services`, `auction-services`, and then `escrow-services`. There are a lot of services, but we are evolving our project.

3. Import the Postman collection located in the `ch8/postman` folder. Execute the request named `AUTH - LOGIN ADMIN` to get a token.

4. In the request named `BID - CREATE`, select the **Authorization** tab, choose the **Bearer Token** option for **Auth Type**, and add the generated token. Then, execute the request twice. The following JSON snippet is the request's payload, which informs the auction ID, user ID, and bid amount. Note that we are using an event notification pattern. The event carries minimal information, that is, only the IDs:

```
{
    "auctionId": "1",
    "userId": 1,
    "amount": 600.00
}
```

The user with the ID of `1` has a fund amount of 1,000.00 registered in their escrow account. Therefore, the first request will execute the whole process, and the auction service console will print `Bid accepted!` The second request will be rejected because the total of reserved bids will be 1,200.00, which is greater than the user's fund of 1,000.00. *Figure 8.11* shows the auction service console with the requests.

```
.bid.kafka.BidProducer               : Place bid: Bid(id=10, auctionId=1, userId=1, amount=600.00, createdAt=2025-03-23T22:50:33.889464)
.bid.kafka.BidProducer               : Bid 10 sent to bids topic to validate user funds!
.bid.kafka.EscrowConsumer            : Escrow 10 processing from escrow topic!
.bid.kafka.EscrowConsumer            :[Bid accepted!]
.bid.kafka.EscrowConsumer            : Escrow 10 processed from escrow topic!
.bid.kafka.EscrowConsumer            : SEND BID 10 STATUS TO THE NOTIFICATION TOPIC!
.ExternalTokenValidationFilter       : x-correlation-id : 822cf18a-7537-4683-ad67-024c8067d5f0

.bid.kafka.BidProducer               : Place bid: Bid(id=11, auctionId=1, userId=1, amount=600.00, createdAt=2025-03-23T22:51:25.167447)
.bid.kafka.BidProducer               : Bid 11 sent to bids topic to validate user funds!
.bid.kafka.EscrowConsumer            : Escrow 11 processing from escrow topic!
.bid.kafka.EscrowConsumer            :[Bid rejected!]
.bid.kafka.EscrowConsumer            : Escrow 11 processed from escrow topic!
.bid.kafka.EscrowConsumer            : SEND BID 11 STATUS TO THE NOTIFICATION TOPIC!
```

Figure 8.11: Auction services API console

Figure 8.12 displays the console output of the escrow services during bid processing.

```
c.p.e.a.d.e.kafka.BidConsumer          : Bid 10 processing from bids topic!
c.p.e.a.d.e.kafka.EscrowProducer       : Escrow 10 sent to escrow   topic!
c.p.e.a.d.e.kafka.BidConsumer          : Bid 10 processed from bids topic!
c.p.e.a.d.e.kafka.BidConsumer          : Bid 11 processing from bids topic!
            .EscrowProducer            : Escrow 11 sent to escrow   topic!
            .BidConsumer               : Bid 11 processed from bids topic!
```

Figure 8.12: Escrow services API console

The figure shows the bid flow within the escrow service. After `BidConsumer` consumes the bid event, `EscrowProducer` publishes an event with the result of the user funds analysis to a Kafka topic, allowing the auction service to consume and act on it.

> **Note**
>
> To visualize messages in Kafka topics, you can download the client tool **Offset Explorer** from `https://kafkatool.com/download.html`.
>
> Kafka also provides native CLI tools such as `kafka-console-consumer.sh` and `kafka-console-producer.sh` for quick testing and debugging directly from the terminal.

As we wrap up the implementation of auction and escrow services, it is essential to highlight the architectural pattern that guides their interaction. While it may seem like a simple producer-consumer setup, it actually incorporates publish-subscribe and event notification patterns. Most importantly, it adheres to the Saga orchestration pattern.

In this process, the auction service initiates a distributed transaction whenever a user places a bid. The escrow service then validates whether the user has enough funds and provides a response. Based on this response, the auction service accepts or rejects the bid, guiding the entire transaction flow. This positions the auction service as the orchestrator and the escrow service as a participant.

Unlike the choreography approach, where services react independently to events, the auction service orchestrates this interaction. It awaits the escrow service's response before making decisions regarding the bid.

The system can easily be enhanced with the message inbox and outbox patterns to strengthen data consistency. These previously discussed patterns help ensure reliable event publishing and processing, making the architecture more robust and fault-tolerant.

Summary

The chapter explored event-driven architecture, emphasizing its asynchronous nature and benefits for modern software systems, especially in a microservices environment. It discussed the core components of event-driven architecture, such as producers, events, event brokers, and consumers, and their role in enabling loose coupling and scalability.

It also covered the fundamentals of events, including their characteristics such as immutability, temporality, and descriptive nature. It also discussed different events—simple, composite, domain, and system events—essential for designing effective event-driven systems. It explored patterns in event-driven systems, such as publish-subscribe, event notification, event-carried state transfer, message inbox and outbox, and Saga. It explained when to use them and the trade-offs involved.

Additionally, the chapter provided a hands-on case study of an online auction system using Spring for Apache Kafka. By implementing a producer and consumer with Kafka as the broker and applying patterns such as Saga orchestration, we demonstrated how to build scalable and resilient services. By combining foundational concepts with a practical guide to implementing an event-driven architecture, this chapter equipped you with the knowledge of building scalable and resilient systems using event-driven architecture.

In *Chapter 9, Pipe-and-Filter and Serverless Architecture*, we will explore serverless architecture, focusing on serverless functions and implementing a service alert with Spring Cloud Function. We will also explore the Pipe and Filter architecture using Spring Batch for efficient batch processing.

Questions

1. What is event-driven architecture, and why is it commonly used in modern applications?

2. What are the key characteristics of events in event-driven architecture?

3. What is the publish-subscribe pattern, and how does it function within event-driven architecture?

4. How does the event-carried state transfer pattern differ from the event notification pattern?

5. What role does Apache Kafka play in implementing event-driven architecture, particularly within the context of the chapter's case study?

6. What are the main components used to produce and consume messages in Spring Kafka?

Get This Book's PDF Version and Exclusive Extras

UNLOCK NOW

Scan the QR code (or go to `packtpub.com/unlock`). Search for this book by name, confirm the edition, and then follow the steps on the page.

Note: Keep your invoice handly. Purchase made directly from packt don't require one.

9

Pipe-and-Filter and Serverless Architecture

This chapter reviews the pipe and filter architecture, highlighting where to use it and where to avoid it. It covers the core functionalities and concepts of the Spring Batch framework and demonstrates how to create a batch-processing application that reads CSV files and populates a database by applying the piper and filter architecture with Spring Batch.

Additionally, we will explore serverless architecture, focusing on **function as a service (FaaS)** and **Spring Cloud Function**. Finally, we will implement a function to send alerts to a Slack channel and deploy the application locally and in the **AWS cloud**. This chapter covers the following topics:

- Reviewing the pipe and filter architecture

- Implementing an application using Spring Batch

- Exploring serverless architecture with FaaS

- Exploring Spring Cloud Function

- Implementing alerts with Spring Cloud Function

By the end of this chapter, you will have acquired a thorough understanding of both the theoretical and practical aspects of the pipe and filter architecture with Spring Batch and serverless applications developing FaaS with Spring Cloud Function, empowering you to build scalable, maintainable data processing pipelines and create portable, cost-effective serverless functions that integrate seamlessly with cloud environments.

Technical requirements

All the code for this chapter can be found on GitHub at `https://github.com/PacktPublishing/Software-Architecture-with-Spring/tree/main/ch9`. Ellipses in the code blocks indicate that parts of the code have been omitted, and the complete code is available on GitHub.

Reviewing the pipe and filter architecture

We provided a comprehensive introduction to the pipe and filter architecture in *Chapter 1, Diving into Software Architecture*. Here, we will briefly review it. *Figure 9.1* illustrates the workflow of the pipe and filter architecture.

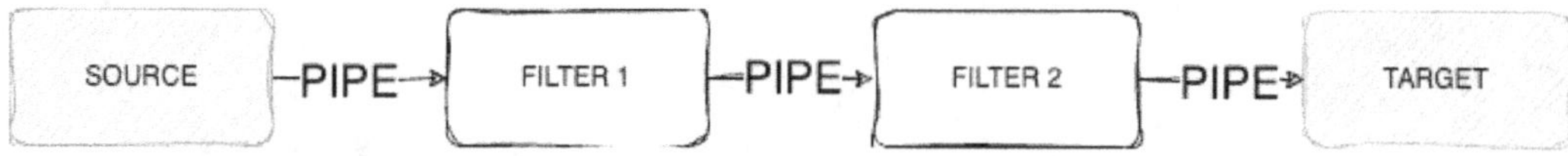

Figure 9.1: Pipe and filter architecture workflow

The pipe and filter architecture comprises a series of processing units, known as filters, which are interconnected by pipes. The output of one filter serves as the input for the next. This structure processes data in stages, offering flexibility, modularity, and scalability. Filters are responsible for specific tasks, such as transforming or aggregating data, while pipes facilitate data transportation between them. But where is the pipe and filter architecture used?

Where to use the pipe and filter architecture

The pipe and filter architecture is commonly used in several areas of software engineering, particularly in scenarios where data needs to be processed sequentially. Here are some of the most prevalent use cases where it is used:

- **Command-line utilities**: One of the most famous and foundational uses of the pipe and filter architecture is in Unix/Linux command-line utilities. Here, different commands (filters) are chained together using pipes (|). In the following command, `cat` reads a file, `grep` filters lines containing a specific term, `sort` orders the lines, and `uniq` removes duplicates, with each command acting as a filter that processes data passed through a pipe:

  ```
  cat file.txt | grep "searchTerm" | sort | uniq > output.txt
  ```

- **Data processing pipelines: Extract, transform, and load (ETL)** processes and Stream processing systems:

  - **ETL processes**: ETL pipelines, commonly used in data warehousing, often employ the pipe and filter architecture. Data is extracted from various sources, transformed by different filters, and finally loaded into a data warehouse.

  - **Stream processing systems**: Systems such as **Apache Flink** and **Apache Beam** use a pipe and filter architecture to process data streams in real time, where data flows through a series of transformations and analyses.

- **Software build systems: Continuous integration/continuous deployment (CI/CD)** pipelines in software development often use the pipe and filter architecture. Each step in the pipeline (for example, code compilation, testing, packaging, and deployment) acts as a filter, and the output from one step becomes the input to the next. Tools such as Jenkins and GitHub Actions are widely used to implement such pipelines. They provide flexibility and automation for seamless integration and deployment workflows.

- **Batch processing:** Batch processing executes tasks in a group without manual intervention. This method collects, processes, and outputs data at scheduled intervals, typically handling large volumes. Generally, it is triggered in predefined schedules, efficiently handling large data volumes, where results are available only after the entire batch is processed. It is commonly used for tasks that do not require immediate user interaction, such as data analysis, report generation, and bulk data transfers.

Batch processing is commonly implemented using a pipe and filter architecture. This combination results in a modular and maintainable system where each processing step can be independently modified or scaled.

The pipe and filter architecture is also used in many other scenarios, such as frameworks, **robotic process automation** (**RPA**), multimedia processing, web servers, and compilers. It is commonly employed in environments where data requires successive processing steps or a modular and scalable design is paramount.

Where to avoid the pipe and filter architecture

We must avoid using the pipe and filter architecture in real-time systems requiring low latency, applications with tightly coupled components or shared state, interactive user applications, and cases where complex workflows or continuous, long-running computations are involved, as the architecture may introduce inefficiencies and performance bottlenecks.

Next, we will learn about the Spring Batch framework, an important tool for developing batch-processing applications that implement the pipe and filter architecture.

Exploring Spring Batch

Another well-known framework from the Spring Framework family, **Spring Batch** is a lightweight, comprehensive framework designed for batch processing. It provides tools and utilities for processing large volumes of data, featuring core functionalities such as the following:

- **Task-oriented framework:** Spring Batch is designed around the concept of a job, which consists of multiple steps. Each step represents a phase in the batch process, such as reading data, processing it, and writing the output.

- **Chunk-oriented processing**: One of the core patterns in Spring Batch is chunk-oriented processing, where large datasets are processed in chunks or segments. For example, data is read in chunks, processed in chunks, and then written in chunks, allowing for more efficient memory management and fault tolerance.

- **Scalability and partitioning**: Spring Batch provides mechanisms for scaling batch jobs to handle large datasets. This includes support for parallel processing, partitioning, and multithreaded steps, which allow batch jobs to be divided and executed concurrently.

- **Transaction management**: Spring Batch integrates with Spring's transaction management capabilities, ensuring that each step or chunk of a job is processed within a transactional context. This ensures data consistency and integrity, mainly when dealing with large-scale data processing.

- **Error handling and restartability**: Spring Batch provides robust error handling mechanisms, allowing jobs to fail gracefully and be restarted from the point of failure. This is critical in long-running batch processes where errors may occur for various reasons, such as network failures or data inconsistencies.

- **Job monitoring and management**: Spring Batch includes tools for monitoring and managing batch jobs. These include the ability to track job execution, log job progress, and manage job life cycles, providing visibility and control over batch processes.

- **Support for various data sources**: Spring Batch can interact with multiple data sources, including relational databases and flat files such as CSV, XML, and message queues. It provides built-in readers and writers for these data sources and allows for custom implementations.

- **Integration with other Spring projects**: Spring Batch seamlessly integrates with other Spring projects, such as Spring Boot, Spring Data, and Spring Cloud. This integration simplifies the development of batch applications by leveraging the broader Spring ecosystem.

Now, let's familiarize ourselves with Spring Batch's core concepts, diving into its domain language:

- `JobLauncher`: The job launcher is the component responsible for launching jobs, often triggered by a scheduler or a manual request.

- `Job`: A job represents the entire batch process. It comprises one or more steps, defining the sequence of actions to be executed.

- `JobParameters`: Job parameters are inputs to the job and define specific configurations or settings for a particular execution.

- `Step`: A step is a phase in the job. It might involve reading, processing, and writing data. Each step can be configured with specific readers, processors, and writers.

- `ItemReader`, `ItemProcessor`, and `ItemWriter`: These are the core components of a chunk-oriented processing step:

  - `ItemReader`: This reads data from the source

- ▪ `ItemProcessor`: This processes the data, applying any necessary business logic or transformations

- ▪ `ItemWriter`: This writes the processed data to the target destination

- `JobRepository`: Spring Batch utilizes a job repository to manage job execution metadata by creating tables in a database to track the job, step, execution status, parameters, and history. This function allows for job resumption, retry, and monitoring while maintaining the integrity and reliability of batch processes. A persistent relational database is recommended for production environments, while an in-memory database such as H2 can be used in non-production settings. The job repository is essential for tracking job and step executions.

The following diagram, *Figure 9.2*, presents the core concepts of Spring Batch.

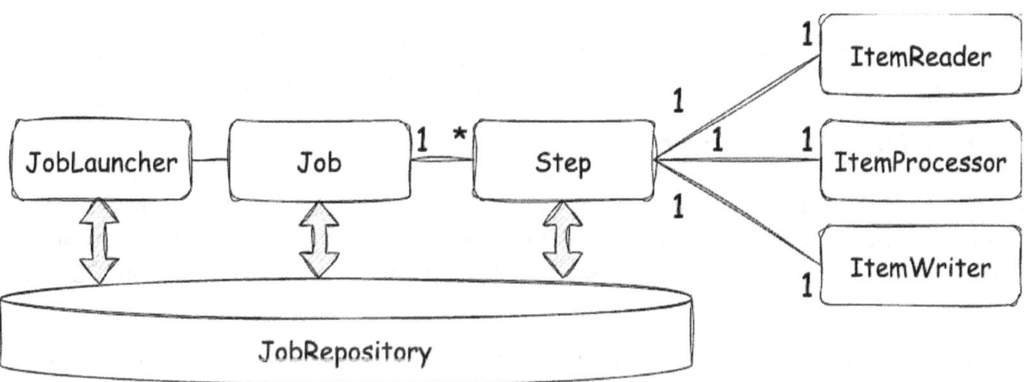

Figure 9.2: Core concepts of Spring Batch

The preceding diagram illustrates the concepts that form the domain language of Spring Batch and its workflow. `JobLauncher` initiates executing `Job`, and the ongoing process's metadata is stored in `JobRepository`. `Job` comprises one or more steps, and each step (`Step`) is associated with a single `ItemReader`, `ItemProcessor`, and `ItemWriter`. Now, let's see how Spring Batch aligns with the pipe and filter architecture.

How does Spring Batch align with the pipe and filter architecture?

In Spring Batch, a job typically consists of multiple steps, each performing a specific processing task, similar to the filters in the pipe and filter architecture. The result of one step can be passed as input to the next step, akin to data flowing through pipes between filters. Spring Batch can be seen as a practical implementation of the pipe and filter architecture, particularly suited for batch processing where data flows through a series of transformation stages.

Now that we understand the pipe and filter architecture and Spring Batch, let's apply this knowledge to our online auction application.

Implementing an application using Spring Batch

It has been amazing to expand our toolbox with the pipe and filter architecture and the Spring Batch framework. Let's put into practice what we have learned by diving into our online auction case study.

Online auction case study

After enabling online transactions, our online application skyrocketed in user and transaction numbers. The application was launched in several countries and was a huge success.

Now, the stakeholders require data reports, which is understandable as data analysis is crucial for any company's success. They will use third-party tools for reports and analysis. However, they need a database with all the company's data.

As our online auction application is built as a microservices architecture, with each service having its own database, we need to create this new database and gather all data within it.

System definition and mission

Gathering data from multiple databases in a new database is complex, mainly because the databases vary – some are relational while others are NoSQL. Additionally, directly querying the databases where the microservices are active is not recommended, as it can overload the database and disrupt the services.

One of the architects suggested that the best approach is for the team responsible for each business domain to handle data extraction. This means the user management team would extract user data from the database to a CSV file, the products team would extract product data, and the auctions team would extract auctions and bids data to CSV files. *Figure 9.3* presents the solution design proposed.

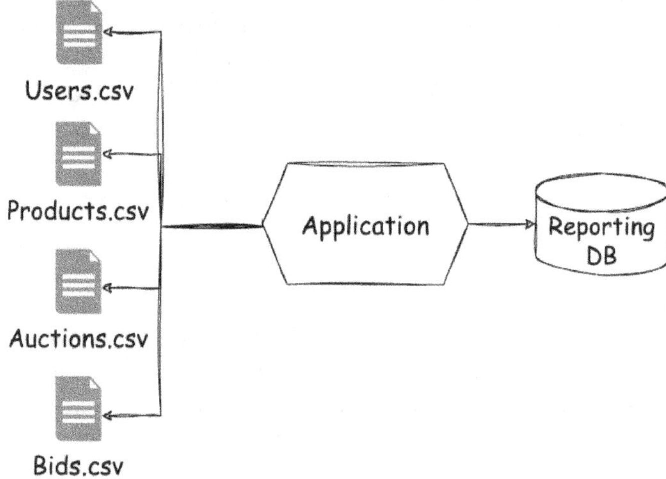

Figure 9.3: Solution design

The proposed solution involves an application that reads CSV files from a directory. These CSV files contain data extracted from the services' database. The `Users.csv` file contains data from the `users` table, the `Products.csv` file from the `products` table, the `Bids.csv` file from the `bids` table, and the `Auction.csv` file from the `auction` table. The application then processes this data and stores it in a reporting database.

We can build the application using the Spring Batch framework, which comprises the pipe and filter architecture. So, before implementing the project, let's set up the environment.

Setting up the environment

To set up the reporting database, run the following command in a terminal in the `ch9/docker/postgres` folder:

```
docker-compose up -d
```

The reporting database will contain the tables from our services together in one database: the `users`, `product`, `bid`, and `auction` tables. Now that our environment is configured and running, let's implement the application.

Implementing the batch application

Let's use the **Spring Initializr** to create the batch application, which we will name `etl-batch-process`. *Figure 9.4* shows a screenshot of the application's dependencies.

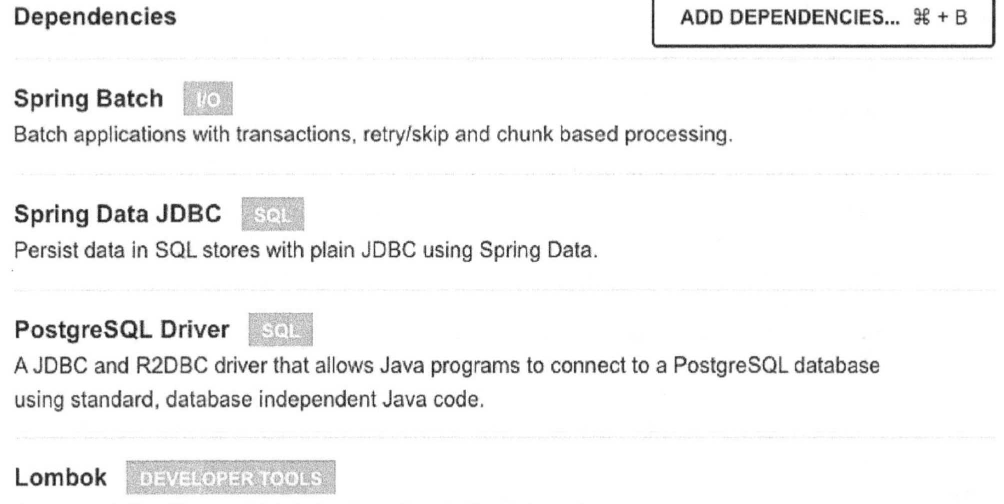

Figure 9.4: Application dependencies

The Spring Batch dependency provides all the batch resources needed to create a batch application, such as batch processing, chunk-based processing, retry and skip, and transactions.

Using pure JDBC or Spring Data JDBC instead of JPA is better when working with batch applications. Thus, you can minimize overhead, reduce complexity, address performance challenges, optimize memory usage, enhance control over database interactions, and achieve more efficient and reliable batch job execution.

The other two dependencies are the PostgreSQL driver, which we will need to connect to the reporting database, and Lombok, which provides annotations that reduce boilerplate code, such as constructors, getters, and setters. *Figure 9.5* shows the sequence of the implementation we will follow to create the component application.

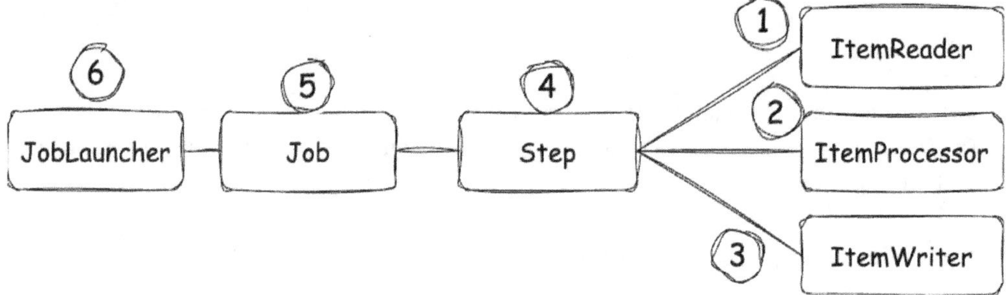

Figure 9.5: Sequence of the component implementation

The implementation process begins with `ItemReader`, followed by `ItemProcessor`, `ItemWriter`, `Step`, `Job`, and finally, `JobLauncher`, which is responsible for initiating the execution of `Job`. This sequence represents the order of the component implementation, so let's start it.

Implementing ItemReader

`ItemReader` is the Spring Batch component that reads the source, which could be a CSV, XML, or database. In the `ch9/data-files` folder, we find four CSV files: `Auctions.csv`, `Bids.csv`, `Products.csv`, and `Users.csv`. The content of these files will be read and saved into the database. Let's work on the `Users.csv` file for learning; its content is presented in the following snippet:

```
id,city,country,email,name,phone_number,state
1,New York,United States,user@wxauction.com,User X,123456789,NY
```

The first line of the CSV file is the header, which defines the names of the columns in the file: `id`, `city`, `country`, `email`, `name`, `phone_number`, and `state`. The subsequent lines contain the data corresponding to each column defined in the header.

The next code snippet presents the attributes from the `User` and `UserDto` classes, mapping the CSV columns:

```
private Long id;
private String name;
private String email;
...
```

The `UserDto` class will handle data from files and, through a process, pass it to the `User` class, which can then be used to save data into the database.

The `UserFieldSetMapper` class presented in the following code snippet implements the `FieldSetMapper` interface:

```
public class UserFieldSetMapper implements
                                  FieldSetMapper<UserDto> {
  public UserDto mapFieldSet(final FieldSet fieldSet)
                               throws BindException {
    return UserDto.builder()
      .id(fieldSet.readLong("id"))
      .name(fieldSet.readString("name"))
      ...
```

The `UserFieldSetMapper` class is a mapper; it maps data obtained from `FieldSet` into a `UserDto` object. `FieldSet` is Spring Batch's abstraction that allows us to bind fields from flat files, similar to how we would handle data from a database. The `fieldSet.readLong("id")` statement reads `Long` data and the `fieldSet.readString("name")` statement reads `String` data.

Similar to the `FieldSetMapper` class, which maps a flat file, other classes, such as `RowMapper`, map rows of a database.

The following code snippet presents the `UserItemReader` class that extends the `FlatFileItemReader` class:

```
@Component
@StepScope
public class UserItemReader extends
                      FlatFileItemReader<UserDto> {
```

The `UserItemReader` class extends `FlatFileItemReader`, which provides essential functionality for reading and parsing flat files. Spring Batch provides various interfaces for dealing with other sources, such as `JdbcCursorItemReader` and `JpaPagingItemReader` for relational databases, `MongoItemReader` for NoSQL documents, `StaxEventItemReader` for XML files, and `JsonItemReader` for JSON Files.

The `@StepScope` annotation ensures that the bean is created and initialized for each step execution, allowing for step-specific configurations such as the late binding of job parameters:

```
public UserItemReader(
  @Value("#{jobParameters['usersFile']}") String
                usersFile){

  ...

    this.setLineMapper(lineMapper());
    this.setResource(new FileSystemResource(usersFile));

  ...
```

The `UserItemReader` constructor receives the path of the `Users.csv` file as a parameter through `@Value("#{jobParameters['usersFile']}")`. It is a **Spring Expression Language (SpEL)** expression used to inject a specific job parameter when the job is started.

The `setResource` method specifies the resource to be processed, in this case, the `Users.csv` file.

The `setLineMapper` sets the `LineMapper` interface through the `lineMapper()` method, which maps lines in flat files to objects. The following code snippet presents its implementation:

```
private LineMapper<UserDto> lineMapper() {
  var defaultLineMapper = new
            DefaultLineMapper<UserDto>();
  var lineTokenizer = new DelimitedLineTokenizer();
  lineTokenizer.setDelimiter(",");
  lineTokenizer.setNames("id","city","country ...
  lineTokenizer.setStrict(false);
  defaultLineMapper.setLineTokenizer(lineTokenizer);
  defaultLineMapper.setFieldSetMapper(new
          UserFieldSetMapper()
  return defaultLineMapper;
}
```

The `lineMapper` method defines how each file line is mapped to the `UserDto` class through the `DefaultLineMapper` class, which implements the `LineMapper` interface.

The `DelimitedLineTokenizer` class is responsible for setting up the file's specificities, such as informing the file's delimiter (in this case, a comma), naming the columns' file, and so on.

Lastly, we pass `UserFieldSetMapper` as a parameter to set `FieldSetMapper`, which, in this case, converts the tokenized data into `UserDto` objects. Now, let's implement `ItemProcessor`.

Implementing ItemProcessor

The `ItemProcessor` interface represents the business logic for processing individual data items during a batch job. It acts as an intermediary between reading data from `ItemReader` and writing data to `ItemWriter`. `ItemProcessor` allows you to apply transformations, validations, or filtering to each item before passing it to the writer. In our use case, we will use it to transform data from the `UserDto` class to the `User` class, as presented in the following code snippet:

```
@Component
public class UserItemProcessor implements
                            ItemProcessor<UserDto, User> {
   public User process(UserDto userDto) throws Exception {
     return User.builder()
       .id(userDto.getId())
       ...
```

The `UserItemProcessor` class implements `ItemProcessor`, which provides the `process` method for transforming `UserDto`, returned by `ItemReader`, into a `User` object that will be used in `ItemWriter`.

Implementing ItemWriter

`ItemWriter` operates similarly to `ItemReader` but performs the opposite function. Instead of reading data, `ItemWriter` writes data to an output resource. It still involves locating, opening, and closing resources but primarily focuses on output operations. This typically means inserting, updating, or sending messages for databases or queues.

The following code snippet shows the `UserItemWriter` class that implements the `ItemWriter` interface:

```
@Component
public class UserItemWriter implements ItemWriter<User> {
   private final JdbcTemplate jdbcTemplate;

   public void write(Chunk<? extends User> users) throws
                                               Exception {
     jdbcTemplate.batchUpdate(
       "INSERT INTO users (id, city, country, email, ...
```

The `write` method takes a chunk of `User` objects that have been read and processed. These objects will be written in a single call to the database, executing the insert operations efficiently in a batch using the `batchUpdate` method from `JdbcTemplate`.

So far, we have the components to read, transform, and write the users' data; now, we will implement the `Step` component, which will orchestrate these components.

Implementing Step

In Spring Batch, `Step` represents a single, independent phase of a batch job. It is a fundamental building block within the Spring Batch framework, encapsulating the logic for a specific task or set of tasks that must be executed as part of the overall job. Each `Step` typically includes reading, processing, and writing data, executed sequentially or conditionally as part of a `Job`. The following code snippet presents the `BatchConfig` class, a Spring configuration class that defines the batch processing setup:

```java
@Configuration
public class BatchConfig {
  private final UserItemReader userItemReader;
  private final ItemProcessor<UserDto, User>
                                    userItemProcessor;
  private final ItemWriter<User> userItemWriter;
  @Bean
  public Step importUsersStep(final JobRepository
          jobRepository, final PlatformTransactionManager
          transactionManager) {
    return new StepBuilder("importUsersStep", jobRepository)
            .<UserDto, User>chunk(100, transactionManager)
            .reader(userItemReader)
            .processor(userItemProcessor)
            .writer(userItemWriter)
            .build();
  }
}
```

The `UserItemReader` class implements the `ItemReader` interface for reading user data, `ItemProcessor` for processing the data, and `ItemWriter` for writing the processed data.

The `importUsersStep` method creates a `Step` using the `StepBuilder` helper class. `StepBuilder` sets up the process chunks of 100 items simultaneously, chaining the reader, processor, and writer, who are responsible for reading, processing, and writing user data.

`JobRepository` is responsible for persisting the state of jobs, steps, and executions, and `PlatformTransactionManager` is an interface in Spring that defines the operations required for transaction management. Now, let's implement the `Job` component.

Implementing Job

In Spring Batch, `Job` represents the entire batch processing workflow. It is the top-level container that orchestrates the execution of one or more `Step` and defines the sequence in which these steps should be executed. `Job` is responsible for managing the life cycle of the batch process, including starting, stopping, and restarting the job and tracking its execution status.

The following code snippet is a method defined in the `BatchConfig` class that defines Job:

```java
public Job importFiles(final JobRepository jobRepository, final
PlatformTransactionManager transactionManager) {
    return new JobBuilder("importFiles", jobRepository)
            .start(importUsersStep(jobRepository, transactionManager))
            .next(importBidsStep(jobRepository, transactionManager))
            .next(importProductsStep(jobRepository,
                                    transactionManager))
...
```

The `importFiles` method is a Spring Bean that defines Job. This Job consists of a sequence of steps (`Step`), starting with `importUsersStep` passed as a parameter to the `start` method, then `importBidsStep` and `importProductsStep` passed as parameters to the `next` method. `JobBuilder` is used to build and return the complete Job, orchestrating the execution of these steps in the specified order.

Implementing JobLauncher

`JobLauncher` is an interface in Spring Batch that is responsible for launching batch jobs. It serves as the primary mechanism for starting a Job and managing its execution, including providing the necessary job parameters and handling the Job life cycle.

The following code snippet is a method defined in the `EtlBatchProcessApplication` class:

```java
@Scheduled(fixedRate = 60000)
public void importFiles() throws Exception {
    JobParameters jobParameters = new
        JobParametersBuilder()
        .addDate("timestamp",
                Calendar.getInstance().getTime())
        .addString("usersFile", USERS_FILE)

        ...

        .toJobParameters();
    JobExecution jobExecution = jobLauncher.run(job,
            jobParameters);
```

The preceding code snippet presented a scheduled method, `importFiles`, that runs every 60 seconds, triggering Job. `JobParameters` is responsible for adding the current timestamp and a filename, `USERS_FILE`, as parameters.

The job is then launched using the `jobLauncher.run()` method with the defined parameters.

All the steps for developing the batch processing application have been completed. Upon execution, the results can be viewed in the screenshot depicted in *Figure 9.6*.

	city		country		email		name	
1	New York		United States		user@wxauction.com		User X	
2	New York		United States		admin@wxauction.com		Admin X	

Figure 9.6: The users table populated by the application

The `users` table was populated with `Users.csv` file data. If you look at a database client, you will note that there are tables with the prefix `batch_`. `JobRepository` created these tables to manage job execution. Now, let's learn about another important architecture: serverless architecture with FaaS.

Exploring serverless architecture with FaaS

Serverless architecture is a cloud computing model in which we focus on writing and deploying code without managing the underlying infrastructure. In this model, cloud providers automatically provision, scale, and manage the resources needed to run the application. Here, we will focus on presenting FaaS and implementing an application with Spring Cloud Function, running it locally on our computer, and then deploying and running it in the cloud provider, AWS. Now, let's proceed with our discussion and learn more about FaaS.

What is FaaS?

FaaS is a serverless model where code runs in response to events without infrastructure management. Applications are split into small, independent functions triggered by events such as HTTP requests or file uploads.

These functions are stateless, short-lived, and designed to execute quickly, making them ideal for tasks that can be handled in isolation.

The benefits of FaaS

The benefits of FaaS include cost efficiency, auto-scaling, reduced complexity, a focus on business value, and a faster time to market.

- **Cost efficiency**: With FaaS, we only pay for the actual time our functions are running, avoiding the cost of idle server resources.

- **Auto-scaling**: FaaS automatically scales in response to demand, ensuring that applications can handle varying loads without manual intervention.

- **Reduced complexity**: With the cloud provider handling the infrastructure, developers are freed from concerns about server maintenance, scaling, and deployment, making the development process more straightforward.

- **Focus on business value**: Developers can concentrate on building functionality and solving business problems rather than dealing with operational concerns.

- **Faster time to market**: FaaS allows developers to build and release features more quickly by removing the overhead of managing infrastructure and simplifying deployments.

Besides these advantages, FaaS has its challenges that we must be aware of before choosing it for a certain functionality.

The challenges of FaaS

There are challenges when using FaaS; let's highlight the main ones:

- **Cold starts**: When a function has not been invoked for some time, it may take longer to execute on its first run, as the cloud provider needs to initialize the environment. This latency can affect performance, particularly for time-sensitive applications. There are strategies to mitigate cold starts, such as keeping functions warm or using provisioned concurrency available on some platforms such as **AWS Lambda**, but these can add complexity and cost.

- **Vendor lock-in**: Each cloud provider implements FaaS differently, which can make it challenging to migrate functions between platforms or maintain multi-cloud deployments.

We can count on the Spring Cloud Function framework for vendor lock-in. Let's find out what Spring Cloud Function is and how it can support us.

Exploring Spring Cloud Function

Spring Cloud Function is a project within the Spring ecosystem that provides a framework for building and deploying serverless applications using Java. We can create functions that can be easily deployed on various serverless platforms such as AWS Lambda, Azure Functions, Google Cloud Functions, or even run locally or in a traditional server-based environment.

The primary goals of Spring Cloud Function are to promote code reuse, enable portability, and simplify the deployment of business logic across different environments. Let's examine its main features:

- **Functional programming**: Spring Cloud Function supports the functional programming paradigm by allowing developers to define business logic using Java's `Function`, `Supplier`, and `Consumer` interfaces.

- **Serverless platform agnostic**: You can create a function once and deploy it to different serverless platforms without having to rewrite or heavily modify your code.

- **Automatic type conversion**: Spring Cloud Function provides built-in support for automatic conversion between various data formats such as JSON, XML, and Java objects, simplifying handling input and output data in your functions.

- **Event-driven architecture support**: The framework supports event-driven programming, allowing functions to be triggered by events such as HTTP requests, messages, or changes in a database. This is particularly useful for building reactive and responsive applications.

- **Custom function composition**: Spring Cloud Function allows you to compose functions by combining multiple functions, enabling complex processing pipelines with minimal boilerplate code.

Spring Cloud Function is a robust framework for building serverless applications, enabling developers to create portable, reusable, and easily deployable functions. It abstracts away the complexities of different serverless platforms, allowing us to focus on writing business logic that can run anywhere, from cloud-based serverless environments to traditional server-based applications. With its deep integration with the Spring ecosystem, Spring Cloud Function provides a seamless development experience for building modern, event-driven applications. Now that we understand serverless architecture and Spring Cloud Function, let's proceed to the application's implementation.

Implementing alerts with Spring Cloud Function

Continuing with our online auction application, the stakeholders required that the users in charge of generating reports and performing data analysis be alerted when the batch application completes populating the report database.

The fictional company *WX-Auction* uses Slack, a collaboration and communication tool. A software engineer suggested a FaaS application that sends alerts to a Slack channel (group) informing when the batch process is completed.

FaaS is a suitable approach because the batch process runs once a day, and building an alert application that keeps running all the time is unnecessary and wasteful of resources and money.

In this hands-on exercise, we will implement the application, run it locally, and then modify it for deployment on the AWS cloud provider.

Let's start by creating the application using Spring Initializr. *Figure 9.7* shows a screenshot displaying the libraries required for the project.

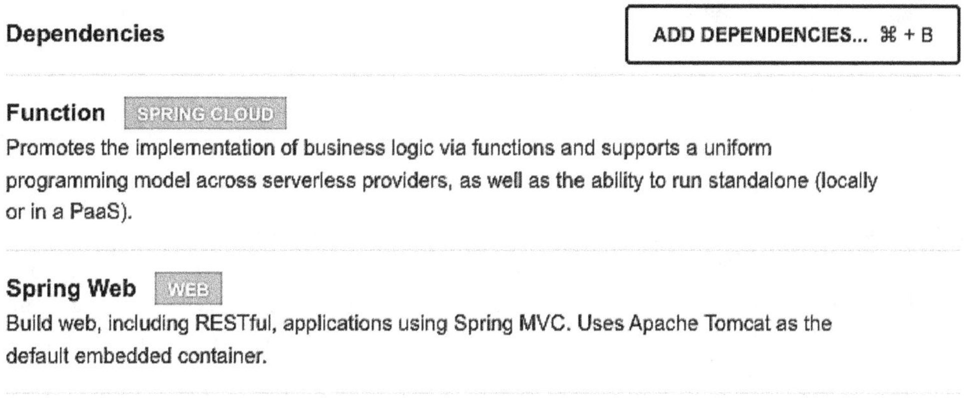

Dependencies   ADD DEPENDENCIES... ⌘ + B

Function SPRING CLOUD

Promotes the implementation of business logic via functions and supports a uniform
programming model across serverless providers, as well as the ability to run standalone (locally
or in a PaaS).

Spring Web WEB

Build web, including RESTful, applications using Spring MVC. Uses Apache Tomcat as the
default embedded container.

Figure 9.7: Application dependencies

We only need to add the Spring Cloud Function and Spring Web MVC dependencies to our project,
called `alert-faas`.

> **Alert**
>
> It's out of the scope of this book to create a step-by-step guide on how to create an account, a
> channel, or an app on Slack. You can access Slack to create an account at `https://slack.`
> `com/get-started#/createnew`, to create a channel at `https://slack.com/`
> `help/articles/201402297-Create-a-channel`, and to create an app and obtain
> a webhook to post messages at `https://api.slack.com/messaging/webhooks`.
>
> If you don't want to set up Slack, use the application version that only prints the message on
> the console, which is also available.

The following code snippet presents a FaaS application through the `SlackAlertFunction`
configuration class:

```
@Configuration
public class SlackAlertFunction {
  @Bean
  public Consumer<Message> alertSlackChannelConsumer() {
    return message -> {
      try {
        restClient.post()
          .uri(slackWebhookUrl)
          .header("Content-Type", "application/json")
          .body(message)
          .retrieve();
        System.out.println("Message sent!");
```

```
      } catch (Exception e) {
       System.out.println("Error: " + e.getMessage());
      }
    };
   }
 }
```

The FaaS application is a configuration class named `SlackAlertFunction`. The function is the `alertSlackChannelConsumer` method. It uses the `Consumer` interface, a functional interface that accepts a single input and doesn't return any value. It will receive a message and use `restClient.post()` to send it to the Slack channel through the webhook defined in the `slackWebhookUrl` variable.

If we want to initiate a call without providing any input and only receive a confirmation that the alert was sent, we can use the `Supplier` functional interface. This interface only produces an output, and the following code snippet demonstrates its use:

```
@Bean
public Supplier<String> alertSlackChannelSupplier() {
  return () -> {
    try {
      String messageContent = "The ETL process is
                          completed! (Supplier Function)";
      String payload = String.format("{\"text\":\"%s\"}",
                                    messageContent);
      restClient.post()
       .uri(slackWebhookUrl)
       ...
```

The updated function, `alertSlackChannelSupplier`, is inside the `SlackAlertFunction` class. The change was to replace the `Consumer` interface with the `Supplier` interface. Since we no longer have input, we created a hardcoded message, `messageContent`, and added it to `payload`. After the function execution, a `String` message is returned.

What about passing an input and receiving an output when calling the function? In this case, we can use the `Function` interface; it accepts one argument and produces a result.

The following code snippet presents the modification to utilize the `Function` interface:

```
@Bean
public Function<Message, String>
                          alertSlackChannelFunction() {
  return message -> {
    try {
      restClient.post()
```

```
                .uri(slackWebhookUrl)
            ...
```

When using `Function<Message,  String>`, we can pass an input (in this case, a `Message` object) and receive an output (in this case, a `String` object).

We have implemented these three functions in our configuration class. That's it! Now, let's run the application locally and test it.

Testing the application

To begin testing, import the Postman collection provided in the `ch09/postman` folder. It contains three requests: consumer, supplier, and function.

Let's call `alertSlackChannelFunction`. The `Function` interface expects an input and provides an output.

Figure 9.8 presents a screenshot of the result of calling `alertSlackChannelFunction`.

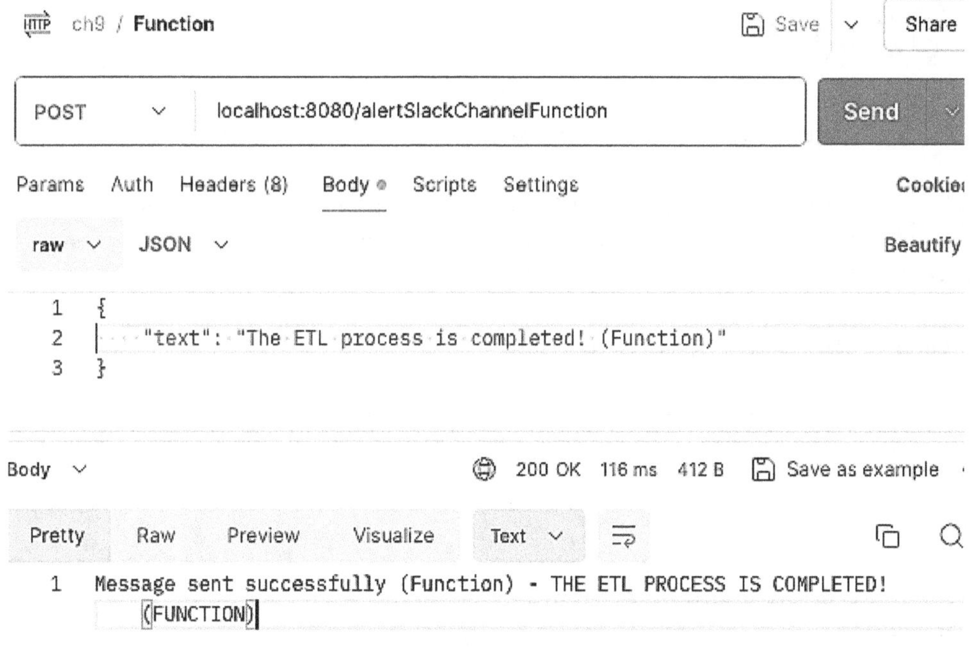

Figure 9.8: Result of calling alertSlackChannelFunction

We sent JSON content to the request body (input) and received the response's raw text (output). What about the results outside of Postman? The messages will be sent to the specified channel if you have configured Slack.

In the screenshot shown in *Figure 9.9*, we can see the messages in the `#wxauction-team` channel.

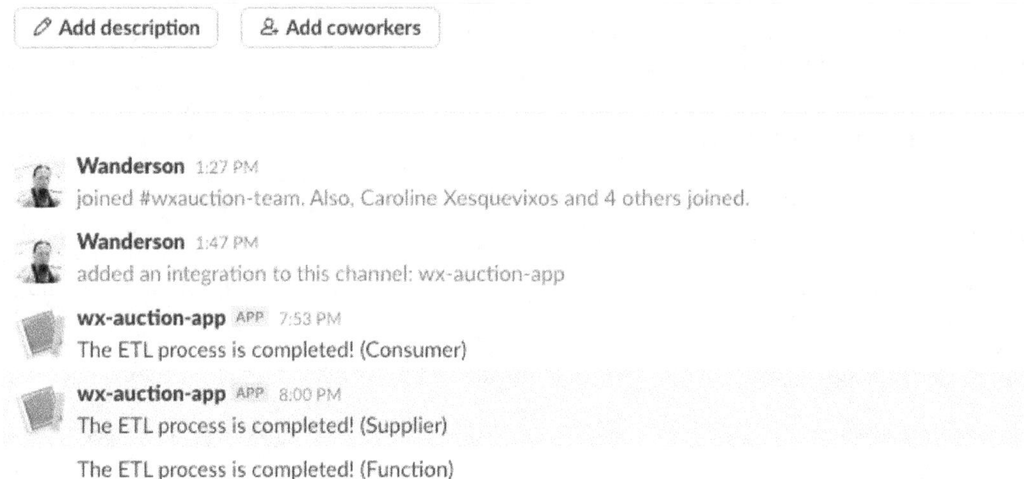

Figure 9.9: Slack's channel with the messages sent by the application

We utilized HTTP requests to invoke the functions, but it's also possible to use events; we can connect a broker to activate the functions through events, similar to what we did in the *Implementing the consumer* section of *Chapter 8*. Now, let's proceed with deploying the application on AWS.

Deploying the application on AWS

We need to make some changes before deploying our application on AWS. As shown in the following configuration snippet, we must add new dependencies to the `pom.xml` file for our application to work on AWS:

```
<dependency>
  <groupId>com.amazonaws</groupId>
  <artifactId>aws-lambda-java-core</artifactId>
</dependency>
<dependency>
  <groupId>org.springframework.cloud</groupId>
  <artifactId>spring-cloud-function-adapter-aws
  </artifactId>
</dependency>
<dependency>
```

```
    <groupId>com.amazonaws</groupId>
    <artifactId>aws-lambda-java-events</artifactId>
</dependency>
```

The `aws-lambda-java-core` dependency provides the foundational classes to implement Lambda functions in Java. The `spring-cloud-function-adapter-aws` dependency bridges Spring Cloud Function with AWS Lambda, making it easier to run Spring-based functions on AWS Lambda. The `aws-lambda-java-events` dependency offers ready-to-use classes for various AWS event types, simplifying working with AWS services in Lambda.

We also need to change the `pom.xml` file in the `<build><plugins>` section, adding the `maven-shade-plugin` plugin and the `spring-boot-thin-layout` dependency to create a package that can be deployed in Lambda AWS:

```
<build>
<plugins>
  <plugin>
    <groupId>org.springframework.boot</groupId>
    <artifactId>spring-boot-maven-plugin</artifactId>
    <dependencies>
      <dependency>
        <groupId>org.springframework.boot.experimental
        </groupId>
          <artifactId>spring-boot-thin-layout</artifactId>
          <version>1.0.31.RELEASE</version>
      </dependency>
    </dependencies>
  </plugin>
  <plugin>
    <groupId>org.apache.maven.plugins</groupId>
    <artifactId>maven-shade-plugin</artifactId>
    ...
```

Finally, we need to add the following configuration in the `application.properties` file:

```
spring.cloud.function.definition=alertSlackChannelFunction
```

The `spring.cloud.function.definition` property ensures that when the Lambda function is called, it will call `alertSlackChannelFunction`. It is essential to set up AWS deployment when the application contains multiple functions. However, even if there's only one function, explicitly setting this property is considered a good practice. Now, create the application JAR with Maven or using your preferred IDE.

Executing the application's deployment on AWS

You are assumed to have an AWS account or have created one to deploy the application. Let's start the deployment process:

1. Log in to the AWS console, search for Lambda, and press *Enter*. Then, click on the **Lambda** result.

2. On the newly loaded screen, click on the **Create Function** button.

3. Set up the configuration as shown in *Figure 9.10*, then click the **Create Function** button:

    - Select the **Author from scratch** option

    - For **Function name**, type `alertSlackChannelFunction`

    - For **Runtime**, select **Java 21**

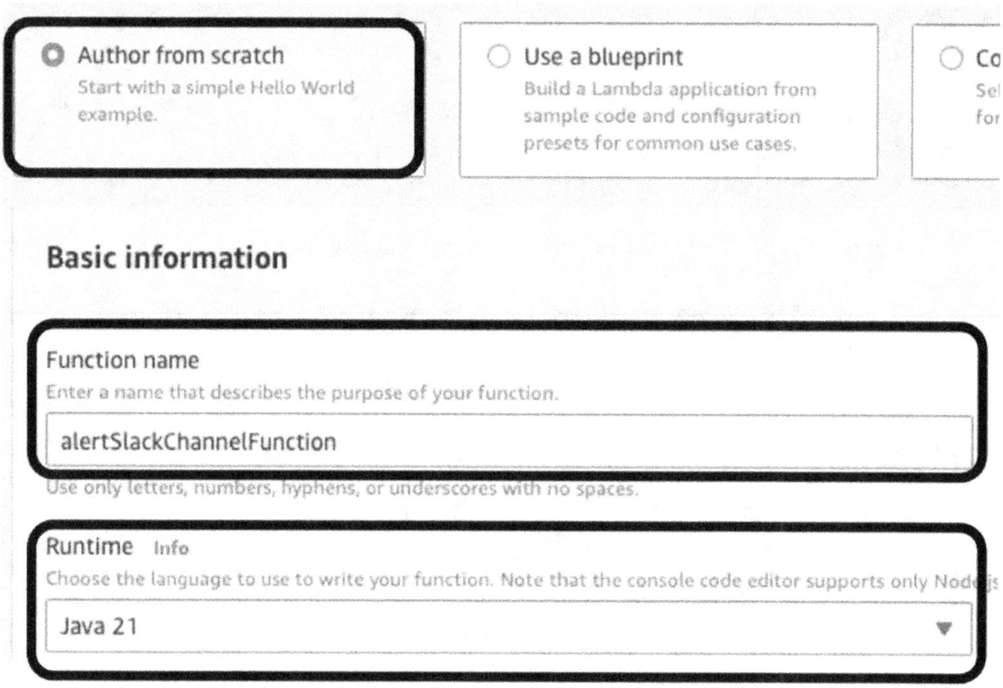

Figure 9.10: The Create Function screen

4. Go to the **Code** tab on the next screen and click the **Upload from** button. Then, upload the application jar named `alerting-faas-0.0.1-SNAPSHOT-aws.jar`.

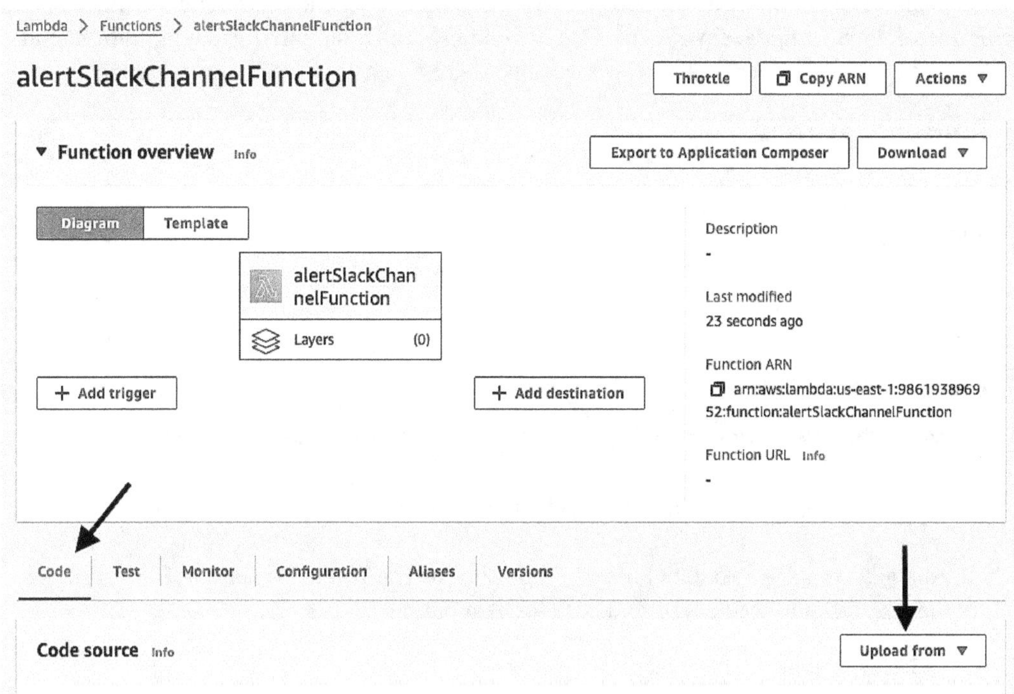

Figure 9.11: Application upload

5. After uploading, in the same **Code** tab, scroll down to the **Runtime settings** section, as shown in *Figure 9.12*, and click the **Edit** button.

Figure 9.12: The Runtime settings section

On the new screen presented, replace the content of the **Handler** input box with `org.springframework.cloud.function.adapter.aws.FunctionInvoker::handleRequest`, as shown in *Figure 9.13*, and click on the **Save** button. This setup is required to seamlessly integrate Spring Cloud Function with AWS Lambda, abstracting AWS Lambda specifics, simplifying configuration, and ensuring that the correct Spring function is invoked based on your application configuration.

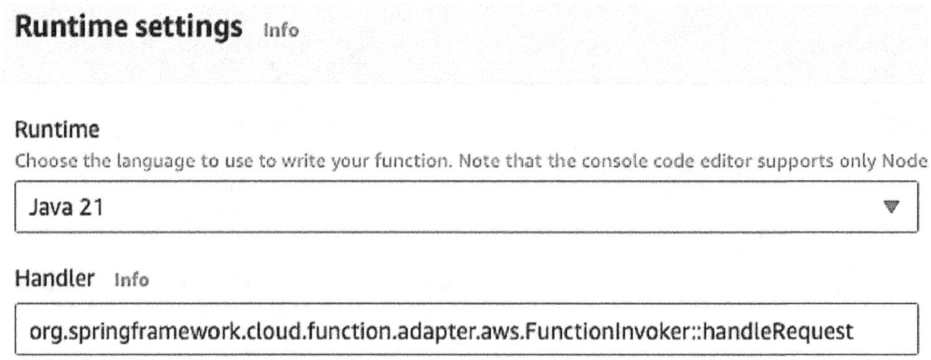

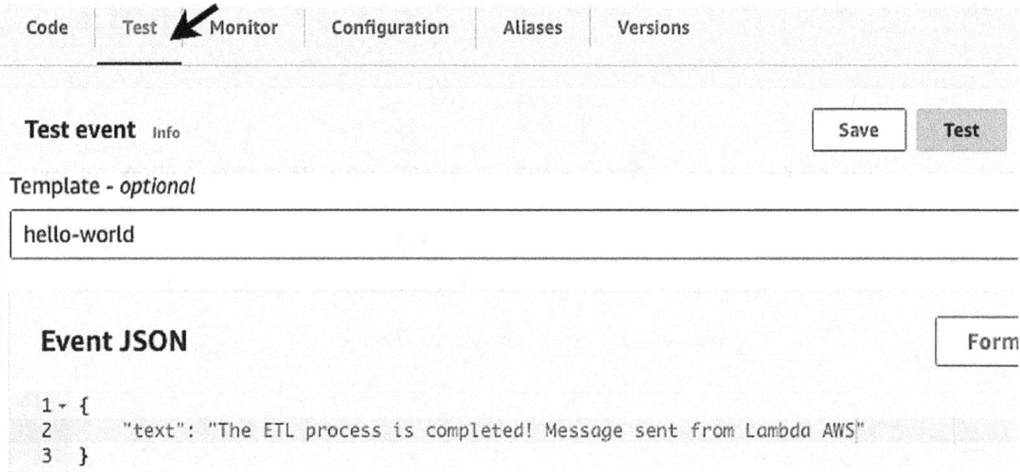

Figure 9.13: Runtime settings configuration screen

1. The setup is complete. Now, it's time to test it. Click on the **Test** tab, enter the JSON as shown in the screenshot in *Figure 9.14*, and click the **Test** button.

Figure 9.14: Test screen

2. The result will be prompted after the function's execution, as illustrated in *Figure 9.15*.

Executing function: succeeded (logs ☑)

  ▼ Details

The area below shows the last 4 KB of the execution log.

```
"Message sent successfully (Function) - THE ETL PROCESS IS COMPLETED! (FUNCTION -
```

Log output

The section below shows the logging calls in your code. Click here ☑ to view the corresponding CloudWatch log group.

```
START RequestId: 36351439-8321-4d96-a955-d622bc082036 Version: $LATEST
2024-09-01T16:10:16.477Z  INFO 2 --- [reporting-faas] [            main]
o.s.c.f.adapter.aws.AWSLambdaUtils        : Received: {"text":"The ETL process is
completed! (Function - AWS)"}
Message sent to Slack successfully. (Function)
END RequestId: 36351439-8321-4d96-a955-d622bc082036
REPORT RequestId: 36351439-8321-4d96-a955-d622bc082036  Duration: 2183.49 ms
```

Figure 9.15: Log of the function execution

3. If you set up Slack's webhook, you can also see the message on the channel, as shown in the screenshot in *Figure 9.16*.

Figure 9.16: Message sent to Slack channel

We've harnessed the power of FaaS with Spring Cloud Function to empower developers by enabling the deployment and execution of individual functions in the cloud without managing the underlying infrastructure. This combination provides unparalleled flexibility, cost efficiency, and automatic scaling, streamlining development and enabling seamless integration across multiple cloud environments for building modern, scalable applications.

Summary

The chapter introduced the pipe and filter architecture and Spring Batch framework, highlighting their advantages, challenges, and typical applications that use the pipe and filter architecture. It also guided you through developing a Spring Batch-based application for an online auction scenario, emphasizing data extraction from CSV files, processing, and storage in a database.

To conclude, the chapter also explored serverless architecture (namely, FaaS) using Spring Cloud Function. We learned about the benefits of FaaS, such as cost efficiency, auto-scaling, and reduced complexity, while addressing challenges such as cold starts and vendor lock-in. Additionally, we discussed how Spring Cloud Function allows us to create reusable, platform-agnostic functions deployable on multiple cloud providers such as AWS Lambda. Finally, we demonstrated building a Slack alert using FaaS and how to run and deploy the function locally and on AWS.

This chapter has equipped you with comprehensive knowledge of pipe and filter and serverless architectures and how to use them with the Spring Batch and Spring Cloud framework in real scenarios to build robust applications.

In *Chapter 10, Security*, we will explore the essential security aspects of software architecture. This will include an in-depth look at OAuth2 and OpenID for seamless authentication and authorization, which enhance our ability to secure and build resilient software systems. Additionally, we will implement an application using what we learned about security.

Questions

1. How does the pipe and filter architecture function, and what are its core components?
2. How does Spring Batch align with the pipe and filter architecture?
3. What are some advantages of Spring Batch in batch processing?
4. What is FaaS, and how does it work?
5. What are the benefits and the challenges of using FaaS?
6. What functional programming paradigms does Spring Cloud Function support?

Get This Book's PDF Version and Exclusive Extras

UNLOCK NOW

Scan the QR code (or go to `packtpub.com/unlock`). Search for this book by name, confirm the edition, and then follow the steps on the page.

Note: Keep your invoice handly. Purchase made directly from packt don't require one.

Part 3: Advanced Topics in Modern Software Development

This part focuses on advanced topics essential for building enterprise-ready applications. It covers key areas such as security, observability, testing, performance optimization, orchestration, and automation. By mastering these concepts, you'll gain the tools and techniques needed to ensure reliability, scalability, and efficiency in complex software systems.

This part has the following chapters:

- *Chapter 10, Security*
- *Chapter 11, Observability*
- *Chapter 12, Testing*
- *Chapter 13, Performance and Optimizations*
- *Chapter 14, Orchestration with Kubernetes*
- *Chapter 15, Continuous Integration and Continuous Deployment*

10
Security

This chapter focuses on essential security practices in software development, emphasizing the importance of integrating security from its conception. It explores principles such as encryption, authentication, and authorization and techniques to safeguard data at rest and in transit. The chapter highlights common threats such as denial-of-service (DoS) attacks, input injection, output encoding, cross-site request forgery (CSRF), and cross-site scripting (XSS) and discusses defense mechanisms to avoid them.

The chapter also introduces security frameworks, including Zero Trust Architecture (ZTA), threat modeling, and the Open Worldwide Application Security Project (OWASP).

In addition, the chapter provides an in-depth discussion of Open Authorization 2.0 (OAuth2) and OpenID Connect (OIDC) for securing user authentication and authorization with a practical implementation utilizing Spring Authorization Server.

This chapter covers the following:

- Reviewing key security topics
- Understanding OAuth2 and OIDC
- Implementing OAuth2 with Spring Authorization

By the end of this chapter, readers will be able to implement robust security measures in their applications, defend against modern threats, and manage user authentication and authorization using industry-standard protocols with OAuth2 and OIDC. This knowledge will equip developers to design and implement robust and secure applications.

Technical requirements

All the code for this chapter can be found on GitHub at `https://github.com/PacktPublishing/Software-Architecture-with-Spring/tree/main/ch10`. Ellipses in the code blocks indicate that parts of the code have been omitted, and the complete code is available on GitHub.

Reviewing key security topics

Security in software development should not be an afterthought but rather a fundamental aspect integrated from the very beginning of a project. Building security into a project from its conception ensures that systems are designed with robust protection mechanisms in mind, creating a solid foundation for safeguarding data, maintaining system integrity, and mitigating risks. When security is treated as a core component of the software development life cycle (SDLC), it becomes significantly more straightforward to manage, reducing the likelihood and impact of vulnerabilities later in the project. Let's understand and explore some crucial measures we must apply to guarantee security in our projects, beginning with securing data.

Securing data

In software architecture, it is crucial to ensure sensitive data's confidentiality, integrity, and availability. Encryption is paramount for protecting data at rest and in transit. However, what exactly is data at rest and in transit?

- **At rest** refers to data or files containing sensitive information stored on physical or virtual devices, such as databases, worksheets, flat files, filesystems, and backups. Encryption at rest secures the data and ensures that these files and their sensitive information remain protected and unreadable without an encryption key. This type of encryption typically employs symmetric encryption algorithms such as **Advanced Encryption Standard** (**AES**), where the same key is used for encryption and decryption.

- **In transit** refers to data transmitted across networks, such as between clients and servers or microservices. The successor to **Secure Sockets Layer** (**SSL**), **Transport Layer Security** (**TLS**) is the most used protocol for encrypting data during transmission. TLS relies on public key cryptography, where public keys are exchanged to establish a session securely.

Spring provides various tools for securing data at rest, such as Java Cryptography Extension (JCE) for AES encryption and BCrypt to hash passwords. For key management, it integrates with Amazon Web Services Key Management Service (AWS KMS) and HashiCorp Vault. For data in transit, it relies on TLS and supports secure communication between services through technologies such as Istio and Linkerd.

Now, it's time to learn about common threats and how to protect our applications against them. Let's start with DoS attacks.

Defending against DoS attacks

A DoS attack occurs when a malicious actor overwhelms a system, network, or web application with excessive requests, causing it to slow down or become unavailable to legitimate users. In a distributed DoS (DDoS) attack, multiple machines are used to send a flood of requests, making it more challenging to defend against. These attacks can target network bandwidth, server resources, or even specific applications by exploiting their weaknesses.

To prevent DoS attacks in a Spring web application or API, you can implement strategies such as the following:

- **Rate limiting**: A technique for determining the number of requests a user or IP can make to your application in a given period. It is essential in preventing DoS attacks because it limits malicious actors overwhelming your system with a flood of requests.

- **Circuit breaker pattern**: A circuit breaker prevents your system from being overwhelmed by halting requests to services that are struggling or failing due to overload. This pattern can block requests when a failure threshold is exceeded and automatically recover when the system stabilizes.

- **Request throttling**: This limits the rate at which requests are processed, slowing down the response time as the limit is approached. This reduces the risk of resource exhaustion in high-traffic scenarios. You can apply this at specific endpoints to protect against abuse.

- **CAPTCHA**: This prevents automated systems from submitting requests in a DoS attack. Integrating Google's reCAPTCHA into login, registration, or password reset forms can mitigate automated DoS attempts.

- **IP blocklisting and allowlisting**: You can allow only trusted IPs (allowlisting) or block specific IP addresses showing malicious behavior (blocklisting). This is especially useful for securing sensitive areas such as admin endpoints. In Spring Security, you can restrict access based on IP address:

```
http.authorizeRequests()
    .antMatchers("/adm/**").hasIpAddress("192.1.1.1")
    .anyRequest().authenticated();
```

The `.antMatchers("/adm/**").hasIpAddress("192.1.1.1")` expression is part of the configuration in Spring Security and restricts access to all URLs under `/admin/` to only clients coming from the IP address 192.1.1.1.

Preventing a DoS attack programmatically in a Spring web application or API requires a multilayered approach, combining rate limiting, request validation, circuit breakers, and security best practices such as IP filtering. Leveraging tools such as Spring Cloud Gateway, Resilience4j, and CAPTCHA integration can provide robust protection against such attacks. Additionally, proactive monitoring, load balancing, and a web application firewall (WAF) are essential to detect and mitigate threats before they cause significant harm.

Ensuring security through input validation and output encoding

Sanitizing inputs with input validation and encoding outputs are essential techniques for preventing injection attacks such as SQL Injection and XSS, which occur when malicious users manipulate input to execute harmful code. Let's explore how to sanitize our inputs and encode outputs.

Sanitizing inputs

Input validation ensures that the data users enter is of the expected format and values. This step is crucial because attackers often exploit unvalidated input fields by injecting malicious data. Proper validation involves checking the data's type, length, and patterns through regular expressions (regexes) to enforce strict patterns for inputs such as emails and phone numbers.

A typical attack regarding input validation is SQL Injection, which occurs when an attacker manipulates an application's SQL queries by injecting malicious SQL code into input fields, allowing the attacker to retrieve, modify, and execute database operations.

The most common case of SQL Injection occurs when the code concatenates SQL statements. In case the application does not sanitize inputs, an attacker could input something such as ' OR '1' = ' into the username field, and the resulting query would be as presented:

```
SELECT * FROM users WHERE username = '' OR '1' = '1' AND password =
'password123';
```

This query would always return true ('1' = '1' is always true), potentially giving the attacker access to the application without needing a valid username and password.

We can prevent such attacks using proper input validation and prepared statements (parameterized queries). The following code snippet presents a JdbcTemplate instance with parameterized queries, represented by ?, that avoid SQL Injection:

```
String sql = "SELECT * FROM users WHERE id = ?";
jdbcTemplate.query(sql, new Object[]{userId}, rowMapper);
```

The userId instance is then safely passed as a parameter without directly concatenating it into the SQL string.

Now, let's explore another crucial item of security: output encoding.

Encoding output

Output encoding ensures that data rendered on web pages is correctly formatted and interpreted as content rather than executable code. This is vital in preventing XSS attacks, where attackers inject malicious JavaScript scripts into web applications, leading to unintended script execution in users' browsers.

For example, if user input is directly rendered without encoding, an attacker could insert a <script> script tag in a comment field that is capable of getting executed by the browser when displayed. To prevent the execution of the code, user input should be encoded before being rendered in HTML, CSS, or JavaScript contexts.

In Spring, we can use libraries such as Thymeleaf, which by default escapes dangerous characters such as <, >, and &, ensuring that any input is treated as plain text, not executable code. The following code snippet uses the Thymeleaf text component:

```
<p th:text="${userComment}"></p>
```

Using the Thymeleaf component, th:text automatically escapes any special characters in userComment, preventing XSS vulnerabilities.

Combining input validation to filter malicious inputs and output encoding to neutralize potential executable code reduces the risk of SQL Injection and XSS attacks. These techniques are foundational to web security and should be applied consistently to all input and output handling in web applications.

Now, let's learn what CSRF is.

Preventing CSRF

A CSRF attack occurs when a malicious site deceives a user into performing unintended actions on a different website from where they are authenticated. The attacker exploits the user's authenticated session to perform actions without their consent. CSRF protection is unnecessary for stateless microservices using token-based authentication but is recommended for stateful web interfaces that rely on cookies.

CSRF protection is enabled by default in Spring Security. However, as the following code snippet shows, we can disable it if necessary:

```
@Bean
public SecurityFilterChain filterChain(HttpSecurity http)
        throws Exception {
  http.csrf(csrf -> csrf.disable())
  ...
```

The `http.csrf(csrf -> csrf.disable())` statement will disable the CSRF for the application.

When CSRF protection is enabled in Spring, a CSRF token is generated for each session and included in forms as a hidden field. The server checks for this token in requests to ensure the request is legitimate.

The following code snippet presents Spring Security's built-in tag, `<input type="hidden" name="${_csrf.parameterName}" value="${_csrf.token}"/>`, to automatically add a CSRF token to forms, ensuring protection against CSRF attacks:

```
<form th:action="@{/submit}" method="post">
  <input type="hidden" th:name="${_csrf.parameterName}"
          th:value="${_csrf.token}" />
  ...
```

By following these practices, Spring Security ensures your application is protected from CSRF attacks, securing any state-changing operations from unauthorized requests.

Presenting important security measures

Here, we will present essential security frameworks and organizations that provide crucial security measures to safeguard applications. We must constantly monitor them to guarantee security. We will introduce ZTA, threat modeling with Spoofing, Tampering, Repudiation, Information disclosure, Denial of service, and Elevation of privilege (**STRIDE**), the OWASP organization and its Top 10 list of the most critical web security risks, and the importance of managing vulnerability and patching.

Introducing ZTA

Zero Trust Architecture (**ZTA**) is a security framework built on the principle of *never trust, always verify*. It assumes that threats can exist inside and outside the network; therefore, no user, device, or system is trusted by default. Access requests must be continuously authenticated, authorized, and validated based on the **principle of least privilege** (**PoLP**). ZTA includes continuous verification, least privilege access, microsegmentation, strong identity verification, encryption, and secure access. It's beneficial for cloud security, remote work, and preventing data breaches, making it essential for maintaining robust security in today's digital environments.

You can access the official publication and detailed information on the National Institute of Standards and Technology (**NIST**) website at `https://www.nist.gov/publications/zero-trust-architecture`.

Now, let's understand threat modeling.

Acknowledging threat modeling

Threat modeling is a proactive security approach that involves identifying potential risks in a system's architecture before exploiting them. It helps visualize how attackers could exploit vulnerabilities. The process includes identifying critical assets such as sensitive data, assessing attack vectors, analyzing potential threat actors, and defining mitigation strategies for each risk.

A popular framework for threat modeling is STRIDE, developed by Microsoft, which defines the following:

- **Spoofing**: When an attacker impersonates another user or system to gain unauthorized access, often by stealing credentials or forging authentication tokens.

- **Tampering**: The unauthorized modification of data, which can involve altering data in transit or modifying stored data.

- **Repudiation**: This happens when a user denies an action, making it hard to prove their involvement without proper logging and accountability.

- **Information disclosure**: Refers to exposing sensitive data to unauthorized users. This can involve unintentional leaks, data breaches, or improperly configured access controls.

- **DoS attacks**: Aim to render a system or service inaccessible to legitimate users by inundating it with excessive requests or consuming resources, thus degrading the service or causing the system to crash.

- **Elevation of privilege**: Occurs when an attacker obtains higher-level permissions than they are supposed to have, enabling them to perform actions as a more privileged user or administrator.

The STRIDE framework allows architects to analyze threats across various attack surfaces systematically. For more information, you can explore the official Microsoft documentation at `https://learn.microsoft.com/en-us/azure/security/develop/threat-modeling-tool-threats`.

OWASP

OWASP is a non-profit organization focused on enhancing web application security by providing free tools, documentation, and guidelines for developers and security professionals. Its most notable contribution is the OWASP Top 10, a regularly updated list highlighting the most critical web security risks, typically revised every 3 to 4 years. Here is an overview of the top 10 risks from the latest version launched in 2021:

1. **Broken access control**: Issues when users can access resources or perform actions beyond their permissions, such as unauthorized access to sensitive data or functionalities, often due to improper enforcement of access controls.

2. **Cryptographic failures**: Issues related to encryption or cryptographic processes that can lead to sensitive data exposure. This includes weak or improper cryptography practices, such as using outdated algorithms or mismanaging encryption keys.

3. **Injection**: Involves injecting malicious data, such as through SQL Injection and XSS, into a web application, typically through input fields.

4. **Insecure design**: Design flaws in the application, such as lack of secure design patterns, weak architecture, or failure to incorporate security measures during the design phase, leading to exploitable vulnerabilities.

5. **Security misconfiguration**: Security settings not properly configured, such as default credentials, overly permissive settings, or missing security patches.

6. **Vulnerable and outdated components**: Outdated software, libraries, or components with known vulnerabilities are often challenging to track, and failing to keep them updated can lead to easily exploitable security risks.

7. **Identification and authentication failures**: Formerly known as broken authentication, this involves flaws in user identification and authentication mechanisms. Common problems include weak passwords, improper session management, or missing **multi-factor authentication (MFA)**, which can lead to unauthorized access.

8. **Software and data integrity failures**: Regarding software updates, critical data, or continuous integration and continuous development (CI/CD) pipelines without verifying integrity. Insecure deserialization and trust issues with third-party software or updates also fall under this category.

9. **Security logging and monitoring failures**: Inadequate logging and monitoring make detecting breaches and other security incidents difficult. This category highlights the importance of comprehensive logging and monitoring to ensure proper **incident response (IR)**.

10. **Server-side request forgery (SSRF)**: SSRF occurs when an application can be tricked into making requests to unintended internal or external systems.

These risks highlight critical vulnerabilities in web applications that developers and security professionals should prioritize to protect against modern threats.

Vulnerability management in software development is an ongoing process that involves identifying, assessing, addressing, and reporting security vulnerabilities in software and hardware. This includes routinely performing vulnerability assessments and penetration testing to identify and resolve security vulnerabilities. It also requires prompt patching of libraries, dependencies, and platforms, mainly when new vulnerabilities are discovered.

Tools such as Dependabot, WhiteSource, and Clair can automate the tracking and patching of vulnerabilities. Regular updates to frameworks and libraries, such as Spring, are essential to ensure that the latest security patches are applied, minimizing the risk from known vulnerabilities.

Now that we comprehend the importance of security and recognize the main threats, let's explore OAuth2 and OIDC, which are crucial to application security.

Understanding OAuth2 and OIDC

OAuth2 and OIDC are two important frameworks – the former for authorization and the latter for authentication. However, before explaining them, we must understand the concepts and differences between entity and identity and the difference between authentication and authorization. So, let's start by demystifying entity and identity.

Clarifying entity and identity

Let's understand entity and identity, two frequently misunderstood and misused terms.

An entity is any object, such as a user, a device, or an application, that can be represented and referenced in a security context. Essentially, it refers to something that exists and interacts with the system.

Identity is the attributes that uniquely identify an entity within a specific context. These attributes can be credentials, such as a username and password, or tokens that represent the entity within a system.

The following table presents a comparison of the two terms:

Entity	Identity
Represents a physical or virtual object such as a user, system, application, and so on.	Represents the information that identifies an entity.
Can be a user, application, or system.	Defined by attributes or credentials that describe the entity, such as username or email.
Does not inherently carry any information about authentication.	Is directly involved in the authentication and identification process.

Table 10.1: Comparison between entity and identity

Now that we have distinguished and understood what entity and identity are, we will analyze the concepts of authentication and authorization and their differences.

Understanding authentication and authorization

Authentication and authorization often need clarification, although they are the heart of application security. Let's clarify each one.

Authentication is the process of verifying a user's identity. For example, when you take a test at a certification center, you must prove that you are the person you claim to be by presenting your ID document. The staff will check your photo and data to confirm your identity. In a system, we use credentials such as username and password for authentication.

There are many methods of authentication used in APIs and web applications; common types are the following:

- **Credential-based authentication**: This category includes basic authentication and digest authentication. Users supply their credentials, such as username and password, in every request. Basic authentication sends credentials encoded in Base64, while digest authentication adds an extra layer of security by hashing the password with a nonce to prevent replay attacks. Both methods are straightforward but require HTTPS to ensure security during transmission.

- **Token-based authentication**: This includes bearer token authentication, **JSON Web Token (JWT)**, and OAuth2. In token-based systems, a token is issued after initial authentication and used in subsequent requests. Bearer tokens are simple strings that act as access keys, while JWT tokens carry user information and claims in a signed, self-contained format, allowing stateless authentication. OAuth2 is a broader framework that we will approach next in the *Exploring the OAuth2 framework* section.

Authorization, on the other hand, is the process of verifying what a user is allowed to do. It is concerned only with the user's permission and not their identity. For example, after entering the venue of a musical concert, you can move to the VIP area. The staff will check your authorization using the ticket to see if it allows access to the VIP area, regardless of who you are. A system will check if you are permitted to execute a specific command, such as making a financial transaction or only accessing transaction records.

Now that the concepts of entity, identity, authentication, and authorization are understood, let's explore OAuth2.

Exploring the OAuth2 framework

OAuth2 is a framework for authorization outlined in RFC 6749 and available at `https://datatracker.ietf.org/doc/html/rfc6749`. It allows third-party applications to access users' resources on other services without exposing their credentials. It is commonly used for delegated access, meaning the user can grant a client limited permissions to act on their behalf. It is a little confusing, so let's explain it another way with an example.

Imagine you want to use a third-party application without creating a new account. You want it to get your data from your Google account. In this scenario, in the OAuth2 context, the third-party application (client) requests your user's data via the Google API (resource server) on your behalf, who is the resource owner. Here, Google will be the authorization server as well. Let's scrutinize each actor of the OAuth2 framework:

- **Resource owner**: The person or entity that owns the resource.

- **Client**: The application that requests access to the resource on behalf of the resource owner.

- **Authorization server**: This authenticates the resource owner and issues access tokens to the client. It can be a third-party provider, such as Google or GitHub, which offers OAuth2-based authentication, or a custom-built authorization server developed by the team that provides full control over security policies and token management.

- **Resource server**: A server that holds protected resources, such as web services or APIs, and validates access tokens.

Figure 10.1 illustrates the actors involved in the basic OAuth2 flow.

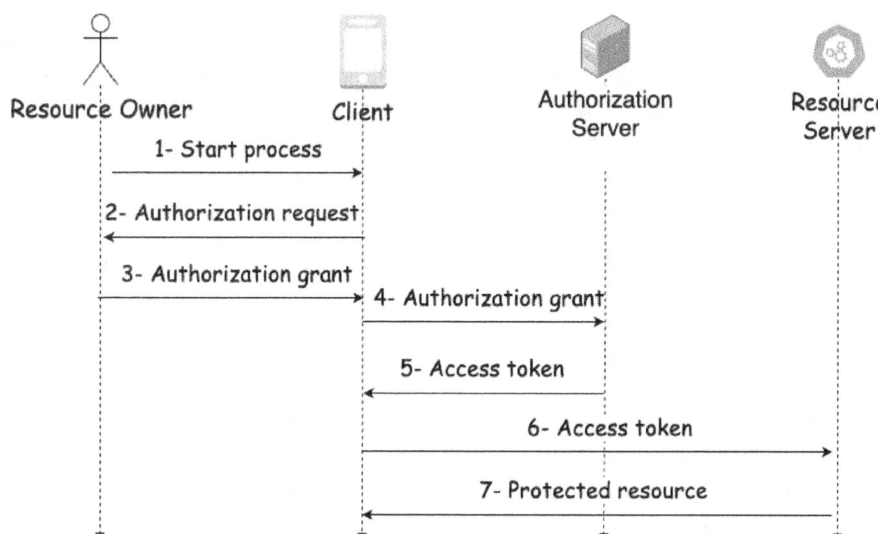

Figure 10.1: OAuth2 flow

The **resource owner** starts the process by triggering some action on the application, such as clicking on an application's button to authenticate via an authorization provider. The **client** then requests authorization or consent from the resource owner. Once the **resource owner** grants permission to the **client**, it forwards this **authorization grant** to the **authorization server**, which returns an access token that the **client** can use to request **protected resources**.

An **access token** is a credential that permits the client to request protected resources from the resource server on behalf of the user. It typically has a short lifespan for security reasons, ensuring its impact is minimized even if a token is compromised. For longer-term access, the authorization server may also provide a refresh token, which can be used to request a new access token without further user interaction.

OAuth2 relies heavily on the secure transmission and storage of access tokens. It is important to use HTTPS to encrypt data in transit and ensure that tokens are stored securely in clients. OAuth2 also mitigates risks by setting token expiration times and limiting the damage of compromised tokens.

Now, let's learn what scopes are.

What are scopes?

Scopes in OAuth2 define specific actions or resources a client can access on behalf of the user. For instance, a scope may limit a client's access to read-only permissions for a user's profile or allow complete data modification. Properly setting scopes ensures the client can only access the minimum required permissions.

Acknowledging grant types

Grant types refer to the different methods or flows by which a client gets an access token from the authorization server. These grant types define how an application can request access to a resource owner's protected resources, depending on the use case and the security requirements. Each grant type handles the exchange of authorization data differently based on the specific interaction between the client, resource owner, authorization server, and resource server. Let's present the most common OAuth2 grant types:

- **Authorization code**: This method of authorization is most suitable for server-side applications. In this process, the client exchanges an authorization code obtained after the user logs in for an access token. This approach offers high security by ensuring that tokens are kept confidential and are not stored in the browser.

- **Implicit**: The implicit grant is primarily used for *single-page applications* (*SPAs*) or mobile apps. In this flow, the client gets the access token directly from the authorization server without a server-to-server code exchange. However, this method is considered less secure and is now deprecated in favor of the authorization code grant with **Proof Key for Code Exchange** (**PKCE**).

- **Client credentials**: This method is utilized for machine-to-machine interactions. To get a token, the client authenticates directly with the authorization server using unique credentials, such as client ID and secret. This authentication process does not involve any user interaction.

- **Resource Owner Password Credentials (ROPC)**: ROPC allows the client to swap the user's credentials for an access token directly. Although this method is generally discouraged due to security vulnerabilities, it can be considered for trusted clients, specifically internal applications.

- **Authorization code with PKCE**: This is an enhanced and more secure version of the authorization code. It is specifically designed for public clients, such as mobile and SPAs. PKCE adds a layer of security by utilizing dynamically generated code challenges and verifiers to prevent the interception of authorization codes. It lessens the risk of unauthorized access and enhances the security of the authorization process.

- **Device code grant**: This is specifically tailored for devices with limited input capabilities, such as **Internet of Things** (**IoT**) devices or smart TVs. In this process, the device presents a unique code to the user, who then authorizes it on a separate device with more advanced input capabilities, such as a phone or computer. This method allows for the secure and convenient authorization of devices with differing input capabilities.

Grant types in OAuth2 define how the client gets an access token from the authorization server to access protected resources. Different grant types are used based on the application and whether a user is involved. Each grant type has its specific flow and security considerations, and the choice of grant type depends on the system's security and user interaction requirements.

OAuth 2.0 is constantly used to secure APIs and is integral to token-based authentication. As we will explore next, it works alongside other protocols such as OIDC for **identity management (IdM)**.

Exploring OIDC

OpenID Connect (OIDC) is an identity layer built on top of the OAuth 2.0 framework. It enables client applications, such as web or mobile apps, to verify a user's identity and obtain basic profile information from an **identity provider (IdP)**, such as Google, Facebook, or other OIDC providers. OIDC adds a standardized way to perform user authentication, allowing applications to authenticate users and retrieve profile data uniformly and securely. This process relies on an ID token containing identity-related claims (such as the user's name, email, and other attributes) in JSON format.

OIDC simplifies verifying users' identities by leveraging the authorization server's authentication and enabling profile information to be retrieved interoperably and REST-like. Additionally, developers can request different claims, such as email or profile, using specific scopes, including OpenID for authentication, profile, or email, depending on the application's needs.

How is OIDC related to OAuth2?

OAuth 2.0 is primarily designed for authorization, enabling applications to access user data with their permission. In contrast, OIDC extends OAuth 2.0 to incorporate user authentication. One key distinction is the addition of the `openid` scope and the ID token, which carries identity-related information in JSON format, allowing the client to confirm the user's identity.

OIDC introduces the concept of *flows* to support various user interactions, while OAuth 2.0 uses the term *grant* to represent the authorization process. For example, OIDC's Authorization Code Flow is often used in scenarios requiring authentication and resource access. These additional features make OIDC a natural extension of OAuth 2.0, enabling secure verification of user identities and providing controlled access to resources.

Both protocols work together in many cases, such as in *single sign-on* (*SSO*) implementations, where users log in to third-party services using providers such as Google or Facebook. This allows applications to obtain user profile data and access other resources securely without exposing credentials to the client application. Now, let's implement both protocols in our application.

Implementing OAuth2 with Spring Authorization

It's time to put our learning into practice. We will use Spring Authorization Server, a framework that offers OAuth2 and OIDC authentication and authorization capabilities for Spring-based applications. It issues clients with access tokens, refresh tokens, and ID tokens following OAuth2 flows.

Online auction case study

As our online auction application grows, we now face a new challenge: third-party clients and external applications are requesting access to our product catalog through APIs. Exposing the product API requires careful consideration of security measures. Relying solely on traditional API keys or basic authentication is no longer sufficient.

System definition and mission

We will implement a robust authentication and authorization mechanism to securely expose our product API to external clients. We will introduce a new component to enforce access control: the authorization server.

The authorization server ensures that any external client requesting product data on behalf of a user is properly registered and authorized to access the API. *Figure 10.2* outlines the essential components we will focus on to implement the OAuth2 flow.

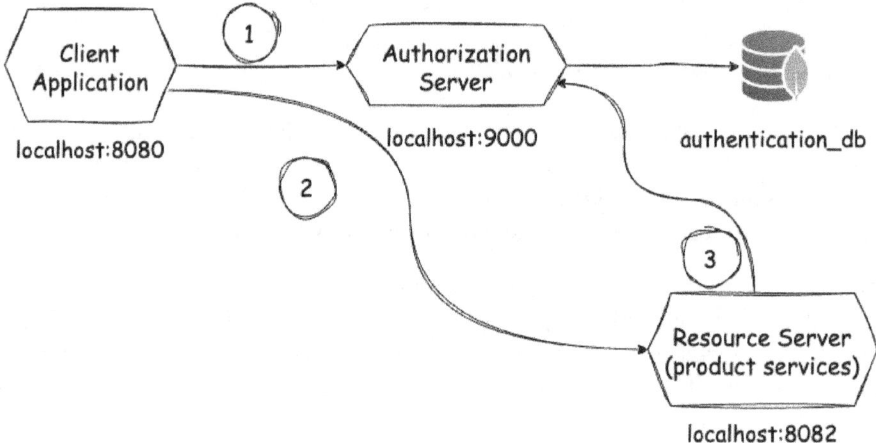

Figure 10.2: Components to implement OAuth2 flow

Let's explain the components' flow:

1. The client requests the authorization server to verify the user's identity and acquire an access token.

2. The authorization server generates an access token upon successful authentication, allowing the client application to access protected resources.

3. The client application transmits the access token to the resource server (product services) to access the requested resource. The resource server verifies the token with the authorization server before granting access.

Then, we will develop two new components, the authorization server and the client application, and adapt the product services to function as resource servers. Let's begin by implementing the authorization server.

Implementing the authorization server

We will utilize the Spring Authorization Server framework to streamline the implementation of our authorization server, leveraging OAuth2 and OIDC. However, understanding the underlying processes for setting it up securely and effectively is crucial when creating the authorization server. We will follow these steps:

1. Create an authorization server project and include the required dependencies.

2. Implement security filters to handle authentication, authorization, and OIDC endpoints.

3. Set up user management to define authentication mechanisms for users and their credentials.

4. Register OAuth2 clients to ensure only authorized applications can request tokens.

5. Manage tokens by implementing encoding, decoding, and validation of access tokens.

6. Configure authorization server settings to enforce security and compliance with OAuth 2.0 specifications.

With the steps outlined, let's begin implementing the authorization server.

Creating the authorization server

Let's set up our authorization server, which we will call `authorization-server`.

The following code snippet presents the dependencies needed to implement an authorization server with Spring Authorization Server:

```xml
<dependency>
    <groupId>org.springframework.boot</groupId>
    <artifactId>spring-boot-starter-oauth2-authorization-
    server</artifactId>
</dependency>
<dependency>
    <groupId>org.springframework.boot</groupId>
    <artifactId>spring-boot-starter-security</artifactId>
</dependency>
<dependency>
    <groupId>org.springframework.boot</groupId>
    <artifactId>spring-boot-starter-web</artifactId>
</dependency>
```

The `spring-boot-starter-oauth2-authorization-server` dependency is a Spring Boot starter that simplifies the implementation of an OAuth2 authorization server in a Spring application. It enables applications to act as an authorization server, issuing access tokens, refresh tokens, and ID tokens while supporting OAuth2 and OIDC flows. It integrates seamlessly with Spring Security, the `spring-boot-starter-security` dependency, providing built-in support for authentication, token management, and client registration.

The `spring-boot-starter-web` dependency enables the creation of RESTful endpoints for handling OAuth2 authorization flows and token management.

Now, let's implement security filters.

Implementing security filter chains to enable OAuth2 and OIDC

We must create a `SecurityFilterConfig` configuration class to configure the security filter chains for the authorization server. The following code snippet presents the `SecurityFilterConfig` class and the first security filter chain, the `authorizationServerSecurityFilterChain` method. It configures security settings for the Spring Authorization Server framework and applies the default OAuth2 authorization server security configurations:

```java
@Configuration
public class SecurityFilterConfig {
@Order(1)
@Bean
SecurityFilterChain authorizationServerSecurityFilterChain
    (HttpSecurity http) throws Exception {

  OAuth2AuthorizationServerConfiguration
    .applyDefaultSecurity(http);
  http.getConfigurer
    (OAuth2AuthorizationServerConfigurer.class)
    .oidc(withDefaults());
  http.exceptionHandling((exceptions) -> exceptions
    .authenticationEntryPoint(
      new LoginUrlAuthenticationEntryPoint("/login")))
      .oauth2ResourceServer(conf ->
        conf.jwt(withDefaults()));

  return http.build();
}
```

The `OAuth2AuthorizationServerConfiguration.applyDefaultSecurity(http)` instruction applies the default security settings for handling HTTP requests in an OAuth2 authorization server, enforcing authentication and token security policies.

The `http.getConfigurer(OAuth2AuthorizationServerConfigurer.class).oidc(Customizer.withDefaults())` instruction enables OIDC support with default values through a customizer, allowing authentication via OIDC-compliant IdPs and enabling features such as user info endpoints and ID tokens.

The `http.exceptionHandling((exceptions) -> exceptions.authenticationEntryPoint(new LoginUrlAuthenticationEntryPoint("/login")))` instruction configures exception handling by redirecting unauthenticated users to the `/login` screen when they try to access protected resources.

The `oauth2ResourceServer(conf -> conf.jwt(Customizer .withDefaults()))` instruction enables the OAuth2 resource server capabilities, allowing the authorization server to validate JWT tokens.

The following code snippet defines the default `SecurityFilterChain` configuration in `SecurityFilterConfig`, enforcing authentication for all requests and restricting access to authenticated users only. It also enables form-based login as the authentication mechanism:

```
@Order(2)
@Bean
SecurityFilterChain defaultSecurityFilterChain
    (HttpSecurity http)throws Exception {
  http.authorizeHttpRequests((authorize) -> authorize
    .anyRequest().authenticated())
    .formLogin(Customizer.withDefaults());
  return http.build();
}
```

The `SecurityFilterChain` configuration ensures that all requests require authentication. If a user not authenticated tries to access a protected resource, an exception is thrown, triggering the authentication entry point defined in the first `SecurityFilterChain` configuration (`authorizationServerSecurityFilterChain`). This redirects the user to the `/login` screen, as previously configured.

Our `SecurityFilterChain` configurations are in place to enforce OAuth2 and OIDC security, handle authentication exceptions by redirecting unauthenticated users to the `/login` screen, and enable JWT-based resource server support. Additionally, they ensure that all requests require authentication. Now, let's implement the code to manage user authentication.

Implementing the user management configuration

Now, let's work on user authentication management. The following code snippet defines the `UserManagementConfig` configuration class, configuring user authentication and security by providing a `UserDetailsService` bean. It retrieves user details from a MongoDB datasource:

```
@Configuration
public class UserManagementConfig {

    private final AuthenticationMongoDatasource
        authenticationRepository;
    ...
    @Bean
    public UserDetailsService userDetailsService() {
      return this::loadUserByUsername;
    }
    private UserDetails loadUserByUsername(String username)
      throws UsernameNotFoundException {
        AuthenticationEntity authentication =
          authenticationRepository.findByUsername(username)
          .orElseThrow(() -> new
          UsernameNotFoundException("User not found with
          username: " + username));
      ...
}
    @Bean
    public BCryptPasswordEncoder passwordEncoder() {
      return new BCryptPasswordEncoder();}
```

The `UserManagementConfig` class is responsible for user authentication. The `userDetailsService` method provides a `UserDetailsService` bean that retrieves user details during authentication. It delegates user lookup to the `loadUserByUsername` method, which fetches user information from the MongoDB database, assigns roles, and returns a `UserDetails` object for authentication and authorization. Additionally, `BCryptPasswordEncoder passwordEncoder()` provides a password encryption mechanism using BCrypt. Now, let's implement the code to register and manage OAuth2 clients.

Implementing registered client configuration

Let's implement the code to register and manage OAuth2 clients, ensuring they can securely authenticate and obtain access tokens from the authorization server.

The following code snippet shows the `RegisteredClientConfig` configuration class to manage registered OAuth2 clients:

```
@Configuration
public class RegisteredClientConfig {

  @Bean
  RegisteredClientRepository registeredClientRepository() {

    RegisteredClient registeredClient =
      RegisteredClient.withId(UUID.randomUUID().toString())
      .clientId("client-application")
      .clientSecret("$2a$10$...")
      .clientAuthenticationMethod(
        ClientAuthenticationMethod.CLIENT_SECRET_BASIC)
      .authorizationGrantType(
        AuthorizationGrantType.AUTHORIZATION_CODE)
      .authorizationGrantType(
        AuthorizationGrantType.REFRESH_TOKEN)
      .redirectUri(
        "http://127.0.0.1:8080/login/oauth2/code/client-server-oidc")
      .scope(OidcScopes.OPENID)
      .scope(OidcScopes.PROFILE)
      .clientSettings(ClientSettings.builder()
      .requireAuthorizationConsent(true).build())
      .build();

    return new
    InMemoryRegisteredClientRepository(registeredClient);
  }
}
```

The `ClientManagementConfig` class registers and manages OAuth2 clients in the authorization server. It defines a `RegisteredClientRepository` bean that stores client details and configurations.

The `registeredClientRepository` method registers an OAuth2 client with the following attributes:

- `withId`: Defines a **unique identifier (UID)** for the client.

- `clientId`: Specifies the UID for the OAuth2 client used for authentication with the authorization server.

- `clientSecret`: Sets a secret key for client authentication.

- `clientAuthenticationMethod`: Defines how the client authenticates. Using `CLIENT_SECRET_BASIC`, the client ID and secret will be validated.

- `authorizationGrantType`: Specifies the OAuth2 authorization flow.

  - The authorization code flow (`AUTHORIZATION_CODE`) follows these steps:

    i. **User requests login**: The client redirects the user to the authorization server's login page.

    ii. **User authenticates and grants consent**: The user logs in and approves the requested permissions (scopes).

    iii. **Authorization code issued**: The authorization server redirects the user to the client with an authorization code.

    iv. **Client exchanges code for token**: The client sends the authorization code and credentials to the authorization server's token endpoint.

    v. **Access token issued**: The authorization server validates the code and responds with an access token and, optionally, a refresh token.

  - The refresh token flow (`REFRESH_TOKEN`) follows these steps:

    i. **Access token issued**: When a user authenticates via the authorization code flow, the authorization server issues both an access token and a refresh token.

    ii. **Access token expires**: The access token has a limited lifespan and eventually expires.

    iii. **Client requests a new token**: Instead of soliciting the user to log in again, the client transmits the refresh token to the authorization server's token endpoint.

    iv. **Authorization server validates the refresh token**: It verifies that the refresh token is valid, unexpired, and associated with the correct client.

    v. **New access token issued**: If valid, the authorization server returns with a new access token and, optionally, a new refresh token.

- `redirectUri`: Defines the URI where the authorization server should send the code and tokens. Breaking down the redirect URI, we have the following:

  - `http://127.0.0.1:8080`: The application URL where the OAuth2 client is running.

  - `/login/oauth2/code`: The default endpoint where Spring Security expects to receive authorization codes.

  - `client-server-oidc`: The client registration ID must match the `registrationId` defined in Spring's OAuth2 client configuration. Note that `client-server` is the client's name.

- `scope`: Specifies the permissions granted to the client.

- `requireAuthorizationConsent`: Determines whether user consent is required before authorization.

Currently, client details are stored in an in-memory repository, but similar to user management, they can also be persisted in a database. Now, let's implement the management of the JWT token.

Implementing the management of the JWT token

The following code snippet presents the `JwtTokenConfig` class. It configures token signing and validation in the Spring authorization server. It defines how JWT tokens are signed, stored, and decoded, ensuring secure token issuance and verification:

```
@Configuration
public class JwtTokenConfig {

  @Bean
  JWKSource<SecurityContext> jwkSource() {
    KeyPair keyPair = generateRsaKey();

    ...

  }


  @Bean
  JwtDecoder jwtDecoder(JWKSource<SecurityContext>
        jwkSource) {
    return OAuth2AuthorizationServerConfiguration
        .jwtDecoder(jwkSource);
  }
  ...

}
```

The `JWKSource<SecurityContext> jwkSource()` method generates and stores cryptographic keys used to sign and verify JWT tokens issued by the authorization server. When a user logs in and receives a token, this method ensures that the token is securely signed using an RSA key pair (public and private keys). The private key is used to sign the token, while the public key allows services to verify its authenticity.

The `JwtDecoder jwtDecoder(JWKSource<SecurityContext> jwkSource)` method validates and decodes JWT tokens issued by the authorization server. When a user makes requests with a JWT token, this method ensures that the token is authentic and untampered by verifying its digital signature using the public key obtained from `JWKSource`.

The last step in concluding the authorization server implementation is coding the configuration defined for the authorization server.

Implementing the settings for the authorization server

Let's implement the code to apply the defined configuration to the authorization server. The following code snippet shows the `AuthorizationServerConfig` class:

```
@Configuration
public class AuthorizationServerConfig {
  @Bean
  AuthorizationServerSettings
        authorizationServerSettings(){
    return AuthorizationServerSettings.builder().build();
  }
}
```

The `AuthorizationServerConfig` class configures the OAuth2 Authorization Server settings in our Spring Authorization Server application. The `authorizationServerSettings` method provides an `AuthorizationServerSettings` bean that defines the authorization server's default configuration. The class manages OAuth2 endpoints, security policies, and protocol compliance.

With the authorization server implementation complete, let's move to the client application's implementation.

Implementing the client application

Now, we will implement the client application, which will request authorization on behalf of a user to access the resource server. The client application's name is `client-application`, and the following code snippet shows the dependency required to implement it:

```
<dependency>
  <groupId>org.springframework.boot</groupId>
  <artifactId>spring-boot-starter-oauth2-client</artifactId>
</dependency>
```

The `spring-boot-starter-oauth2-client` dependency enables OAuth2 client capabilities. It allows the application to authenticate users via external IdPs such as Google, GitHub, or a custom authorization server.

The following configuration snippet defines the OAuth2 client registration in the `application.yaml` file, enabling the application to authenticate via an OIDC-compliant authorization server:

```
spring:
  security:
    oauth2:
      client:
        registration:
          client-server-oidc:
            provider: spring
```

```
        client-id: client-application
        client-secret: secret
        authorization-grant-type: authorization_code
        redirect-uri: "http://127.0.0.1:8080/login/oauth2/code/
        {registrationId}"
        scope: openid, profile
        client-name: client-application-oidc
    provider:
      spring:
        issuer-uri: http://localhost:9000
```

This client configuration registration must match the details previously configured in the registered client configuration within the authorization, as follows:

- `client-server-oidc`: This is the registration that identifies the OAuth2 client configuration in Spring Security.

- `provider`: Specifies a custom name for the IdP.

- `clientId`: Specifies a UID for the OAuth2 client used for authentication with the authorization server.

- `clientSecret`: Sets a secret key for client authentication.

- `authorization-grant-type`: Specifies the OAuth2 authorization flow.

- `redirectUri`: Defines the URI where the authorization server should send the code and tokens. Breaking down the redirect URI, we have the following:

  - `http://127.0.0.1:8080`: The application URL where the OAuth2 client is running.

  - `/login/oauth2/code`: The default endpoint where Spring Security expects to receive authorization codes.

  - `{registrationId}`: A placeholder for the client registration ID, which will be dynamically replaced with `client-server-oidc` in the OAuth2 authentication flow.

- `scope`: Specifies the permissions requested from the authorization server.

- `client-name`: Provides a user-friendly name for this client configuration.

- `issuer-uri`: Specifies the authorization server's issuer URL, which is used to discover endpoints for authentication and token management.

In the client-application project, we also define a `ProductController` class, which is a controller and is shown in the following code snippet:

```java
@RestController
public class ProductController {
  public RestClient webClient;

  @GetMapping("products")
  public ProductResponse getProducts(
    @RegisteredOAuth2AuthorizedClient(
      "client-server-oidc") OAuth2AuthorizedClient client) {
    return webClient
      .get()
      .uri("http://127.0.0.1:8082/v1/products")
      .header("Authorization", "Bearer %s"
        .formatted(client.getAccessToken()
        .getTokenValue()))
      .retrieve()
      .body(ProductResponse.class);
  }
}
```

The `getProducts` method requests that the resource server (product services) fetch product data. It includes the bearer token obtained from the authorization server in the request header to authenticate the request.

Now, let's implement the resource server, ensuring it enforces OAuth2 security and validates access tokens before serving protected resources.

Implementing the resource server

We will implement the resource server by adapting the product services to use OAuth2 security. This will ensure that only authenticated clients with a valid access token can access protected product data.

The following code snippet shows the required dependencies to configure product services as an OAuth2 resource server:

```xml
<dependency>
  <groupId>org.springframework.boot</groupId>
  <artifactId>spring-boot-starter-oauth2-resource-
    server</artifactId>
</dependency>

<dependency>
```

```
   <groupId>org.springframework.security</groupId>
   <artifactId>spring-security-oauth2-jose</artifactId>
</dependency>
```

The `spring-boot-starter-oauth2-resource-server` dependency enables the application to validate and process OAuth2 access tokens.

The `spring-security-oauth2-jose` dependency provides support for JWT token handling, including token signature verification and decoding, allowing the resource server to authenticate requests securely.

The following configuration snippet was added to the `properties.yaml` file to configure the resource server for OAuth2 authentication:

```
spring:
  security:
    oauth2:
      resourceserver:
        jwt:
          issuer-uri: http://localhost:9000
```

The configuration specifies the authorization server details, which is responsible for issuing JWT tokens and exposing the public key required for token validation. The resource server must validate and decode incoming JWT tokens by verifying their digital signature. Instead of using the private key directly, it retrieves the public key from the authorization server, as defined by the `issuer-uri` property. This ensures that only tokens issued by the trusted authorization server are accepted, enabling the resource server to authenticate requests securely.

Our implementation is complete. The authorization server, the client application, and the resource server are fully configured. Let's proceed with testing to ensure they function correctly together.

Testing the authentication and authorization flow

Now that the authorization server, client application, and resource server have been fully implemented, we must verify that they work together as expected. The testing process will ensure that tokens are correctly issued, validated, and used to secure access to protected resources:

1. Set up the databases using the Docker Compose file in the `ch11/docker-resources` directory.

2. Start the authorization server, client application, and resource server located in the `ch11` directory.

3. Open a browser and go to the following URL: `http://localhost:8080/products`. It will redirect you to the default authorization server's login page at `http://localhost:9000/login`, as shown in *Figure 10.3*.

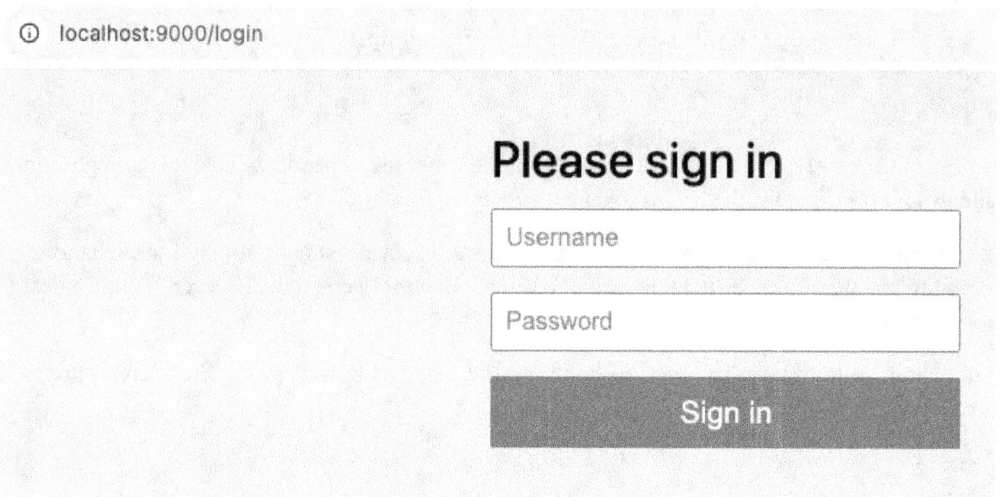

Figure 10.3: Login page

4. Log in using `admin@wxauction.com` as the username and `test123` as your password. Then, click the **Sign In** button.

5. Since our configuration requires consent, a consent screen will appear, as shown in *Figure 10.4*. Please click on the **profile** checkbox and then click the **Submit Consent** button.

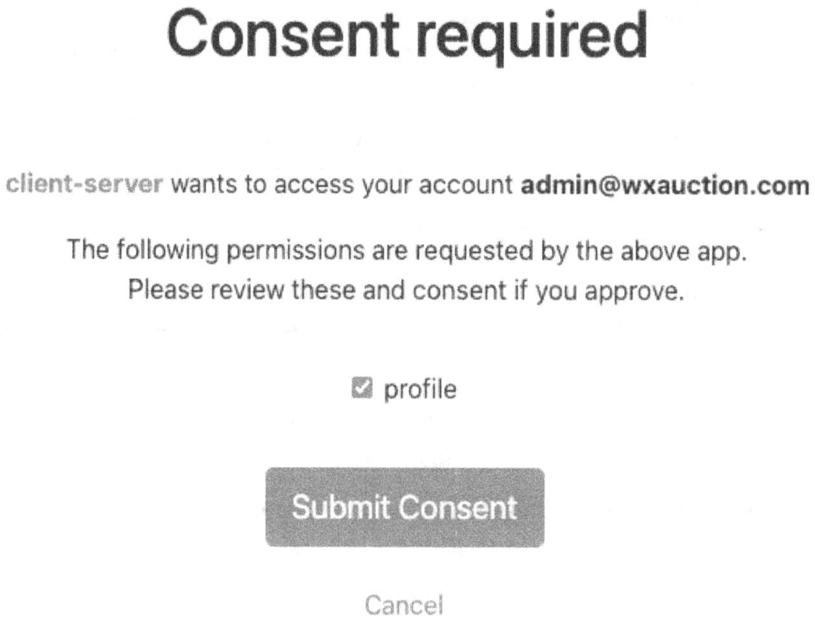

Figure 10.4: Consent screen

6. After consent, the data is returned from the resource server and is shown in *Figure 10.5*.


```
Pretty-print ☑

[
  {
    "id": 1,
    "name": "Old car",
    "description": "Fancy old car",
    "userId": 1,
    "photoBase64": null
  },
```

Figure 10.5: Product's list returned from the resource server

We have successfully implemented and tested our authorization server, client application, and resource server, ensuring security through OAuth2 and OIDC. The authentication flow works as intended, issuing access, refresh, and ID tokens for secure service communication. This implementation lays a strong foundation for expanding security policies and enhancing access control mechanisms.

Summary

This chapter provided a comprehensive exploration of security in software development, emphasizing the importance of integrating security from the beginning of the project. The reader learned about core security concepts, including encryption for protecting data at rest and in transit. The chapter also explained defensive techniques such as input validation and output encoding to protect against SQL Injection and XSS, alongside strategies to prevent CSRF and DoS attacks.

In addition, the chapter introduced advanced frameworks such as ZTA and OWASP, focusing on the most critical web security vulnerabilities. It further demonstrated the implementation of OAuth2 and OIDC for authentication and authorization using Spring Authorization Server.

This chapter covered theoretical concepts and practical implementation strategies for securing data and applications and defending against common security threats.

In *Chapter 11, Observability*, we will examine observability and its pillars and highlight how it differs from traditional monitoring. We'll implement observability in our applications using tools such as **Elasticsearch, Logstash, Kibana (ELK)**, Micrometer, OpenTelemetry, Zipkin, and **application performance monitoring (APM)**.

Questions

1. What is the importance of integrating security from the beginning of a project?

2. What is encryption, and how does it protect data at rest and in transit?

3. What is output encoding, and how does it prevent XSS attacks?

4. What is the OWASP Top 10, and why is it important?

5. What are OAuth2 and OIDC, and how do they enhance authentication and authorization?

6. Which framework streamlines the implementation of OAuth2 and OIDC in our Spring Boot applications?

Get This Book's PDF Version and Exclusive Extras

Scan the QR code (or go to `packtpub.com/unlock`). Search for this book by name, confirm the edition, and then follow the steps on the page.

Note: Keep your invoice handly. Purchase made directly from packt don't require one.

11

Observability

This chapter explores the essential components of observability in modern software systems, particularly within microservices and distributed architectures. It discusses the three pillars of observability: **logs**, **metrics**, and **traces**. The chapter highlights the significance of these pillars in gaining deeper insights into system reliability and performance, surpassing traditional monitoring methods.

This chapter integrates our online auction application with observability tools such as **Elasticsearch**, **Logstash**, **Kibana**, **Micrometer**, **OpenTelemetry**, and **Zipkin**.

Additionally, it delves into **Application Performance Monitoring (APM)** and explores how to integrate an online auction application with **New Relic**. It also compares the initial observability approach with an APM tool such as New Relic.

This chapter covers the following:

- Unraveling observability

- Implementing the three pillars of observability

- Introducing application performance monitoring

By the end of this chapter, you will be able to implement comprehensive observability in your applications; monitor system performance using logs, metrics, and traces; and troubleshoot issues effectively with tools such as ELK, OpenTelemetry, and Zipkin, as well as APM tools such as New Relic. This knowledge will enable you to ensure system reliability, detect and troubleshoot issues, and optimize performance in distributed architectures.

Technical requirements

All the code for this chapter can be found on GitHub at `https://github.com/PacktPublishing/Software-Architecture-with-Spring/tree/main/ch11`. Ellipses in the code blocks indicate that parts of the code have been omitted, and the complete code is available on GitHub.

Unraveling observability

The rise of microservices, distributed architectures, and cloud-native technologies has made systems more complex. Services now operate across multiple nodes and diverse infrastructures, making traditional management methods inadequate and troubleshooting in distributed environments much more challenging.

Maintaining system reliability and performance in this ever-changing landscape requires more than just monitoring set metrics. When issues cascade across services or unexpected latency spikes occur, you need deeper visibility, where observability becomes essential. Let's understand what observability is.

What is observability?

Observability refers to the capability to assess a system's internal state by analyzing its external outputs, such as logs, metrics, and traces. The more observable a system is, the faster and more precisely we can trace a performance issue back to its root cause without needing to conduct further tests or write additional code.

Observability involves comprehensively collecting and analyzing data to understand system performance deeply. It goes beyond traditional monitoring capabilities, which focus on tracking predefined metrics such as CPU usage, memory, and uptime, to assess system health and detect issues based on set thresholds.

As mentioned earlier, observability relies on three pillars: logs, metrics, and traces. These three pillars offer a complete system view and support efficient troubleshooting and performance optimization. Let's look into them to gain a full understanding:

- **Logs** are records of events within a system or network. They offer insights into how applications function and can be used to diagnose issues, pinpoint performance bottlenecks, and identify potential security risks.

- **Metrics** are numerical datasets created by measuring events, such as performance and behavior. Typically, metrics are gathered by monitoring specific system parameters, such as CPU usage, memory utilization, error rates, latency, and response time. Metrics provide quantitative insights for evaluating and optimizing a network or system's performance.

- **Traces** record events in a causal order, demonstrating how one event triggers or leads to another. By observing the sequence of events and their relationships, tracing systems help to understand the flow of a request through a system, allowing for the identification of delays, failures, or bottlenecks. Tracing is essential in distributed systems, as analyzing the sequence of events across multiple services is necessary to determine the root cause of any issue.

Logs, metrics, and traces provide a comprehensive view of a system's performance. *Figure 11.1* presents the role of the three pillars of observability.

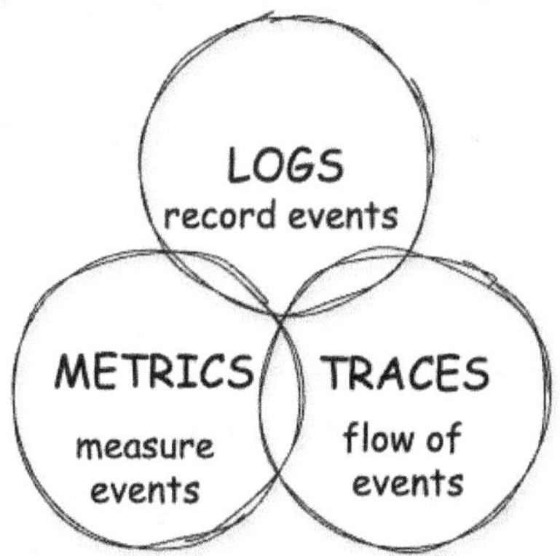

Figure 11.1: Three pillars of observability

Logs, metrics, and traces are interconnected pillars of observability that revolve around events. Logs capture individual events; metrics are derived from measuring system behaviors, over time often related to events; and traces represent the flow of events with their causal relationships across a system.

Let's use response time as an example to illustrate how logs, metrics, and traces can provide complete visibility into a system's internal state.

When an event occurs, logs record the event details, such as when the request was made and what actions were taken. For instance, if a request took 50 milliseconds to complete, the log entry will capture that this event occurred and when it started and ended.

The metric associated with this event, in this case, the response time, will quantify the 50 milliseconds and assess whether that value is typical, fast, or slow compared to the system's usual performance. It enables tracking over time to identify patterns, such as whether the response time of 50 milliseconds is an outlier or consistent with other events.

Finally, traces provide a visual map or tree of the request's journey through the system, highlighting each service or component it interacted with. If the request took 50 milliseconds, traces will help identify which parts of the system contributed to this duration—whether it was a database call, an external API, or another service. This allows you to pinpoint precisely where time was spent and understand the root cause of the delay, making it easier to optimize or troubleshoot the system.

Logs, metrics, and traces provide a comprehensive understanding of what happened and why. Now, let's implement them in our online auction application.

Implementing the three pillars of observability

Now, we will implement the three pillars of observability in our online auction application. Let's start by applying the first pillar of observability: logs.

We will utilize the famous **Elasticsearch, Logstash, and Kibana (ELK)** stack to manage our application's logs.

Managing logs with ELK

ELK is a robust open source stack widely used for centralized logging, log analysis, and data visualization. Each component plays a distinct role, so let's explore them:

- **Elasticsearch:** This is a highly scalable, distributed search and analytics engine designed to store, index, and query vast amounts of data in near-real time. It is built on top of **Apache Lucene**, offers advanced full-text search capabilities, and supports complex queries and aggregations. Its primary purpose is to provide a fast, efficient way to search, analyze, and visualize large datasets, enabling businesses to extract actionable insights. It is popular for log analysis, monitoring, and search-driven applications. Its main features are as follows:

  - **Distributed architecture:** Ensures high availability and scalability by distributing data across multiple nodes, making the system resilient to malfunctions

  - **Real-time data processing:** Indexes data almost instantly, allowing queries to be performed on the latest data

  - **Full-text search:** Supports tokenization, stemming, relevance scoring, and other advanced search features to ensure precise and meaningful search results

  - **Aggregations and analytics:** Enables powerful aggregations to summarize data and perform statistical analysis, which is helpful for dashboards and reporting

  - **RESTful API:** Provides a simple, HTTP-based API for seamless integration with various applications

  - **Speed and performance:** Optimized for fast search and retrieval, even across large datasets

- **Logstash:** This is a robust data processing pipeline. It collects, filters, transforms, and enriches data from various sources before sending it to destinations such as Elasticsearch for indexing. Logstash supports multiple input types and can ingest information from files, databases, message brokers, APIs, and syslogs. It processes data in real time, ensuring low-latency streaming, and can forward processed data to other systems. Logstash handles structured and unstructured data formats, offers fault tolerance, and has a modular design with customizable plugins. It is commonly used for log aggregation, metric collection, and handling application and security events for real-time threat detection.

- **Kibana**: Kibana is a web-based tool that works with Elasticsearch, allowing users to visualize and explore data. It enables the creation of interactive dashboards, making it valuable for real-time monitoring, log analysis, and system performance tracking. With flexible querying, users can explore data, set alerts, and share reports, aiding in trend monitoring and anomaly detection.

ELK provides tools for managing and analyzing logs, allowing users to monitor applications' health and performance effectively. *Figure 11.2* shows how ELK functions along with services.

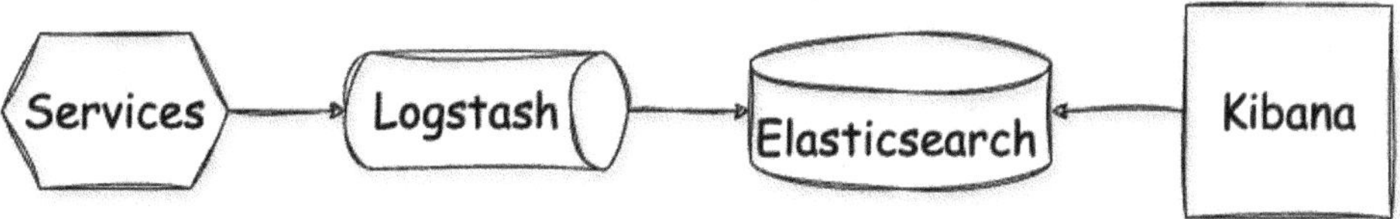

Figure 11.2: ELK functioning along with services

Figure 11.2 illustrates the flow of log data through the ELK stack, starting from services that generate logs. These logs are sent to Logstash, where the data is transformed and enriched, ensuring it is ready for indexing and storage. Next, the enriched data is passed to Elasticsearch, which allows for fast querying and aggregation, enabling real-time searching across vast datasets. Finally, the data is visualized and analyzed through Kibana, which connects to Elasticsearch, completing the pipeline for effective observability and analysis.

Kibana provides a visual interface for creating dashboards, graphs, and charts that help users monitor application health, detect anomalies, and troubleshoot issues efficiently. This pipeline ensures a seamless process from log generation to data visualization, enabling comprehensive observability and real-time insights into system performance. Let's start by setting up the ELK stack to have our logs centralized and visualize them in Kibana.

Setting up the ELK stack

The `docker-compose` file for running ELK is in the `ch11/docker/observability` folder on GitHub. Since it is an ordinary Docker setup, we won't discuss the details of the file itself. Instead, we will discuss the configuration files that set up these tools.

Let's begin with the `logstash.conf` file, which instructs Logstash to process incoming logs from Spring Boot applications and send them to Elasticsearch. The following configuration snippet shows what this looks like:

```
input {
  tcp {
    port => 5000
    codec => json_lines
  }
}
```

```
filter {
  json {
    source => "message"
  }
}
output {
  elasticsearch {
    hosts => ["elasticsearch:9200"]
    index => "online-auction-logs-%{+YYYY.MM.dd}"
  }
  stdout { codec => rubydebug }
}
```

The Logstash configuration defines how logs are received, processed, and outputted. The following sections outline its components and their functions:

- **Input block**: The `input` block specifies how Logstash will receive the data from applications. In the preceding configuration, it will listen for incoming connections on TCP on port `5000` in JSON format.

- **Filter block**: The `filter` block processes incoming logs. Here, the `json` filter is used to parse JSON content within the message field of each log. If logs are encapsulated within a message field, this filter extracts individual JSON elements and converts them into structured fields for easier querying and analysis in Elasticsearch.

- **Output block**: The `output` block sends processed logs and the standard output to Elasticsearch on port `9200`. Logs are stored in `online-auction-logs-YYYY.MM.dd`, creating a new daily index for log retention and querying performance. Additionally, logs are sent to the standard output using the `rubydebug` codec for easy debugging. The rubydebug codec outputs the log event as a Ruby-style hash, essentially a key-value representation of the structured log data. Each event is printed with its fields, including metadata, making inspecting and validating the log's content easy.

> **Attention**
>
> If you use macOS, you must disable AirPlay Receiver to run Logstash on port `5000`. To do this, type `AirPlay Receiver` into Spotlight search and disable it.

Once Logstash is set up, we can refactor the application to send logs to Logstash for visualization in Kibana.

Refactoring the application to support logs

Logstash is the only thing we need to configure, so now we will configure the services to send logs to Logstash. We will use Logback to integrate the logging with Logstash. The default Spring Boot logging framework is Logback, which streamlines configuration and integration with Spring applications. It delivers high-performance logging with a faster startup time and lower memory usage. Logback offers various appenders for different needs, including compatibility with log aggregation tools such as Logstash.

The following dependency needs to be added to the project's `pom.xml` file:

```xml
<dependency>
    <groupId>net.logstash.logback</groupId>
    <artifactId>logstash-logback-encoder</artifactId>
    <version>8.0</version>
</dependency>
```

The `logstash-logback-encoder` dependency enables applications that use Logback to produce JSON-format logs, facilitating seamless integration with Logstash and efficient indexing in Elasticsearch for easy visualization through tools such as Kibana.

The following configuration snippet shows the `logback-spring.xml` file in the `src/main/resources` application's folder. It configures Logback to send logs to Logstash:

```xml
<configuration>
<appender name="LOGSTASH"
class="net.logstash.logback.appender.LogstashTcpSocketAppender">
    <destination>localhost:5000</destination>
    <encoder class="net.logstash.logback.encoder.
      LoggingEventCompositeJsonEncoder">
    <providers>
    ...
    <root level="info">
      <appender-ref ref="LOGSTASH" />
    </root>
</configuration>
```

This Logback configuration is designed to send logs to Logstash via a TCP connection on localhost port `5000`. It uses `LogstashTcpSocketAppender` to ensure that logs are transmitted in a format compatible with Logstash.

The specified encoder is `LoggingEventCompositeJsonEncoder`, which formats the log events into JSON. This structured JSON format makes it easier for Logstash to process the logs and forward them to Elasticsearch for indexing and analysis.

The `root` element sets the default log level to `INFO`, ensuring that all logs of level `INFO` and above are sent to the LOGSTASH appender for processing.

In the last step, we will enhance the controller to send logs. The following code snippet presents the refactored `AuthenticationController` class, which includes the `createAuthenticationToken` method modified to send logs.

```
@Slf4j
public class AuthenticationController {

@PostMapping
public ResponseEntity<AuthenticationResponse>
createAuthenticationToken(@RequestBody
    AuthenticationRequest authenticationRequest,
    @RequestHeader HttpHeaders headers)
    throws Exception {
    log.info("START PROCESS OF AUTHENTICATION");
    final Optional<String> token = generateTokenUseCase
        .execute(
            authenticationRequest.getUsername(),
            authenticationRequest.getPassword());
    log.info("END PROCESS OF AUTHENTICATION");
    return ResponseEntity.ok(
        new AuthenticationResponse(token.get()));
}
```

`@Slf4j` is a Lombok annotation that simplifies logging in Java applications by eliminating the need to declare a logger instance manually. The statement `log.info` is a method from the SLF4J API, enabled through `@Slf4j`, to log messages. Because Logback is configured with a Logstash appender, these messages will be sent to Logstash.

That's the magic of working with ELK through Spring Boot applications: the simplicity. Without a line of code, we set up the application to send logs to Logstash. Now, let's run the application, perform some tests, and visualize the logs in Kibana.

Visualizing logs in Kibana

Once the ELK stack and the online auction application are up and running, begin by making requests to generate a token. The services will already have sent logs to Logstash, which forwards them to Elasticsearch. Now, let's access the Kibana console to adjust and visualize the logs:

1. Access Kibana through this URL: `http://localhost:5601`.

2. On the left menu, click on the **Stack Management** link or access it through the URL `http://localhost:5601/app/management`.

3. Click on **Index Management** to see the `online-auction-logs-%{+YYYY.MM.dd}` index that we set up in the block output in the `logstash.conf` file.

4. On the left side menu, click **Data Views**, then click the **Create data view** button and fill in the fields as shown in *Figure 11.3*. To conclude, click the **Save data view to Kibana** button.

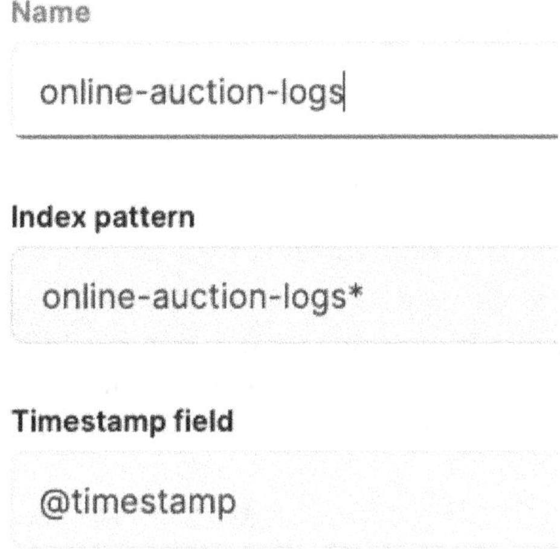

Figure 11.3: Data view's information

5. To view the logs, click the hamburger menu and then the **Discover** link, as shown in *Figure 11.4*.

Figure 11.4: Kibana Discover screen

Let's take a closer look at the Kibana **Discover** screen to understand how we can leverage it:

- Box 1 allows us to select the index to which the log was sent.

- Box 2 contains the fields that we can use for filtering.

- Box 3 allows us to input our filter using the **Kibana Query Language** (**KQL**) syntax. In this case, we used the `"message: "* PROCESS OF AUTHENTICATION"` KQL syntax to find the messages that the authentication services logged.

- Box 4 displays the results of our filter.

- Box 5 provides a visualization of the data over time.

The application now has centralized logging, aggregating log events from various components into a single platform. This improves visibility, enables faster troubleshooting, and allows correlation, analysis, anomaly detection, and real-time monitoring. The structured JSON logs also enhance filtering and querying in Elasticsearch for proactive monitoring and alerting in Kibana. Let's now work on implementing the second pillar of observability in our application: metrics.

Managing metrics with Micrometer and OpenTelemetry

We previously implemented logs using ELK as part of our observability strategy. Now, we will focus on another critical pillar of observability: metrics. To achieve this, we will utilize two essential tools: **Micrometer** for collecting application metrics and **OpenTelemetry** to export these metrics to a centralized observability platform. Let's begin by understanding these tools.

Introducing Micrometer

Micrometer is a framework for collecting application metrics that work with various monitoring systems, such as Prometheus and Elasticsearch. It offers a unified instrumentation interface, allowing you to use counters, gauges, timers, and distribution summaries that can be sent to multiple monitoring platforms. Micrometer is especially effective for Spring Boot applications, as it is integrated by default with Spring Boot Actuator, facilitating the collection of JVM metrics, HTTP request performance data, and custom application metrics.

Introducing OpenTelemetry

OpenTelemetry is an open source observability framework designed to collect, process, and export telemetry data from applications and infrastructure, including metrics, logs, and traces. It provides a unified standard for gathering observability data, helping developers and operations teams monitor the performance and health of distributed systems, microservices, and cloud-native applications.

The core components of OpenTelemetry are the following:

- **Software Development Kits (SDKs) and APIs**: Language-specific libraries such as Java, Python, and Go for instrumenting applications to generate telemetry data. Instrumentation refers to integrating code, using libraries that can automatically capture telemetry, such as HTTP requests, or allowing manual instrumentation in the code.

- **OpenTelemetry Collector**: A vendor-agnostic data pipeline that collects, processes, and exports telemetry data to various backends, such as Elasticsearch, Prometheus, Zipkin, and Jaeger. It plays a central role in the OpenTelemetry ecosystem, making it easy to gather telemetry data from multiple sources and forward it to different observability platforms. OpenTelemetry Collector works by defining three main components:

- **Receivers**: Collect data from different sources, such as **OpenTelemetry Protocol** (**OTLP**) and Prometheus

- **Processors**: Process data through batching, filtering, and enhancing before forwarding to exporters

- **Exporters**: Send data to monitoring systems or backends such as Zipkin, Elasticsearch, and Prometheus

- **Instrumentation libraries**: Tools such as Micrometer for Java applications automatically instrument frameworks such as Spring Boot, generating telemetry data with minimal code changes.

- **OpenTelemetry Protocol**: OTLP efficiently transmits telemetry data between services, collectors, and backends.

OpenTelemetry addresses the challenge of observing complex distributed systems by offering a vendor-neutral solution that avoids lock-in, supporting multiple backends such as Zipkin, Jaeger, Prometheus, and ELK. It ensures standardized instrumentation, enabling consistent data collection across various programming languages and frameworks. Additionally, it provides complete observability by supporting logs, metrics, and traces within a unified framework.

> **Why integrate Micrometer and OpenTelemetry?**
>
> Integrating Micrometer and OpenTelemetry in a Spring Boot application is a powerful strategy for achieving comprehensive observability. Micrometer captures critical metrics, such as HTTP requests and JVM performance, with minimal configuration. OpenTelemetry is a unified data pipeline that exports these metrics, traces, and logs to various backends. This integration ensures complete visibility by correlating metrics with traces and logs, helping to identify and troubleshoot performance issues effectively. Additionally, it avoids vendor lock-in by supporting multiple platforms such as Zipkin, Jaeger, Prometheus, and ELK. Combining Micrometer's ease of use with OpenTelemetry's flexibility creates a scalable, future-proof observability solution tailored for modern distributed systems.

With a clear understanding of the strengths of Micrometer and OpenTelemetry, the next step is to set up OpenTelemetry Collector.

Setting up OpenTelemetry Collector

OpenTelemetry Collector is available through the docker-compose file in the ch11/docker/ observability folder. Here, we will analyze its configuration.

The following configuration snippet is the otel-collector-config.yml file that configures OpenTelemetry Collector:

```yaml
receivers:
  otlp:
    protocols:
      http:
        endpoint: "0.0.0.0:4318"
processors:
  cumulativetodelta: {}
  filter:
    metrics:
      exclude:
        match_type: regexp
        metric_names:
          - "jvm.gc.pause"
exporters:
  elasticsearch:
    endpoints: ["http://elasticsearch:9200"]
service:
  pipelines:
    metrics:
      receivers: [otlp]
      processors: [cumulativetodelta, filter]
      exporters: [elasticsearch]
```

Open Collect acts as a central pipeline for collecting, processing, and exporting telemetry data to the chosen observability platforms. The following sections outline its components and their functions:

- **receivers block**: The receivers block collects incoming telemetry data from sources. The OTLP receiver listens for incoming telemetry data using the HTTP protocol on port 4318 and accepts requests from any network interface.

- **processors block**: The `processors` block modifies or filters telemetry data before exporting it. The `cumulativetodelta` processor converts cumulative metrics, such as counters that keep increasing, into delta metrics, which only track changes between exports. This is useful when backends expect delta values, that is, values that change for a specific metric, such as memory usage over a particular time window, instead of cumulative ones. The filter processor excludes specific metrics using a regular expression match. Here, metrics named `jvm.gc.pause` are excluded from the export. This is typically done to reduce noise or exclude irrelevant data.

- **exporters block**: The `exporters` block sends telemetry data to external backends. The `elasticsearch` exporter sends metrics to an Elasticsearch instance running at `http://elasticsearch:9200`. This allows the metrics to be stored, searched, and visualized using tools such as Kibana.

- **pipelines block**: A pipeline within a service block defines how data flows from receivers through processors to exporters. This metrics pipeline receives telemetry data via the OTLP receiver, processes it using `cumulativetodelta` and filter processors, and exports the results to Elasticsearch.

With OpenTelemetry Collector configured and ready to process and export telemetry data, the next step is to refactor the application to support metrics collection, enabling seamless integration with the observability pipeline.

Refactoring the application to support metrics

Once OpenTelemetry Collector is configured and running, we must make some refactors in our application to support metrics. The following dependency, `micrometer-registry-otlp`, needs to be added to the project:

```
<dependency>
   <groupId>io.micrometer</groupId>
   <artifactId>micrometer-registry-otlp</artifactId>
   <scope>runtime</scope>
</dependency>
```

The `micrometer-registry-otlp` library enables Micrometer to export metrics using the OTLP, integrating the Micrometer's metrics collection with the OpenTelemetry ecosystem. It allows metrics from a Spring Boot application to be sent to OpenTelemetry Collector, which can forward the data to monitoring platforms such as Elasticsearch, Prometheus, or Grafana.

The following configuration snippet is the `application.properties` file with the properties related to metrics export:

```
management.endpoints.web.exposure.include=*
management.otlp.metrics.export.enabled=true
management.otlp.metrics.export.url=http://localhost:4318/v1/metrics
management.otlp.metrics.export.step=10s
```

Let's analyze the purpose of each property:

- The `management.endpoints.web.exposure.include` property ensures that all actuator endpoints are exposed

- The `management.otlp.metrics.export.enabled` property enables metrics export via the OTLP. It ensures that the application is configured to send metrics data to an OTLP-compatible backend

- The `management.otlp.metrics.export.url` property specifies the URL of OpenTelemetry Collector where the metrics will be sent

- The `management.otlp.metrics.export.step` property defines the interval at which metrics are collected and sent to the OTLP endpoint

Now, let's set up the configuration to visualize the metrics in Kibana.

Configuring and visualizing metrics in Kibana

Once OpenTelemetry Collector and the online auction application are operational, start making requests to generate a token. Now, let's access the Kibana console to adjust and visualize the application's metrics.

1. Access Kibana through the URL `http://localhost:5601`.

2. On the left menu, click on the **Stack Management** link or access it through the URL `http://localhost:5601/app/management`.

3. On the left-side menu, click **Data Views**, then click the **Create data view** button and fill in the fields as shown in *Figure 11.5*. To conclude, click the **Save data view to Kibana** button.

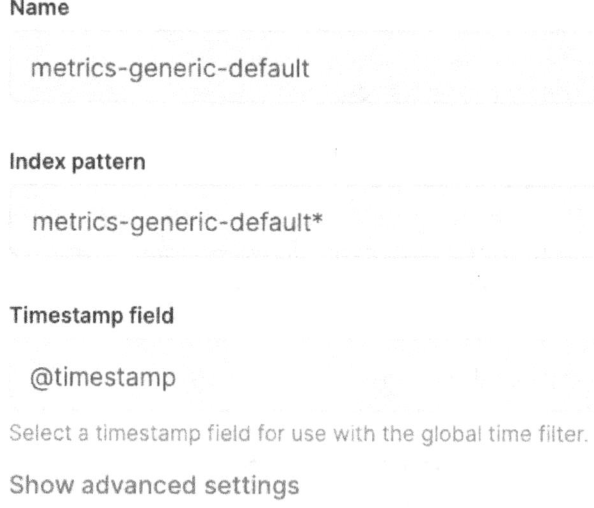

Figure 11.5: Data view information

4. To view the metrics, click on the hamburger menu and select the **Discover** link. The Discover screen in *Figure 11.6* displays filtered logs, showing only the gateway services logs with an HTTP status code of 503.

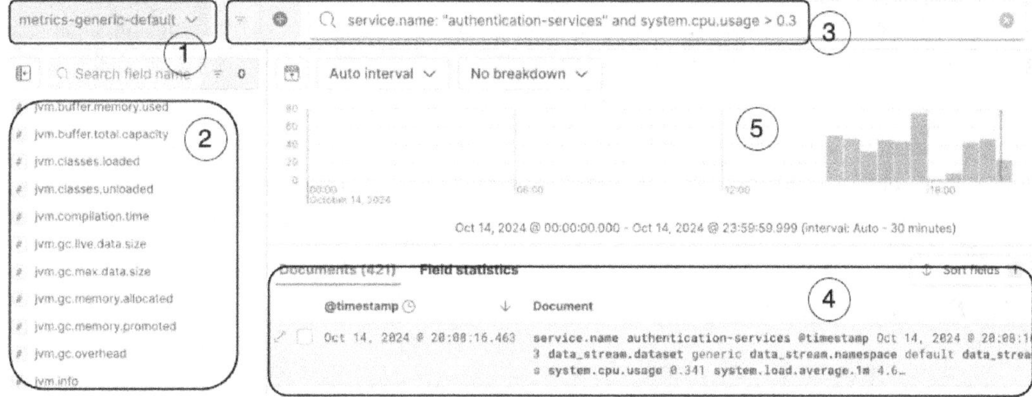

Figure 11.6: Kibana displaying filtered logs

Let's analyze the Kibana **Discover** screen to understand how to leverage it:

- Box 1 allows you to select the index to which the metric is configured to be sent.

- Box 2 contains the fields available for filtering the metric's data.

- Box 3 is where you can enter your filter using the KQL syntax. In this instance, we used the `resource.attributes.service.name : "gateway-services"` and `attributes.httpStatusCode : 503` KQL syntax to filter for metrics related to the authentication services where system CPU usage exceeds 0.3.

- Box 4 displays the results of our filter.

- Box 5 provides a visualization of the data over time.

The application now features centralized logging and metrics, which provide valuable insights into system events and performance trends. Using Kibana, we can create interactive dashboards that offer real-time insights into metrics data, making it easier to visualize trends, monitor system health, and detect anomalies. Its powerful querying capabilities and customizable visualizations such as charts, graphs, and gauges allow us to track **key performance indicators** (**KPIs**) effectively. Additionally, Kibana supports alerting, ensuring that teams are notified when metrics exceed predefined thresholds, which helps facilitate proactive issue resolution. Next, we will focus on implementing the third pillar of observability: traces.

Managing traces with OpenTelemetry and Zipkin

In monolithic applications, all components are closely connected and typically run in the same memory space. This makes it easier to understand, troubleshoot, and track the sequence of actions using logs and metrics. Identifying performance issues, errors, or failures can be achieved by examining logs or analyzing metrics within the same system. Therefore, traces are beneficial but not as essential since the connections between components are more straightforward.

Tracing is crucial for monitoring and diagnosing issues in microservices. Due to their distributed nature, a single request often interacts with multiple components. Tracing helps identify performance bottlenecks, track errors, and contribute to system observability. It allows teams to gain insights and ensure reliability as services scale or evolve.

Understanding distributed tracing

Distributed tracing is a method to monitor how a specific request moves through various distributed system components. It allows us to track the journey of a request between systems, helping to ensure that the user's request is fulfilled efficiently.

Distributed tracing is built upon two core concepts:

- **Span ID**: It tracks individual requests. Each service request has a unique span ID. As they move through various components, more span IDs are generated.

- **Trace ID**: It correlates spans and tracks an incoming request, traversing various services involved in fulfilling it.

Figure 11.7 illustrates a request, highlighting the trace ID and its related spans.

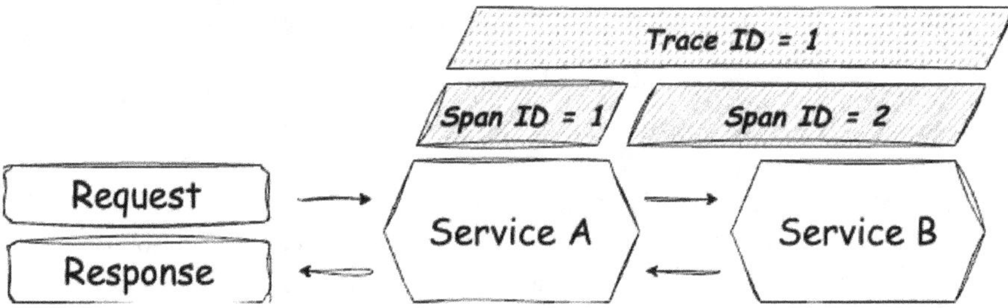

Figure 11.7: The request flow between the services with trace ID and spans ID

As illustrated in *Figure 11.7*, when a request is initiated in a distributed system, a trace ID is generated to track the entire request life cycle across services. Within this trace, individual spans are created for each service interaction, such as the transition from service A to service B, with each span representing a single unit of work. These spans, uniquely identified as span ID = 1 and span ID = 2, correlate under the same trace ID, providing a comprehensive view of the request's flow and timing across the system. Now, let's learn about Zipkin, a system that helps us with distributed tracing.

What is Zipkin?

Zipkin is a distributed tracing system that collects and displays trace data. It captures timing information to troubleshoot latency issues, monitor request flow, and understand service interactions. Zipkin provides a comprehensive view of how requests move through services, helping to identify bottlenecks or errors. It also pinpoints latency by showing processing times and enables seamless tracing context propagation through trace and span IDs.

It also includes a dependency diagram visualizing traced request flows across applications. This feature is useful for identifying patterns, error paths, or interactions with outdated services.

Applications must be instrumented using a tracer or instrumentation library, such as OpenTelemetry, to send data to Zipkin. The data can be sent via HTTP or messages and stored in memory or on a persistent backend, such as Elasticsearch.

Now, let's apply our new learning and add tracing to our online auction application.

Setting up Zipkin

We will now add the third and last pillar of observability: tracing. Let's start by configuring OpenTelemetry Collector. The following configuration snippet presents the `otel-collector-config.yml` file:

```yaml
receivers:
  otlp:
    protocols:
      http:
        endpoint: "0.0.0.0:4318"
exporters:
  zipkin:
    endpoint: "http://zipkin:9411/api/v2/spans"
service:
  pipelines:
    traces:
      receivers: [otlp]
      exporters: [otlp, zipkin]
```

The `zipkin` exporter is configured to send trace data to a Zipkin server. When a distributed tracing system collects trace data, it sends it to Zipkin via the `/api/v2/spans` endpoint.

The `traces` pipeline defines how traces are processed. It specifies that the pipeline should receive trace data from the `otlp` receiver and then export it to the `otlp` and `zipkin` exporters. This means trace data will be sent to another service via the OTLP protocol and to the Zipkin server for further visualization.

This configuration allows OpenTelemetry Collector to receive trace data via HTTP and export it to an OTLP endpoint and Zipkin. The main point is that Zipkin serves as an exporter, enabling the trace data to be visualized through its user interface, which assists in distributed tracing.

Zipkin has now been added to the `docker-compose` file to enable distributed tracing. Given its straightforward setup, we will not delve into the configuration details, as they are minimal and require little explanation. Now, let's refactor our services to enable distributed tracing and capture their interactions.

Refactoring the application to support traces

We have configured OpenTelemetry Collector to work with Zipkin; with Zipkin up and running, let's add the necessary dependencies, Micrometer and OpenTelemetry, to enable distributed tracing in our setup:

```
<dependency>
  <groupId>io.micrometer</groupId>
  <artifactId>micrometer-tracing-bridge-otel</artifactId>
</dependency>
<dependency>
  <groupId>io.opentelemetry</groupId>
  <artifactId>opentelemetry-exporter-otlp</artifactId>
</dependency>
```

- The `micrometer-tracing-bridge-otel` dependency acts as a connector between Micrometer's tracing API and OpenTelemetry's backend. It enables Micrometer's tracing features, such as spans, while transmitting the trace data to OpenTelemetry. This integration combines Micrometer's vendor-neutral API for metrics and traces with OpenTelemetry's standardized tracking system. Consequently, traces from your Spring Boot application, collected by Micrometer, are smoothly exported through OpenTelemetry collectors.

- The `opentelemetry-exporter-otlp` dependency lets your application send collected traces and metrics data to an OTLP endpoint. It allows seamless transmission of observability data, including traces, metrics, and logs, to OpenTelemetry Collector or other OTLP-compatible services. The OTLP protocol ensures consistent communication, supporting comprehensive observability by collecting data from various services, centralizing it for further processing, and forwarding it to backends such as Zipkin, Prometheus, or Elasticsearch.

The following configuration snippet shows the properties in the `application.properties` file needed to set up tracing in our application:

```
management.tracing.enabled=true
management.tracing.sampling.probability=1.0
management.otlp.tracing.endpoint=
http://localhost:4318/v1/traces
```

The configuration enables tracing in the application through the `management.tracing.enabled` property. `management.`The `tracing.sampling.probability` property ensures that 100% of the requests are sampled and traced. `management.`The `otlp.tracing.endpoint` property specifies the endpoint to which trace data will be sent, in this case, OpenTelemetry Collector running locally on port `4318`. This setup ensures that all traces are captured and sent to the specified tracing endpoint for analysis.

The configuration and refactoring to trace the interactions in our services is complete. Now, let's visualize the traces in Zipkin.

Visualizing the traces in Zipkin

Once the application runs, it will send the traces and spans, and we can visualize them in Zipkin. Let's follow these steps:

1. Execute the `http://localhost:8072/authentication/v1/api/auth` request to get a token. The complete request is provided on GitHub.

2. Access Zipkin at `http://localhost:9411/zipkin`. Then, click **RUN QUERY** to see the requests, as shown in *Figure 11.8*.

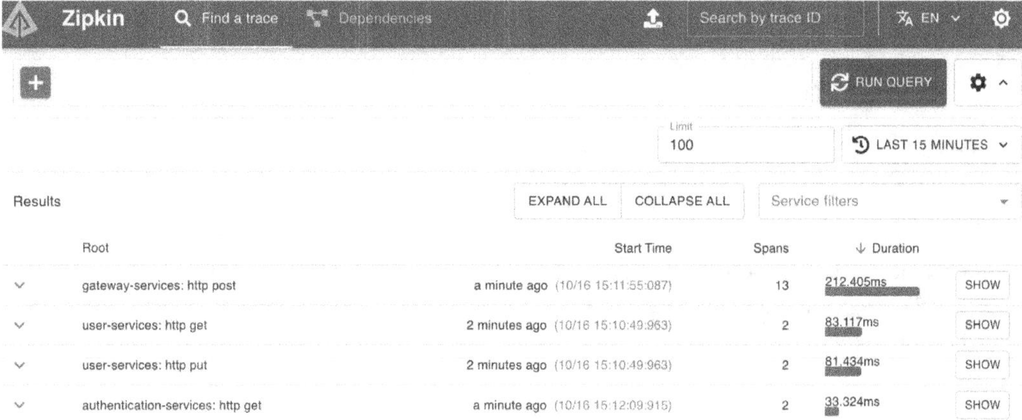

Figure 11.8: Zipkin presenting the request from the last 15 minutes

3. Click on the **Show** button to display the tracing of a request. *Figure 11.9* presents the traces screen showing the details of the request. It starts with the gateway services passing through authentication services to get the token. It also highlights the total duration of the request and the duration of each request between the services. We can also see the request's trace ID comprising 13 spans.

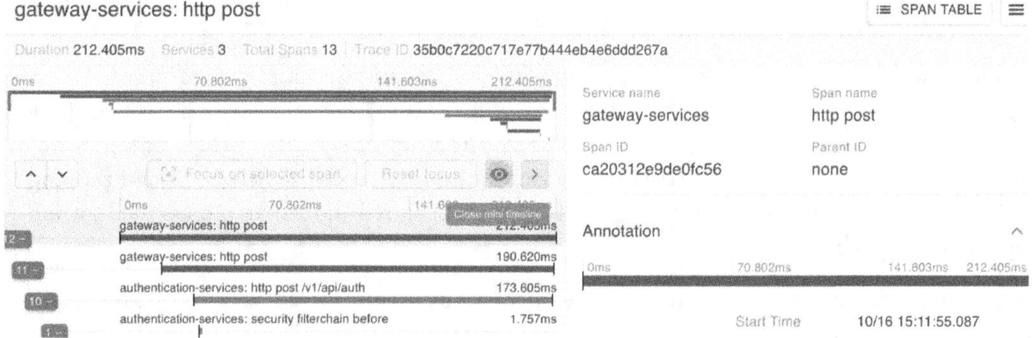

Figure 11.9: Traces screen

4. Click **Dependencies** at the top to access the dependencies screen. *Figure 11.10* shows a Zipkin dependency diagram that visualizes the interactions between different microservices in a system. This diagram helps you understand the overall architecture and data flow, allowing you to identify how the services are connected and trace potential bottlenecks or errors in their interactions.

Figure 11.10: Dependency's services screen

Now, our online auction application applies the three pillars of observability: logs, metrics, and traces. We can visualize logs and metrics through ELK and traces through Zipkin. Now, let's consider another vital tool for observability: APM.

Introducing application performance monitoring

While ELK, Micrometer, OpenTelemetry, and Zipkin are excellent tools for logging, metrics, and tracing, APM serves as an alternative that provides a comprehensive, all-in-one solution for monitoring application performance. APM includes capabilities for logs, metrics, traces, and infrastructure insights, requiring less manual effort and offering deeper functionality. But what exactly is APM?

What is APM?

APM is a set of tools and practices for monitoring and managing software applications' performance and availability. It offers real-time insights into application behavior, tracking metrics such as response times, resource usage (CPU, memory, and throughput), error rates, and user experience. By monitoring key application components, including the server, database, and frontend, APM helps identify performance bottlenecks, diagnose issues, and ensure optimal user experience.

APM tools typically capture metrics, traces, and logs to give a complete view of the application's health. This enables developers and operations teams to proactively identify issues, such as delayed response times or system errors, and address them before they affect end users. Examples of APM tools include New Relic, Dynatrace, and Datadog, which integrate with various environments to deliver detailed analytics on application performance. Here, we will implement observability through the New Relic tool.

Implementing and visualizing observability with New Relic

An account on New Relic is required to follow along with these steps. If you don't have one, please create an account and follow the setup steps:

1. Access the URL `https://one.newrelic.com`.

2. On the main page, click **All Entities** on the left, and follow the steps to set up full stack observability in your environment.

3. Now, let's set up the New Relic Java agent. To download it, execute the following `curl` command. You can find more information in the documentation at `https://docs.newrelic.com/install/java`.

   ```
   curl -O https://download.newrelic.com/newrelic/java-agent/
   newrelic-agent/current/newrelic-java.zip
   ```

4. Unzip the downloaded `newrelic-java.zip` file.

5. In the `newrelic` folder, there is a configuration file named `newrelic.yml`. Create six copies of `newrelic.yml` with the following names:

    - `newrelic-authentication-services.yml`
    - `newrelic-user-services.yml`
    - `newrelic-service-discovery-services.yml`
    - `newrelic-product-services.yml`
    - `newrelic-gateway-services.yml`
    - `newrelic-configuration-services.yml`

    In these configuration files, change the following keys: `license_key` and `app_name`. The license key can be retrieved from the New Relic website, then set `license_key` with your license key. `app_name` should correspond to the application's name as specified in the file. For example, for the `newrelic-authentication-services.yml` file, `app_name` must be set to `authentication-services`.

6. To run our application, we must pass the following parameters to the JVM: `javaagent`, indicating the path to the New Relic agent, and `newrelic.config.file`, specifying the configuration file for the New Relic agent. The following is an example of the command line used to run the authentication services:

    ```
    java -javaagent:/path/to/newrelic/newrelic.jar
    -Dnewrelic.config.file=/path/to/newrelic/newrelic-
    authentication-services.yml
    -jar authentication-services.jar
    ```

7. Execute the `http://localhost:8072/authentication/v1/api/auth` request a few times; this will send data to New Relic.

8. When the application starts, it displays the following log related to New Relic in the console, as shown in *Figure 11.11*. This means that the New Relic agent is activated for the application.

```
2024-10-06T15:51:34,349-0300 [28356 1] com.newrelic INFO: New Relic Agent: Loading configuration file "/Users/wanderson/newrelic/newrelic-authentication-services.yml"
2024-10-06T15:51:34,387-0300 [28356 1] com.newrelic INFO: Using default collector host: collector.newrelic.com
2024-10-06T15:51:34,387-0300 [28356 1] com.newrelic INFO: Using default metric ingest URI: https://metric-api.newrelic.com/metric/v1
2024-10-06T15:51:34,387-0300 [28356 1] com.newrelic INFO: Using default event ingest URI: https://insights-collector.newrelic.com/v1/accounts/events
2024-10-06T15:51:34,627-0300 [28356 1] com.newrelic INFO: New Relic Agent: Writing to log file: /Users/wanderson/newrelic/logs/newrelic_agent.log
```

Figure 11.11: Log about New Relic

9. Visit the New Relic website, click on **APM & Services**, and then select the name of the service to view its metrics, as illustrated in *Figure 11.12*.

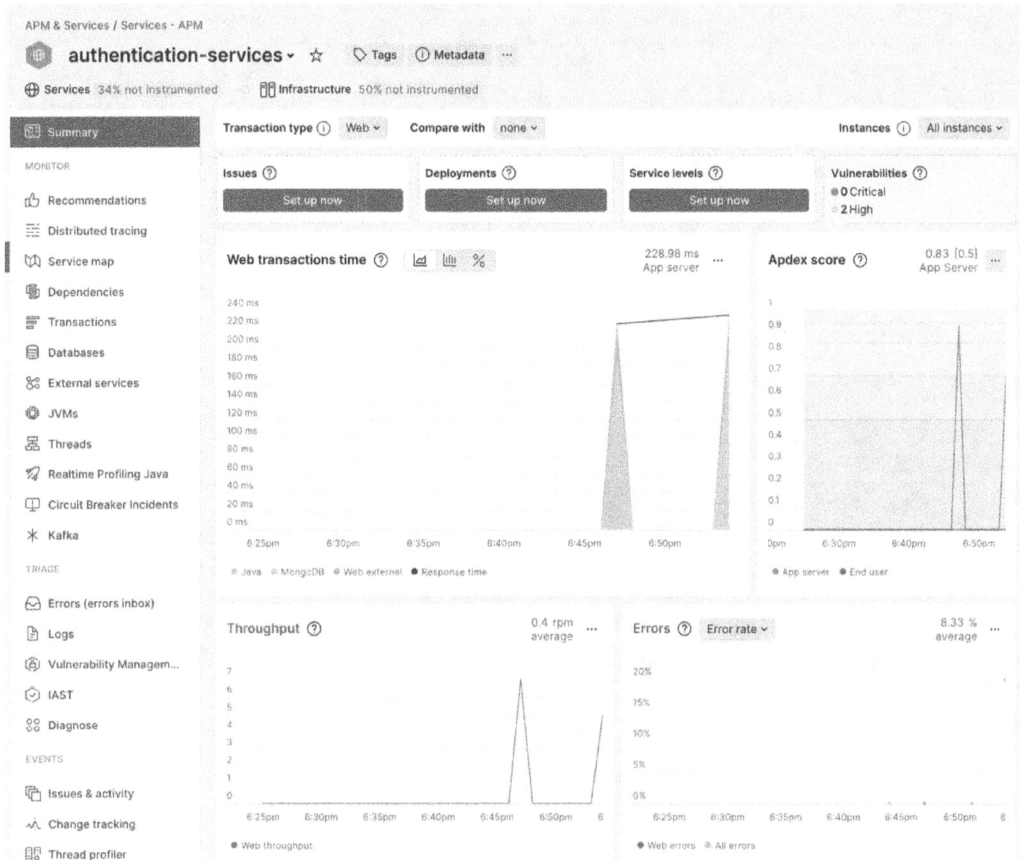

Figure 11.12: Metrics screen

10. Click on **Distributed tracing** and then on the request to see the tracing, as presented in *Figure 11.13*.

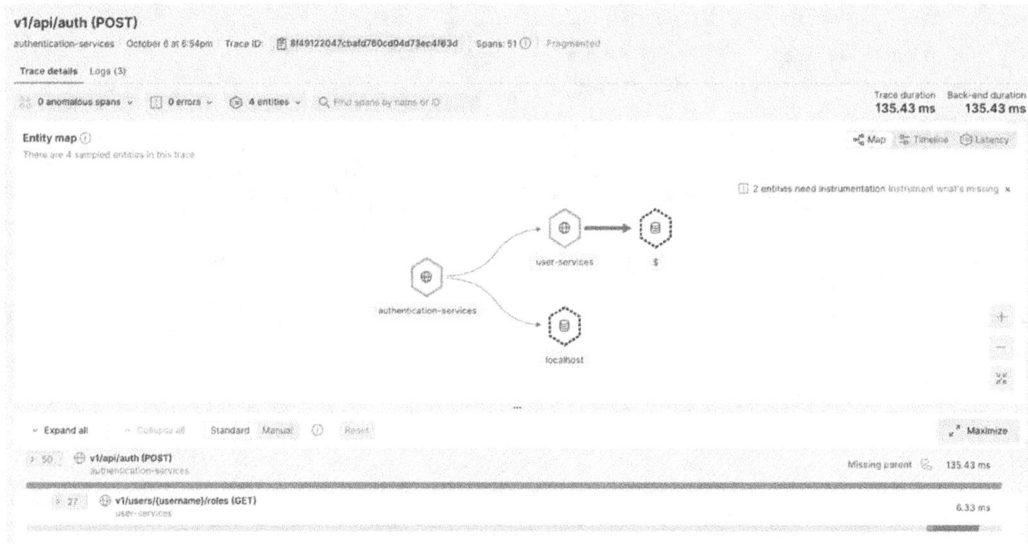

Figure 11.13: Distributed tracing screen

11. To visualize the logs, click on **Logs**, as presented in *Figure 11.14*.

Figure 11.14: Logs screen

As a leading SaaS-based APM tool, New Relic offers features such as logs, metrics, traces, and user experience monitoring, making it a strong choice for achieving optimal performance and reliability in distributed environments.

To conclude, both approaches are valid for implementing observability in our applications. We leverage powerful open source tools that enhance our observability capabilities when using ELK, Micrometer, OpenTelemetry, and Zipkin. However, these tools require more manual configuration and management. They offer greater flexibility and control but can also make implementation and management more challenging.

On the other hand, New Relic is an all-in-one, out-of-the-box APM solution with integrated logs, metrics, and traces. It is easier to set up and use with minimal configuration. It provides seamless observability with advanced features and requires less maintenance, but it comes with a cost because it's a SaaS solution.

The use of both approaches, APM tools alongside open source observability solutions, is a widespread practice globally, particularly among companies that prioritize robust system observability. However, adoption trends may vary, with open source tools being more popular among organizations focusing on cost-efficiency and flexibility, while APM tools tend to be favored by those valuing ease of integration and vendor support.

Summary

This chapter comprehensively explored observability in modern software systems, emphasizing the importance of deep visibility across distributed architectures. You learned about the three pillars of observability—logs, metrics, and traces—and how they contribute to system performance monitoring and troubleshooting. The chapter also explained how to implement observability using tools such as ELK for centralized logging, Micrometer, OpenTelemetry for metrics, and Zipkin for distributed tracing.

In addition, the chapter introduced advanced topics such as APM with New Relic. It demonstrated how to integrate it to provide a complete view of application performance in a distributed environment, from logs to traces.

This chapter's theoretical concepts and practical implication strategies provided insights into enhancing observability in distributed systems to improve application reliability and performance.

In *Chapter 12, Testing*, we will introduce and emphasize the significance of software testing. We will explore the testing pyramid, various types of testing, the principles of **Test-Driven Development (TDD)**, and tools and frameworks for automated testing.

Questions

1.   What is observability in modern software systems?

2.   What are the three pillars of observability?

3.   How do logs contribute to observability?

4.   What role do metrics play in observability?

5.   Why are traces essential in distributed systems?

6.   What is the difference between conventional monitoring and observability?

Get This Book's PDF Version and Exclusive Extras

Scan the QR code (or go to `packtpub.com/unlock`). Search for this book by name, confirm the edition, and then follow the steps on the page.

Note: Keep your invoice handly. Purchase made directly from packt don't require one.

12

Testing

This chapter explores automated testing in modern software development, highlighting its role in ensuring quality, enabling faster releases, and supporting continuous delivery in Agile and DevOps-driven environments. It also presents a practical exploration of the testing pyramid—a foundational model that categorizes testing into three levels: unit, integration, and **end-to-end** (**E2E**) tests—with hands-on examples of unit and integration tests using tools such as **JUnit 5**, **Mockito**, **Testcontainers**, **MockMvc**, **RestAssured**, and Spring Boot's testing support for loading full application contexts.

In addition, it also covers performance testing with **JMeter**, **Test-Driven Development** (**TDD**), and **Behavior-Driven Development** (**BDD**) approaches, demonstrating how they improve code quality and align testing with business requirements.

This chapter covers the following:

- Boosting software quality with automated testing
- Understanding and implementing the test pyramid
- Boosting applications with performance tests
- Exploring test-driven development
- Introducing behavior-driven development

By the end of this chapter, you will have theoretical and practical knowledge of how to implement automated testing strategies that enhance software quality, speed up feedback loops, and support scalable, dependable applications.

Technical requirements

All the code for this chapter can be found on GitHub at `https://github.com/PacktPublishing/Software-Architecture-with-Spring/tree/main/ch12`. Ellipses in the code blocks indicate that parts of the code have been omitted, and the complete code is available on GitHub.

Boosting software quality with automated testing

In today's world, software touches nearly every aspect of daily life. We use applications for countless tasks, so we may quickly look for alternatives when software fails or is slow. As innovation speeds up, maintaining high quality while delivering software faster becomes crucial. Let's explore automated testing further. It helps bridge the gap between fast-paced development cycles and user expectations.

Applying automated testing effectively

Automated testing is essential for supporting fast-paced development, **Continuous Integration (CI)**, and **Continuous Delivery (CD)** workflows. While its benefits—such as faster feedback, safe refactoring, and reduced manual work—are well known, its effectiveness depends on how strategically and practically it's applied. When implemented with careful consideration, automated testing can yield substantial benefits; however, without a well-defined strategy, it may quickly become burdensome, leading to neglected or unreliable tests.

Engaging in strategic planning, selecting the right tools, and integrating testing into the development workflow is crucial to achieving effective automated testing. This ensures that the tests remain relevant, maintainable, and capable of providing meaningful feedback.

Engineers must recognize that testing is essential for software quality. The team needs to value tests and not just create them to tick a box. It's not rare to see tests being overlooked to save time by reducing automated test development. As a result, code in production frequently breaks due to simple errors, such as `NullPointerException`. Therefore, testing needs to become part of the company culture, and everyone should understand the benefits of it. The team should require automated tests for every new feature or bug fix submitted through a pull request, along with defining a target test coverage percentage.

To maximize the benefits of automated testing, we can follow these steps:

- **Define testing goals and coverage**: Begin by identifying the critical areas of the code base that require testing. Prioritize core functions, business logic, and features that involve complex interactions. For APIs, create unit tests to verify the status codes, ensure errors are handled correctly, and confirm that the correct responses are provided. Additionally, check that the required fields in requests are being correctly managed.

- **Select the right testing tools**: Select tools that align with the project's technology stack and those that are compatible with CI tools such as Jenkins or GitHub Actions, such as the following:

  - JUnit, Mockito, AssertJ, and Hamcrest for unit tests

  - Testcontainers for isolating components such as databases and message brokers in integration tests

  - Selenium for UI and E2E tests in web applications

  - Postman or RestAssured for API testing

  - JMeter for performance testing

  - JaCoCo or SonarQube for coverage tests

- **Organize tests using the test pyramid**: The test pyramid is a model that emphasizes having more unit tests, fewer integration tests, and even fewer E2E tests. This structure ensures fast, reliable feedback without the overhead of too many complex tests.

- **Review and maintain tests regularly**: Automated tests require maintenance to stay effective. Teams should regularly update and refactor tests as the application evolves, removing obsolete tests and adjusting to new functionality.

- **Leverage TDD**: TDD is a methodology that employs the writing of tests before the code implementation. The process begins with creating a test that initially fails. Then, code is written to make the test succeed. Once the test passes, the code is refined and optimized for better organization and clarity. This technique ensures thorough test coverage for new functionality and helps define requirements more clearly.

- **Automate with CI**: Integrate tests into your CI pipeline so they run automatically on each code change. This ensures that tests are consistent and that the team receives rapid feedback on the impact of changes.

By following these steps and carefully selecting options that fit our projects appropriately, we can adopt automated testing practices that improve software quality and streamline development processes. Now that we recognize the importance of automated tests in delivering quality software, let's delve deeper into the test pyramid.

Understanding and implementing the test pyramid

Mike Cohn introduced the test pyramid in his book, *Succeeding with Agile*, which serves as a visual guide to different testing layers and provides a basic structure for the proportion of tests at each level. *Figure 12.1* illustrates the test pyramid with its layers.

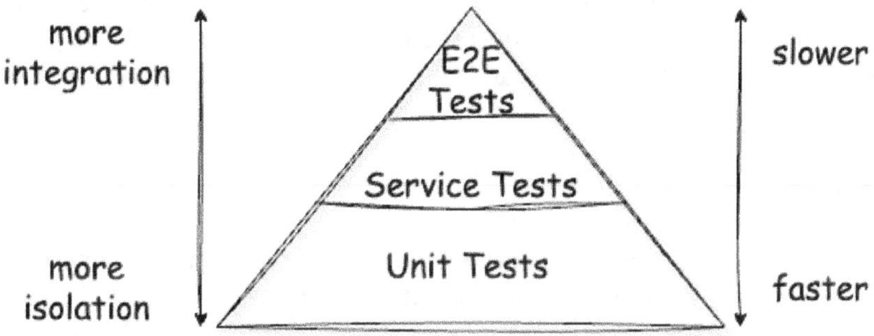

Figure 12.1: Test pyramid

The test pyramid contains three layers arranged from bottom to top: **unit tests**, **service (or integration) tests**, and **E2E tests**. The tests at the bottom of the pyramid are more isolated and faster than those at the top, which are more integrated and slower.

The core idea behind the test pyramid is useful when building an effective test suite. The two primary principles should guide our approach:

- Implement tests that vary in scope and focus

- As you move up the pyramid, the number of tests should decrease

To create a balanced, efficient, and maintainable test suite, focus on developing many fast and targeted unit tests and only include a moderate layer of service or integration tests. Limit your E2E tests to a small number of tests. Thus, you will avoid creating a test ice cream cone structure, as presented in *Figure 12.2*.

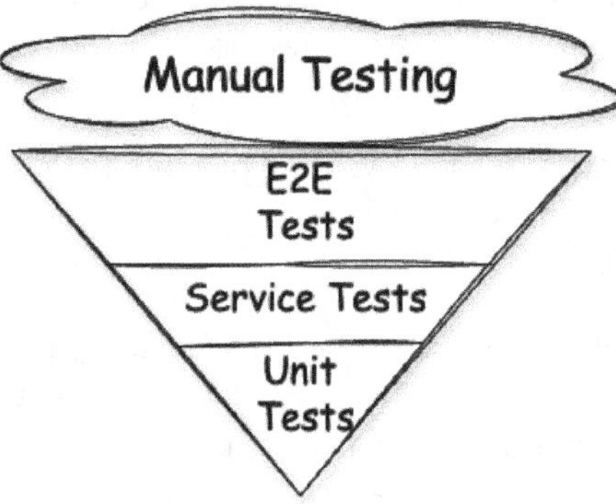

Figure 12.2: Test ice cream cone anti-pattern

The test ice cream is an anti-pattern in software testing that prioritizes tests at the top of the pyramid. This often leads to slower and harder-to-maintain test suites.

Cohn's test pyramid offers a helpful starting point for test distribution, but the terminology can feel restrictive and ambiguous in modern development practices. As systems become more complex, many teams benefit from adapting the pyramid to fit their specific context, adding or redefining layers, and clarifying testing goals across unit, integration, and E2E tests. Now, let's explore each layer of the test pyramid, beginning with unit tests.

Exploring unit testing

Unit tests focus on verifying individual components or units of code in isolation to confirm that they function as intended. Typically, this involves testing methods or classes to verify that each behaves correctly under specific conditions. By isolating units for testing, we can quickly identify bugs, verify functionality, and ensure that the minor pieces of the application function as intended before integrating them with other components.

Unit testing plays a crucial role in detecting errors early in the development cycle, which reduces the cost of bug fixes later. Characteristics of unit testing are as follows:

- **Fast**: Unit tests should run quickly, providing immediate feedback to developers

- **Isolated**: Unit tests do not depend on external components such as databases, APIs, and message brokers

- **Repeatable**: Each test should consistently yield the same result, regardless of the environment in which it is executed

Unit tests are the cheapest to write and maintain, but they are incredibly valuable because they provide fast feedback during development, helping to catch issues early in the lifecycle.

Unit tests usually replace external components such as databases and APIs with test doubles. A **test double**, a generic term for mock, refers to any case where a production object is replaced for testing purposes.

Should we use solitary or sociable tests?

When implementing unit tests, we can choose between **solitary** and **sociable testing** approaches. Solitary tests isolate the unit entirely by replacing dependencies with a test double, focusing solely on the unit's functionality to identify issues precisely. Sociable tests allow interaction between a unit and related components, verifying that they work together as expected without heavily using a test double. Thus, they are suitable for integration or component testing.

The choice between the two depends on the context: sociable tests are useful for stable interactions, while solitary tests are ideal for isolating specific unit behaviors. Mixing the approaches is no problem.

> **Note**
>
> What should unit testing test? Unit tests should focus on a class's public interface and observable behavior, such as verifying that input X produces result Y, rather than on internal details. This approach keeps tests resilient to refactoring, ensuring they validate outcomes instead of implementation specifics. Avoid testing private methods or trivial code such as getters and setters. By prioritizing meaningful tests, unit testing becomes a powerful tool for enhancing code quality and supporting refactoring without adding unnecessary overhead.

Implementing unit tests

Let's use a specific example from the auction context to write a unit test. We will use a class named `AuctionBid`, which models a user's bidding behavior. It is presented in the following code snippet:

```java
public class AuctionBid {
  private final String bidder;
  private BigDecimal highestBid;
```

```java
    public AuctionBid(String bidder) {
      this.bidder = bidder;
      this.highestBid = BigDecimal.ZERO;
    }
    public void placeBid(BigDecimal amount) {
      if (amount.compareTo(getHighestBid()) <= 0) {
        throw new IllegalArgumentException("Bid must be
          higher than current highest bid");
      }
      this.highestBid = amount;
    }
    public BigDecimal getHighestBid() {
      return highestBid;
    }
    public String getBidder() {
     return bidder;
    }
  }
```

The `AuctionBid` class keeps track of a bidder's highest bid and enforces the business rule that any new bid must be higher than the current highest bid through the `placeBid` method. It is ideal for unit testing because it does not depend on external systems such as databases or APIs, and we will focus solely on verifying the correctness of the business logic.

The following code snippet is the test class, `AuctionBidTest`, which includes unit tests that validate both valid and invalid bidding through the `givenHigherBid_whenPlaceBid_thenUpdatesHighestBid` and `givenLowerOrEqualBid_whenPlaceBid_thenThrowsException` methods:

```java
Public class AuctionBidTest {

  @Test
  void givenHigherBid_whenPlaceBid_thenUpdatesHighestBid(){
    AuctionBid bid = new AuctionBid("Alice");
    bid.placeBid(new BigDecimal("100.00"));

      assertThat(bid.getHighestBid()).isEqualByComparingTo(
          new BigDecimal("100.00"));
  }
  @Test
  void
  givenLowerOrEqualBid_whenPlaceBid_thenThrowsException(){
    AuctionBid bid = new AuctionBid("Bob");
    bid.placeBid(new BigDecimal("150.00"));
```

```
    assertThatThrownBy(() -> bid.placeBid(new
      BigDecimal("100.00"))).isInstanceOf(
        IllegalArgumentException.class)
      .hasMessage("Bid must be higher than current highest
        bid");
  }
```

Let's explore the `AuctionBidTest` class's technical elements to understand better how unit tests are structured and executed in Java with Junit 5, the most used testing framework in modern Java applications.

The `@Test` annotation, provided by JUnit 5, designates a method as a test case. When the test suite is executed, methods annotated with `@Test` are automatically discovered and run by the testing framework. Each method should verify a specific behavior or scenario.

The `assertThat` and `assertThatThrownBy` methods are part of **AssertJ**, an assertion library that comes with the `spring-boot-starter-test` dependency, which is included by default in Spring Boot projects. AssertJ offers a fluent and expressive API for writing assertions, making tests more readable and failure messages more helpful.

The `assertThat` method verifies expected values or conditions, allowing for readable and expressive test code. It can be used to check object equality, collection contents, or numeric comparisons.

The `assertThatThrownBy` method is designed to assert that a specific code block throws an expected exception. It allows additional validations to be chained, such as the type of exception and its message.

These methods enhance test clarity and provide more descriptive failure messages than traditional assertion approaches. Now, let's understand what mocks and spies are and how to apply them in our unit tests.

Understanding mocks and spies in unit tests

When writing unit tests, it's common to isolate the class under test by replacing its dependencies with test doubles. Two commonly used types of test doubles are mocks and spies, and while they may look similar at first glance, they behave quite differently.

A mock is a fully stubbed object and doesn't execute any real logic unless explicitly instructed. It's useful when you want to simulate behavior and verify interactions without relying on any internal implementation.

A spy, on the other hand, wraps a real object and allows partial mocking. By default, a spy calls the actual methods of the real object unless a method is specifically stubbed. This is helpful when you want to test real behavior while still being able to override specific parts if needed.

The following code snippet is a unit test method that uses `mock`:

```
@Test
void mock_shouldReturnStubbedValueAndNotCallRealLogic(){
  AuctionBid mockBid = mock();
  when(mockBid.getHighestBid()).thenReturn(new
    BigDecimal("999.00"));
  BigDecimal result = mockBid.getHighestBid();
  assertThat(result).isEqualTo(new BigDecimal("999.00"));
}
```

Instead of using a real `AuctionBid` object, this test creates a mock of the class using Mockito with `mock()`, giving full control over its behavior.

The when method defines how the mock should respond to method calls. In this case, when `mockBid.getHighestBid()` is invoked, it returns a predefined `BigDecimal` value of `999.00`. Finally, `assertThat(result).isEqualTo(new BigDecimal("999.00"))` verifies that the returned value matches the expected one.

The following code snippet presents a unit test using `spy` instead of `mock`:

```
@Test
void givenStubbedHighestBid_whenPlaceBidLower_thenException
    (){

  AuctionBid realBid = new AuctionBid("Charlie");
  AuctionBid spyBid = spy(realBid);

  doReturn(new BigDecimal("200.00"))
    .when(spyBid)
    .getHighestBid();

  assertThatThrownBy(() -> spyBid.placeBid(new
    BigDecimal("150.00")))
    .isInstanceOf(IllegalArgumentException.class)
    .hasMessage("Bid must be higher than current highest
      bid");
}
```

In this test, a real `AuctionBid` instance is wrapped with a spy using `spy(realBid)`. The `getHighestBid()` method is stubbed using `doReturn(...)` to simulate a scenario where the highest bid is already set to `200.00`. When `placeBid(150.00)` is called, the actual `placeBid` method is invoked because it was not stubbed. Inside `placeBid`, the validation correctly calls the `getHighestBid()` method, meaning the stubbed value is used. As a result, the comparison inside `placeBid` checks against the stubbed value, `200.00`, not the real field value. This leads to the expected behavior where the validation fails, throwing an `IllegalArgumentException`. This example shows how spies combine real behavior and controlled stubbing, allowing tests to simulate specific internal states without altering the original class implementation.

As shown, mocks are ideal when you want complete control over behavior without relying on the object's internal logic. At the same time, spies are helpful when you want to verify interactions or override specific behavior while still retaining access to the actual implementation. Choosing between a mock and a spy depends on the intent of the test: use mocks when testing behavior in isolation and spies when you need actual logic but also want the flexibility to intercept or verify specific calls.

Implementing unit tests for business logic

Let's explore a unit test that validates the logic of the `GetUserRolesUseCase` class within the user services API. We will create unit tests for the `execute` method, which returns roles for an existing user or the ANONYMOUS role if the user does not exist. The following code snippet presents the code of the `GetUserRolesUseCase` class:

```java
public class GetUserRolesUseCase {

  private final UserRepository userRepository;

  public GetUserRolesUseCase(UserRepository userRepository)
  { this.userRepository = userRepository;}
  public List<String> execute(String username) {

    List<String> roles = new ArrayList<>();
    Optional<User> user =
      userRepository.findByUsername(username);
    user.ifPresentOrElse(usr ->
      usr.getRoles().forEach(role ->
        roles.add(role.getName())), () ->
          roles.add("ANONYMOUS"));
    return roles;

  }
}
```

The following code snippet is the `GetUserRolesUseCaseTest` class, the unit test class created to test the execute method from the `GetUserRolesUseCase` class:

```java
public class GetUserRolesUseCaseTest {
  @Test
  void givenUserExists_whenExecute_thenReturnsRoles(){

    UserRepository mockRepository = mock();
    GetUserRolesUseCase useCase = new
```

```java
        GetUserRolesUseCase(mockRepository);

    Set<Role> roles = Set.of(new Role(1L, "ROLE_USER"), new
        Role(2L, "ROLE_ADMIN"));

    User user = new User(1L, "Alexander", …

    when(mockRepository.findByUsername(
        "alexander@example.com"))
        .thenReturn(Optional.of(user));

    List<String> result =
        useCase.execute("alexander@example.com");

    assertThat(result).containsExactlyInAnyOrder(
        "ROLE_USER", "ROLE_ADMIN");
}

    @Test
    void givenNoUser_whenExecute_thenReturnsAnonymousRole(){

    UserRepository mockRepository = mock();
    GetUserRolesUseCase useCase = new
        GetUserRolesUseCase(mockRepository);

    when(mockRepository.findByUsername(
        "not_exist@example.com"))
        .thenReturn(Optional.empty());
    List<String> result =
        useCase.execute("not_exist@example.com");

    assertThat(result).containsExactly("ANONYMOUS");
    }
}
```

The `GetUserRolesUseCaseTest` class contains two test methods: `givenUserExists_whenExecute_thenReturnsRoles` and `givenNoUser_whenExecute_thenReturnsAnonymousRole`.

The `givenUserExists_whenExecute_thenReturnsRoles` test verifies that the use case correctly retrieves roles for a user found by their username. Instead of relying on a real database, it uses a Mockito mock of `UserRepository` to isolate the logic, providing full control over its behavior and ensuring the test runs independently of external systems. The mock is injected into a new instance of `GetUserRolesUseCase`, and its behavior is defined using `when(...).thenReturn(...)` to return predefined roles. The `assertThat(result).containsExactlyInAnyOrder(...)` assertion confirms that the method returns the expected roles, regardless of order.

The `givenNoUser_whenExecute_thenReturnsAnonymousRole` test follows the same approach but simulates the absence of a user by returning `Optional.empty()`. It verifies that the use case correctly returns a default role of `ANONYMOUS` when no user is found. The assertion checks that the result contains exactly that role.

Together, these tests validate the entire business logic in isolation, covering both the successful and fallback scenarios, and ensuring correctness without relying on external infrastructure such as a database. Now, let's implement unit tests for RESTful controllers.

Implementing unit tests for RESTful controllers

Unit testing RESTful controllers is essential to ensure that endpoints correctly handle input, delegate tasks appropriately, and return the expected HTTP status codes. To achieve this, we can utilize MockMvc, a powerful utility provided by Spring. MockMvc allows us to simulate HTTP requests to the controllers and verify the results without starting an entire web server.

The following code snippet defines the `UserControllerTest` class, which is responsible for verifying the behavior of the `UserController` component:

```
@WebMvcTest(UserController.class)
@AutoConfigureMockMvc(addFilters = false)
class UserControllerTest {
  @Autowired
  private MockMvc mockMvc;
  @MockBean
  private GetUsersUseCase getUsersUseCase;
  @Test
  void getUsers_shouldReturnListOfUsers_whenUsersExist()
      throws Exception {
    List<User> users = List.of(new User(1L, …
    when(getUsersUseCase.execute()).thenReturn(users);
    mockMvc.perform(get("/v1/users")
      .accept(MediaType.APPLICATION_JSON))
      .andExpect(status().isOk())
      .andExpect(jsonPath("$", hasSize(2)))
      .andExpect(jsonPath("$[0].name").value("Alice"))
      .andExpect(jsonPath("$[1].email")
      .value("bob@example.com"));
  }
```

The code uses the `@WebMvcTest(UserController.class)` annotation to load only the web layer of the Spring Boot application, which includes controllers and related components, without initializing the full application context. To simplify testing and avoid security-related errors, the `@AutoConfigureMockMvc(addFilters = false)` annotation disables security filters, ensuring that endpoints can be tested without authentication.

The `MockMvc` object is injected using `@Autowired`, enabling the test to simulate HTTP requests to controller endpoints without starting a real server. To isolate the controller logic, `GetUsersUseCase` is mocked with `@MockBean`, which internally creates a Mockito mock and either replaces the existing Spring bean with a mock or, if the bean does not exist, registers a new mock bean in the application context, allowing the use of standard Mockito stubbing and verification.

The line `mockMvc.perform(get("/v1/users"))` simulates an HTTP GET request to the `/v1/users` endpoint, allowing the test to interact with the controller as if it were handling a real request. The call to `.accept(MediaType.APPLICATION_JSON)` specifies that the test expects a JSON-formatted response. Following that, the chain of `.andExpect(...)` methods asserts the status code is `200` (OK) and uses JSONPath expressions to verify specific elements in the returned JSON payload, ensuring that the data structure and content match the expected output.

With MockMvc, we can write concise and expressive unit tests for controller endpoints, ensuring they behave correctly under various input and output scenarios. Now, let's explore the next test pyramid layer: test integration.

Exploring integration testing

Integration testing is a stage of software testing in which individual units or components are combined and tested as a group. It verifies that an application interacts correctly with external components such as databases, APIs, event systems, file storage, authentication, notification services, caching, and configuration management. These tests confirm that the application handles data, responses, permissions, messages, and secrets as expected, ensuring smooth integration and data consistency across all components in production-like conditions.

Unlike unit tests, which focus on isolated functionality within a single component, integration tests assess the behavior of interconnected parts of the application.

In integration testing, we can also use a test double, which is similar to unit testing. For example, suppose we want to verify that our code saves data to the database, but the function first calls an API and we do not need to test it. In that case, we can mock it since our primary focus is to ensure the code is correctly saved to the database.

But is it a good idea to use real components such as databases and APIs in our integration tests?

Avoiding real components in integration tests

Creating integration tests with real components such as databases and APIs can be beneficial, but using simulated environments is usually more practical. The term *real components* refers to real databases or APIs in environments such as development or even production. While real components provide the most accurate production-like conditions, they can introduce challenges.

Real components may be unavailable or unstable, leading to unreliable tests and false negatives, ultimately disrupting the CI/CD pipeline. Setting up, tearing down, and interacting with real components significantly increases test execution time, slowing down the CI/CD process. Managing data consistency, state cleanup, and environment isolation in real databases is challenging and may result in flaky tests or environmental conflicts. Additionally, using real components in CI/CD can incur additional infrastructure costs, especially when relying on managed services or cloud-hosted databases and APIs.

The integration test's purpose is to test and verify the interaction with components. If it is not recommended to use real components, how should we test these components in a way that we have a reliable test?

Simulating real components in integration tests

To achieve reliable integration testing without relying on real components, you can simulate dependencies using tools that provide realistic, isolated environments for databases, APIs, and other services:

- **Use mock servers for external APIs**: Tools such as WireMock or MockServer allow you to simulate API responses, mimicking the behavior of third-party services. These mock servers let you define responses for different endpoints and scenarios, ensuring consistent behavior without dependency on external availability.

- **Use Testcontainers for infrastructure testing**: Testcontainers is a great library that lets you spin up isolated, disposable instances of any infrastructure component available as a Docker container. While it is commonly used for databases such as PostgreSQL, MySQL, or MongoDB and message brokers such as Kafka and RabbitMQ, it can also run services such as LocalStack and MinIO. LocalStack emulates AWS services such as S3, DynamoDB, and SQS, making it ideal for testing cloud interactions locally without hitting actual AWS endpoints. MinIO offers an S3-compatible API and can be used to simulate object storage behavior in a controlled environment. Using Testcontainers to orchestrate these components ensures consistent, production-like environments for your tests without relying on shared infrastructure or external availability.

Using these techniques, integration tests can closely simulate real interactions, ensuring reliability and consistency while avoiding dependency on live production systems. This approach reduces the risk of false negatives and keeps CI/CD pipelines fast and stable. Now, let's implement an integration test using Testcontainers.

Implementing integration tests with Testcontainers

We will now implement an integration test for the `execute` method of the `GetUserRolesUseCase` class, which is the same method for which we've implemented unit tests. In our unit test, we used a test double to simulate the repository behavior. Now, we will use Testcontainers to provide a PostgreSQL database since we've already learned the cons of using an actual database in our integration tests.

Why use Testcontainers instead of the H2 in-memory database? Testcontainers can provide the same database that the service uses in a production environment, making our tests closer to real situations. For instance, with Testcontainers, we could create and work with procedures, functions, and some features that the H2 database does not provide.

The following configuration snippet presents the dependencies required to be added to the `user-services` API:

```
<dependency>
  <groupId>org.springframework.boot</groupId>
  <artifactId>spring-boot-testcontainers</artifactId>
  <scope>test</scope>
</dependency>

<dependency>
  <groupId>org.testcontainers</groupId>
  <artifactId>junit-jupiter</artifactId>
  <scope>test</scope>
</dependency>
<dependency>
  <groupId>org.testcontainers</groupId>
  <artifactId>postgresql</artifactId>
  <scope>test</scope>
</dependency>
```

The `spring-boot-testcontainers` module adds native Spring Boot 3.1+ integration with Testcontainers, allowing us to use annotations such as `@ServiceConnection` so that Spring automatically configures properties such as the data source URL, username, and password based on the running container.

The `junit-jupiter` module integrates Testcontainers with JUnit 5, enabling support for annotations such as `@Testcontainers` and `@Container`, which manage the container lifecycle during test execution.

The `postgresql` module from Testcontainers provides the `PostgreSQLContainer` class used to spin up isolated PostgreSQL instances inside Docker containers for database integration tests.

Regarding configuration, in real-world scenarios, integration tests often require different configuration settings than the production environment—for example, disabling security filters, enabling test-specific beans, or connecting to test containers.

The following configuration snippet is the `application-test.properties` file in the `src/test/resources` folder:

```
eureka.client.enabled=false
management.otlp.metrics.export.enabled=false
management.tracing.enabled=false
```

The `eureka.client.enabled` property disables the Eureka client, preventing the application from registering with a Eureka server or attempting service discovery.

The `management.otlp.metrics.export.enabled` property disables the export of metrics to the **OpenTelemetry (OTLP)** collector.

The `management.tracing.enabled` property turns off distributed tracing.

We will load a database using Testcontainers, so we must populate the database for the tests. Then, we must create the `init.sql` file in the `src/test/resources` folder. It contains instructions for inserting data into the tables, such as the SQL instruction in the following code snippet:

```
INSERT INTO users ( city, country, email, name, phone_number, state)
VALUES ('New York', 'United States', 'user@wxauction.com', 'User X',
'123456789', 'NY');
```

Now, let's check the integration test class, `GetUserRolesUseCaseIntegrationTest`, presented in the following code snippet:

```
@SpringBootTest
@Testcontainers
@ActiveProfiles("test")
@Sql({"/init.sql"})
public class GetUserRolesUseCaseIntegrationTest{
  @Container
  @ServiceConnection
  static PostgreSQLContainer<?> postgres =
    new PostgreSQLContainer<>("postgres:16-alpine");
  @Autowired
  private UserJpaDatasource userJpaDatasource;
  private GetUserRolesUseCase getUserRolesUseCase;
  ...
  @Test
  void givenUserExists_whenExecute_thenReturnsRoles() {
    String username = "admin@wxauction.com";
```

```
    List<String> roles =
      getUserRolesUseCase.execute(username);
    assertThat(roles).contains("ROLE_ADMIN");
  }
  ...
```

Although `@SpringBootTest` typically loads the entire application context and is often associated with E2E testing, in this case, it is used to facilitate a real database interaction through `GetUserRolesUseCase`. Different application parts may require different testing strategies: repository classes with `@DataJpaTest`, controllers with `@WebMvcTest`, and complete workflows with `@SpringBootTest` for full E2E scenarios.

When using `@ActiveProfiles("test")`, Spring first loads the default `application.properties` and then overrides its values with those from `application-test.properties`. The base configuration is not ignored but extended or replaced by the test profile settings.

The `@Testcontainers` annotation enables integration with the Testcontainers library, allowing containers defined with `@Container` to be automatically started and stopped for the test lifecycle.

The `@Sql({"/init.sql"})` annotation runs the specified SQL script, `init.sql`, before the test executes, initializing the database with the required schema and test data to ensure consistent and repeatable test conditions. The `@Container` annotation marks `PostgreSQLContainer` as a managed Testcontainers resource, ensuring it is automatically started before the tests and stopped afterward.

The `@ServiceConnection` annotation, introduced in Spring Boot 3.1, tells Spring to automatically configure application properties, such as `spring.datasource.url`, `username`, and `password`, using the running container, eliminating the need for manual property setup.

`PostgreSQLContainer` specifies the `postgres:16-alpine` Docker image and, when annotated with `@Container`, is automatically started before the tests and stopped afterward by the Testcontainers framework—eliminating the need for manual `start()` and `stop()` calls.

The `givenUserExists_whenExecute_thenReturnsRoles` integration test method mirrors the previous unit test in purpose but differs in execution. Instead of using a test double, it interacts with the actual application context and database setup, verifying the real behavior of `GetUserRolesUseCase` in an integrated environment.

To execute the integration test, go to the project folder and run the following command:

```
mvn clean test -Dtest=GetUserRolesUseCaseIntegrationTest
```

Observe in the console that the tables are created, data is inserted, and the `userRepository.findByUsername` instruction in the `execute` method of `GetUserRolesUseCase` interacts with the database to perform the specified query using Testcontainers.

Testcontainers is a powerful integration testing tool that provides realistic, isolated environments using Docker containers. By spinning up actual instances of databases, message brokers, and other components, Testcontainers ensures that tests are highly accurate and closely reflect production conditions. Now, let's implement an integration test for the persistence layer.

Implementing integration tests for the persistence layer

Implementing integration tests for the persistence layer is crucial to validate that custom queries, entity mappings, and data access behaviors function correctly with the underlying database. Even though Spring Data JPA abstracts much of the data access logic, it's essential to test custom queries and ensure they return accurate results, respect entity relationships, and adhere to schema constraints. These tests assist in identifying potential issues such as incorrect JPQL or native SQL, mismatches between entity attributes and database columns, or unintended behavior introduced by joins and fetch strategies.

The following code snippet defines the `UserJpaRepository` interface, a Spring Data JPA repository responsible for managing user entities:

```java
public interface UserJpaRepository extends
                          JpaRepository<UserEntity, Long> {
  @Query("SELECT u FROM UserEntity u WHERE u.email =
          :username")
  Optional<UserEntity> findByUsername(String username);
}
```

The repository extends `JpaRepository` to provide standard CRUD operations and declares a custom query method, `findByUsername`, which retrieves a user by their email address. The following code snippet is `UserJpaRepositoryIntegrationTest`, the test class that tests the `UserJpaRepository` interface:

```java
@DataJpaTest
@Testcontainers
@AutoConfigureTestDatabase(replace =
        AutoConfigureTestDatabase.Replace.NONE)
@Sql("/init.sql")
public class UserJpaRepositoryIntegrationTest{
  @Container
  @ServiceConnection
  static PostgreSQLContainer<?> postgres =
    new PostgreSQLContainer<>("postgres:16-alpine");
  @Autowired
  private UserJpaRepository userJpaRepository;

  @Test
  void findByUsername_shouldReturnUser_whenEmailExists() {
```

```
    String email = "admin@wxauction.com";
    Optional<UserEntity> result =
      userJpaRepository.findByUsername(email);
    assertThat(result).isPresent().get()
      .extracting(UserEntity::getEmail).isEqualTo(email);
  }
}
```

The `UserJpaRepositoryIntegrationTest` class closely resembles the previously discussed `UserJpaDatasourceIntegrationTest` class, with the key distinction being its use of the `@DataJpaTest` annotation instead of `@SpringBootTest`. Provided by Spring Boot, `@DataJpaTest` is specifically tailored to test JPA components in isolation. It is considered a lightweight integration test because it loads only the parts of the application context related to persistence—such as repositories, entity mappings, and `EntityManager`—without initializing the full Spring Boot application context. As a result, tests annotated with `@DataJpaTest` tend to be faster and more focused than those using `@SpringBootTest`, which brings up the entire application context, including web, security, and other non-persistence-related components. Now, let's implement a full stack integration test.

Implementing full stack integration tests

Now, we will implement a full stack integration test using RestAssured and Testcontainers. The test covers multiple application layers—from RESTful API endpoints through business logic to the persistence layer—ensuring E2E correctness and integration across the system.

This test ensures the application behaves correctly across all layers—from handling HTTP requests at the API layer to executing business logic and persisting data in the database. RestAssured is ideal for this scenario because it issues actual HTTP requests, enabling full validation of routing, filters, serialization, and security configurations. Unlike MockMvc, which operates within the Spring context and simulates HTTP interactions, RestAssured interacts with the application as an actual client would.

The following configuration snippet includes the `rest-assured` dependency, which is required to use the RestAssured library for writing and executing HTTP-based integration tests:

```xml
<dependency>
  <groupId>io.rest-assured</groupId>
  <artifactId>rest-assured</artifactId>
  <version>5.5.1</version>
  <scope>test</scope>
</dependency>
```

The following code snippet defines the `UserControllerIntegrationTest` class, which uses RestAssured to send a request to the `/v1/users/{username}/roles` endpoint. It verifies that the application correctly returns the associated roles for the specified user:

```java
@SpringBootTest(
    classes = UserServicesApplication.class,
    webEnvironment= SpringBootTest.WebEnvironment.RANDOM_PORT
)
@Testcontainers
@Sql("/init.sql")
public class UserControllerIntegrationTest {
    @LocalServerPort
    private int port;
    @Container
    @ServiceConnection
    static PostgreSQLContainer<?> postgres =
        new PostgreSQLContainer<>("postgres:16-alpine");
    @Test
    void getUserRoles_shouldReturnRoles_whenUserExists() {

        RestAssured.baseURI = "http://localhost";
        RestAssured.port = port;
         given()
            .accept(ContentType.JSON)
            .header("traceparent", "00-abcdef1234567890abc")
            .when()
            .get("/v1/users/admin@wxauction.com/roles")
            .then()
            .log().all()
            .statusCode(200)
            .body("roles", not(empty()))
            .body("roles", hasItem("ROLE_USER"));
    }
}
```

The `@SpringBootTest` annotation is configured with `classes = UserServicesApplication.class` and `webEnvironment = SpringBootTest.WebEnvironment.RANDOM_PORT`. They tell Spring to start the full application context on a random port, making it suitable for full stack integration tests.

The `@LocalServerPort` annotation injects the port used at runtime, which is then assigned to `RestAssured.port`. Additionally, `RestAssured.baseURI` is set to `http://localhost`, ensuring that RestAssured sends HTTP requests to the correct base address of the locally running Spring Boot test server.

Within the `getUserRoles_shouldReturnRoles_whenUserExists` test method, RestAssured is used to send a `GET` request to the `/v1/users/admin@wxauction.com/roles` endpoint. The `.accept(ContentType.JSON)` line sets the `Accept` header. A `traceparent` header is also added to simulate distributed tracing.

After the request is sent using `.when().get(...)`, the response is validated using `.then()` with chained assertions, such as `.statusCode(200)`, which asserts that the HTTP response status should be `200` (OK). Next, `.body("roles", not(empty()))` checks that the `roles` field in the JSON response is not empty. Then, `.body("roles", hasItem("ROLE_USER"))` confirms that the list includes `ROLE_USER`.

The `.log().all()` call is helpful during test development or debugging, as it logs the complete request and response data to the console.

This test is a complete setup for integration testing with RestAssured in a Spring Boot application. It covers application bootstrapping, containerized database usage, a real HTTP request, and response verification. Now, let's explore the final layer of the test pyramid: E2E tests.

Exploring E2E testing

E2E tests assess an application's complete workflow by examining the entire system from beginning to end. At the top of the test pyramid, E2E tests validate critical user interactions by ensuring all components, such as UI, backend, and database, work together as expected. By mimicking actual user actions, E2E tests help catch integration issues across the application and verify that essential workflows, such as user registration, checkout, or data processing, function correctly from the user's perspective.

Due to their slower execution times and higher maintenance needs, E2E tests should focus only on mission-critical paths rather than covering every possible interaction. Tools such as Selenium, Cypress, and Playwright are commonly used for automating E2E tests, with options for parallel execution to reduce test duration. To make these tests manageable, best practices include limiting dependencies on specific test data and running the most important ones as part of the CI/CD pipeline to catch integration issues early in development.

E2E provides valuable insight into the end user experience but is resource-intensive. To ensure robust coverage without sacrificing test efficiency, faster, lower-level tests, such as unit and integration tests, should be balanced with E2E tests.

While the test pyramid emphasizes establishing a solid foundation for functional correctness through unit, integration, and E2E tests, performance tests go beyond this framework to assess non-functional aspects such as speed, responsiveness, and system stability under load; let's explore performance tests and how to boost applications.

Boosting applications with performance testing

Imagine it's Black Friday, one of the year's busiest shopping days. Customers are flooding your online store, eager to grab deals and fill their carts with discounts they've been waiting for all year. But as they click through the pages and add items to their carts, something starts to happen—pages slow down, some users are met with loading errors, and a few even get completely timed out. What should have been a record-breaking day for sales has turned into a frantic scramble to restore performance, leaving customers frustrated and likely to take their business elsewhere.

This scenario sheds light on the importance of performance testing. While functional tests ensure our application works, performance tests ensure it works well under pressure. They verify that our system meets expected responsiveness, stability, and scalability standards under different workloads. Performance testing allows us to identify bottlenecks, such as slow response times, excessive resource consumption, and potential system failures when the application is under heavy load. By catching these issues early, we can optimize resources and fine-tune our application's resilience and responsiveness when it matters most, giving us confidence that our system can handle spikes in traffic and unexpected loads.

The main types of performance tests include the following:

- **Load testing**: Simulate normal to high user loads to ensure the application can manage expected traffic levels

- **Stress testing**: Push the system to its breaking point to observe its behavior under intense conditions

- **Scalability testing**: Evaluate the application's ability to scale up or down in response to increased or decreased workloads

- **Endurance testing**: Run the system for an extended period under a typical load to check for memory leaks or stability issues over time

Performance testing is vital for applications expected to handle a significant number of users or high transaction rates, such as e-commerce sites, social media platforms, or financial applications. Teams often conduct performance tests on days when they anticipate a surge in application usage, such as Black Friday.

Performance testing enhances user satisfaction, minimizes downtime, and ensures a smoother experience under peak loads by identifying and resolving performance issues early. Let's implement load testing with Jmeter.

Implementing load testing with JMeter

We will use **Apache JMeter** to conduct load testing and simulate multiple users accessing the endpoint, `http://localhost:8072/authentication/v1/api/auth`, to obtain a token. Let's start the implementation:

1. Download Apache JMeter from `https://jmeter.apache.org/download_jmeter.cgi` and extract it to a directory.

2. Launch JMeter by running the `jmeter` executable in the `bin` folder.

3. Create a new test plan. Right-click on the test plan, select **Add**, then choose **Threads (Users)**, and finally, select **Thread Group**. This thread group defines the number of users and the test duration. Enter the configuration in the following list, as shown in *Figure 12.3*:

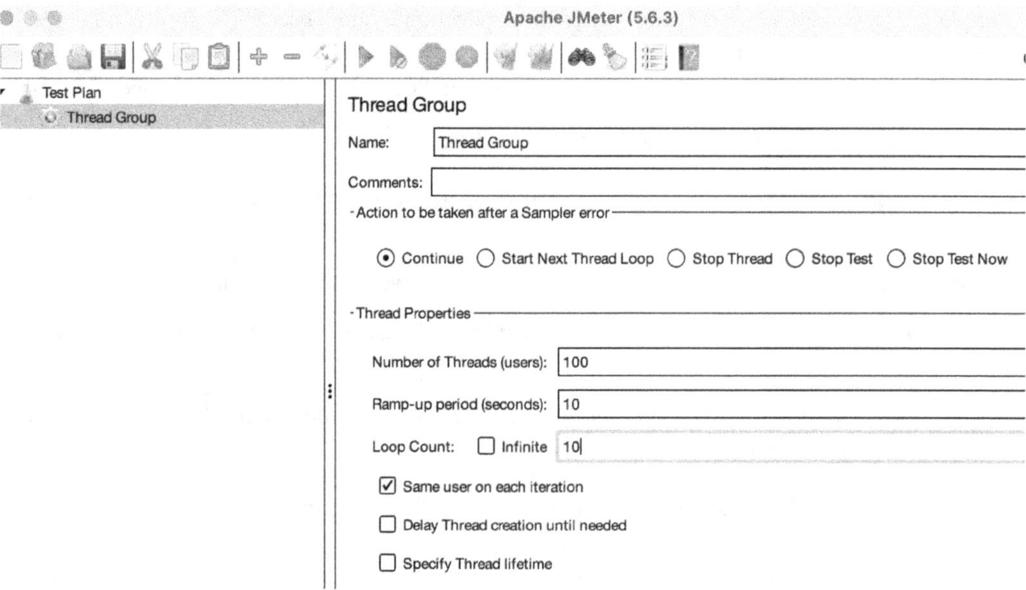

Figure 12.3: Thread Group configuration

- **Number of Threads (users)**: Set the setting to `100` to simulate 100 concurrent users

- **Ramp-Up period (seconds)**: Set the setting to `10` seconds so that JMeter will initiate all threads within that time frame

- **Loop Count**: Set it to `10`; each user will send 10 requests

4. Create a new HTTP request. Right-click on **Thread Group**, select **Add**, then choose **Sampler**, and finally, select **HTTP Request**. Enter the configuration in the following list, as shown in *Figure 12.4*:

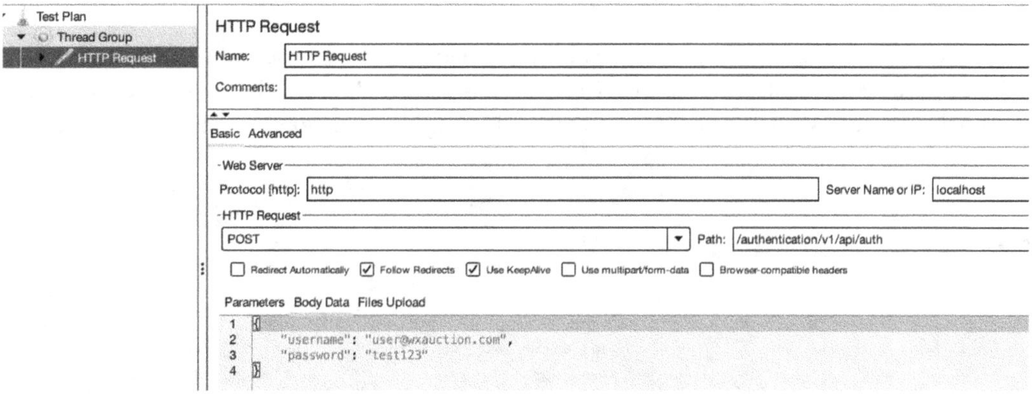

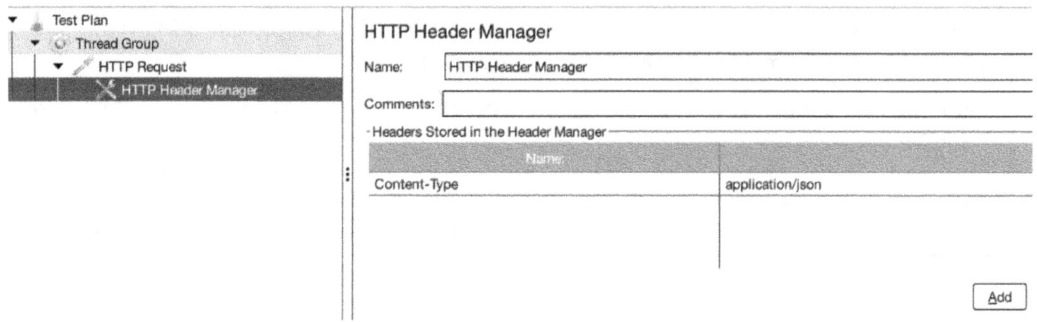

Figure 12.4: HTTP Request configuration

- **Protocol** [http] : Enter http
- **Server Name or IP**: Enter localhost
- **Port Number**: Specify the port 8072
- **HTTP Request**: Set to **POST**
- **Path**: Enter /authentication/v1/api/auth

5. Create a new HTTP request manager. Right-click on **HTTP Request**, select **Add**, then choose **Config Element**, and finally select **HTTP Request Manager**. Enter the following configuration, as shown in *Figure 12.5.*

Figure 12.5: HTTP Header Manager configuration

The following is the pair-value header:

- **Name**: `Content-Type`

- **Value**: `application/json`

6. Now, let's validate the response; we will check whether the response code is `200`. Create a response assertion. Right-click on **HTTP Request**, select **Add**, then choose **Assertions**, and finally, select **Response Assertion**. Enter the following configuration, shown in *Figure 12.6*:

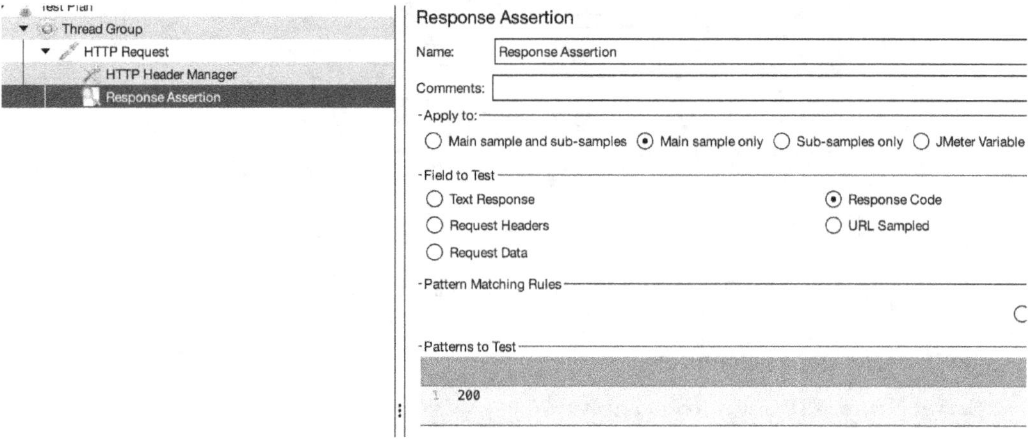

Figure 12.6: Response Assertion

Use the following **Response Assertion** values:

- **Field to Test**: Select **Response Code**

- **Patterns to Test**: Enter `200`

7. Now, let's add a listener to capture and view results. Right-click on **Thread Group**, select **Add**, then choose **Listener**, and finally, select **Summary Report**. This will provide insights into the application, such as response times, throughput, and success rates.

8. Verify that the online auction application is running, then click the **Start** button in JMeter to begin the load test.

JMeter will simulate 100 users making requests to the authentication services to get a token, providing metrics on response times, throughput, and error rates in the summary report and table results.

Analyzing the load testing results

After completing the loading test, let's delve into the results in the summary report illustrated in *Figure 12.7*. This will help us uncover critical insights. This report provides an overview of the performance indicators, including response times, error rates, throughput, and system resource usage under load. By thoroughly examining these metrics, we can pinpoint bottlenecks, evaluate whether performance meets the expected thresholds, and identify areas that may require optimization to ensure stability and responsiveness under heavy user demand.

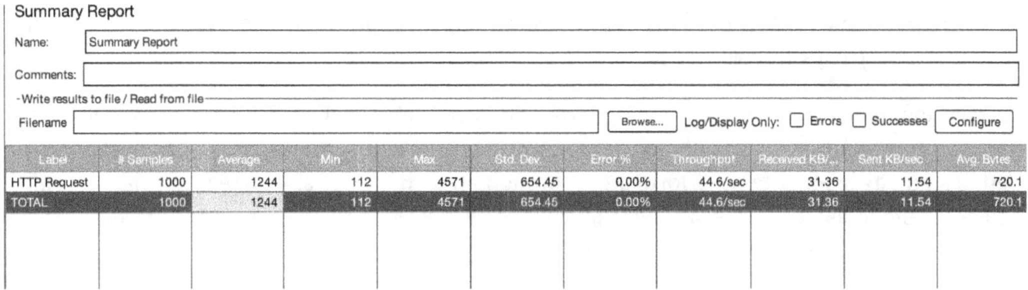

Summary Report

Name: Summary Report

Comments:

Write results to file / Read from file

Filename   Browse...   Log/Display Only: ☐ Errors ☐ Successes   Configure

Label	# Samples	Average	Min	Max	Std. Dev	Error %	Throughput	Received KB/...	Sent KB/sec	Avg. Bytes
HTTP Request	1000	1244	112	4571	654.45	0.00%	44.6/sec	31.36	11.54	720.1
TOTAL	1000	1244	112	4571	654.45	0.00%	44.6/sec	31.36	11.54	720.1

Figure 12.7: Loading the test's summary report

Let's analyze each column from the summary report with their results:

- **# Samples**: The test was sent to the server with 1,000 HTTP requests, a good sample size for understanding the average performance.

- **Average**: The average response time for HTTP requests was 1,244 milliseconds, which indicates the typical time it takes for requests to be processed. Depending on the system's expectations, this could be considered slow if the target is sub-second responses.

- **Min** (minimum): The fastest response time recorded was 112 milliseconds. This could represent instances where the server had fewer loads or responded quickly due to optimized processing paths.

- **Max** (maximum): The slowest response time was 4,571 milliseconds, which indicates occasional latency spikes. These could be due to temporary resource constraints or peak server loads.

- **Std. Dev.** (standard deviation): The standard deviation was 654.45 milliseconds, showing reasonably high variability in response times. This high deviation suggests inconsistent response times, possibly due to fluctuating server load, network issues, or backend processing delays.

- **Error %**: No errors were recorded. This indicates that all requests were successfully processed, which is a positive outcome for reliability.

- **Throughput**: The throughput was 44.6 requests per second. This metric reflects the capacity of the server to handle requests under the current configuration. Higher throughput is generally desired for high-load scenarios.

- **Received KB/sec**: The average rate at which data is received from the server was 31.36 KB per second. This information helps us understand the data flow from the server side and could inform bandwidth considerations.

- **Sent KB/sec:** The data sent rate was 11.54 KB per second, reflecting the outgoing data from JMeter to the server. This metric can help assess whether the load generation requires considerable bandwidth.

- **Avg. Bytes:** The average response data size was 720.1 bytes per request, which gives an idea of the response payload size.

The server handles requests reliably with no errors, showing stable performance under average load. However, response times vary, with occasional slowdowns reaching 4.5 seconds. A high standard deviation suggests inconsistent performance. Throughput is moderate at 44.6 requests per second, sufficient for moderate loads but may need testing for higher demands. Optimization, caching, and load balancing could help achieve more consistent and faster response times.

Performance testing like this helps ensure applications can reliably handle real-world traffic, providing a smoother user experience. Now, we can shift focus to development practices that drive quality from the start, such as TDD and BDD. These approaches emphasize writing tests early and help define functionality through test scenarios, fostering more precise requirements and robust code.

Exploring Test-Driven Development

TDD is an approach where tests are intentionally written before the code itself, but it's more than just *writing tests first*—TDD is a disciplined methodology that guides the entire development process. In TDD, development follows a structured cycle: the process begins with creating a test for the desired functionality. Then, code is written to ensure the test succeeds. Once the test passes, the code is refined to enhance its organization and clarity. *Figure 12.8* illustrates this TDD workflow.

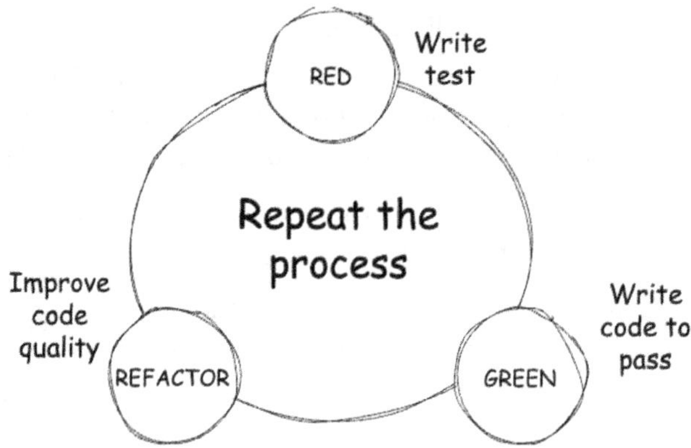

Figure 12.8: TDD process

The process when working with TDD is as follows:

1. *Red*: Start by writing a test defining a small functionality piece. Since the feature doesn't exist yet, the test will initially fail, signaling that code is needed to make it pass.

2. *Green*: Write the minimal amount of code required to pass the test. The goal is to keep the code simple and focus on meeting the test requirements.

3. *Refactor*: Once the test passes, improve the code's structure and efficiency without changing its behavior. Refactoring is crucial in TDD, as it enhances readability, maintains clean code, and minimizes duplication.

TDD promotes a continuous feedback loop. We define precise requirements by writing tests before code, resulting in higher code quality and better test coverage. It also fosters incremental development, ensuring that each feature is fully validated before proceeding. TDD is commonly used in Agile and modern software development practices to ensure software meets functional requirements with fewer defects.

Having explored TDD and its focus on test-first design, we now move to BDD, which builds upon TDD principles with a stronger emphasis on defining behaviors through collaboration and shared understanding.

Introducing Behavior-Driven Development

BDD emphasizes testing a system's overall behavior rather than verifying individual functions. Rather than focusing solely on isolated code units, BDD aims to ensure that the software aligns with business requirements and meets user expectations.

BDD builds on TDD while incorporating a business perspective, making it particularly compatible with *domain-driven design* (*DDD*). This approach utilizes a narrative style for tests, written in a manner easily understandable by everyone—developers, testers, and business stakeholders alike. The goal is to establish a ubiquitous language. This shared vocabulary reflects the core concepts of the domain, making the tests clear and relevant to both technical and non-technical team members.

A common way to structure these behavior-focused tests is through the *given-when-then* (*GWT*) format. Let's look at this format:

- *Given*: Set up the initial context

- *When*: Describe the action taken

- *Then*: Outline the expected outcome

Using GWT in BDD allows teams to write tests that describe each feature's behavior in a straightforward, human-readable way. This helps ensure the application meets technical requirements and business expectations, aligning development closely with real-world needs.

The GWT pattern can absolutely be used in tests such as unit tests. Although GWT is often associated with BDD, its structured format makes it highly versatile and practical for organizing any type of test, from isolated units to complex integrations.

Applying the GWT pattern in our tests

To demonstrate the GWT pattern, let's get the previous unit test example, the *findByUsername_shouldReturnUser_whenUserExists()* method. The following code snippet is the test method refactored to the GWT pattern:

```
@Test
void givenAnExistingUsername_whenFindByUsername_thenReturnsUser() {
  // Given
  String name = "testUser";
  UserEntity userEntity = new UserEntity();
  userEntity.setName(name);
  when(userJpaRepository.findByUsername(name)).thenReturn(
    Optional.of(userEntity));
  // When
  Optional<User> result =
    userJpaDatasource.findByUsername(name);
  // Then
  assertTrue(result.isPresent());
  assertEquals(name, result.get().getName());
}
```

The first change is the method name; in GWT, we use the `given..._when..._then...` syntax; in this case, the method's name changed to `givenAnExistingUsername_whenFindByUsername_thenReturnsUser()`. It clearly outlines the scenario: *Given an existing username* describes the setup, *when finding by username* specifies the action being tested, and *then returns user* indicates the expected result. This naming convention makes the method self-explanatory and easy to understand:

- In the `Given` section, you set up the initial conditions or context required for the test. This often involves preparing objects, initializing data, or mocking dependencies to create the code's state so it runs correctly. Here, it builds and sets up the `UserEntity` object and mocks the `userJpaRepository.findByUsername` method.

- The `When` section executes the behavior or action being tested. This step directly calls the method or performs the action you want to validate, here, `userJpaDatasource.findByUsername`. It's often a single instruction or a sequence of calls focused on the functionality being tested.

- The `Then` section verifies that the outcome matches the expected result. Here, we use assertions to check that the state, values, or behaviors are correct. This part confirms that the action performed in the `When` section led to the desired outcome.

The GWT pattern clarifies and structures tests, making them easy to read and understand. By clearly separating setup, execution, and verification, GWT ensures that tests are maintainable and effectively communicate the intent to all team members, including those who may not be deeply technical. This approach improves collaboration and provides a shared language for describing system behaviors.

Summary

This chapter explored automated testing in modern software development, emphasizing quality in fast-paced delivery cycles. You learned about the test pyramid and its layers—unit, integration, and E2E tests—and their roles in ensuring software reliability. Practical examples demonstrated how to implement effective tests using tools such as JUnit 5 and Mockito for unit testing, Spring Boot's test utilities for loading full application contexts, Testcontainers for stable and isolated integration tests, and MockMvc and RestAssured for validating API behavior at different layers.

The chapter also covered performance testing using JMeter to assess system stability and scalability and introduced TDD and BDD, which foster code quality through test-first design and business-aligned requirements using the GWT pattern.

This chapter's theoretical concepts and practical implication strategies provided a solid foundation for developing automated testing strategies that enhance software quality in agile development.

In *Chapter 13, Performance and Optimizations*, we will explore the intricacies of the *Java Virtual Machine (JVM)* and garbage collection. We will also use tools to identify bottlenecks and conduct insightful performance analyses. Additionally, we will discuss how to apply caching to improve response times and performance and introduce asynchronous and non-blocking communication through reactive programming.

Questions

1. What is the primary benefit of automated testing in software development?
2. What is the test pyramid, and why is it important?
3. Why should we avoid using actual databases or APIs in integration tests?
4. How does Testcontainers improve integration tests compared to in-memory databases?
5. What is a test double, and when is it used?
6. How does load testing differ from stress testing?

Get This Book's PDF Version and Exclusive Extras

UNLOCK NOW

Scan the QR code (or go to `packtpub.com/unlock`). Search for this book by name, confirm the edition, and then follow the steps on the page.

Note: Keep your invoice handly. Purchase made directly from packt don't require one.

13

Performance and Optimizations

This chapter covers **Java Virtual Machine** (**JVM**) and **Garbage Collector** (**GC**) optimization techniques to improve application efficiency and scalability. It begins by revisiting the JVM architecture to build a foundational understanding of its components and how they manage memory and resources. The chapter also presents strategies for tuning the GC and explores practical heap sizing and configuration approaches, ensuring minimal latency and improved throughput.

This chapter also explores caching strategies to improve application performance, minimize response times, and alleviate server load. It approaches **virtual threads** and **reactive programming** with **Spring WebFlux**, presenting a non-blocking, event-driven approach to developing highly scalable and responsive applications.

This chapter covers the following topics:

- Optimizing the JVM and GC

- Caching to improve performance

- Introducing reactive programming with WebFlux

By the end of this chapter, you will have acquired practical and theoretical knowledge to optimize JVM performance, implement effective caching strategies, and embrace reactive programming for modern Java applications.

Technical requirements

All the code for this chapter can be found on GitHub at `https://github.com/PacktPublishing/Software-Architecture-with-Spring/tree/main/ch13`. Ellipses in the code blocks indicate that parts of the code have been omitted, and the complete code is available on GitHub.

Optimizing the JVM and GC

The JVM is the core runtime environment for executing Java applications, and its performance directly influences application efficiency and scalability. We will explore strategies for optimizing the JVM and configuring the GC to minimize latency, improve throughput, and reduce memory overhead. But first, let's take a step back and revisit the JVM and GC.

Revisiting the JVM

The JVM is pivotal in the Java ecosystem, providing a consistent execution environment across diverse hardware and **operating systems (OSs)**. Understanding how the JVM manages memory and CPU resources is essential for performance-critical applications. The JVM architecture is illustrated in *Figure 13.1*.

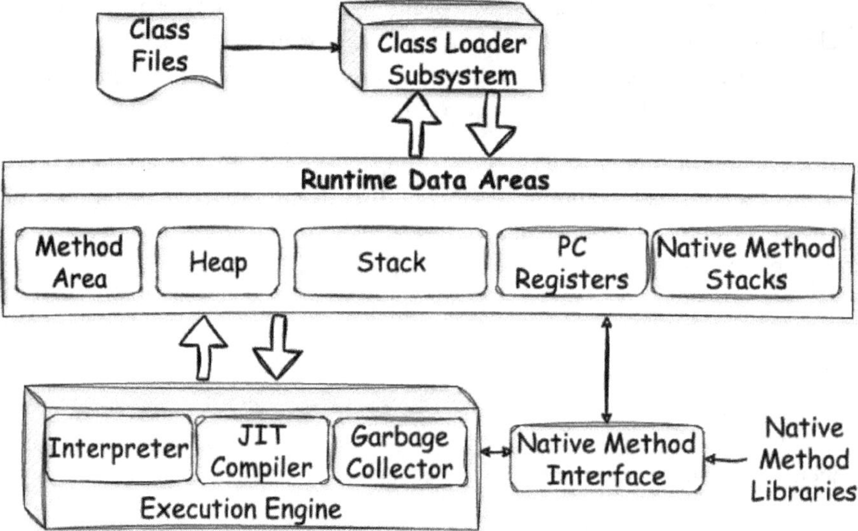

Figure 13.1: JVM architecture

The diagram shows the architecture of the JVM. The class files contain the compiled bytecode, which the Class Loader subsystem is responsible for loading into memory. The runtime data areas manage various memory regions, including the Method Area, Heap, Stack, **Program Counter Registers (PC Registers)**, and Native Method Stacks. Each area serves a distinct purpose during program execution.

The execution engine includes the interpreter, **Just-In-Time (JIT) compiler**, and the GC, which handle bytecode execution and memory management.

The Native Method interface facilitates the integration of native libraries, enabling interactions between Java code and platform-specific features. This groundwork paves the way for a closer examination of one of the JVM's essential components: the GC, which plays a pivotal role in managing memory efficiently and ensuring optimal application performance.

Unraveling the GC

The GC automatically manages memory in Java applications, reclaiming space from unused objects. While this simplifies development, the GC can impact performance due to pauses during collection. *Figure 13.2* shows the Java memory heap and its generations.

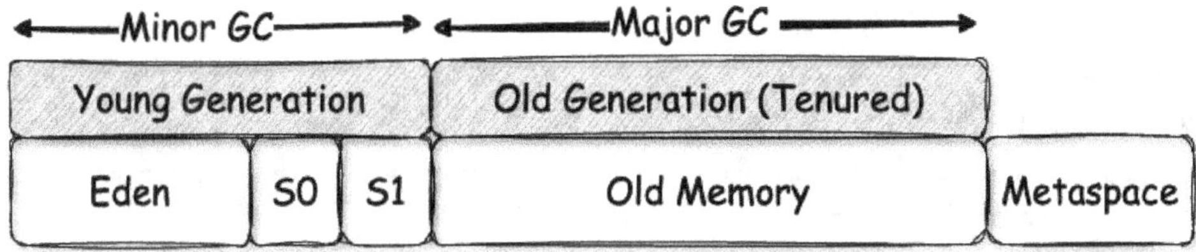

Figure 13.2: Java memory heap and its generations

The diagram illustrates the memory structure of the Java heap, managed by the GC. The heap is divided into the Young Generation, Old Generation (Tenured), and Metaspace.

Objects are first allocated to the Young Generation, specifically in Eden space. If they survive the Minor GC garbage collection process in the Eden space, they are moved to survivor spaces (S0 or S1). These survivor spaces serve as temporary storage for objects still in use. Objects are moved back and forth between S0 and S1 during subsequent Minor GCs. If an object continues to survive multiple GC cycles in the survivor spaces, it is promoted to the Old Generation, where long-lived objects reside.

Minor GC occurs frequently in the Young Generation to reclaim space by removing short-lived objects, which makes it relatively fast. Major GC, the process of garbage collection, operates in the Old Generation to clean up long-lived objects, but it is slower and can cause application pauses.

The Metaspace, introduced in Java 8, stores class metadata in native memory and is not directly managed by the GC. The GC ensures efficient memory usage and prevents memory leaks by automatically reclaiming unused space in these regions, with the generational model optimizing the process for short-lived and long-lived objects.

Building on this understanding of the Java heap and its management by the GC, the next step is to explore strategies for tuning the GC to reduce pauses, enhance efficiency, and tailor its behavior to meet the application's specific performance needs.

Exploring JVM GCs

The GC manages memory but can cause performance issues due to stop-the-world pauses, especially during Major GC in the Old Generation. Stop-the-world is a JVM event in which all application threads are paused to allow the GC to perform specific tasks, such as memory cleanup.

Modern JVMs offer advanced collectors to minimize pauses and enhance efficiency. Let's highlight some GCs:

- **G1 GC**: Designed for large applications, it minimizes pauses and adapts dynamically to system conditions. We can enable it with the `-XX:+UseG1GC` JVM parameter.

- **Shenandoah GC**: This performs concurrent garbage collection with memory compaction, reducing pause times. We can enable it with the `-XX:+UseShenandoahGC` JVM parameter.

- **Z GC (ZGC)**: ZGC focuses on achieving extremely low pause times, making it ideal for applications requiring high responsiveness. It scales efficiently from small to very large heaps and can be enabled with the `-XX:+UseZGC` JVM parameter.

- **C4 GC (Azul Platform Prime)**: C4 stands for **Continuously Concurrent Compacting Collector** and is a pause-free GC designed for ultra-low latency and extreme scalability. It eliminates stop-the-world pauses, making it ideal for large heaps and real-time systems. It requires the Azul JVM.

Selecting the right GC requires understanding your application's throughput, latency, and scalability needs. We can configure the JVM to optimize performance by evaluating each GC's trade-offs. Now, let's learn how to determine appropriate values for heap sizing.

Determining appropriate values for heap sizing

While the JVM provides default heap settings, they are often insufficient or inefficient for specific workloads. Determining appropriate values for heap size parameters requires a combination of application profiling, workload analysis, and system constraints. Here are some approaches and suggestions that we can take to set the correct values for our applications:

- **Analyze application behavior**: Profile your application using tools such as VisualVM to understand its memory usage patterns. Analyze memory allocation trends, object lifetimes, and potential memory leaks. Determine if your application is memory-intensive or CPU-intensive, as this directly impacts optimal heap size allocation.

- **Monitor GC performance**: Analyze GC events to pinpoint issues. Frequent Minor GCs may indicate insufficient Young Generation space, while prolonged Major GC pauses often result from excessive object promotion to the Old Generation. Optimize heap regions by adjusting the Young-to-Old Generation size ratio with `-XX:NewRatio=<value>` and tuning the Survivor space within the Young Generation using `-XX:SurvivorRatio=<value>`.

- **Load testing and fine-tuning**: Conduct load testing to replicate production scenarios and monitor performance metrics such as latency, throughput, and GC pause times. Based on these metrics, gradually adjust heap sizes. Evaluate memory utilization during steady-state and peak loads to ensure adequate headroom for unexpected memory spikes.

- **Set initial and maximum heap sizes**: Use `-Xms<size>` to set the initial heap size and `-Xmx<size>` to set the maximum heap size. For applications with stable memory requirements, set `-Xms` equal to `-Xmx` to minimize the overhead of heap resizing during runtime.

- **Leverage random access memory (RAM) proportions**: For memory-constrained environments such as containers, we can configure heap sizes as a percentage of total available RAM using `-XX:InitialRAMPercentage=<value>` for the initial heap and

   `-XX:MaxRAMPercentage=<value>` for the maximum heap. A common guideline is to allocate 50-70% of available memory to the heap, leaving the rest for OS and non-heap memory requirements such as Metaspace or native thread stacks.

- **Account for non-heap memory**: Remember that heap memory is only part of the total memory consumed by the JVM. Non-heap memory such as Metaspace, thread stacks, and direct buffers also requires careful consideration, particularly in memory-constrained environments such as Docker or Kubernetes. If needed, adjust Metaspace size using

   `-XX:MetaspaceSize=<size>` and `-XX:MaxMetaspaceSize=<size>` to prevent uncontrolled growth when the application uses many classes or dynamic proxies.

Continuously profiling and tuning heap parameters helps achieve a balanced configuration that reduces GC overhead and enhances performance. Once familiar with heap sizing approaches, let's analyze case studies that can provide practical insights into how JVM tuning resolves challenges.

Analyzing case studies of JVM tuning

To fully grasp the impact of JVM tuning, it's helpful to see how specific configurations and optimizations might be applied in a scenario. Let's approach case studies of JVM tuning to address performance challenges.

Improving latency in a high-traffic web application (Case Study 1)

A large-scale e-commerce application experienced significant latency during peak traffic periods. Users reported slow response times, particularly during flash sales when the application handled a high volume of concurrent requests.

The root cause identified was long GC pauses during Major GC in the Old Generation. The application used the default Parallel GC, which focused on throughput but caused stop-the-world events that blocked request processing.

A possible approach to address the issue could be the following:

- **GC selection**: Switch to the G1 GC using

  `-XX:+UseG1GC`, designed to minimize GC pause times.

- **Target pause time**: Set the `-XX:MaxGCPauseMillis` option to target a maximum GC pause duration.

- **Heap sizing**: Adjust the initial and maximum heap settings with `-Xms<Value>` and `-Xmx<Value>` to ensure a consistent heap size and avoid the overhead associated with resizing.

- **Region size**: In the G1 GC, the heap is divided into equally sized regions, each serving as a flexible unit for memory allocation and garbage collection. The size of these regions can significantly impact performance, as smaller regions improve memory allocation granularity. Still, it may increase management overhead, while larger regions reduce overhead but can lead to less efficient memory use. We can configure the region size using the `-XX:G1HeapRegionSize=<value>` JVM parameter. Choosing the optimal region size depends on the application's memory footprint and behavior.

With the latency challenges of high-traffic web applications addressed, let's turn to a different context: optimizing performance for a data-intensive analytics platform.

Scaling a data-intensive analytics platform (Case Study 2)

A big data analytics platform faced severe performance bottlenecks while processing massive datasets. The application frequently ran out of memory and experienced long garbage collection pauses, disrupting workflows and delaying critical analytics tasks.

The root cause was identified as an overwhelmed Old Generation due to the accumulation of large, long-lived objects. The platform's memory-intensive operations required a GC capable of handling a large heap with minimal impact on execution.

A possible approach to address the issue could be the following:

- **GC selection**: Adopt ZGC for its low-pause characteristics and scalability

- **Heap scaling**: Set heap size dynamically using `-XX:InitialRAMPercentage=<value>` and `-XX:MaxRAMPercentage=<value>` to allocate memory based on available system resources

- **GC logging**: Enable detailed GC logs with `-Xlog:gc*` for real-time monitoring and fine-tuning

- **Max pause time**: Configure minimal pause durations using

  `-XX:MaxGCPauseMillis`

After scaling a data-intensive platform, let's explore how JVM tuning can address memory constraints in containerized microservices architectures.

Optimizing memory usage in a microservices architecture (Case Study 3)

A microservices-based payment processing system deployed in a Kubernetes cluster frequently exceeded container memory limits, leading to pod restarts and service disruptions. This issue impacted the reliability of payment processing during peak transaction loads.

The problem was traced to inefficient heap size configurations and suboptimal garbage collection in containers' constrained memory environment.

A possible approach to address the issue could be the following:

- **GC selection**: Switch to the Shenandoah GC using `-XX:+UseShenandoahGC` for concurrent garbage collection and memory compaction

- **Heap size management**: Configure heap sizes as percentages of container memory using `-XX:InitialRAMPercentage=<value>` and `-XX:MaxRAMPercentage=<value>`

- **Metaspace tuning**: Prevent uncontrolled growth by setting `-XX:MetaspaceSize=<value>` and `-XX:MaxMetaspaceSize=<value>`

These case studies demonstrate how JVM tuning can resolve performance bottlenecks and enhance application reliability. By carefully selecting GCs, optimizing heap configurations, and exploring advanced JVM options, systems can achieve improved scalability, reduced latency, and efficient resource utilization. Next, we'll explore JVM profiling and GC analysis tools.

Exploring JVM profiling and GC analysis tools

To effectively optimize the performance of the JVM, it is crucial to thoroughly understand memory usage, GC behavior, and potential application bottlenecks. There are several powerful tools available that offer in-depth analysis and advanced features. Here are some recommended tools for profiling and analyzing garbage collection:

- **VisualVM**: A lightweight, free tool for real-time CPU, memory, and thread monitoring. Features include GC insights, heap dump analysis, and live application profiling.

- **Java Flight Recorder (JFR) and Java Mission Control (JMC)**: Low-overhead tools for continuous profiling, ideal for production monitoring. JFR captures runtime data efficiently, while JMC analyzes recordings for GC pauses, thread activity, and CPU usage.

- **Eclipse Memory Analyzer Tool (MAT)**: Open source tool for identifying memory leaks and optimizing memory usage. It offers object references, dependency graphs, and detailed reports, scaling effectively for large heap dumps.

Leveraging these tools is essential for diagnosing issues, optimizing memory, and enhancing Java application efficiency. While garbage collection and memory profiling help manage runtime behavior, another crucial aspect of performance lies in reducing redundant computations and database access. In this context, we now turn to caching techniques, which play a crucial role in boosting responsiveness and reducing latency.

Caching to improve performance

Let us imagine a situation in which a library has a certain book that almost all members are eager to read. Each time a reader requested it, the librarian would fetch it from the storage room, a long walk away. One day, the librarian decided to keep the book at the front desk instead. Now, when readers asked for it, they handed it over instantly, saving time and effort. A cache works similarly by storing frequently accessed data in a fast, easily accessible location, improving system performance and reducing the need for repeated, time-consuming operations. To better understand cache, let's answer the question: What is cache?

What is caching?

Caching is the process of storing copies of data in a temporary storage location, often referred to as a cache, to allow faster access. Instead of repeatedly fetching data from a database or an external API, a cache provides quick access to frequently requested information. *Figure 13.3* illustrates the flow of caching applied in our product service.

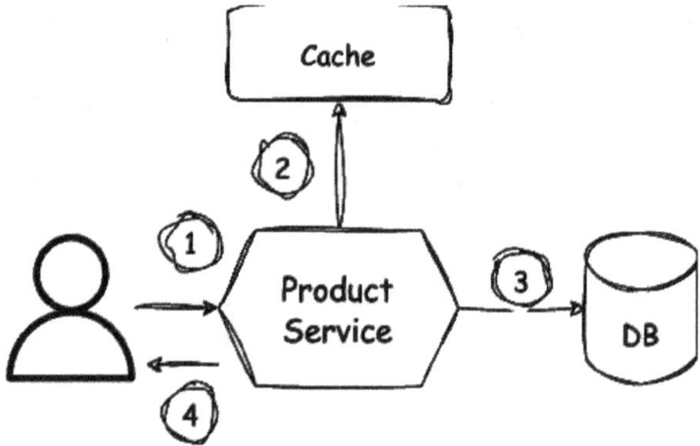

Figure 13.3: The flow of a product service with cache

The diagram depicts the flow of a product service utilizing a cache to optimize performance:

1. The client requests the product service to retrieve the product list.

2. Before querying the database, the product service checks the cache to see if the requested data is already cached. This step aims to avoid unnecessary database access.

3. This step occurs only if the data is not in the cache, prompting a request to the database to retrieve it.

4. The product service responds to the user with the requested data. Simultaneously, it may store the retrieved data in the cache to handle future requests for the same data more efficiently, reducing database queries.

Let's explore the benefits of applying caching in our systems, from accelerating response times to reducing server load and enhancing overall scalability.

Benefits of caching

Caching enhances system performance by reducing database load, minimizing latency, and delivering faster response times to clients. It is especially advantageous for systems with high-read operations or applications requiring low-latency responses. Key benefits include the following:

- **Improved performance**: Caching can drastically increase your application's speed by reducing time spent on expensive operations such as database queries or network calls

- **Reduced load**: Offloading frequent requests to the cache minimizes the load on databases and APIs, enabling them to handle more requests or focus on critical tasks

- **Cost efficiency**: Caching can reduce resource usage and lower costs associated with data processing or database scaling for cloud-hosted applications

- **Enhanced scalability**: A well-implemented caching strategy allows applications to scale effectively, handling more concurrent users without significant performance degradation

While caching provides numerous benefits, it also introduces challenges, such as cache invalidation to maintain data consistency and cache eviction to manage space limitations and data freshness. Strategies such as cache invalidation mechanisms can effectively address these issues. Let's explore these strategies further.

Unraveling cache invalidation strategies

Caching systems must be kept fresh and accurate. Cache invalidation is the process of clearing outdated data from the cache. Common strategies include the following:

- **Cache eviction policies**: These are strategies for managing limited cache space by deciding which data to remove when the cache is full. Some common policies include the following:

  - **Least recently used (LRU)**: LRU removes data that hasn't been accessed for the longest time.

  - **First-in-first-out (FIFO)**: FIFO evicts the oldest data added to the cache, regardless of how often it is accessed.

  - **Least frequently used (LFU)**: LFU removes data accessed the least number of times.

- **Time-based expiry**: Time-based expiry is a caching strategy in which data is automatically invalidated after a specified duration, referred to as **time-to-live (TTL)**. This method ensures that cached data stays fresh and relevant.

- **Write-through cache**: A write-through cache is a strategy that immediately updates the cache whenever changes are made to the backend, ensuring data consistency and eliminating stale data. While this method benefits scenarios requiring strong consistency in read and write operations, the extra update step may result in slightly higher latency for write operations.

Now, let's check the best practices when applying caching in our systems.

Applying the best practices for caching

Best practices for caching are essential to ensure effective performance improvements while avoiding common pitfalls. Here are some recommended approaches:

- **Choose the right data to cache**: It is crucial to choose the right data to cache. Focus on caching information that is accessed frequently but does not change often, such as product details or user profiles. This approach ensures the cache remains useful without becoming a bottleneck for updates.

- **Set appropriate expiry times**: Based on the volatility of the cached data, define realistic TTL values to set appropriate expiry times. This prevents stale data from being served to users and keeps the cache updated.

- **Avoid over-caching**: Excessive caching can lead to memory overuse, increased maintenance complexity, and stale data issues. Striking a balance between caching and system resources is critical.

- **Ensure fault tolerance (FT)**: Design the system to handle cache misses effectively. This includes implementing a reliable fallback mechanism to retrieve data from the source whenever the cache is unavailable or outdated.

Following these practices, we can implement caching solutions that enhance performance, maintain data accuracy, and provide a seamless user experience. Now, let's see the types of caching we can apply to our systems.

Recognizing the types of caching

Depending on a system's specific needs and architecture, various types of caching exist, each suited to different use cases. Let's examine some of the most common types of caching and their applications:

- **In-memory caching**: This is the practice of storing data in RAM to facilitate fast access. Tools such as Redis and Memcached are commonly used for in-memory caching. Typical use cases include session management and storing frequently accessed database rows.

- **API caching**: This refers to storing the responses from frequently accessed API endpoints to minimize redundant computations and database queries. It can be implemented at different levels, including on the client, server, or through intermediaries such as API gateways or reverse proxies such as NGINX or AWS API Gateway.

- **Database caching**: Database caching refers to storing query results or objects to reduce the frequency of database lookups. Effective implementation can utilize features such as query caching and materialized views.

- **Content delivery network (CDN)**: A CDN refers to storing static assets such as HTML, images, CSS, and JavaScript files on servers distributed across various geographical locations. Examples of CDN caching providers are Cloudflare, Akamai, and AWS CloudFront.

- **Browser caching**: Browser caching allows web browsers to store resources locally on a user's device, reducing server load and improving page load times. Configured with HTTP headers such as Cache-Control for caching policies and ETag for resource freshness, browser caching improves the overall user experience by making web applications more efficient and responsive.

Caching is crucial for enhancing software performance. Selecting the right approach based on the use case ensures efficient, scalable systems that enhance user experience while optimizing resource usage. Now, let's implement a cache in our online auction application.

Implementing a cache at the application level

Application-level or local cache stores frequently accessed or computationally expensive data within the application using specialized libraries or frameworks. In this hands-on exercise, we will explore integrating **Spring Cache,** a convenient abstraction for managing cache, with **Caffeine,** a high-performance in-memory caching library.

This combination leverages the simplicity of Spring Cache and the advanced features of Caffeine, such as time-based expiration, size-based eviction, and asynchronous cache loading. We will use our product service to apply caching when getting the product list. Let's get started!

1. Add the following `Caffeine` dependency to the `pom.xml` file in the product services API. Spring Cache is part of the Spring Framework and works with Spring Boot out of the box:

```
<dependency>
    <groupId>com.github.ben-manes.caffeine</groupId>
    <artifactId>caffeine</artifactId>
</dependency>
```

2. Add the `@EnableCaching` annotation to the `ProductServicesApplication` class to enable cache in the application, as shown in the following code snippet:

```java
@EnableCaching
public class ProductServicesApplication {
```

3. The following code snippet presents the configuration class to set up `CaffeineCacheManager`:

```java
@Configuration
public class CacheConfig {

  @Bean
  public CacheManager cacheManager() {
    CaffeineCacheManager cacheManager =
    new CaffeineCacheManager("products");
    cacheManager.setCaffeine(Caffeine.newBuilder()
    .expireAfterWrite(10, TimeUnit.MINUTES)
    .maximumSize(100));
    return cacheManager;
  }
}
```

The `CacheConfig` class configures caching for the application using Caffeine as the caching provider. The `cacheManager` bean creates a `CaffeineCacheManager` instance with the cache name `products`. Then, it sets an expiration time of 10 minutes after a cache entry is written and limits the cache size to a maximum of 100 entries. These settings ensure efficient memory usage and automatic removal of stale or least-used data.

4. The following code snippet represents a service layer we must add to the `datasources` package. This addition is necessary to avoid violating the clean architecture of the project by adding Spring annotations at a higher level; in this case, in the use-case classes. Previously, we directly called the use-case classes from the controllers; now, the controllers will call the service layer first, which will then interact with the use-case classes:

```java
@Service
public class ProductServiceImpl implements ProductService {
  @Cacheable("products")
  public List<ProductResponse> getAllProducts() {
    List<Product> products = getProductsUseCase.execute();
    return products.stream().map …
  }

  @CacheEvict(value = "products", allEntries = true)
  public ProductResponse addProduct(
    ProductRequest productRequest) {
    …
```

The @Cacheable ("products") annotation caches the result of the getAllProducts method in the products cache. If the cache already contains the data, the method is skipped, and the cached data is returned, improving performance by avoiding repetitive computations. The @CacheEvict(value = "products", allEntries = true) annotation clears all entries in the products cache when the addProduct method is called, ensuring the cache remains consistent and does not serve outdated data after a new product is added. These annotations enable seamless caching and consistency management within the application.

When you run the project and make a request to retrieve the product list, you will notice that a SQL Hibernate log appears in the console the first time you do this. The log will not be displayed for subsequent requests because the data is being retrieved from the cache instead of querying the database. If you add a new product, the cache will be cleared. As a result, the next time you request the product list, it will query the database again.

In a microservices architecture, application-level caching presents a significant limitation. When multiple instances of a service, such as a product service, are running, changes made to the cache in one instance—such as adding or removing a product—are not propagated to the other instances. This lack of synchronization can lead to inconsistencies in the cached data across the service instances, undermining the system's reliability. To address this issue and ensure consistency in a distributed environment, we can implement a distributed cache using a solution such as Redis, which provides centralized caching and synchronization across all instances.

Implementing a distributed cache with Redis

Implementing a distributed cache with Redis ensures consistency and scalability in microservices architectures. Unlike application-level caching, Redis acts as a centralized caching solution accessible to all service instances, allowing them to share and synchronize data efficiently. To integrate Redis with Spring Boot in a straightforward and idiomatic way, we will use the native support provided by the spring-boot-starter-data-redis dependency. This starter leverages Lettuce, the default Redis client, and integrates seamlessly with the Spring Cache abstraction. It is lightweight, widely adopted, and well suited for use cases focused on caching. Let's apply the distributed cache in our product services API using **Spring Data Redis**, building on the previous application-level cache implementation:

1. Let's leverage the previous code of the product services API, removing the Caffeine dependency and the CacheConfig class, then add the following Spring Data Redis dependency in the pom.xml file:

```xml
<dependency>
  <groupId>org.springframework.boot</groupId>
  <artifactId>spring-boot-starter-data-redis</artifactId>
</dependency>
```

2. In the `resources` folder, configure Redis in the `application.properties` file:

```
spring.cache.type=redis
spring.redis.host=localhost
spring.redis.port=6379
spring.redis.timeout=60000
spring.redis.lettuce.pool.max-active=10
spring.redis.lettuce.pool.min-idle=2
```

This configuration connects to a Redis server running on `localhost:6379` and sets a connection timeout of 60 seconds. The connection pool is configured to allow up to 10 active connections, with at least 2 kept idle to ensure responsiveness during high-load scenarios.

3. The following code snippet presents the `CacheConfig` configuration class for setting up the Redis-based `CacheManager` class:

```java
@Configuration
public class CacheConfig {

  @Bean
  public CacheManager cacheManager(
    RedisConnectionFactory redisConnectionFactory) {
      RedisCacheConfiguration config =
      RedisCacheConfiguration.defaultCacheConfig()
        .entryTtl(Duration.ofMinutes(10))
        .serializeValuesWith(
            RedisSerializationContext.SerializationPair
            fromSerializer(
                new GenericJackson2JsonRedisSerializer()));
      return
        RedisCacheManager.builder(redisConnectionFactory)
      .cacheDefaults(config).build();
    }
}
```

The `CacheConfig` class sets up caching in the application using Spring Data Redis, which integrates seamlessly with Spring Cache through the `@EnableCaching` annotation. The `cacheManager` bean creates a `RedisCacheManager` class backed by a `RedisConnectionFactory` class, which is provided as a method parameter to establish the connection to the Redis server. The configuration defines a default TTL for cached entries using `.entryTtl(Duration.ofMinutes(10))` and specifies JSON serialization for cache values with `.serializeValuesWith(SerializationPair.fromSerializer(new GenericJackson2JsonRedisSerializer()))`, ensuring that the data stored in Redis remains both structured and readable. This setup enables the application to use Redis as a centralized, distributed cache backend, allowing consistent and efficient cache management across multiple service instances.

The migration from the application-level cache to a distributed cache is complete. Since we are using Spring Cache annotations, no further changes are needed.

4. When you request the list of products, it is saved to Redis, as illustrated in *Figure 13.4*.

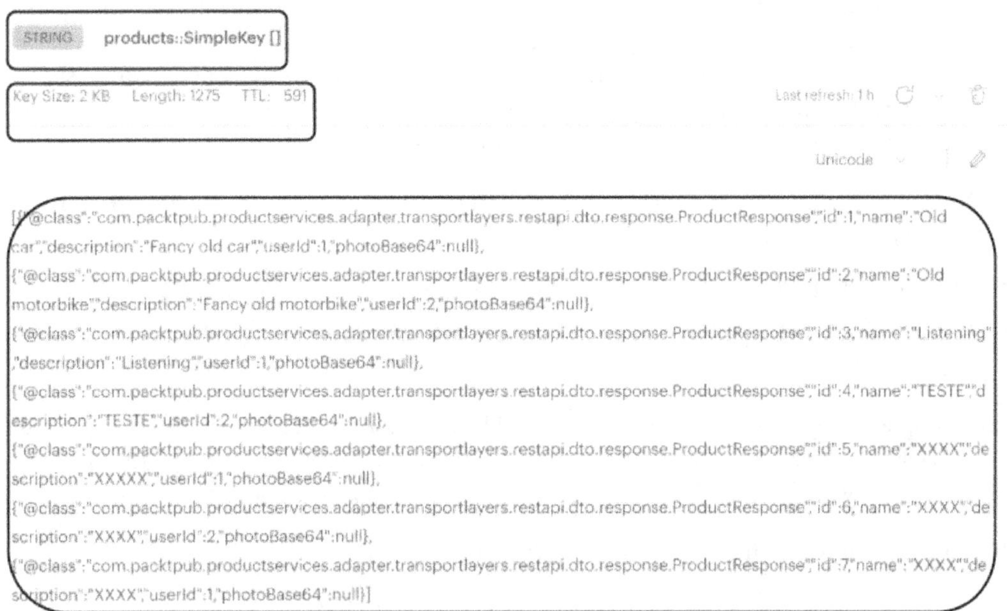

Figure 13.4: Products cached in Redis

The figure shows the **Redis Insight** client connected to the Redis server. It can be downloaded at `https://redis.io/insight/`. We can see that a key named `products::SimpleKey []` was created. This key represents a cached result managed by Spring Cache, using the default `SimpleKey` class for methods without parameters. The value stored is a serialized list of `ProductResponse` objects in JSON format. The entry also shows a TTL, indicating how long the cached data will remain in Redis before expiring. Now, let's shift to another programming paradigm: reactive programming.

Introducing reactive programming with WebFlux

Reactive programming is a paradigm designed to handle asynchronous data streams focusing on non-blocking, event-driven systems. Unlike traditional imperative programming models, reactive programming allows systems to react to changes in data or events in real time, making it especially suitable for modern applications that demand high performance and scalability.

Why reactive programming?

Traditionally, web servers handle requests using a thread pool, where each thread is dedicated to a single request. For instance, if a server has three threads, it can process three requests simultaneously, while a fourth request must wait until one of the threads becomes available. However, this model can lead to inefficiencies, as threads may remain idle while waiting for external operations, such as database responses. This idle time consumes memory and CPU resources without accomplishing meaningful work, which can create resource limitations as the number of threads increases. Reactive programming addresses these challenges by offering the following:

- **Non-blocking I/O**: Operations do not block threads while waiting for external resources, allowing for better resource utilization

- **Asynchronous processing**: Tasks are executed independently, enhancing system responsiveness

- **Backpressure handling**: Ensures producers and consumers work at compatible speeds to avoid overwhelming resources

Reactive programming enables asynchronous, non-blocking task handling. Threads can switch to other tasks while waiting for operations to complete, which optimizes resource usage. This method enhances scalability and performance without endlessly adding more threads or resources.

Adhering to the Reactive Streams specification

Reactive programming builds on the **Reactive Streams specification**, a standard defining the interaction between asynchronous components. You can find more information at `https://www.reactive-streams.org/`. Its core interfaces include the following:

- **Publisher**: The primary component that produces data asynchronously and emits items to its subscribers when requested, ensuring a non-blocking data flow.

- **Subscription**: This manages the contract between a publisher and a subscriber. It allows subscribers to request data at their own pace and provides mechanisms for backpressure to prevent overwhelming the system with data.

- **Subscriber**: Consumes data emitted by the publisher. It defines four methods, `onSubscribe`, `onNext`, `onError`, and `onComplete`, to handle events such as receiving data, errors, or completion signals.

- **Processor**: A hybrid component that acts as a subscriber and a publisher. It consumes data from one source, processes or transforms it, and produces data for another subscriber, enabling a modular pipeline for reactive transformations.

Figure 13.5 provides a visual representation of the interaction between the core components of the Reactive Streams specification.

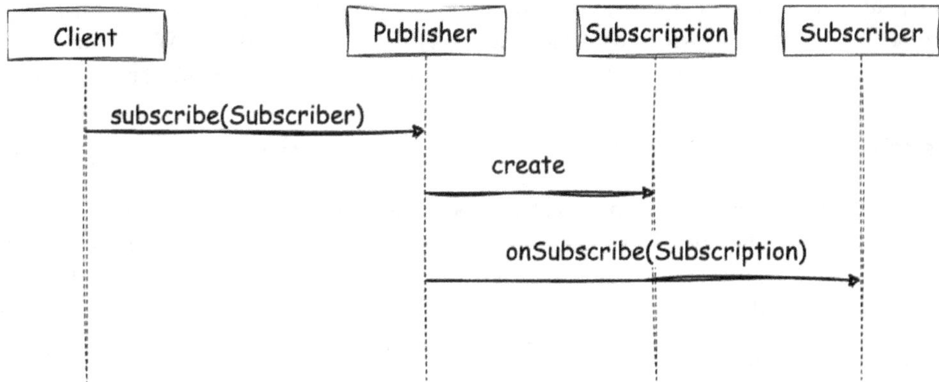

Figure 13.5: Components of the Reactive Streams specification

The client asks the publisher to start sending data by subscribing to it. The publisher then creates a subscription, which links the publisher and the subscriber, which will receive the data. The subscription is sent to the subscriber, allowing it to control how much data it wants to receive and when. This setup ensures that data flows smoothly without overwhelming the system. Now, let's learn about Spring WebFlux.

What is Spring WebFlux?

Spring WebFlux, introduced in Spring 5, implements the Reactive Streams API, offering a robust framework for building reactive applications. It is the reactive counterpart to the traditional Spring MVC framework and is built on **Project Reactor**, a library compliant with Reactive Streams. Spring WebFlux provides two programming models:

- **Annotation-based programming**: Spring WebFlux supports annotation-based request handling similar to Spring MVC, using annotations such as `@Controller`, `@RequestMapping`, and `@GetMapping`. This structured approach simplifies the transition from Spring MVC, enabling developers to adopt reactive programming with a minimal learning curve.

- **Functional programming**: Spring WebFlux also introduces a functional, declarative programming style by leveraging routing and handler functions. Instead of annotations, developers define routes programmatically using the `RouterFunction` and `HandlerFunction` APIs. This approach promotes a more concise, modular, and testable design, allowing for greater flexibility in processing HTTP requests, especially in reactive, event-driven applications. The functional style is particularly beneficial for building lightweight and scalable microservices.

Spring WebFlux's core concepts include handling data streams using Mono and Flux. Mono represents a single-value or empty asynchronous stream, ideal for operations expecting one or no result. At the same time, Flux handles a sequence of 0 to N asynchronous elements, suitable for streaming multiple items. These reactive types, provided by Project Reactor, form the foundation of WebFlux's reactive programming model. Now, let's convert the authentication services to the reactive model using WebFlux.

Converting authentication services to be reactive

Converting authentication services to a reactive model can significantly improve scalability and responsiveness by leveraging non-blocking I/O and asynchronous processing. This transformation allows the system to handle more concurrent requests with fewer resources, making it ideal for high-traffic environments and resilient to heavy workloads. In the following steps, we will convert the authentication services to a reactive model using Spring WebFlux:

1. Remove the `spring-boot-starter-web` Spring MVC dependency and add the `spring-boot-starter-webflux` dependency, as shown in the following configuration snippet:

    ```
    <dependency>
      <groupId>org.springframework.boot</groupId>
      <artifactId>spring-boot-starter-webflux</artifactId>
    </dependency>
    ```

2. Remove the `spring-boot-starter-data-mongodb` dependency and add the `spring-boot-starter-data-mongodb-reactive` dependency, as shown in the following configuration snippet. This replacement is needed because the former uses blocking operations that are incompatible with the reactive model, in contrast with the latter, which employs non-blocking I/O:

    ```
    <dependency>
      <groupId>org.springframework.boot</groupId>
      <artifactId>spring-boot-starter-data-mongodb-reactive
      </artifactId>
    </dependency>
    ```

3. The following code snippet shows the modifications applied to the `createAuthenticationToken` method in the `AuthenticationController` class to handle token creation in a reactive model:

    ```
    @PostMapping
    public Mono<AuthenticationResponse>
      createAuthenticationToken(@RequestBody
     Mono<AuthenticationRequest> authenticationRequestMono){
        return authenticationRequestMono
        .flatMap(authenticationRequest ->
          generateTokenUseCase.execute(
    ```

```
            authenticationRequest.getUsername(),
            authenticationRequest.getPassword())
        .map(AuthenticationResponse::new)
        );
    }
```

The method's return type, encapsulated in the Mono object, ensures the response is sent asynchronously once the entire reactive pipeline completes. This enables the server to continue processing other tasks concurrently while the token generation and response creation are being completed.

The @RequestBody Mono<AuthenticationRequest> annotation is received as a Mono object, a reactive publisher representing a single asynchronous computation or value. Unlike traditional blocking approaches, the body is not fully materialized upfront; instead, it is processed as it becomes available.

The flatMap operator handles the operation's asynchronous nature. It processes the incoming AuthenticationRequest object as soon as Mono emits it.

The .map(AuthenticationResponse::new) step transforms the token once emitted into an AuthenticationResponse object. The entire chain of operations remains non-blocking and reactive, meaning no thread is waiting for the result at any point.

Additionally, the Mono pipeline is lazy, meaning it executes only when subscribed, ensuring efficient resource utilization while maintaining a non-blocking, reactive flow.

4. The following code snippet shows the changes in the execute method from the GenerateTokenUseCase class:

```
public Mono<String> execute(String username, String password) {
  return authenticationManagerRepository.authenticate(
  username, password)
  .flatMap(authentication ->
  userRepository.getRolesByUsername(username)
    .collectList()
    .doOnNext(authentication::setRoles)
    .thenReturn(authentication)
  )
  .flatMap(authentication ->
  Mono.just(tokenRepository.generate(authentication))
  );
}
```

The method's return type encapsulated in the `Mono` object ensures the response is sent asynchronously.

The method starts by invoking `authenticationManagerRepository.authenticate`, which returns a `Mono` object representing the result of the asynchronous authentication process. Once the authentication is successful, the `flatMap` operator chains the next asynchronous step. This step involves fetching the user's roles from `userRepository.getRolesByUsername`, which emits a `Flux<String>` representing the roles. The `.collectList()` operator converts the emitted roles into a `Mono<List<String>>`.

Once the roles are collected, `doOnNext` sets them on the authentication object without altering the flow. The `thenReturn(authentication)` step ensures that the modified authentication object is passed to the next stage of the reactive pipeline.

Finally, another `flatMap` operator generates a token for the authenticated user. The `tokenRepository.generate(authentication)` method is invoked, and its result is wrapped in a `Mono<String>` to be returned as the final output of the method. The entire pipeline is lazy and only executes when subscribed, maintaining an entirely reactive, non-blocking flow from authentication to token generation.

5. The following code snippet shows the changes in the `AuthenticationJpaDatasource` interface:

```java
@Repository
public interface AuthenticationJpaDatasource
    extends ReactiveCrudRepository<AuthenticationEntity, Long> {
  Mono<AuthenticationEntity> findByUsername(String username);
}
```

We must switch from `MongoRepository` to the `ReactiveCrudRepository` interface because the latter supports non-blocking, asynchronous interactions essential for reactive applications. The `ReactiveCrudRepository` interface works well with the reactive stack, enabling non-blocking I/O with MongoDB, which improves scalability and resource efficiency.

6. The following code snippet shows the changes in the `getRolesByUsername` method from the `UserRestApi` class:

```java
public class UserRestApi implements UserRepository {
  private final WebClient webClient;

  public Flux<String> getRolesByUsername(String username) {
  return webClient.get()
  .uri("http://USER-
    SERVICES/v1/users/{username}/roles", username)
  .retrieve()
  .onStatus(status -> status != HttpStatus.OK,
    clientResponse ->
```

```
clientResponse.bodyToMono(String.class)
.flatMap(errorBody -> Mono.error(new
  RuntimeException("Error: " + errorBody))))
.bodyToFlux(String.class);
}
...
```

To align with a reactive model, we should replace `RestClient` with `WebClient`. The `WebClient` class is non-blocking and improves efficiency and scalability for high-concurrency applications.

The method returns a `Flux<String>`, a non-blocking stream of roles. The `webClient.get()` method initiates a non-blocking and async request to the user service endpoint to obtain the user's roles. The `retrieve()` method is used to extract the response, and `onStatus` handles error scenarios by checking if the response status is different from 200. In case of an error, the response body is mapped into a `Mono` object containing the error message and rethrown as a `RuntimeException` exception.

The `bodyToFlux(String.class)` method extracts the roles from the response body as a stream (`Flux`), ensuring the entire process is asynchronous and non-blocking.

7. The following code snippet shows the changes in the `SecurityConfiguration` class:

```
@EnableWebFluxSecurity
public class SecurityConfiguration {


    private final ReactiveUserDetailsService
reactiveUserDetailsService;
@Bean
public SecurityWebFilterChain
securityWebFilterChain(ServerHttpSecurity http) {...
  @Bean
  public ReactiveUserDetailsService
  reactiveAuthenticationManager() {...
    @Bean
    public ReactiveOAuth2UserService<OAuth2UserRequest,
    OAuth2User>
    reactiveOAuth2UserService() {
      return new CustomOAuth2UserService();
      }
```

The `@EnableWebFluxSecurity` annotation enables and configures security in reactive Spring WebFlux applications.

The `securityWebFilterChain` method is used for Spring WebFlux, providing a reactive, stateless security configuration using `ServerHttpSecurity`. Previously, the application relied on Spring MVC and used `UserDetailsService`, `OAuth2UserService`, and `AuthenticationManager`. Now, we have switched to a reactive version using `ReactiveUserDetailsService`, `DefaultReactiveOAuth2UserService`, and `ReactiveAuthenticationManager`.

The conversion to a reactive paradigm using Spring WebFlux is completed. Now, let's compare Spring MVC and Spring WebFlux.

Comparing Spring MVC and Spring WebFlux

To compare the performance of authentication services using Spring MVC and Spring WebFlux, let's analyze their behavior under intensive token requests. *Figure 13.6* shows the VisualVM threads tab for both implementations.

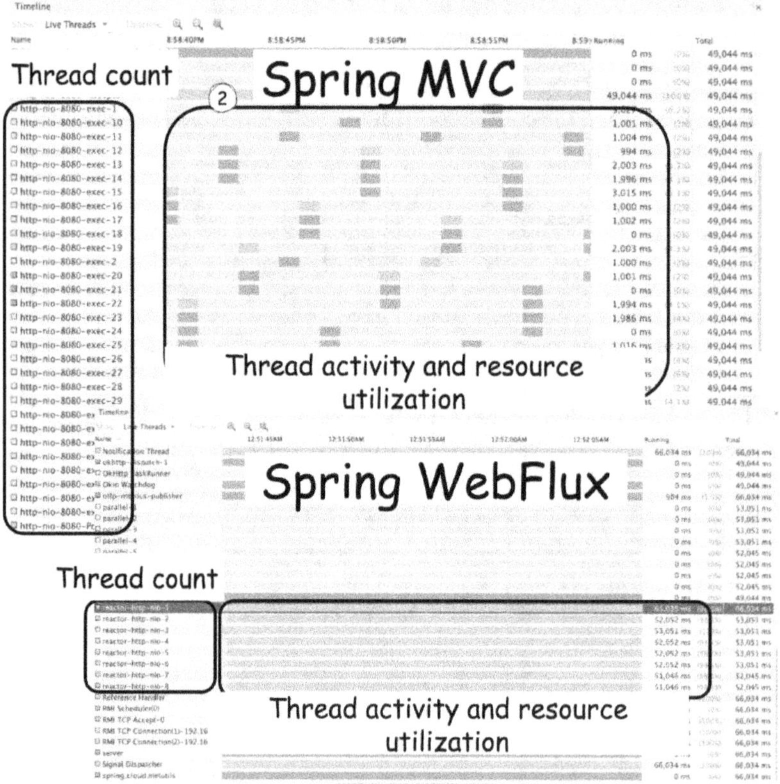

Figure 13.6: Authentication services using Spring MVC and Spring WebFlux

The figure presents the VisualVM's threads tab with the result of the Spring MVC and Spring WebFlux authentication services. Let's analyze the results:

- **Thread count**: Spring MVC uses a thread-per-request model (`http-nio-*` threads), creating many threads to handle requests. This can lead to high resource consumption, even for idle or waiting threads, and scalability challenges under heavy loads. Spring WebFlux, in contrast, employs an event-driven, non-blocking model (`reactor-http-*` threads), requiring fewer threads and scaling more efficiently.

- **Thread activity and resource utilization**: In Spring MVC, many threads remain in a waiting or blocked state due to its blocking architecture, leading to significant idle time and inefficient resource usage. In contrast, Spring WebFlux's non-blocking approach ensures threads are actively handling asynchronous tasks, minimizing idle time and enhancing resource efficiency.

Spring MVC's blocking thread-per-request model can limit scalability in high-concurrency scenarios due to resource inefficiencies. Spring WebFlux's reactive programming model offers better resource utilization and scalability, making it more suitable for heavy workloads. With these differences in mind, should we use Spring MVC or Spring WebFlux?

> **Spring MVC or Spring WebFlux?**
>
> The choice depends on the specific use case and workload. Spring MVC is best suited for smaller applications with low-to-moderate concurrency. Proper thread pool tuning, monitoring, and avoiding long-blocking operations in request handlers are essential to prevent overload. In contrast, Spring WebFlux is ideal for high-concurrency applications, especially those handling real-time, streaming, or reactive APIs. To fully leverage its benefits, ensure the application is non-blocking end-to-end, using reactive database drivers such as R2DBC or MongoDB.

Comparing reactive programming with virtual threads

Virtual threads, introduced in Java's Project Loom, are a lightweight threading model designed to address the limitations of traditional platform threads. Unlike platform threads, which rely on OS-level resources, virtual threads are handled by the JVM and are far less resource-intensive. This allows the creation of a vast number of threads without the overhead typically associated with platform threads. The main features of virtual threads include the following:

- **Thread-per-task model**: Developers can adopt a traditional blocking programming style without worrying about resource limitations, as each task can have its own thread

- **Seamless integration**: Virtual threads work transparently with existing Java code, libraries, and frameworks, requiring minimal code changes

- **Blocking calls support**: They efficiently handle blocking I/O by suspending and resuming threads without consuming OS-level resources

Reactive programming and virtual threads aim to improve scalability and resource utilization, but they achieve these goals differently and cater to distinct use cases, as shown in *Table 13.1*.

Aspect	Reactive Programming	Virtual Threads
Programming model	Non-blocking, event-driven; relies on callbacks and streams.	Blocking, imperative; follows a traditional thread-per-task model.
Learning curve	Steeper due to the need to understand asynchronous concepts such as Mono and Flux.	Minimal for Java developers familiar with blocking code.
Resource utilization	Optimized by using fewer threads with asynchronous task switching.	Lightweight threads reduce resource consumption even for blocking calls.
Code complexity	Higher, as it requires chaining and composing asynchronous calls.	Lower, with code resembling traditional synchronous programming.
Ecosystem support	Requires reactive libraries and frameworks such as Reactor and WebFlux.	Works seamlessly with existing libraries, even blocking ones.
Use case	Best for high-concurrency applications with streaming or event-driven workloads.	Suitable for applications that need high concurrency but prefer simpler code.

Table 13.1: Comparison between reactive programming and virtual threads

Reactive programming is ideal for systems requiring end-to-end non-blocking behavior, such as real-time data streams or highly scalable APIs. However, it introduces complexity and may necessitate refactoring.

Virtual threads are perfect for applications that need high concurrency without the complexity of reactive programming or when integrating with blocking libraries is a requirement. The choice ultimately depends on the application's requirements, team expertise, and the desired balance between performance and simplicity.

Enabling virtual threads in Spring Boot applications

As of Spring Boot 3.2 and Spring Framework 6.1, virtual threads can be used with Spring MVC, enhancing concurrency and scalability while maintaining a familiar blocking programming model. Let's enable virtual threads in the user services API.

We must add the following property to the `application.properties` file to enable virtual threads:

```
spring.threads.virtual.enabled=true
```

The `spring.threads.virtual.enabled=true` property enables virtual threads for the embedded Tomcat server. It allows request handling in Spring MVC to run on virtual threads, significantly boosting scalability in I/O-heavy applications without switching to a reactive stack.

To check if virtual threads were enabled in the user services API, let's leverage Spring Actuator. Open a browser and enter the following URL: `http://localhost:8081/actuator/threaddump`. *Figure 13.7* shows the JSON thread dump of the user services API:

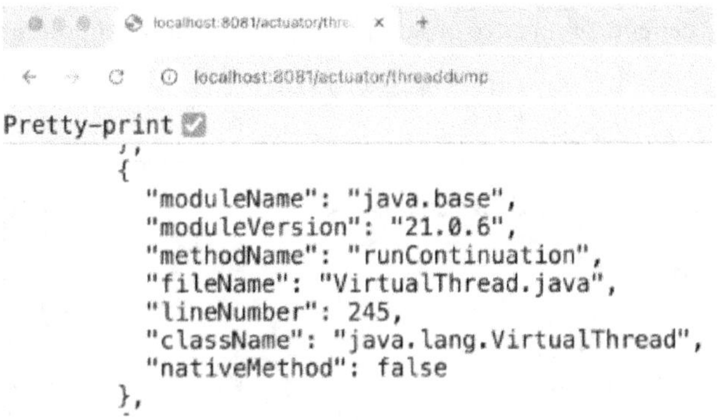

Figure 13.7: JSON thread dump of the user services API

As shown in the figure, the presence of the `filename: VirtualThread.java` and `className: java.lang.VirtualThread` entries confirms that virtual threads are being used.

Summary

This chapter explored strategies for enhancing Java application performance by optimizing the JVM and GC, focusing on reducing latency, improving throughput, and tailoring configurations to application-specific needs. Readers gained insights into JVM architecture, memory management, and advanced tuning techniques such as heap sizing and GC selection.

The chapter also introduced caching as a critical tool for improving responsiveness and scalability, with practical implementations using Spring Cache and Redis. It explored reactive programming with Spring WebFlux, showcasing how non-blocking, event-driven paradigms enable scalable, high-performance applications. To conclude, it discussed virtual threads and how to enable them in Spring Boot projects.

By combining theoretical knowledge with practical techniques, this chapter provided a comprehensive foundation for optimizing JVM performance, implementing efficient caching strategies, and adopting reactive programming for modern Java systems.

In *Chapter 14, Orchestration with Kubernetes*, we will explore the power of Kubernetes, examine its fundamental concepts, and gain hands-on experience installing and deploying applications using MiniKube.

Questions

1. What is the role of the GC in the JVM, and why is it important to tune it?

2. What are some key parameters for tuning JVM heap memory?

3. How does caching improve application performance?

4. What is the difference between application-level caching and distributed caching?

5. What are the key benefits of reactive programming over traditional programming models?

6. How does Spring WebFlux differ from Spring MVC?

Get This Book's PDF Version and Exclusive Extras

Scan the QR code (or go to `packtpub.com/unlock`). Search for this book by name, confirm the edition, and then follow the steps on the page.

Note: Keep your invoice handly. Purchase made directly from packt don't require one.

14

Orchestration with Kubernetes

This chapter introduces Kubernetes as a powerful, open source container orchestration platform. It begins by exploring the architecture of a Kubernetes cluster and its components. The chapter also highlights Kubernetes' benefits, such as automation, scalability, and reliability, while addressing its drawbacks and evaluating scenarios where it is most effective.

The chapter delves into managing container images with a registry, creating Kubernetes manifests, and deploying them into a Kubernetes cluster. It establishes a comprehensive approach to leveraging Kubernetes for modern application deployment and management by covering these critical aspects.

This chapter covers the following:

- Understanding the Kubernetes
- Managing container images with a registry
- What are Kubernetes manifests?
- Deploying the application into the Kubernetes

By the end of this chapter, you will have a solid understanding of Kubernetes' capabilities, how to deploy containerized applications using manifests, and how to manage these deployments effectively in a Kubernetes environment.

Technical requirements

All the code for this chapter can be found on GitHub at `https://github.com/PacktPublishing/Software-Architecture-with-Spring/tree/main/ch14`. Ellipses in the code blocks indicate that parts of the code have been omitted, and the complete code is available on GitHub.

Understanding the Kubernetes

Kubernetes, often called **K8s** or **kube,** is an open source platform for container orchestration. It streamlines and automates tasks such as deploying, managing, and scaling containerized applications, reducing the need for manual intervention.

In Greek, the term *Kubernetes* means helmsman or pilot. The abbreviation *K8s* represents the eight letters between *K* and the letter *s*. Developed by Google, Kubernetes was released as an open source project in 2014. It combines Google's expertise in large-scale workloads with contributions from the open source community. Let's delve deeper into Kubernetes to understand the Kubernetes cluster.

What is a Kubernetes cluster?

A Kubernetes cluster consists of multiple nodes, which are individual machines that work together to run containerized applications. It forms the basis of Kubernetes architecture and facilitates applications' management, deployment, and scaling in a distributed environment. A cluster has two main components: the control plane and the worker nodes. *Figure 14.1* illustrates the Kubernetes cluster.

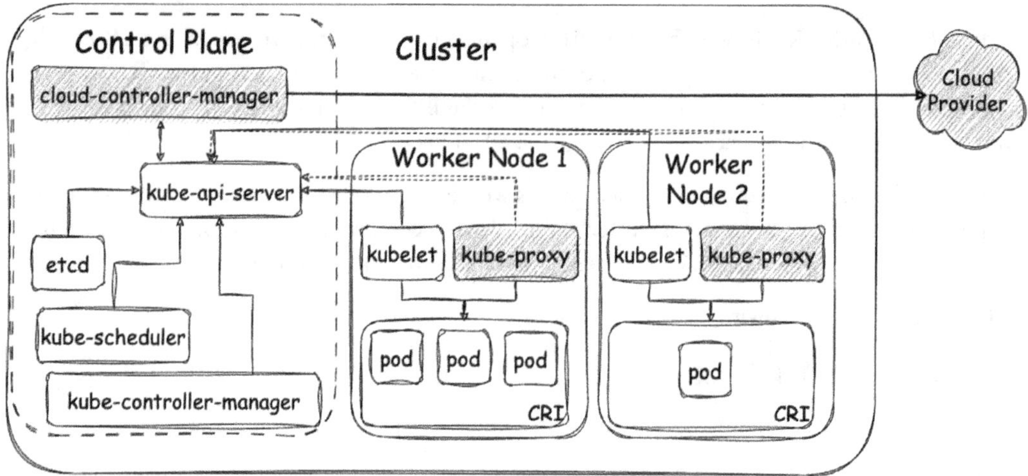

Figure 14.1: Kubernetes cluster

Let's explore the components that comprise the Kubernetes cluster illustrated in the figure:

- **Control plane:** The control plane functions as the brain of the cluster. It manages the system's desired state by scheduling workloads, managing nodes, and monitoring their health. It is also responsible for ensuring that a specified number of application replicas run across the nodes and that the applications operate as intended. The control plane includes the following key components:

  - **Cloud controller manager:** `cloud-controller-manager` integrates the cluster with a cloud provider's API and manages cloud-specific tasks such as node deletion, route setup, and load balancer operations. It combines multiple control loops into a single process, can scale horizontally for performance and reliability, and is not used in on-premises or standalone environments.

- **Api server**: `kube-api-server` exposes the Kubernetes API, handling communication between users and the cluster.

- **Controller manager**: `kube-controller-manager` runs various controller processes as a single binary to simplify operations. Controllers handle specific tasks such as monitoring node availability, managing one-off tasks through `Job` objects, maintaining `EndpointSlice` links between Services and Pods, and creating default Service accounts for new namespaces. It ensures the cluster is in its desired state.

- **Scheduler**: `kube-scheduler` assigns newly created Pods without a node to suitable nodes. Its decisions consider resource requirements, hardware and software constraints, affinity and anti-affinity rules, data locality, workload interference, and deadlines.

- **etcd**: This is a robust key-value store that holds configuration data and state information for the Kubernetes cluster, including details about nodes, Pods, services, and other resources.

- **Worker nodes**: These are the machines, whether virtual or physical, where the applications run. Each worker node contains the following:

  - **kubelet**: `kubelet` is a service that communicates with the control plane to receive instructions. It ensures that containers are running as specified by continuously monitoring their status and restarting them if necessary to maintain the desired state.

  - **kube-proxy**: `kube-proxy` manages network rules to enable communication between Pods. It maintains network connectivity within the cluster by handling routing, load balancing, and forwarding traffic to the appropriate services.

  - **Container runtime**: This is a core component of Kubernetes that manages the execution and lifecycle of containers. Kubernetes supports container runtimes such as containerd, CRI-O, and other implementations compatible with the **Container Runtime Interface (CRI)**.

What does "desired state" mean?

In Kubernetes, the desired state is the user-defined configuration of an application's infrastructure, including the number of replicas, resource allocations, and networking rules. Kubernetes monitors the system and corrects any discrepancies between the actual and desired states to maintain proper cluster operation.

Understanding the components of a Kubernetes cluster is essential for grasping how the control plane and worker nodes work together to maintain the desired state of containerized applications. Now, let's explore Kubernetes's modular architecture, which organizes various features and components into distinct categories.

Categorizing the Kubernetes components

Kubernetes is a powerful container orchestration platform designed to simplify containerized applications' deployment, scaling, and management. Its modular architecture organizes components into distinct categories, making them easier to understand and manage. Each component is tailored to address specific aspects of application management, enabling Kubernetes to handle both simple deployments and complex distributed systems.

The key categories—core components, networking, workloads, storage, and configuration—work together to provide a comprehensive solution. This organization allows us to focus on specific tasks while maximizing Kubernetes' capabilities. Here's an overview of the categorized components that form the backbone of Kubernetes:

- **Core components**:

  - **Pods**: The smallest and most basic deployable unit in Kubernetes, a Pod represents a single instance of a running process in a cluster. Pods can encapsulate one or more tightly coupled containers, shared storage volumes, and a unique IP address for internal communication. They serve as the foundation for scaling and orchestrating applications and provide a logical layer for managing containerized workloads.

  - **Namespaces**: These are logical partitions within a Kubernetes cluster that enable the isolation and organization of resources such as Pods, services, and deployments. They are useful for managing environments such as development, staging, and production, limiting resource consumption, and ensuring security through **role-based access control** (**RBAC**) policies.

  - **Deployments**: These are controller resources used to manage stateless applications by defining their desired state, such as the number of replicas and container configurations. Deployments enable developers to perform rolling updates, ensuring zero downtime during application upgrades, and support rollbacks to previous versions in case of failures. They also provide self-healing capabilities by automatically replacing failed Pods.

  - **ReplicaSets**: These resources are responsible for maintaining a specified number of Pod replicas to ensure high availability and fault tolerance. ReplicaSets monitor the cluster's state and automatically create or terminate Pods to match the desired replica count. While commonly managed by Deployments, they can also be used independently for more straightforward use cases or legacy applications.

- **Networking components**:

  - **Services**: A Service in Kubernetes abstracts a group of Pods, presenting them as a single, stable network endpoint. This setup facilitates seamless communication between components within a Kubernetes cluster. Services decouple workloads from individual Pod instances, ensuring traffic is properly routed even when Pods are created or terminated dynamically. Various services offer internal and external communication flexibility, such as `ClusterIP`, `NodePort`, `LoadBalancer`, and `ExternalName`.

- **Ingress**: This component is a specialized API resource that manages external HTTP and HTTPS access to Kubernetes Services. It allows for advanced routing with features such as path-based and host-based rules, TLS/SSL termination, and load balancing. Ingress simplifies exposing applications to the internet while supporting custom configurations through annotations, providing fine-grained control over behavior.

- **Network Policies**: These establish and enforce firewall rules at the Pod level to regulate network traffic flow between Pods and external endpoints. Network Policies define the permitted traffic based on criteria such as labels, namespaces, and IP ranges. This method strengthens security and minimizes the chances of lateral movement within the cluster and unauthorized access.

- **Service meshes**: These are advanced networking frameworks, such as Istio and Linkerd, that operate at the application layer to offer features such as traffic routing, observability, and security. Service meshes simplify the implementation of complex functionalities, including retries, failovers, distributed tracing, service discovery, and mutual TLS authentication. These features enhance the reliability and manageability of microservices architectures.

- **Workload components**:

  - **StatefulSets**: These are Kubernetes workload API objects designed to manage stateful applications that require stable and unique network identities, persistent storage, and consistent deployment order. StatefulSets ensure that each Pod in the set maintains a unique identifier and hostname, making them ideal for databases, distributed systems, and other state-dependent workloads.

  - **DaemonSets**: These ensure that a single Pod runs on every node or a subset of nodes in the cluster, typically for cluster-wide tasks such as log collection, monitoring, or network policy enforcement. DaemonSets automatically add or remove Pods as nodes are added or removed, ensuring consistent service across the cluster.

- **Jobs/CronJobs**:

  - **Jobs**: These handle one-off tasks expected to terminate upon completion, such as data processing or database migration. They ensure that a task runs to completion, retrying failed tasks when necessary.

  - **CronJobs**: These schedule recurring tasks to run at specified intervals, similar to traditional cron jobs in Unix systems. They are useful for periodic workloads such as backups, report generation, or maintenance tasks.

- **Autoscalers**:

  - **Horizontal Pod Autoscaler (HPA)**: This dynamically adjusts the number of Pod replicas based on resource usage metrics such as CPU and memory or custom metrics, ensuring that applications can handle varying workloads efficiently.

- **Vertical Pod Autoscaler (VPA)**: This optimizes Pod resource requests and limits by monitoring usage over time and automatically adjusting CPU and memory allocations to prevent over-provisioning or under-utilization.

- **Custom resource definitions (CRDs)**: You can enable users to extend Kubernetes by defining custom resource types tailored to specific use cases. CRDs allow developers to create and manage their API resources, integrating custom functionality into Kubernetes while leveraging its native API server and controller patterns.

- **Storage components**:

  - **Persistent volumes (PVs)**: These represent a piece of storage provisioned by a Kubernetes cluster. PVs abstract the underlying storage implementation and support various backends, such as local storage, **Network File System (NFS)**, cloud storage, or network storage systems.

  - **Persistent volume claims (PVCs)**: These act as requests for storage by applications. PVCs specify the required storage size and access mode, such as read-write and other parameters. Kubernetes binds a PVC to a suitable PV, providing seamless access to storage for Pods while decoupling applications from the underlying storage infrastructure.

  - **Storage classes**: These define the different storage options provided in a Kubernetes cluster, such as SSDs, HDDs, or provisioners for cloud and network storage. Storage classes enable dynamic provisioning of PVs based on specific criteria, such as performance, replication policies, or availability zones. Using storage classes, administrators can simplify storage management while ensuring applications receive the appropriate storage type for their needs.

- **Configuration and Secrets**:

  - **ConfigMaps**: These allow the storage and management of non-sensitive data as key-value pairs that can be easily injected into Pods. They separate configuration from application code, enabling developers to change settings—such as environment variables, command-line arguments, and configuration files—without the need to rebuild container images. This approach promotes flexibility and consistency across different environments, including development, staging, and production.

  - **Secrets**: These are Kubernetes resources created to securely store sensitive information, such as API keys, passwords, tokens, and certificates. Secrets encrypt data at rest and control access through RBAC policies. They can be injected into Pods either as environment variables or mounted as files, which ensures secure and streamlined access to sensitive information without exposing it in application code or container images.

By classifying Kubernetes components into core, networking, workload, storage, and configuration groups, we can better understand its modular architecture as a versatile container orchestration platform. Now, let's discuss why Kubernetes is essential.

Why is Kubernetes essential?

Our online auction application's microservices currently utilize Docker Compose to run various components, including databases. While Docker Compose is an excellent tool for managing microservices in development or small-scale environments, it has limitations in production settings where reliability, scalability, and automation are critical. This is where Kubernetes is essential, as it effectively addresses these needs.

Kubernetes is a powerful framework for running resilient distributed systems. It handles scaling, failover, and deployment strategies such as canary deployments, allowing you to focus on building applications rather than managing infrastructure. Additionally, Kubernetes provides essential automation for maintaining system stability in production environments. For example, if a container crashes, Kubernetes detects the issue and promptly replaces the container, ensuring continuous uptime. This automation removes the burden of manual intervention and guarantees that applications remain operational despite failures.

By simplifying and automating container management, Kubernetes empowers us to deploy applications efficiently, maintain high availability, and scale seamlessly, making it the ideal choice for production-grade systems. Kubernetes provides features such as the following:

- **Service discovery and load balancing**: Kubernetes makes containers accessible using DNS names or unique IP addresses and efficiently distributes network traffic to maintain stability, even during periods of high demand.

- **Storage orchestration**: It automatically mounts storage systems of your choice, whether local or cloud-based.

- **Automated rollouts and rollbacks**: This feature ensures your applications remain in the desired state by automating the deployment process. It also gradually implements updates or rolls back to previous versions if issues arise.

- **Automatic resource optimization**: It efficiently allocates resources by aligning the CPU and memory requirements of containers with the available nodes, optimizing resource utilization throughout the cluster.

- **Self-healing capabilities**: It restarts failed containers, replaces unhealthy ones, and removes non-responsive ones. It also ensures that containers are ready before making them available to clients.

- **Secret and configuration management**: This feature safely stores and manages sensitive data such as passwords, API keys, and tokens. It also updates configurations and secrets without requiring a rebuild of container images or exposing sensitive information.

- **Batch processing**: It manages batch jobs and **continuous integration** (CI) workloads while handling container failures seamlessly.

- **Horizontal scaling**: It easily scales applications up or down via commands, user interfaces, or automatic triggers, such as CPU utilization.

- **IPv4/IPv6 dual-stack support**: It allocates IPv4 and IPv6 addresses to Pods and services for flexible networking.

- **Extensibility**: It enables the addition of custom features without modifying the Kubernetes source code.

Kubernetes has transformed application deployment and management. It offers a powerful, scalable, and resilient platform that meets the demands of production-grade systems. Its comprehensive features, such as automated rollouts, self-healing, secret management, and horizontal scaling, make it an indispensable tool for running containerized applications. By abstracting the complexities of infrastructure management, Kubernetes allows us to focus on innovation and efficiency.

While Kubernetes provides significant benefits, it also presents challenges.

What are the Kubernetes drawbacks?

Kubernetes offers numerous benefits but has certain drawbacks that must be considered when deciding whether it's the right tool for your project:

- **Steep learning curve**: It requires a significant understanding of concepts and configurations.

- **Complexity**: Managing and debugging large-scale clusters can be challenging.

- **Overhead**: It has resource and cost overhead for smaller applications.

While Kubernetes provides a robust platform for managing containerized applications, these drawbacks make it less ideal for all use cases. These challenges underscore the importance of carefully evaluating whether Kubernetes aligns with your project's needs.

Analyzing when to use and not to use Kubernetes

Use Kubernetes when your applications require high availability and scalability to handle varying workloads effectively. It is particularly well suited for managing microservices architectures, especially those with complex networking needs. Additionally, Kubernetes is beneficial in environments where automating deployments and rollbacks is a crucial aspect of the development and operations workflow.

On the other hand, avoid using Kubernetes for simple applications that demand minimal scaling, as the complexity may outweigh the advantages. It may not be ideal for small teams that lack the expertise to manage and maintain Kubernetes effectively.

With this foundation, the subsequent step in the Kubernetes workflow involves managing container images with a registry, which is essential for ensuring seamless and efficient deployments. Let's next discuss how to manage container images.

Managing container images with a registry

An image registry is a centralized service that stores, manages, and distributes container images. It acts as a repository where developers can push their container images after building them and pull these images when deploying applications in different environments. Image registries are essential in containerized workflows as they simplify sharing, versioning, and deploying container images. There are three types of image registries—public, private, and self-hosted registries:

- **Public registries**: These are widely accessible and host various container images. They are ideal for sharing commonly used images or accessing resources contributed by the community. Registries that offer public repositories include Docker Hub, known for its extensive collection of official and community images; Quay.io, which supports public and private repositories with advanced security and analytics; and GitHub Container Registry, integrated with GitHub for managing and sharing project-related images.

- **Private registries**: Designed for use within organizations or specific projects, these registries provide enhanced security, restricted access, and better control over container images. Registries that offer private repositories include Docker Hub, which supports private repositories with restricted access for specific collaborators; Amazon **Elastic Container Registry** (**ECR**), a cloud-based option integrated with AWS services; and Harbor, an open source registry offering advanced vulnerability scanning and image signing features.

- **Self-hosted registries**: These allow us to host and manage our own registries, providing complete control over the infrastructure and policies. Docker Registry is an open source, lightweight option for private image storage, while Harbor offers self-hosted deployments with advanced features such as access control and vulnerability scanning.

Image registries streamline container workflows by centralizing the storage and distribution of images, making them essential for CI/CD pipelines, production deployments, and secure image management. Selecting the appropriate registry depends on scalability, integration requirements, and security needs.

Now we understand the role and types of image registries, we will explore how to create container images and push them to Docker Hub's registry.

Creating and pushing images to Docker Hub

Let's create and push the images to the Docker Hub registry. We will use the authentication services to outline the process. Once the image is built, it will be tagged and pushed to Docker Hub, making it accessible for deployment in any environment. To proceed, you need to create an account, which you can do at `https://hub.docker.com`.

> **Alert**
>
> When you execute the commands, replace the Docker Hub username `wxesquevixos` with your username.

Let's follow these steps to create and push the image:

1. A Dockerfile is required to create images. The Dockerfile is located in the application's root folder. The specifics of Dockerfile creation will not be detailed here, as they were thoroughly discussed in *Chapter 6, Microservices Architecture.*

2. Open a Terminal console and navigate to the `authentication-services` project folder at `ch14/authentication`. Then, execute the following command and enter your Docker Hub credentials to log in:

    ```
    docker login
    ```

3. Once you are logged in, let's proceed to build the authentication services image. Execute the following command:

    ```
    docker build --platform linux/amd64,linux/arm64 -t wxesquevixos/
    authentication-services:latest .
    ```

4. Now, we need to push the application's image to Docker Hub. Execute the following command:

    ```
    docker push wxesquevixos/authentication-services:latest
    ```

After uploading your application's image, you can view it by visiting your Docker Hub account at `https://hub.docker.com/repositories`, as illustrated in *Figure 14.2.*

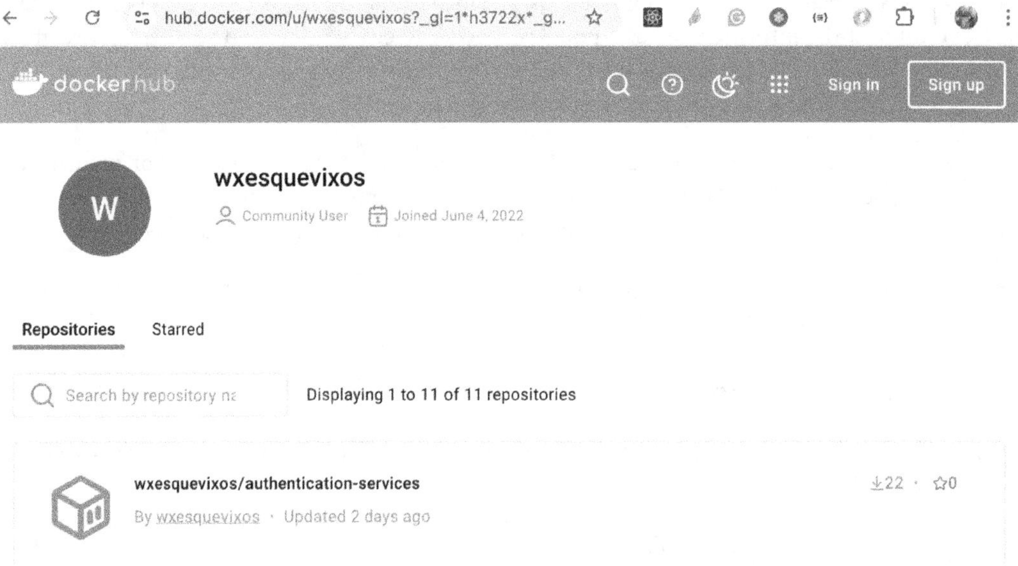

Figure 14.2: Docker Hub repository with the application's image+

The application's image has been successfully uploaded to Docker Hub, making it ready to be pulled and deployed in any Kubernetes environment.

Now, we will create the necessary Kubernetes manifests to deploy the application, including configurations for Deployment, Service, and Ingress resources.

What are Kubernetes manifests?

Kubernetes manifests are configuration files written in YAML or JSON format that define the desired state of a Kubernetes resource. They are blueprints for configuring and operating applications, services, and other components. By enabling declarative configuration, manifests allow us to specify the system's desired state, and Kubernetes automatically manages and corrects any deviations to maintain that state. Unlike the imperative approach, which requires direct commands to modify resources, declarative manifests ensure deployments are more predictable and repeatable, providing consistency across environments. Manifests facilitate automation, seamlessly integrating with CI/CD pipelines and other tools to streamline workflows.

Kubernetes manifests can define various resource types according to an application or cluster's specific needs. Common resource types include Pods, Deployments, Services, Ingress, ConfigMaps, Secrets, PVCs, Jobs, CronJobs, and CRDs.

Kubernetes manifests are fundamental for managing and deploying applications in a Kubernetes cluster.

Once we understand the purpose and importance of Kubernetes manifests, we are prepared to create the manifests required for our application's deployment.

Crafting the application's manifests

Now, we will craft the Kubernetes manifests required to deploy the authentication services and their associated components. These manifests are critical for defining how the application is deployed, exposed, and interacts with external resources. Specifically, we will cover the following manifests: `Deployment`, `Service`, and `Ingress`, which can be found in the `ch14/kubernetes` directory. Let's start with the `Deployment` manifest.

Deployment manifest

The Deployment defines the desired state of the authentication service, including container specifications, replicas, and resource configurations.

The following configuration snippet of the `authentication-services-deployment.yml` file is the `Deployment` manifest for authentication services:

```yaml
apiVersion: apps/v1
kind: Deployment
metadata:
```

```
    name: authentication-services
    labels:
      app: authentication-services
spec:
  replicas: 2
  selector:
    matchLabels:
      app: authentication-services
  template:
    metadata:
      labels:
        app: authentication-services
    spec:
      containers:
        - name: authentication-services
          image: wxesquevixos/authentication-services:latest
          ports:
            - containerPort: 8080
          env:
            - name: MONGODB_URL
              value: "mongodb://auction_
  app:auction123@192.168.100.89:27017/autentication_db?authSource=admin"
            - name: USER-SERVICES
              value: "http://user-services.default.svc.cluster.local"
```

The `kind` field specifies that it is a `Deployment` resource and the `metadata.name` field names it as `authentication-services`. The `metadata.labels` field categorizes it with the label `app:authentication-services`.

`spec.replicas` defines the Pod's number—in this case, two replicas will be created.

`spec.selector.matchLabels` ensures the `Deployment` manages Pods with the label `app:authentication-services`.

`template.metadata.labels` assigns the label `app:authentication-services` to the Pods.

`template.spec.containers` defines the container configuration, where the container name is `authentication-services`, and the image specifies the Docker image. In this case, it will pull the image, `wxesquevixos/authentication-services:latest`, that we pushed to Docker Hub.

`ports.containerPort` exposes port `8080` in the container.

The env defines environment variables where `MONGODB_URL` specifies the connection string for the external MongoDB database, and `USER-SERVICES` specifies the URL for the `user-services` endpoint within the cluster.

The URL `http://user-services.default.svc.cluster.local` is the fully qualified domain name for a Kubernetes Service within the cluster. Here's what each part represents:

- `user-services`: The name of the Service

- `default`: The namespace where the Service is deployed, in this case, the default namespace

- `svc`: Indicates that this is a `Service` resource

- `cluster.local`: The default DNS for the Kubernetes cluster

This URL allows Pods within the cluster to communicate with the `user-services` Service in the default namespace.

> **Alert**
>
> Sensitive environment variables must be stored in a `Secret` manifest to enhance security and prevent exposure. In our example, we will leave it in the `Deployment` manifest.

After creating and understanding the `Deployment` manifest, let's create the `Service` manifest.

Service manifest

The Service provides stable networking for the Deployment and enables other components within the cluster to communicate with it by name, abstracting the underlying Pod IPs.

The following configuration snippet is the `Service` manifest `authentication-services-deployment.yml` file:

```yaml
apiVersion: v1
kind: Service
metadata:
  name: authentication-services
spec:
  selector:
    app: authentication-services
  ports:
    - protocol: TCP
      port: 80
      targetPort: 8080
  type: ClusterIP
```

The `kind` field specifies that the resource defined in the manifest is a Service.

`spec.selector` routes traffic to Pods with the label `app: authentication-services`.

`spec.ports` maps the Service ports. The protocol specifies the use of TCP for communication. It exposes port `80` for the Service, and `targetPort` forwards traffic to port `8080` in the container.

`type` sets the Service type as `ClusterIP`, making it accessible only within the cluster using its DNS name, `authentication-services.default.svc.cluster.local`.

Now, let's create the `Ingress` manifest to route external HTTP and HTTPS traffic.

Ingress manifest

Ingress manages external HTTP and HTTPS access to services within a cluster, enabling routing based on URLs, hostnames, and SSL termination.

The following configuration snippet is the `Ingress` manifest `authentication-services-ingress.yml` file:

```
apiVersion: networking.k8s.io/v1
kind: Ingress
metadata:
  name: authentication-services-ingress
  annotations:
    nginx.ingress.kubernetes.io/enable-cors: "true"
    nginx.ingress.kubernetes.io/cors-allow-origin: "*"
    nginx.ingress.kubernetes.io/cors-allow-methods: "GET,
POST, PUT, DELETE, OPTIONS"
    nginx.ingress.kubernetes.io/cors-allow-headers: "Authorization,
Content-Type"
spec:
  ingressClassName: nginx
  rules:
    - host: authentication-services.com
      http:
        paths:
          - path: /v1/api/auth
            pathType: Prefix
            backend:
              service:
                name: authentication-services
                port:
                  number: 80
```

The `kind` field specifies that it is an `Ingress` resource and `metadata.name` names it.

The `annotations` field configures NGINX Ingress with CORS settings to allow cross-origin requests and specify allowed origins, methods, and headers.

`spec.ingressClassName` specifies the Ingress controller, which is NGINX. The `rules` field defines the routing rules, where the `host` field is used to route traffic for `authentication-services.com`. Additionally, the `paths` field directs requests that match `/v1/api/auth` to the `authentication-services` Service on port `80`.

Since we will use MongoDB as an external resource outside of Kubernetes, we will create a `Service` manifest to enable the authentication services to access it.

External Service manifest for MongoDB

Running databases outside Kubernetes optimizes resources, simplifies backup and recovery with tools such as Amazon RDS or MongoDB Atlas, and avoids Kubernetes overhead for StatefulSets and scaling. It also enhances security with private networks and firewalls, improves reliability with proven configurations, and supports large-scale production environments.

We will keep MongoDB and PostgreSQL external to Kubernetes to leverage these benefits.

The following configuration snippet is a Service that provides access to external resources:

```
apiVersion: v1
kind: Service
metadata:
  name: mongodb-service
spec:
  type: ExternalName
  externalName: 192.168.100.89
  ports:
    - port: 27017
      targetPort: 27017
```

The `kind` field specifies that it is a `Service` resource, and `metadata.name` names it as `mongodb-service`.

`spec.type` defines the `Service` type as `ExternalName`, allowing it to connect to an external resource.

`externalName` specifies the external MongoDB database's IP address.

The `ports` field maps port `27017` for MongoDB communication.

Since MongoDB will be used as an external resource outside of Kubernetes, this `Service` manifest enables authentication services to access it.

By crafting the `Deployment`, `Service`, `Ingress`, and external `Service` manifests, we have defined the essential components for deploying and managing the authentication service and its dependencies in Kubernetes. These manifests establish the configuration, networking, and external connectivity required for seamless integration and scalability.

With the manifests ready, the next step is to deploy these resources into the Kubernetes cluster to bring the authentication service and its related components to life. Let's move on to deploying these resources in Kubernetes.

Deploying the application into the Kubernetes

Now that we have completed the steps to containerize the application using a Dockerfile and pushed its image to the container registry, Docker Hub, as well as created the required Kubernetes `Deployment`, `Service`, and `Ingress` manifests, we are ready to proceed with the next phase.

In this phase, we will refactor the application, install minikube to create a local Kubernetes cluster, deploy the prepared manifests, and test the application to ensure it runs as expected. Let's refactor our application and understand why this extra step is necessary.

Refactoring the application

For simplicity, we will focus on the authentication services API to illustrate the process of deploying an application in Kubernetes, removing Spring Cloud dependencies in favor of Kubernetes-native features such as service discovery and traffic routing.

Now let's refactor the authentication services:

> **Spring Cloud Patterns and Kubernetes**
>
> To retain familiar Spring Cloud patterns while integrating with Kubernetes resources, we can use Spring Cloud Kubernetes. It allows Spring Boot applications to seamlessly integrate with the Kubernetes ecosystem by mapping concepts like service discovery and externalized configuration to native Kubernetes resources such as Services, ConfigMaps, and Secrets. To learn more, visit: `https://spring.io/projects/spring-cloud-kubernetes`.

1. Remove the following dependencies from the `pom.xml` file: `spring-cloud-starter-netflix-eureka-client`, `spring-cloud-starter-loadbalancer`, and `spring-cloud-starter-config`.

2. As we have removed the configuration services, we must add the authentication services properties back to the `application.properties` file. The `user-services.url` property was added to define the `USER-SERVICES` placeholder, for which Kubernetes will inject the address to the user services through an environment variable:

```
user-services.url=${USER-SERVICES}
```

3. In the `BeansConfiguration` class, refactor the `restClient` method, as shown in the following code snippet. It removes the `@LoadBalanced` annotation and the `CustomLoadBalancerInterceptor` class:

```java
@Bean
public RestClient restClient() {
    return RestClient.create();
}
```

4. In the `UserRestApi` class, we added the `userServiceUrl` variable to retrieve its value from the environment variable defined by the `user-services.url` property:

```java
@Service
public class UserRestApi implements UserRepository {

    @Value("${user-services.url}")
    private String userServiceUrl;

    private final RestClient restClient;

    public List<String> getRolesByUsername(String
      username) {
      RoleResponse result = restClient.get()
        .uri(userServiceUrl + "/v1/users/" + username +
            "/roles")
        .retrieve()
      ...
```

These changes streamline the application by leveraging Kubernetes-native features. Now, let's set up minikube.

Setting up minikube

minikube is a lightweight Kubernetes implementation specifically designed for local development and testing. It creates a single-node Kubernetes cluster on the local machine, allowing developers to experiment with Kubernetes features, deploy applications, and test configurations in a controlled environment. minikube is ideal for developers because it supports Ingress, DNS, and storage features. It closely mimics a complete Kubernetes cluster while being resource-efficient and straightforward to set up.

> **minikube installation**
>
> Please follow the instructions at `https://minikube.sigs.k8s.io/docs/start` to install minikube. You will also find extensive documentation about minikube there.

1. After installing minikube, we can start it. Open a Terminal console and execute the following command. *Figure 14.3* shows a screenshot of the terminal with minikube running:

```
minikube start
```

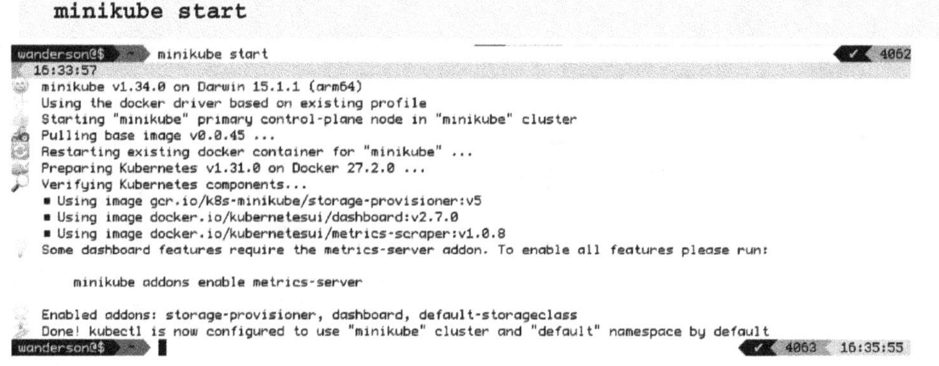

Figure 14.3: minikube started

2. minikube provides a dashboard where we can see all the Kubernetes components that were previously discussed. To access the dashboard, execute the following command. *Figure 14.4* shows a screenshot of it:

```
minikube dashboard
```

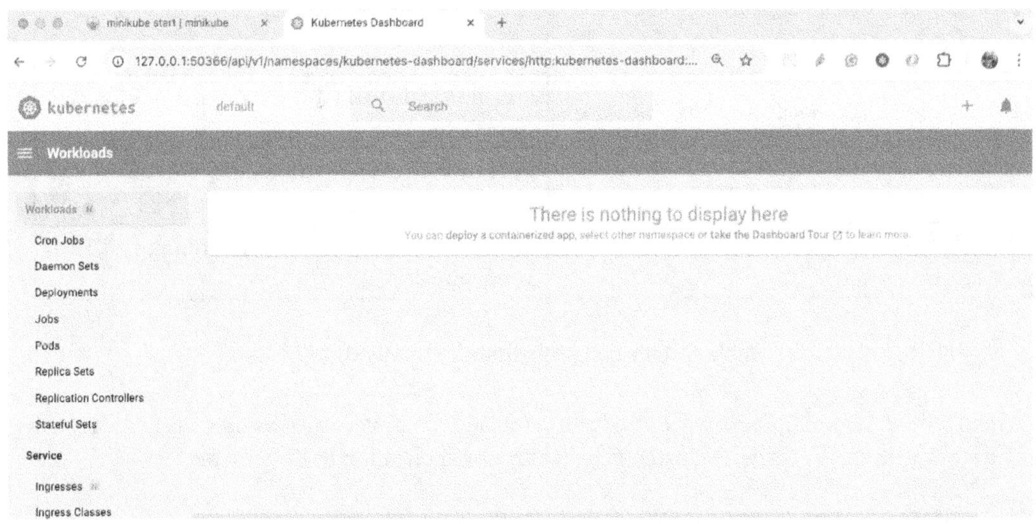

Figure 14.4: minikube's dashboard

3. Run the following command in another terminal to initiate the minikube tunnel. This is crucial for exposing `LoadBalancer` services by creating a network tunnel that routes traffic from the host to the cluster. It also makes services accessible externally and simulates production behavior:

```
minikube tunnel
```

With minikube set up, let's explore essential Kubernetes commands to enhance application deployment and management.

Presenting essential kubectl commands

Essential `kubectl` commands are crucial for efficiently managing Kubernetes resources. They enable tasks such as applying manifests, managing Pods and services, scaling deployments, and troubleshooting. The following table highlights the most useful commands, serving as a foundational toolkit for deploying and maintaining applications in a Kubernetes cluster.

Command	Description
`kubectl get <resource>`	Lists the resources of a specified type in the cluster, such as Pods, services, or deployments
`kubectl apply -f <file|directory>`	Deploys or updates resources defined in a manifest file or directory
`kubectl delete -f <file|directory>`	Deletes resources defined in a manifest file or directory

Command	Description
`kubectl describe <resource> <name>`	Displays detailed information about a specific resource
`kubectl logs <pod-name>`	Fetches the logs of a specific Pod for debugging purposes
`kubectl exec -it <pod-name> -- <command>`	Executes a command inside a running Pod, such as opening a shell

Table 14.1: Essential Kubernetes commands

With minikube set up and the essential Kubernetes commands presented, we now have the foundational tools to work with the Kubernetes cluster. Let's deploy our application to Kubernetes.

Deploying the application in Kubernetes

Installing the authentication service in Kubernetes involves deploying its resources using manifest files that define how the application will operate within the cluster. This process includes creating a Deployment to manage the Pods, a Service to enable internal communication, and an Ingress to allow external access.

> **Alert**
>
> The `ch14/kubernetes` folder on GitHub contains manifests for PostgreSQL, user, and product services. You can deploy them by following the same process outlined for deploying the MongoDB and authentication services manifests.

Let's perform the steps outlined to deploy the authentication service in Kubernetes successfully:

1. To set up MongoDB and PostgreSQL, open a terminal, navigate to the `ch14/docker-resources/` directory, and run the following command:

   ```
   docker-compose up -d
   ```

2. To install the Ingress controller, execute the following command in a terminal. Kubernetes Ingress controllers direct external HTTP/HTTPS traffic to cluster services based on `Ingress` resource rules. They act as reverse proxies, load balancers, and support tools such as NGINX and Traefik. `Ingress` classes link resources to specific controllers, ensuring flexible and scalable traffic management:

   ```
   kubectl apply -f https://raw.githubusercontent.com/kubernetes/
   ingress-nginx/controller-v1.11.3/deploy/static/provider/cloud/
   deploy.yaml
   ```

3. Go to the terminal where you initialized the minikube tunnel and enter your machine's password if prompted, and press Enter.

4. Open another terminal and execute the following command to find out your IP:

```
ifconfig | grep "inet " | grep -v 127.0.0.1 | awk '{print $2}'
```

5. Navigate to the `ch14/kubernetes/databases` folder and open the `mongodb-external-service.yaml` file. Replace the IP `192.168.100.89` with the IP address you got in step 3.

6. Execute the following command to deploy the Service into Kubernetes and make MongoDB accessible to the applications in Kubernetes:

```
kubectl apply -f mongodb-external-service.yaml
```

7. Execute the following command to check that the services were deployed, as shown in *Figure 14.5*. The `mongodb-service` of the `ExternalName` type maps to an external IP address of `192.168.100.89` on port `27017/TCP`:

```
kubectl get service
```

```
NAME                     TYPE           CLUSTER-IP     EXTERNAL-IP       PORT(S)      AGE
kubernetes               ClusterIP      10.96.0.1      <none>            443/TCP      16m
mongodb-service          ExternalName   <none>         192.168.100.89    27017/TCP    10m
```

Figure 14.5: MongoDB service deployed

8. Navigate to the `ch14/kubernetes/authentication` folder and open the `authentication-services-deployment` file. Replace the IP `192.168.100.89` with the IP address you got in step 3.

9. Execute the following command to deploy the authentication service using its `Deployment` manifest:

```
kubectl apply -f authentication-services-deployment.yaml
```

10. Execute the following command to apply the `Service` manifest for the authentication service:

```
kubectl apply -f authentication-services-service.yaml
```

11. Execute the following command to apply the `Service` manifest for the authentication service:

```
kubectl apply -f authentication-services-ingress.yaml
```

12. Go to the terminal where you initialized the minikube tunnel and enter your machine's password if prompted, and press Enter.

13. The application has been deployed to Kubernetes, and we need to configure our local system to resolve the DNS by adding entries to the `/etc/hosts` file. Add the following line to it:

```
127.0.0.1  authentication-services.com
```

The application and its dependencies have been successfully deployed to Kubernetes, and the authentication service is now fully operational within the cluster. We have ensured a scalable and reliable deployment by leveraging Kubernetes' powerful features, such as Ingress controllers for external access and Services for internal communication.

Now, let's test the application to verify that all components function as expected and that the authentication service is accessible internally and externally.

Testing the application

We will request a token from the authentication service to test the application deployed in Kubernetes. This will confirm that the service is properly deployed, accessible, and functioning as expected:

1. Navigate to the `ch14/postman` folder and import the `ch14.postman_collection.json` file to Postman.

2. To obtain the token, submit the request at `http://authentication-services.com/v1/api/auth`. *Figure 14.6* illustrates a token request made to the authentication service.

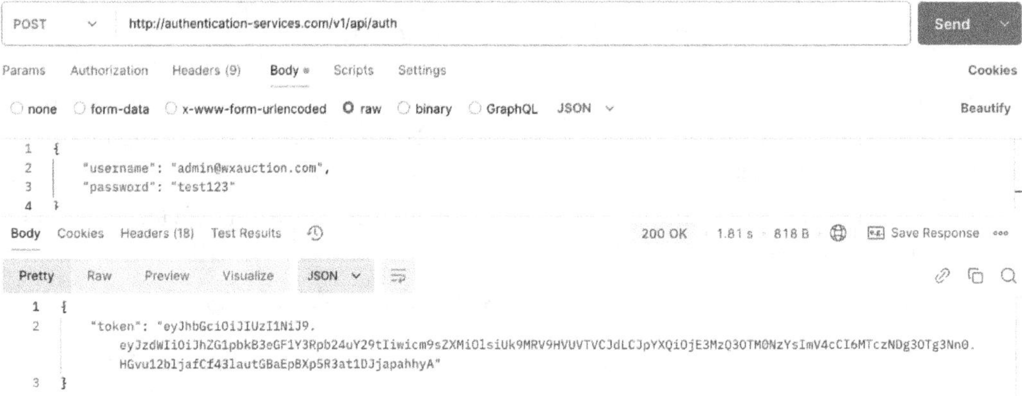

Figure 14.6: Authentication services request to get a token

The authentication service's deployment and testing in Kubernetes have been successfully completed. By utilizing Kubernetes-native features and following best practices, we ensured a scalable, reliable, and production-ready setup. Testing confirmed that the authentication service is functioning as expected, providing a solid foundation for further development and integration with other services in the cluster.

Summary

This chapter provided an in-depth exploration of Kubernetes as a container orchestration platform, highlighting its ability to streamline application deployment, management, and scaling. You were introduced to the Kubernetes architecture, including the control plane and worker nodes, and gained a clear understanding of its role in managing distributed systems and maintaining the desired state of applications.

The chapter also covered essential Kubernetes features such as service discovery, load balancing, automated rollouts, self-healing, and horizontal scaling, showcasing their benefits for production-grade systems. Additionally, it examined managing container images with registries, crafted Kubernetes manifests, and deployed the authentication services into minikube for local Kubernetes setups.

This chapter combined foundational concepts with practical applications to equip you with the knowledge to use Kubernetes to deploy scalable, reliable, and efficient containerized applications.

In *Chapter 15, Continuous Integration and Continuous Deployment*, we will explore the fundamentals of CI/CD, examine its key concepts and principles, and gain hands-on experience setting up and automating a CI/CD pipeline using Jenkins.

Questions

1. What is Kubernetes and why is it important?
2. What are the main components of a Kubernetes cluster?
3. What are Kubernetes manifests and what are they used for?
4. What is the purpose of the `Deployment` manifest in Kubernetes?
5. How does the `Service` manifest work in Kubernetes?
6. What is the function of the `Ingress` manifest in Kubernetes?

Get This Book's PDF Version and Exclusive Extras

Scan the QR code (or go to `packtpub.com/unlock`). Search for this book by name, confirm the edition, and then follow the steps on the page.

Note: Keep your invoice handly. Purchase made directly from packt don't require one.

15

Continuous Integration and Continuous Deployment

This chapter introduces **continuous integration and continuous deployment (CI/CD)** as essential practices for modern software development, as even the best-designed software architectures require effective delivery mechanisms to ensure that changes are integrated smoothly, tested consistently, and deployed reliably. It begins by highlighting the challenges of traditional development models and explains how CI/CD addresses these issues by automating key stages of the release process to improve efficiency, collaboration, and quality. The chapter presents the principles of CI/CD, such as version control, automated builds, and testing, while explaining the distinctions between continuous delivery and continuous deployment.

Additionally, the chapter provides a detailed walkthrough of implementing a CI/CD pipeline using Jenkins, covering the setup of environment configurations, GitHub integration, and Docker containerization. By exploring these components, the chapter establishes a comprehensive approach to building robust CI/CD workflows, ultimately enhancing the reliability and speed of software delivery.

This chapter covers the following:

- Understanding CI/CD
- Setting up the environment and GitHub
- Building a CI/CD pipeline with Jenkinsfile
- Setting up Jenkins and the CI/CD pipeline

By the end of this chapter, you will have a solid understanding of CI/CD practices, how to build and automate software delivery pipelines using Jenkins, and how to manage these pipelines effectively for streamlined and reliable deployments in a modern development environment.

Technical requirements

All the code for this chapter can be found on GitHub at `https://github.com/PacktPublishing/Software-Architecture-with-Spring/tree/main/ch15`. Ellipses in the code blocks indicate that parts of the code have been omitted, and the complete code is available on GitHub.

Understanding CI/CD

In traditional software development, teams often followed a linear approach known as the waterfall model. Developers would work on large portions of code over extended periods before integrating their changes. This process frequently resulted in integration hell, where merging changes from different team members led to conflicts and delays. Additionally, testing was typically conducted manually at the end of the development cycle, making it difficult to detect and address issues early.

In the early 2000s, the rise of Agile and DevOps methodologies addressed these challenges by promoting iterative development and faster feedback loops. This shift led to the emergence of CI, which minimizes integration issues by enabling frequent and automated code merging and testing. Soon after, CD and continuous deployment emerged to streamline staging, release, and production processes. Let's explore the concepts and practices of CI/CD to better understand their significance and impact on software development workflows.

Exploring CI/CD

CI/CD focuses on automating key stages of the software release process to optimize and accelerate development. In some contexts, the letter *D* in *CI/CD* can also mean delivery. The primary distinction between *continuous delivery* and *continuous deployment* is how changes are released to the production environment. In continuous delivery, changes require manual approval before they are promoted to production. On the other hand, continuous deployment allows changes to move through the pipeline and into production without any manual intervention. *Figure 15.1* illustrates the CI/CD pipeline flow.

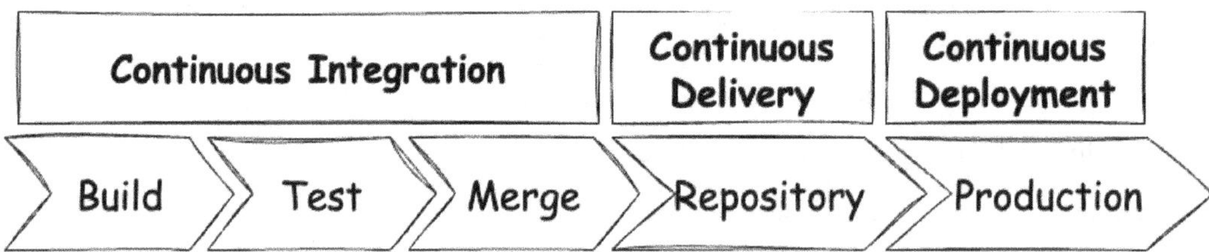

Figure 15.1: CI/CD process flow

Let's clarify the CI/CD pipeline flow illustrated in *Figure 15.1* by presenting a use case involving a company that develops a microservices-based application using Jenkins for its CI/CD pipeline (Jenkins is an open source automation tool designed to support CI/CD processes by automating software projects' building, testing, and deployment):

1. **Continuous integration**:

   - Developers commit their changes to a GitHub repository.

   - GitHub triggers the Jenkins pipeline through a webhook setup.

   - The pipeline executes unit tests, conducts code quality checks using tools such as SonarQube, and builds a Docker image for the service.

2. **Continuous delivery**:

   - After the build passes, the pipeline automatically deploys the Docker image to a staging environment.

   - At this stage, the deployment to production must be manually triggered after the software is validated as working as expected.

3. **Continuous deployment**:

   - In a continuous deployment setup, the manual approval from continuous delivery is removed. Instead, once the staging tests pass, the build is automatically deployed to Kubernetes for production. This means that updates to the production environment occur without any manual intervention.

In this scenario, Jenkins optimizes the entire CI/CD pipeline, facilitating efficient code integration, testing, and deployment. Let's examine the core principles of CI/CD to better understand how it enhances the software development life cycle.

Examining the core principles of CI/CD

Understanding the core principles of CI/CD is essential for enhancing the efficiency of our software development life cycle. These fundamentals improve development and deployment workflows, enabling us to deliver software faster and with higher quality:

- **Versioned centralized source repository**: A centralized source repository plays a crucial role in **source code management** (**SCM**). It contains all the essential files and scripts to create builds, including the application's source code, database schemas, libraries, configuration files, and versioning information. Additionally, it should house test scripts and build automation scripts to streamline the development process.

- **Frequent, small code merges and iterations**: Making small, regular changes to the repository and merging them into the main branch helps prevent hidden conflicts and simplifies debugging. Avoid large, infrequent commits, which can lead to delays and risks.

- **Automated build and self-testing**: The build process should be automated and run with a single command, packaging the application and compiling code dependencies. The CI/CD pipeline must include automated tests that cause a build to fail if any tests fail. Static analysis tools can help maintain code quality and security compliance.

- **Stable and consistent testing environments**: Code should be tested in an environment that mimics production. New code must not be tested in the live environment; instead, it must be tested in cloned environments to identify issues early and ensure results reflect real-world conditions.

- **Transparent collaboration and visibility**: All team members should have access to the latest builds, repository updates, and logs. Clear version history and real-time CI/CD status help developers monitor progress and stay updated on changes.

- **Reliable and low-risk deployments**: Deployments should be reliable and routine, giving teams the confidence to release updates anytime. Effective testing should catch issues before production. Smaller, incremental deployments reduce the risk of large-scale failures and simplify rollbacks.

Adhering to these CI/CD principles can enhance software quality, minimize errors, and optimize the delivery process. Now, let's check the benefits and challenges of CI/CD.

Recognizing the benefits and challenges of CI/CD

By automating the workflow from code integration to deployment, CI/CD enables teams to deliver updates and new features more frequently and efficiently. This approach helps detect and address issues early, minimizing downtime and improving overall software quality. Here are some benefits that CI/CD provides:

1. **Higher code quality**: Automated testing frameworks, such as JUnit or Selenium, catch bugs early, ensuring a more stable and reliable code base.

2. **Improved collaboration**: CI/CD encourages frequent code integration, promoting collaboration and continuous improvement among developers.

3. **Reduced manual effort**: Automation reduces time-consuming manual processes, allowing developers to concentrate on creating new features instead of performing repetitive tasks.

4. **Lower risk**: Small, incremental deployments lower the chances of large-scale failures, making rollbacks simpler and more manageable if issues arise.

5. **Increased transparency**: CI/CD pipelines provide real-time visibility into the software's health, making it easier for teams to monitor progress and identify bottlenecks.

6. **Faster time-to-market**: Automating integration, testing, and deployment accelerates the release cycle. For example, teams using tools such as Jenkins or GitHub Actions can automatically build and test code with every commit, significantly speeding up the feedback loop.

Adopting CI/CD offers significant benefits but poses challenges, such as complex pipeline configurations and time-consuming build failures. Strong infrastructure and monitoring tools are essential for effective automation. Despite these challenges, CI/CD is vital for agile teams, enhancing feedback loops and collaboration and ensuring alignment with user expectations.

Presenting popular CI/CD automation tools

In modern software development, CI/CD tools are crucial in automating builds, tests, and deployments, enabling teams to deliver reliable software quickly and efficiently. Here are some of the most popular CI/CD tools, each offering unique features that cater to different needs:

- **Jenkins** is a popular open source automation server known for its role in CI and continuous deployment. Its extensive plugin ecosystem supports project building, deployment, and automation across various programming languages. Jenkins simplifies complex workflows with pipelines as code using Jenkinsfiles and integrates seamlessly with version control systems such as GitHub, GitLab, and Bitbucket, enhancing source code management and CI.

- **GitHub Actions** is a built-in CI/CD tool for GitHub repositories that automates workflows triggered by Git events, such as pushes and pull requests. It allows developers to create custom workflows using YAML files for tailored automation. The tool also features a marketplace of reusable actions, making it easier to set up and accelerate the creation of pipelines with pre-built components for common tasks.

- **GitLab CI/CD** is an integrated feature of the GitLab platform that provides a comprehensive DevOps solution, covering version control, CI/CD automation, container registry management, and monitoring. It seamlessly integrates with GitLab repositories for efficient code collaboration and deployment. Pipelines are configured using YAML files for flexible automation, and it supports Docker containers, making it suitable for containerized applications. This tool is ideal for teams looking for an all-in-one solution for version control, CI/CD, and project management.

- **CircleCI** is a versatile CI/CD tool that is available in cloud and on-premises versions. It is recognized for its ease of use and high performance. It supports workflows across various environments, including Docker, Linux, Windows, and macOS, allowing for flexible development setups. CircleCI enables parallel test execution for faster feedback and integrates well with Docker and Kubernetes, making it ideal for containerized applications. The pipeline configuration is managed through intuitive YAML files, simplifying process automation.

Now that we acknowledge the importance of CI/CD and know some CI/CD tools, let's implement a CI/CD pipeline using Jenkins, one of the most widely used automation tools. We'll demonstrate the process by focusing on the authentication services for our online auction project. Let's begin by setting up the environment and creating the GitHub project.

Setting up the environment and GitHub

To ensure that our pipeline can pull code from the project's GitHub repository during execution, we must set up the necessary environment and GitHub project. This process will involve configuring a public URL, creating a GitHub repository, and setting up webhooks to trigger pipeline runs automatically. Let's start by creating a public URL for our local development.

Creating a public URL for local development

Creating a public URL for our local development environment allows external services to interact with our application. This URL ensures that code pushed to GitHub can trigger our CI/CD pipeline. This process occurs through webhooks, which send requests to a specified endpoint.

We will use the **ngrok** tool to create a secure, temporary public URL that forwards requests to our local server. It supports HTTPS and includes a web interface for inspecting and debugging incoming requests.

> **Setting up ngrok**
>
> Create an account at https://dashboard.ngrok.com/signup and follow the instructions at `https://dashboard.ngrok.com/get-started/setup` to set up ngrok and get started.

It will provide session details after setting up and running ngrok, as illustrated in *Figure 15.2*.

```
ngrok

👋 Goodbye tunnels, hello Agent Endpoints: https://ngrok.com/r/aep

Session Status                online
Account                       wandersonxs@gmail.com (Plan: Free)
Version                       3.19.0
Region                        South America (sa)
Latency                       19ms
Web Interface                 http://127.0.0.1:4040
Forwarding                    https://8af5-2804-1680-1236-aa00-5c8e-9c98-aee5

Connections                   ttl      opn      rt1      rt5      p50      p90
                              10       0        0.00     0.00     30.09    30.31
```

Figure 15.2: ngrok session details

Forwarding is our most important detail, as it exposes localhost:8080 by creating a publicly accessible URL. Copy and save this URL. We will use it to configure the GitHub webhook in the *Setting up GitHub* section. So, let's set up GitHub.

Setting up GitHub

To automate the deployment process, we need to create a new GitHub repository named `authentication-services` for the project. We will push the code to this repository, which is in the `ch15/authentication-services` folder. *Figure 15.3* shows a screenshot of the authentication services pushed to GitHub.

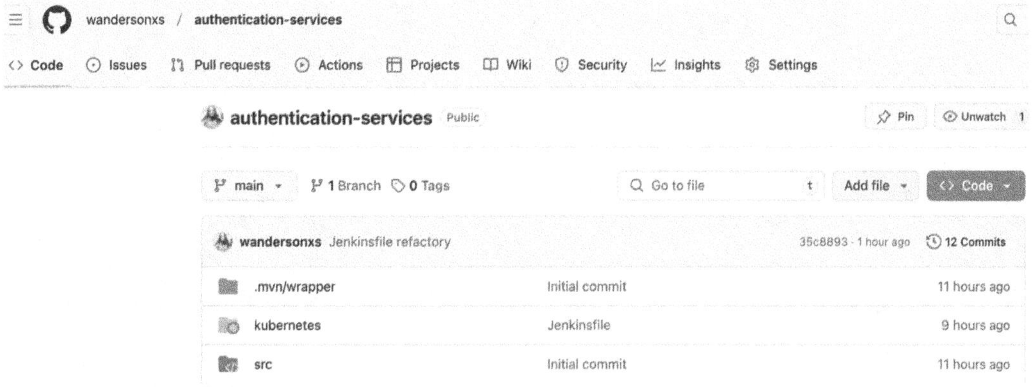

Figure 15.3: Authentication services' GitHub repository

The figure illustrates the project pushed to the `wandersonxs` GitHub account in the `authentication-services` repository. Now, let's create a webhook to trigger our CI/CD pipeline in Jenkins whenever a merge is made to the `main` branch.

Creating a webhook to trigger the pipeline

Webhooks enable external services to receive notifications about specific events. In this context, we want to trigger our CI/CD pipeline in Jenkins whenever a push or merge occurs to the `main` branch of our project. So, let's follow the steps:

1. Go to **Settings**, choose **Webhooks** from the left menu, and click the **Add Webhook** button.

2. On the next screen, follow the instructions to complete the form on the screen and click the **Add webhook** button. *Figure 15.4* displays the completed screen with the necessary information, as described in the list that follows:

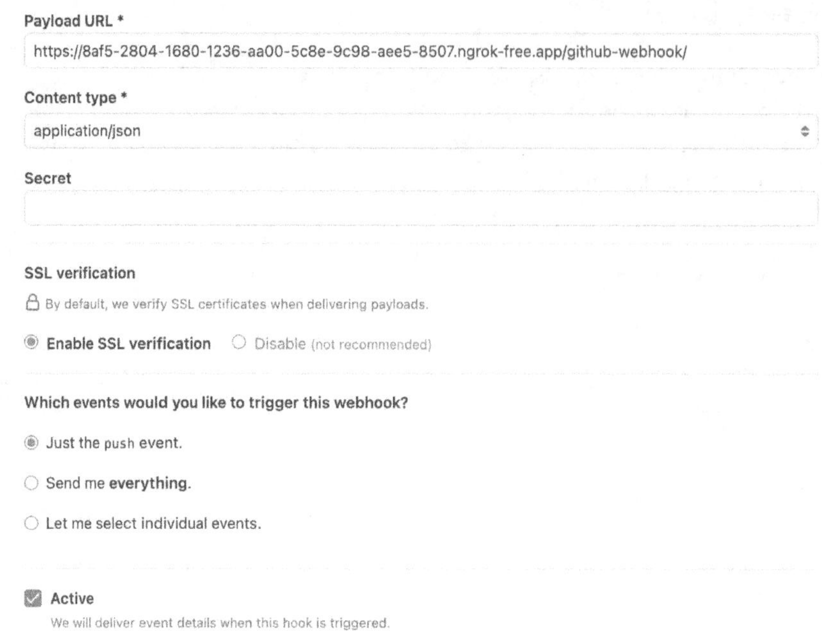

Figure 15.4: Webhook to trigger the Jenkins CI/CD pipeline

3. **Payload URL**: Enter the forwarding URL provided by ngrok, adding `/github-webhook` at the end.

4. **SSL verification**: Select the **Enable SSL verification** option.

5. **Which events would you like to trigger this webhook?**: Choose the **Just the push event** option.

6. **Active**: Keep it marked.

After setting up our GitHub repository and webhook, we can craft the Jenkinsfile to build our CI/CD pipeline.

Building a CI/CD pipeline with Jenkinsfile

Creating CI/CD pipelines involves establishing a structured and automated process that simplifies the key stages of software delivery, including building, testing, and deploying applications. By utilizing Jenkins, we can create a Jenkinsfile that serves as a blueprint for managing this workflow. This approach ensures consistency, reliability, and scalability across various development environments. We will implement a Jenkinsfile, the core component for building CI/CD pipelines with Jenkins.

Defining the Jenkinsfile

The Jenkins configuration file that defines the complete workflow of a pipeline and facilitates the automation of CI/CD processes is the **Jenkinsfile**. It specifies the stages and steps involved in building, testing, and deploying an application, serving as a blueprint for Jenkins to orchestrate the entire process. Written in Groovy-based syntax, it typically follows the declarative pipeline format, which provides a clear and structured approach for defining complex workflows.

One key advantage of a Jenkinsfile is that it can be committed to the same version control repository as the application's code base, ensuring that the pipeline evolves alongside the source code. Treating the pipeline configuration as code enhances maintainability, traceability, and collaboration, making the workflow easier to review and manage. Now, we will delve into the structure of a Jenkinsfile and explore how its components work together to create an efficient CI/CD pipeline.

Understanding the Jenkinsfile

The Jenkinsfile structure comprises various blocks, each serving a distinct purpose in defining the CI/CD pipeline. These blocks specify different aspects of the pipeline, such as where it runs, the key phases of execution, the steps performed within each phase, and additional configurations for user input and notifications. *Table 15.1* outlines the main blocks of a Jenkinsfile, highlighting their roles and indicating whether they are required or optional.

Block	Purpose	Required/Optional
`pipeline`	Root block that defines the entire pipeline	Required
`agent`	Defines the environment where the pipeline runs, specifying options such as a node, Docker container, or other execution platforms	Required
`environment`	Declares environment variables used in the pipeline	Optional
`stages`	Defines the main phases of the pipeline, such as build, test, and deploy, outlining the sequential steps of the CI/CD process	Required
`stage`	Defines a single phase of the pipeline, such as the build stage, specifying the tasks to be performed during that phase	Required
`steps`	Commands that are executed during the stage	Required
`post`	Specifies actions to be executed after the pipeline has completed, such as sending notifications or performing cleanup tasks	Optional

Block	Purpose	Required/Optional
`input`	Adds manual approval steps in the pipeline	Optional
`parameters`	Allows for user input during pipeline execution	Optional
`options`	Adds additional configurations to the pipeline, such as specifying timeouts, enabling retries, or setting resource limits	Optional

Table 15.1: Main blocks of a Jenkinsfile

The table presents the main blocks of a Jenkinsfile, briefly explaining each one and whether it is required or optional. Now, let's create the Jenkinsfile for our authentication services and delve deeper into the blocks to clarify them better.

Crafting the Jenkinsfile

Now, we will create the Jenkinsfile for the authentication services application and explore its blocks to understand them better.

The complete Jenkinsfile is found in the `ch15/authentication-services` directory. Here, we will break it down block by block to provide a detailed explanation of each component, helping you understand how the different parts work together to define a fully functional CI/CD pipeline:

1. The `pipeline` block defines the overall structure of the Jenkins pipeline and serves as the root block that encloses all other blocks. It is a required component that outlines the entire CI/CD process:

    ```
    pipeline {
    ```

2. The `agent` block specifies where the pipeline or individual stages will run, such as on a specific node, Docker container, or another environment. It is a required block that determines the execution environment for the pipeline. There are three options for agents:

    *   `any`: Use any available agent

    *   `none`: No agent – useful if agents are specified in each stage

    *   `Custom`: Specify a particular node or label

    We will use `agent any` for simplicity and flexibility. This will allow the pipeline to run on any node that meets the basic requirements for Docker and Maven:

    ```
    pipeline {
        agent any
    ```

3. The `environment` block defines global environment variables that are accessible throughout the entire pipeline. These variables can be customized or overridden within specific stages as needed. This block is optional but helpful in maintaining consistent values across multiple steps. The following `environment` block defines three variables: DOCKER_IMAGE for the Docker image name, DOCKER_TAG for the image version tag, set to `latest`, and GITHUB_REPOSITORY_URL for the project's GitHub URL:

```
environment {
    DOCKER_IMAGE = 'wxesquevixos/authentication-services'
    DOCKER_TAG = 'latest'
    GITHUB_REPOSITORY_URL = 'https://github.com/…
}
```

4. The `stages` block contains multiple `stage` blocks, each representing a distinct pipeline phase, such as build, test, or deploy. This block is required, as it defines the main phases of the CI/CD process, with each `stage` block functioning as an independent step within the pipeline. Our Jenkinsfile includes the `Checkout` stage to retrieve the project's code from the GitHub repository, followed by `Build` to compile the application and `Test` to run unit tests. The `Build Docker Image` stage creates a Docker image, while `Push Docker Image` uploads it to Docker Hub. Finally, the `Deploy to Minikube` stage deploys the application to Minikube:

```
stages {
    stage('Checkout') {
        steps {
            echo 'Checking out code...'
            git branch: 'main',
            url: "${GITHUB_REPOSITORY_URL}"
        }
    }
    stage('Build') {
        steps {
            echo 'Building the application...'
            sh 'mvn clean package -DskipTests'
        }
    }
    stage('Test') {
        steps {
            echo 'Running tests...'
            sh 'mvn test'
        }
    }
    stage('Build Docker Image') {
        steps {
```

```
                echo 'Building Docker image...'
                sh """
                        docker build -t ${DOCKER_IMAGE}:
                          ${DOCKER_TAG} .
                    """
            }
        }
        stage('Push Docker Image') {
            steps {
                echo 'Pushing Docker image to Docker Hub...'
                withCredentials([usernamePassword(credentialsId:
                'dockerhub-credentials', usernameVariable:
                'DOCKER_USERNAME', passwordVariable:
                'DOCKER_PASSWORD')]) {
                  sh '''
                  echo $DOCKER_PASSWORD | docker login -u
                    $DOCKER_USERNAME --password-stdin
                  docker push ${DOCKER_IMAGE}:${DOCKER_TAG}
                  '''
                }
            }
        }
        stage('Deploy to Minikube') {
            steps {
                echo 'Deploying to Minikube...'
                sh """
                kubectl apply -f kubernetes/authentication-services-
                        deployment.yaml
                kubectl apply -f kubernetes/authentication-services-
                        service.yaml
                kubectl apply -f kubernetes/authentication-services-
                        ingress.yaml
                """
            }
        }
```

5. The steps block, required within a stage, contains the specific commands or actions to execute during that pipeline phase. The Deploy to Minikube stage defines the application's deployment process to Minikube. Its steps block prints a message using the echo command and runs shell commands using kubectl to apply the deployment, service, and ingress resources:

```
    stage('Deploy to Minikube') {
        steps {
            echo 'Deploying to Minikube...'
            sh """
```

```
        kubectl apply -f kubernetes/authentication-services-
    deployment.yaml
        kubectl apply -f kubernetes/authentication-services-
        service.yaml
        kubectl apply -f kubernetes/authentication-services
        ingress.yaml
        """
    }
  }
}
```

6. The `post` block is an optional section that defines actions to be executed after the pipeline or individual stages are complete. It contains sub-blocks such as `always`, which runs regardless of the outcome; `success`, which runs only when the pipeline or stage succeeds; `failure`, which runs only when it fails; and `unstable`, which runs if the pipeline or stage becomes unstable, such as when tests fail:

```
post {
  success {
    echo 'Pipeline completed successfully!'
  }
  failure {
    echo 'Pipeline failed. Please check the logs.'
  }
}
```

We created and explored the structure and components of a Jenkinsfile, highlighting how each block plays a crucial role in defining an efficient CI/CD pipeline. With this foundation in place and our Jenkinsfile created, we will set up and walk through the step-by-step implementation of the CI/CD pipeline in Jenkins.

Setting up Jenkins and the CI/CD pipeline

In *Chapter 15, Orchestration with Kubernetes*, we manually performed the entire process of deploying authentication services. This process involved pulling the code from GitHub, creating Docker images, pushing those images to Docker Hub, and deploying the services into Minikube. This process is time-consuming, prone to human error, and not scalable for frequent updates or larger teams. To address these issues, we will implement automation to streamline this workflow using CI/CD pipelines with Jenkins, which will provide us with the following capabilities:

1. **Automate code integration**: Automatically pull the latest code from GitHub whenever changes are merged into the `main` branch

2. **Build and test**: Use Maven to compile the application and run tests to maintain code quality

3. **Containerize and push**: Build Docker images for the updated services and push them to Docker Hub

4. **Deploy**: Deploy the updated authentication services seamlessly into Minikube

By the end of this chapter, we'll have a fully automated CI/CD pipeline that ensures our authentication services are built, tested, and deployed efficiently, reducing manual effort and enabling faster iterations.

> **Note**
>
> Before you start, make sure that your environment is properly set up. Minikube should be running correctly and configured for external access to MongoDB, as outlined in *Chapter 15, Orchestration with Kubernetes*. Additionally, ensure that Docker, Maven, and Java are installed and configured on your system, as these tools are crucial for building and testing the project during the pipeline execution.

Now, let's start setting up Jenkins.

Setting up Jenkins

We have completed several steps so far: we created a public URL using ngrok, set up a GitHub repository, configured webhooks to trigger events, and created the Jenkinsfile. Now, it's time to set up Jenkins, a powerful automation tool that will serve as the engine for our CI/CD pipeline.

> **Jenkins installation**
>
> Visit https://www.jenkins.io/download/ to download and install Jenkins for your platform.

Once Jenkins is installed and initialized, let's proceed with its configuration:

1. To start Jenkins, follow the instructions provided in the installation. For macOS users, follow these instructions to run Jenkins locally on port `8080`:

    ```
    /opt/homebrew/opt/jenkins/bin/jenkins
    --httpListenAddress\=127.0.0.1 --httpPort\=8080
    ```

2. Copy the admin's password generated and printed in the console, as shown in *Figure 15.5*.

```
Jenkins initial setup is required. An admin user has been created and a password generated.
Please use the following password to proceed to installation:

ae80f18920724acabfea24ae75a29f34

This may also be found at: /Users/wanderson/.jenkins/secrets/initialAdminPassword
```

Figure 15.5: Admin password

3. *Figure 15.6* shows the screen to unlock Jenkins. Paste the generated admin password copied from the console and click on the **Continue** button. You can also find the admin password in the `initialAdminPassword` file in the `/USER_HOME/.jenkins/secrets` directory.

Figure 15.6: Unlock Jenkins screen

4. On the **Customize Jenkins** screen, as shown in *Figure 15.7*, click on the **Install suggested plugins** option.

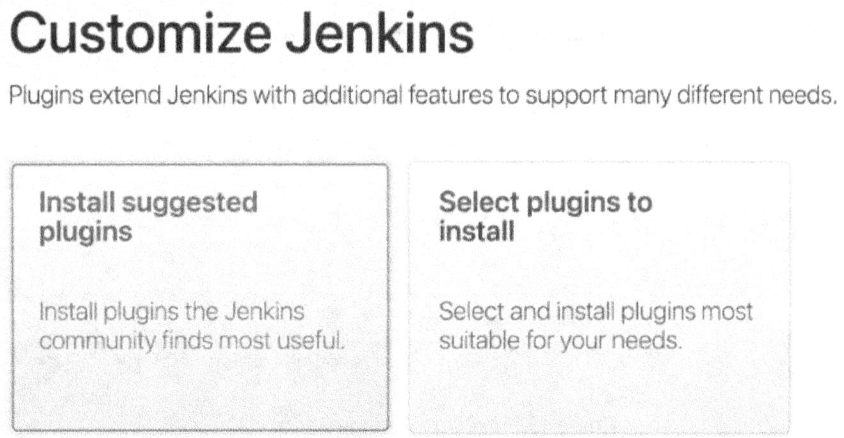

Figure 15.7: Customize Jenkins

5. After the plugin installation, you can create or skip an admin user on the **Create First Admin User** screen, as shown in *Figure 15.8*. I strongly recommend making one. Fill out the form and click on the **Save and Continue** button.

Figure 15.8: Create First Admin User

6. *Figure 15.9* presents the **Instance Configuration** screen. Enter the Jenkins URL in the input field: `http://localhost:8080/`. Proceed by clicking on the **Save and Finish** button.

Figure 15.9: Instance Configuration

7. On the next screen, click the **Start using Jenkins** button. You will be redirected to the Jenkins **Dashboard** screen, as shown in *Figure 15.10*.

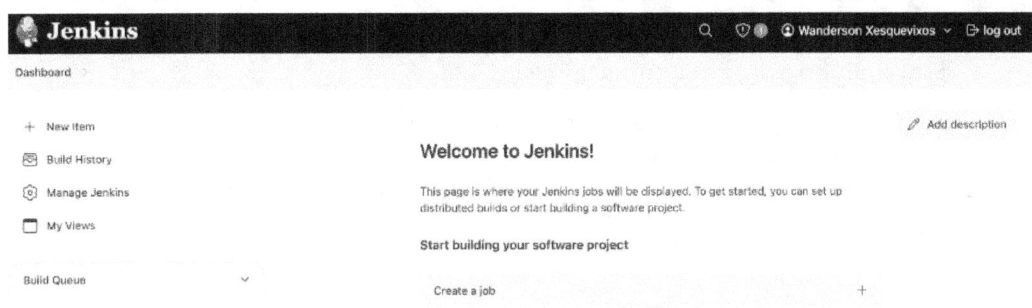

Figure 15.10: Jenkins setup is complete

Once Jenkins is installed and configured, the next step is to set up a pipeline to automate your build, test, and deployment processes.

Setting up the pipeline

With Jenkins installed and configured, the next step is to set up the pipeline, which is the core automation workflow for building, testing, and deploying our project. A Jenkins pipeline outlines the steps the project will follow whenever a new change is pushed to the `main` branch of the linked GitHub repository. Let's proceed with the following steps:

1. With Jenkins initialized, enter the following URL in your browser: `http://localhost:8080`.

2. On the main Jenkins screen, click on the **Create a job** option.

3. Enter the project name `authentication-services` on the next screen, select the **Pipeline** option, and click **OK**. *Figure 15.11* illustrates the screen for creating the job.

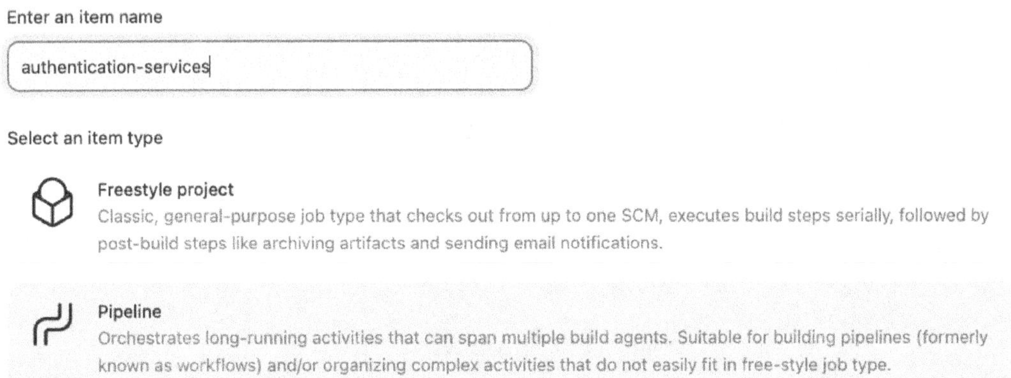

Figure 15.11: Creating the pipeline

4. On the next screen, click the **Build Triggers** menu and select the **GitHub hook trigger for the GITScm polling** option, as illustrated in *Figure 15.12*.

When Jenkins receives a GitHub push event, the GitHub plugin verifies whether the repository matches the one defined in the job's SCM configuration. If they match, the plugin triggers a one-time polling by the Git plugin. The Git plugin then detects changes and initiates the build.

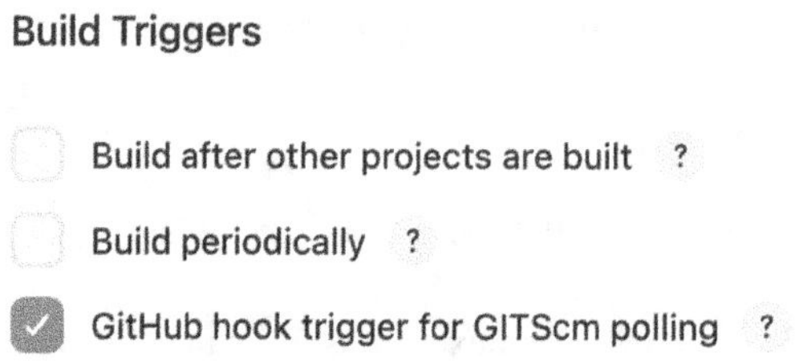

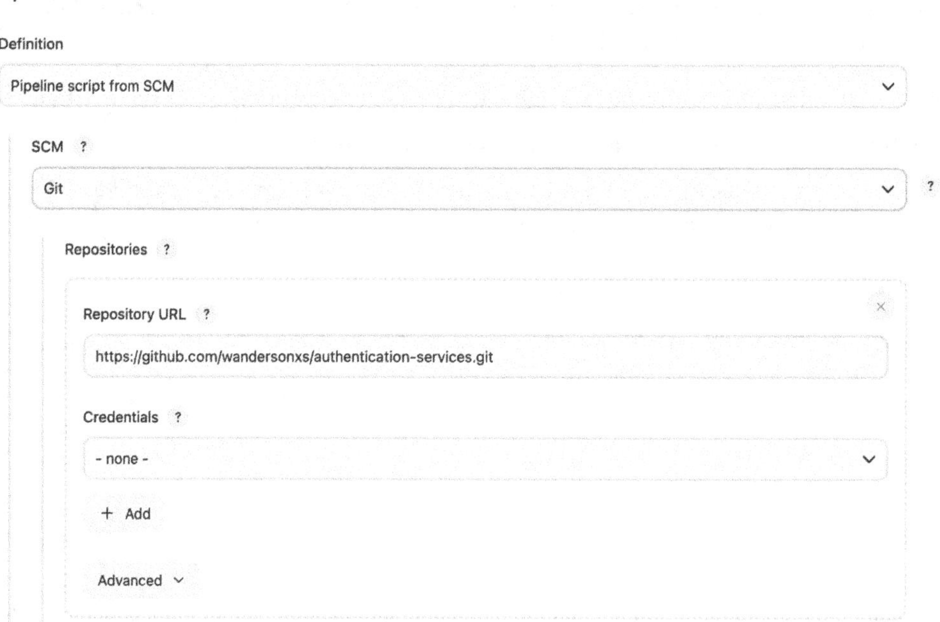

Figure 15.12: Build Triggers section

5. Click on the **Pipeline** menu and complete the form according to the instructions. *Figure 15.13* shows the **Pipeline** section filled in, as described in the list that follows:

Figure 15.13: Pipeline section

6. **Definition**: Select the **Pipeline script from SCM** option. When you do, Jenkins will use the Jenkinsfile from the source code repository to define the pipeline steps.

7. **SCM**: Select the **Git** option. The Git plugin enables essential Git operations in Jenkins projects. It supports polling, fetching, checking out, and merging content from Git repositories.

8. **Repository URL**: Enter the URL or path of the Git repository, similar to the format used in the Git `clone` command. For our example, it will be `https://github.com/wandersonxs/authentication-services.git`.

9. **Credentials**: Since the repository is public, it should be kept as - **none** -.

10. Scroll down in the **Pipeline** section, as shown in *Figure 15.14*, and complete the form, as described in the list that follows:

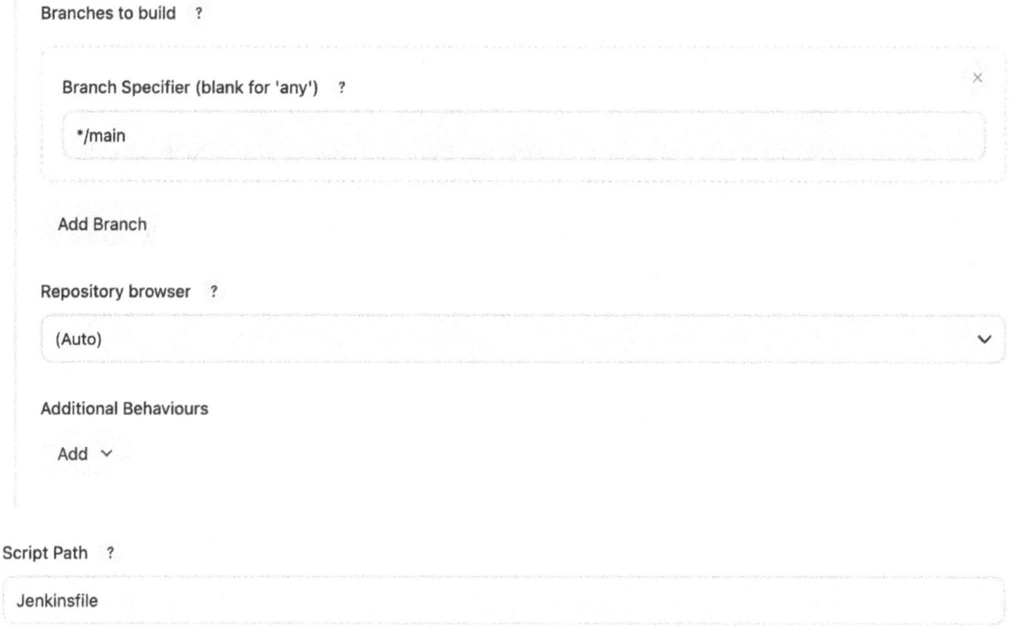

Figure 15.14: Pipeline section

11. **Branch Specifier (blank for 'any')**: We must specify the branch we want to start the pipeline when something is pushed. Fill out with `*/main`.

12. **Script Path**: This specifies the location of the Jenkinsfile within the repository. By default, it takes the Jenkinsfile from the project's root directory if you set it to **Jenkinsfile**. Keep it as **Jenkinsfil14.**

13. Click on the **Save** button.

14. Click on the **Dashboard** menu at the top left or visit `http://localhost:8080`. *Figure 15.15* presents the **Dashboard** screen with our `authentication-services` job created.

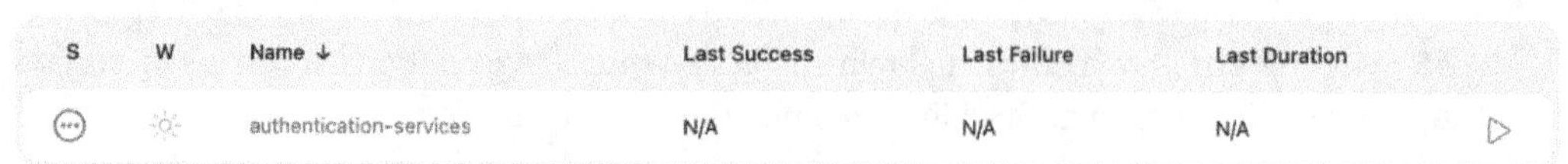

Figure 15.15: Dashboard screen with job created

Our pipeline has been created and configured; however, an additional step is still needed. As you recall, we have a stage for creating and pushing the image to Docker Hub, so we must provide the necessary credentials. Let's set this up in Jenkins.

Setting up Docker Hub credentials

We will set up the credentials in Jenkins to enable the pipeline to push the project image to Docker Hub. Let's follow these steps:

1. On the **Dashboard** screen, click the **Manage Jenkins** menu and select **Credentials, System, and Global credentials (unrestricted)**. Finally, click the + **Add Credentials** button.

2. Fill out the form according to the instructions. *Figure 15.16* shows the credentials form filled in, as described in the following list:

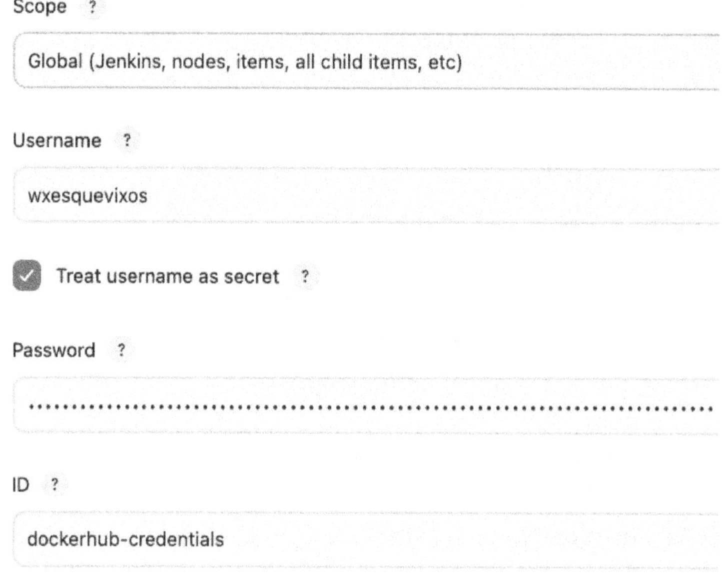

Figure 15.16: Global credentials form

    i.   **Scope**: Choose the **Global** option. **Global** means the credentials are accessible to all jobs and users across Jenkins. In contrast, **System** means the credentials are only accessible to Jenkins system processes, such as pipeline scripts, and cannot be accessed through the UI for jobs.

    ii.   **Username**: Provide your Docker Hub username.

    iii.   **Password**: Provide your Docker Hub password.

    iv.   **ID**: Fill it out with `dockerhub-credentials`. This field is an internal unique ID identifying these credentials from jobs and other configurations.

3.   Click on the **Save** button. The Docker Hub credentials were created as presented in *Figure 15.17*.

Global credentials (unrestricted)

Credentials that should be available irrespective of domain specification to requirements matching.

ID	Name	Kind
dockerhub-credentials	dockerhub-credentials	Username with password

Figure 15.17: Credentials for Docker Hub

Having fully configured Jenkins, it's time to test the pipeline to ensure it runs as expected. We must verify that each stage—from fetching the code to building, testing, and deploying—functions smoothly.

Starting the pipeline manually

With Jenkins set up and the pipeline configured, you're now ready to trigger your first build. We'll walk you through starting the pipeline manually to ensure everything functions as intended. This will help verify that Jenkins can fetch the latest code, execute the defined stages, and complete the pipeline process successfully. By running the pipeline manually, we can also catch any issues early before relying on automated triggers from GitHub. Let's begin by running the pipeline and observing its execution!

1.   Access the Jenkins **Dashboard** screen, click on the `authentication-services` project, and then click on the **Build Now** menu. *Figure 15.18* illustrates the pipeline process started.

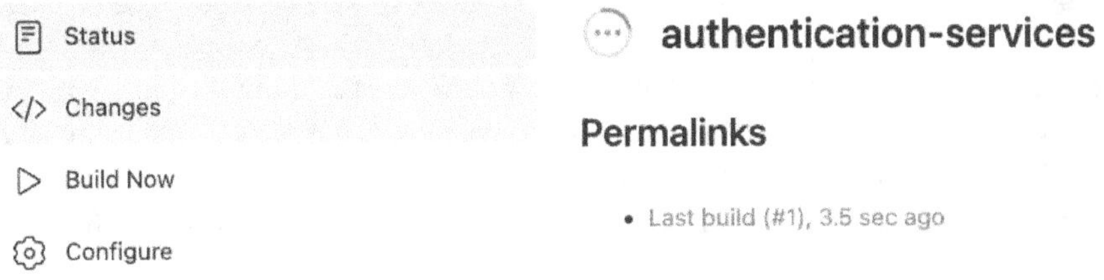

Figure 15.18: Pipeline started

2. Click on the **Stages** menu to monitor the pipeline's progress. *Figure 15.19* illustrates Jenkins' view of the stages representing the execution progress. Each block corresponds to a stage in the pipeline, including steps such as **Checkout SCM, Checkout, Build, Test, Build Docker Image, Push Docker Image, Deploy to Minikube**, and **Post Actions**. Green checkmarks indicate the successful completion of these stages.

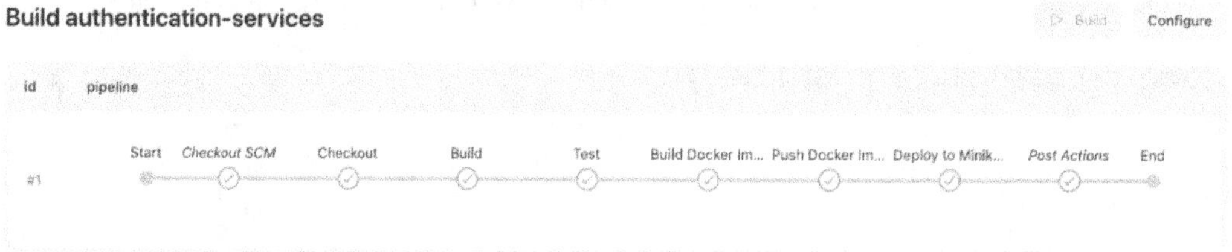

Figure 15.19: Jenkins pipeline stages overview for authentication services

3. We can check the Kubernetes dashboard as well. You can start it through the `minikube dashboard` command.

4. *Figure 15.20* presents the authentication services deployed and running in Minikube.

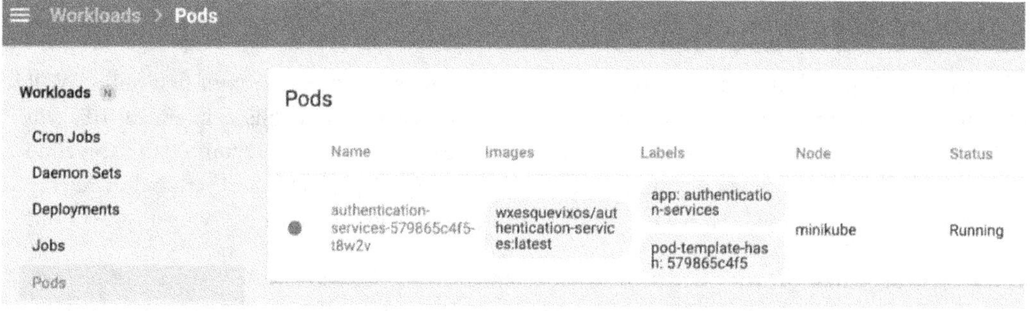

Figure 15.20: Authentication services deployed and running in Minikube

By starting the pipeline manually, we verified that each stage—from checkout to deployment—was executed successfully, confirming that our setup was functioning as expected. Now that the manual run is complete, it's time to transition to an automated process. The pipeline starts automatically whenever a push is made to the `main` branch of the `authentication-services` project on GitHub.

Starting the pipeline automatically after pushing changes to GitHub

Automation plays a vital role in creating an efficient CI/CD process by continuously testing and deploying code changes without requiring manual intervention. Now, we will test whether the pipeline triggers automatically after a push to the project's `main` branch on GitHub.

> **Note**
>
> Ensure ngrok is running and configure GitHub's webhook to the same URL.

Let's start the process by verifying that the pipeline will be triggered automatically:

1. Access the `authentication-services` project we pushed to GitHub in the *Setting up the environment and GitHub* section, make any modifications, and push it to the `main` branch on GitHub. I pushed the project with the comment `Update to test pipeline execution`.

2. Go to the Jenkins **Dashboard** screen to see that **Build Executor Status** is running, as shown in *Figure 15.21*. In this example, the build ID is 2.

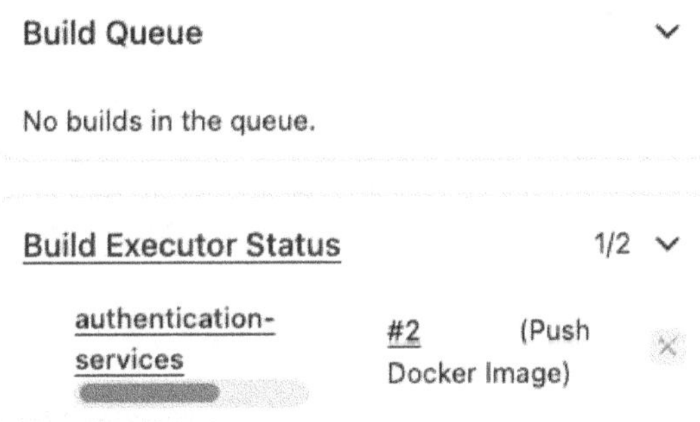

Figure 15.21: Build Executor Status for authentication services

3. Go to the **Dashboard** screen and click on the **#2** link. The number may vary depending on how many times the process has been run. Figure 15.22 presents the **Dashboard** screen with the link to click.

Figure 15.22: Dashboard screen

4. The following screen, shown in *Figure 15.23*, illustrates the details of the Jenkins build process triggered by a GitHub push. It provides information on the build's runtime, repository details, and changes made. Note that the changes reflect our commit comments pushed to GitHub.

Figure 15.23: Details of the Jenkins build process

We implemented a complete CI/CD pipeline using Jenkins to automate our authentication services' building, testing, and deployment. The process began with setting up Jenkins and configuring a pipeline that triggers GitHub pushes. We also securely integrated our Docker Hub credentials to publish images.

To verify our setup, we manually ran the pipeline and monitored its stages, confirming that each step—from checking out the source code to deploying in Minikube—executed successfully. Finally, we tested the automated workflow to ensure that every push to the `main` branch seamlessly triggers the pipeline.

This automated CI/CD setup enhances development efficiency, reduces manual effort, and enables faster, more reliable deployments. It lays the foundation for a scalable and resilient workflow.

Summary

This chapter provided an in-depth exploration of CI/CD, emphasizing their role in automating software development workflows and improving code quality, collaboration, and release frequency. You were introduced to key CI/CD principles, such as automated builds, self-testing, small and frequent code integrations, and reliable deployments. The chapter also covered the differences between continuous delivery and continuous deployment, illustrating their processes through an example pipeline using Jenkins. Additionally, it provided step-by-step instructions for configuring Jenkins, integrating GitHub webhooks, building Docker images, and deploying the authentication services into Minikube.

By combining foundational concepts with a practical guide to building a Jenkins CI/CD pipeline, this chapter equipped you with the knowledge to implement efficient, automated pipelines for streamlined software delivery and deployment.

Questions

1. What is CI/CD?
2. What is the main objective of CI?
3. What is the main objective of CD?
4. What distinguishes continuous delivery from continuous deployment?
5. What are some benefits of implementing CI/CD?
6. What role do Jenkins and Jenkinsfile play in CI/CD pipelines?

Get This Book's PDF Version and Exclusive Extras

Scan the QR code (or go to `packtpub.com/unlock`). Search for this book by name, confirm the edition, and then follow the steps on the page.

Note: Keep your invoice handly. Purchase made directly from packt don't require one.

16
Unlock Your Exclusive Benefits

Your copy of this book includes the following exclusive benefit:

- ⟳ Next-gen Packt Reader
- 📄 DRM-free PDF/ePub downloads

Follow the guide below to unlock them. The process takes only a few minutes and needs to be completed once.

Unlock this Book's Free Benefits in 3 Easy Steps

Step 1

Keep your purchase invoice ready for *Step 3*. If you have a physical copy, scan it using your phone and save it as a PDF, JPG, or PNG.

For more help on finding your invoice, visit `https://www.packtpub.com/unlock-benefits/help`.

> **Note**
>
> If you bought this book directly from Packt, no invoice is required. After *Step 2*, you can access your exclusive content right away.

Step 2

Scan the QR code or go to `packtpub.com/unlock`.

On the page that opens (similar to *Figure 16 .1* on desktop), search for this book by name and select the correct edition.

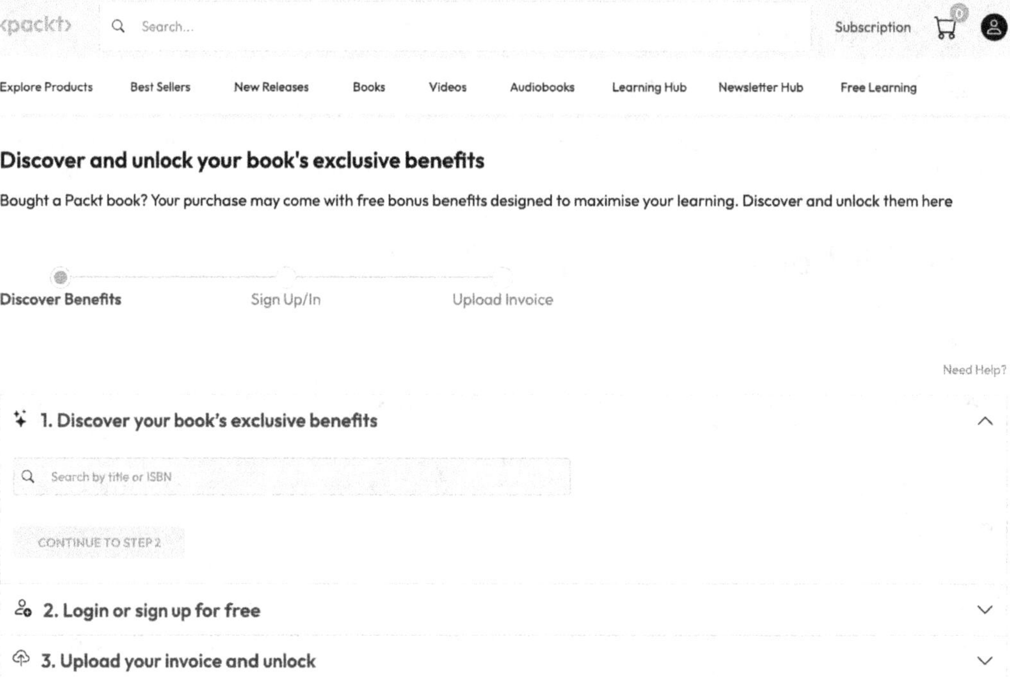

Figure 16.1: Packt unlock landing page on desktop

Step 3

After selecting your book, sign in to your Packt account or create one for free. Then upload your invoice (PDF, PNG, or JPG, up to 10 MB). Follow the on-screen instructions to finish the process.

Need help?

If you get stuck and need help, visit
`https://www.packtpub.com/unlock-benefits/help`
for a detailed FAQ on how to find your invoices and more. This QR code will take you to the help page.

> **Note**
>
> If you are still facing issues, reach out to `customercare@packt.com`.

Index

A

O

P

T

V

W

Y

Z

packtpub.com

Subscribe to our online digital library for full access to over 7,000 books and videos, as well as industry leading tools to help you plan your personal development and advance your career. For more information, please visit our website.

Why subscribe?

- Spend less time learning and more time coding with practical eBooks and Videos from over 4,000 industry professionals

- Improve your learning with Skill Plans built especially for you

- Get a free eBook or video every month

- Fully searchable for easy access to vital information

- Copy and paste, print, and bookmark content

Did you know that Packt offers eBook versions of every book published, with PDF and ePub files available? You can upgrade to the eBook version at packtpub.com and as a print book customer, you are entitled to a discount on the eBook copy. Get in touch with us at customercare@packtpub.com for more details.

At www.packtpub.com, you can also read a collection of free technical articles, sign up for a range of free newsletters, and receive exclusive discounts and offers on Packt books and eBooks.

Other Books You May Enjoy

If you enjoyed this book, you may be interested in these other books by Packt:

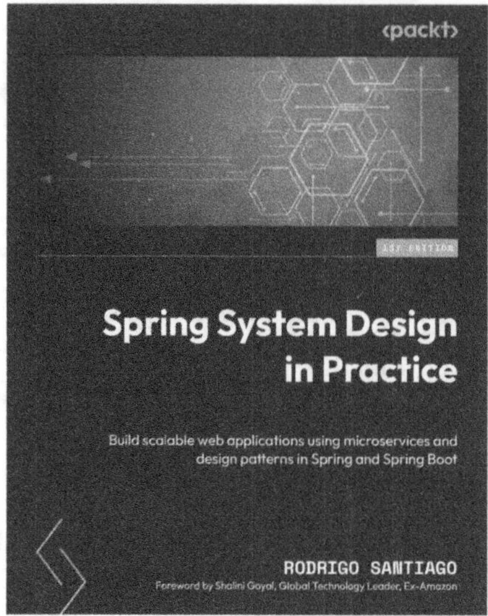

Spring System Design in Practice

Rodrigo Santiago

ISBN: 978-1-80324-901-8

- Implement microservices for scalable, resilient web systems

- Break down business goals into well-structured product requirements

- Weigh tradeoffs between writing asynchronous vs. synchronous services and SQL vs. NoSQL storage

- Accelerate service development and reliability through the adoption of test-driven development

- Identify and eliminate hidden performance bottlenecks to maximize speed and efficiency

- Achieve real-time processing and responsiveness in distributed environments

React Key Concepts

Maximilian Schwarzmüller

ISBN: 978-1-83620-227-1

- Build modern, user-friendly, and reactive web apps
- Create components and utilize props to pass data between them
- Handle events, perform state updates, and manage conditional content
- Add styles dynamically and conditionally for modern user interfaces
- Use advanced state management techniques such as React's Context API
- Utilize React Router to render different pages for different URLs
- Understand key best practices and optimization opportunities
- Learn about React Server Components and Server Actions

Packt is searching for authors like you

If you're interested in becoming an author for Packt, please visit `authors.packtpub.com` and apply today. We have worked with thousands of developers and tech professionals, just like you, to help them share their insight with the global tech community. You can make a general application, apply for a specific hot topic that we are recruiting an author for, or submit your own idea.

Share your thoughts

Now you've finished Software Architecture with Spring, we'd love to hear your thoughts! Scan the QR code below to go straight to the Amazon review page for this book and share your feedback or leave a review on the site that you purchased it from.

`https://packt.link/r/1835880614`

Your review is important to us and the tech community and will help us make sure we're delivering excellent quality content.

www.ingramcontent.com/pod-product-compliance
Lightning Source LLC
Chambersburg PA
CBHW080357030726
47598CB00010B/2778